Competition Policy in Regulated Industries

Approaches for Emerging Economies

Paulina Beato and Jean-Jacques Laffont
Editors

Published by the Inter-American Development Bank
Distributed by The Johns Hopkins University Press

Washington, D.C.
2002

©2002   **Inter-American Development Bank**
1300 New York Avenue, N.W.
Washington, D.C. 20577

Produced by the IDB Publications Section.

To order this book, contact:
IDB Bookstore
Tel: 1-877-PUBS IDB/(202) 623-1753
Fax: (202) 623-1709
E-mail: idb-books@iadb.org
www.iadb.org/pub

Cataloging-in-Publication data provided by the
Inter-American Development Bank
Felipe Herrera Library

Competition policy in regulated industries : approaches for emerging economies / Paulina Beato and Jean-Jacques Laffont, editors.

     p. cm.   Includes bibliographical references.
     ISBN: 193100336X

     1. Competition--Latin America.   2. Industrial concentration--Latin America.   3. Antitrust law--Latin America.   I. Beato, Paulina. II. Laffont, Jean-Jacques, 1947-   III. Inter-American Development Bank.

338.6048 C677--dc21   LCCN: 2002115376

Contents

Foreword

Competition Policy in Regulated Industries: Approaches for Emerging Economies is part of a larger effort of the Inter-American Development Bank to find new ways to improve the efficiency of infrastructure services in emerging economies. The Bank's agenda includes two main goals in this regard: increasing competitiveness and promoting regional integration.

A competitive environment in infrastructure sectors enhances infrastructure productivity and yields economywide benefits. During the past two decades, the countries of Latin America enacted important reforms in infrastructure services, encompassing changes both in ownership patterns and in operating terms. Regulatory frameworks have also evolved from monopoly and public ownership settings lacking specific regulations, to private participation scenarios with competition and regulation playing complementary roles. However, even though competition is a pivotal feature of all public services reform processes, a high degree of vertical and horizontal concentration pervades the industrial structure of many of the region's countries. Furthermore, mergers and acquisitions that are taking place in the context of an increasingly global economy, without the appropriate legislation to promote competition and restrain market control, have often led to reduced levels of competition *for the market* or *in the market*. This book makes the case that enhancing competition in infrastructure sectors demands the appropriate mix of three policies: structural reforms that separate competitive and noncompetitive segments; competition regulations that preclude abuse of dominant position and control mergers and acquisitions; and appropriate regulations for ensuring that prices of and access to essential facilities (the noncompetitive segments of the industry) are nondiscriminatory and fair.

The Inter-American Development Bank has actively promoted infrastructure reform in Latin American and Caribbean countries. The Bank has also financed private projects aimed at fostering the implementation of reforms in the power, gas, water, and transport sectors. The Bank is developing a comprehensive approach to foster development of transnational infrastructure projects to support integration. This book discusses how competition and liberalization in the infrastructure sectors are critical for transnational projects and regional integration. Regulations and reforms in the energy and transportation sectors of the European Union provide useful lessons for Latin America. Structural reforms and regulatory changes required for infrastructure market integration take time because some agents are reluctant to lose their capacity to control and manipulate infrastructure markets. Acknowledging the brakes that losers and winners may put on the integration process, it must nevertheless continue to go forward because society must not forgo the increase in efficiency and welfare associated with a larger regional market.

Carlos M. Jarque
Manager, Sustainable Development Department
Inter-American Development Bank

Editors' Introduction

Paulina Beato and Jean-Jacques Laffont

In developing countries, regulation and liberalization of economic infrastructure services raise specific questions.[1] One key concept in analyzing regulation and competition policy is the marginal cost of public funds; that is, the social cost of raising one unit of account. This cost includes a deadweight loss because government revenue is raised by means of distortionary taxes. In developed countries, a common estimate of the average deadweight loss of taxes is 0.3, meaning that it costs citizens 1.3 units of account when the government raises 1 unit of account.[2] In developing countries, extreme inefficiency and corruption of tax systems hinder governments from investing in infrastructure services and affect the cost of all types of public interventions, particularly policies that deal with regulation and competition.

Although the auditing of costs is an essential instrument for regulatory and competition agencies, many developing countries lack sophisticated accounting systems and appropriately trained auditing staffs and administration (Trebilcock 1996). As a result of political and social impediments, auditors' salaries seldom provide sufficient incentive to invest the effort required to inhibit corruption. Moreover, lack of computerized systems, as well as other technological advances, makes it harder for auditors to uncover cost padding and evaluate real costs. Finally, limited liability constraints make it difficult to impose high penalties for wrongdoing.

---

[1] Sometimes referred to as public utilities, economic infrastructure services include telecommunications, electricity, gas, transport, and post. Since it is generally agreed that public utilities should be privatized whenever possible, this book does not focus on issues related to privatization.

[2] The deadweight loss depends on the type of tax used because tax systems are seldom optimized.

The low internal costs of side transfers have led to widespread corruption in many developing countries. When two parties (such as a firm and an auditor, or a bidder and the organizer of an auction) design side transfers to arrange a private deal, they must take into account the costs of being identified and the necessity of using indirect compensation, which is less efficient than money. In developing countries, the expected cost of side transfers is less than in developed countries because they are more difficult to identify and social norms may place a positive value on certain types (such as those that occur within families, villages, or ethnic groups). Accordingly, fighting corruption in developing countries becomes more difficult (Tirole 1992).

Credit market inefficiencies and sheer lack of wealth make limited liability constraints more binding. They also make it difficult to borrow and attract foreign capital, resulting in many problems associated with regulation and competition policy. Because banking sector regulations and competition policy are complementary, inefficient regulations that make borrowing costly or impossible may cause an effective competition policy to destroy the rents that allow firms to invest or may create other instabilities.[3]

Governments of developed countries have two characteristics that are often missing in developing nations: constitutional control and ability to enter into long-term contracts. Without the checks and balances found in well-functioning democracies—supreme courts, government auditing bodies, separation of powers, and independent media[4]—it is easier for interest groups to exert undue influence on their government. Lack of democracy and well-functioning political institutions increases the uncertainty of future regulations and hinders the government and regulatory agencies from making credible, long-term policy commitments. Consequently, the economic policies of developing countries are more sensitive to ratchet effects and renegotiations.

Weakness of the rule of law is also characteristic of many developing countries. Legal and contractual enforcement are often poor, and biases toward self-enforcing contracts can lead to frequent renegotiations.

Finally, many developing countries experience difficulty in attracting the foreign capital needed to liberalize and deregulate public utilities. This, in turn, affects developing countries' recommendations for promoting competition in infrastructure services.

---

[3] Mishkin (1997) concludes that developing countries may need to move slowly in financial liberalization to prevent excesses in a lending boom.

[4] See Beasley and Burgess (2001) for an empirical study of government responsiveness to media activity.

BOX 1. REREGULATING NEW ZEALAND'S TELECOMMUNICATIONS INDUSTRY

New Zealand's Ministerial Inquiry into Telecommunications of June 2000 stated: "The existing system of relying on the courts, arbitration, or industry self-regulation to resolve disputes relating to such matters as terms and conditions of interconnection, number allocation and portability, and access to billing information has resulted in, and has the potential to continue to result in, significant delays; Changes of the regime are therefore required. The Inquiry considers that, consistent with the view held by most other countries, industry-specific regulation is warranted."

Structuring Regulatory Agencies That Favor Competition

When considering how to structure regulatory agencies that favor competition, the initial question is whether responsibility for regulation and competition policy should be incorporated into a single agency. In this regard, the recent experiences of New Zealand and Australia are instructive.

New Zealand's novel approach to regulation used only general competition laws, enforced by courts and an industrywide competition authority, to regulate first telecommunications and then power. Self-regulation by the industry was introduced, with councils composed of industry participants who negotiated the main rules and access conditions.

Although the country's experience cannot be considered an immediate failure, the government now recognizes the need to maintain regulatory control in industries that are not sufficiently competitive—even telecommunications, the most competitive industry discussed in this book (box 1). The concern is that such light control of the industry will not prevent abuse of dominant position. The number of cases brought before the courts since the regulation was put into place shows that the industry's rapidly changing, technology intensive characteristics make it difficult to determine whether a firm is guilty of abusing its dominant position. Moreover, the procedures are cumbersome, involving long delays. Relying solely on competition laws has proven inefficient, even when these laws are highly developed and well enforced. Accordingly, one can safely conclude that relinquishing regulation is not the best option.

Integrating regulation and general competition policy into a single agency is possible only in countries that have opted for a multi-industry regulatory agency, as has Australia. This country's regulation is organized around the Australian Competition and Consumer Commission (ACCC, a federal multisector agency), specialized agencies, and regionally coordinated sectoral and functional bureaus. The ACCC handles product safety, consumer protection, mergers, restrictive trade practices, and access. It also has taken over a significant portion of the specialized regulator's duties. For example, the regulatory body in charge of telecommunications was dismantled following creation of the ACCC.[5] The Utility Regulators Forum, created in 1997, ensures coordination of regulatory activities within the ACCC.

The Australian solution thus integrates regulation and competition at the federal level, even when regional agencies are used. This system contrasts with that of the United States, where multisector regulations are the states' responsibility, specialized regulations are the federal government's responsibility, and competition policy is handled separately.

Integrated regulatory agencies—at least for telecommunications, electricity, gas, and transport industries—are a sound option for many developing countries that lack human resources. Economies of scope are larger between the regulatory agencies of those industries than between regulation and competition policy agencies. To avoid creating a too powerful agency, the general recommendation is to create a competition policy agency separate from integrated regulatory agencies established at the federal level. Exceptions to federal regulation could include large countries or involve water distribution. While technology calls for federal regulation to save on costs, accountability requires more decentralized institutions.

In chapter 1, Aubert and Laffont address these structural issues, elaborating on three questions: Should states be federally regulated or should regulation be decentralized to states? Should regulators assume responsibility for all industries, as they do in Costa Rica, Jamaica, and Panama, or should they handle separate industries, as they do in Argentina, Brazil, and Colombia? Should a single entity deal with pricing, quality, and competition, as in Australia, or should several entities handle these matters, as in most Latin American countries?

The authors propose that sound advice on these structural issues must take into account political constraints, initial conditions, and industry characteristics. The various options implemented in developed countries and the experiences of many Latin American countries (Argentina, Bolivia, Brazil,

---

[5] However, a regulator is in charge of universal service obligations.

BOX 2. BOLIVIA'S BALANCED COMPROMISE

Bolivia recently established a regulatory system that constitutes a balanced compromise between a multisector agency and specialized regulators. It comprises sector-specific branches supervised by a coordinating entity. The structure is similar to a multisector agency with specialized units; however, the branches are more independent, making the structure more acceptable to ministries reluctant to transfer their regulatory power to a multisector agency. Such a system may reduce the threat of regulatory capture by industry, but it may not insulate agencies from political interference, given their strategic importance.

Chile, and Peru) suggest that the trade-offs are complex (box 2). They involve balancing differentiation versus coordination, constructive versus destructive regulatory competition, local versus government control, local versus federal corruption, industry-specific expertise versus shared resources, and diversifying versus consolidating the risk of institutional failure.

Trade-offs in Breaking Up Monopolies

Formerly, long-distance telecommunications and electricity generation industries were considered natural monopolies in their entirety. Today, however, segments of these industries are considered potentially competitive and are being opened to competition. Other segments, such as the electricity transmission grid and the local telecom loop, are still considered natural monopolies and remain regulated (with new forms of regulation eventually applied).

Three types of market structures can be envisioned for these industries: vertical disintegration, vertical integration, and competition in infrastructures. In vertical disintegration, the firm controlling the bottleneck (the natural monopoly segment) is not allowed to compete in the services that use the bottleneck as input. For example, the local telephone company, which owns the local loop, is not allowed to compete in long-distance services, which need the local loop to access consumers. In vertical integration, the firm controlling the bottleneck is one competitor among the many that provide services using the bottleneck as input. In competition in infrastructure, vertically integrated firms may compete, each controlling a bottleneck and providing the service.

The contrast between vertical disintegration and vertical integration rests on a comparison of the economies of scope that vertical integration makes possible and the problems of bias that it raises. Economies of scope are likely to be independent of the characteristics of developing countries (at least for given technologies), but favoritism is more difficult to fight, in which cases, preference should be given to vertical disintegration.[6]

The distinction between vertical integration and competition in infrastructure rests on an assessment of the fixed costs associated with competition in providing the bottleneck (such as local telephony) and the gains that can be expected from competition (Auriol and Laffont 1992). The comparison is difficult in developing countries, where the high cost of public funds makes both the duplication of fixed costs and the information rents resulting from monopolistic provision of the bottleneck more expensive.

Choosing among market structures is further complicated by the dynamics of the industry involved, which may be moving toward competition. In telecommunications, for example, vertical disintegration may, in fact, delay the emergence of competition among vertically integrated firms that provide both local and long-distance telephony. However, for railways,[7] gas, and electricity, vertical disintegration of track, pipeline, and transmission grid from transport or generation can be a viable option if competition in services is introduced.

In chapter 2, Serra takes a close look at the decisions competition authorities in Chile have made to promote competition and prevent monopolistic practices in infrastructure services. The country's antitrust law vaguely defines conduct that constitutes a violation of the law and situations that pose a risk to the efficient development of markets; the law is equally ambiguous in specifying which powers and instruments are available to antitrust institutions. Three out of the five cases presented—external communications network, electrical transmission system, and gas pipeline—are natural monopolies, resulting from the heavy economies of scale involved in their development. The other two cases—maritime ports and refuse

---

[6] However, one should also consider the importance of transaction costs; they may be higher in cases of vertical disintegration because of the lack of enforceability of contracts and the lack of strong commitments, which lead to constant renegotiations (see Ordover, Pittman, and Clyde 1994). In small countries and in such industries as electricity, one should consider that only a vertical structure provides a critical level of business that can attract foreign investment.

[7] In some cases, competition is possible by roads or (for large countries) between vertically integrated firms that are interconnected with reciprocal access rules.

dumps—have essential facility status. Because Chile has a scarcity of natural bays, maritime ports are considered essential. Refuse dumps are also deemed essential because of restrictions imposed by environmental protection agencies, coupled with the location of neighboring communities.

The antitrust commissions' rulings demonstrate that vertically integrated monopolies pose a risk to competition in services that are allowed to compete. The commissions have arbitrated various measures to reduce the likelihood that integrated monopolies can prevent or destroy market competition. Specifically, they have investigated and penalized anticompetitive conduct, promoted the entry of new providers of essential input, imposed standards of transparency on integrated monopolies, demanded autonomy for business units that provide nonregulated services, and restricted vertical integration.

Recent decisions are stricter than older ones in setting restrictions on vertical integration. Formerly, only legal unbundling was recommended, while more recent decisions have recommended complete separation of competitive and noncompetitive segments. In addition, the commissions have called on appropriate government agencies to avoid free price negotiation of essential facilities (electrical transmission, access to local telecommunications networks, and gas transport) and to regulate such rates.

All of these cases involve choosing between a single regulated entity that owns the railway track, gas pipeline, or electricity grid and customers who share ownership of the bottleneck and agree on rules for using it. The choice is between the inefficiency of regulation and the free-rider problems of joint ownership. In a country where regulation is easily captured, the latter option may be preferable, despite the lack of consumer representation it may entail.

Market power of producers, especially foreign producers, creates unique problems for the gas industry. In Europe, it is argued that, for supply by Algeria, Norway, and Russia, a vertically integrated network operator who also owns gas fields may enhance consumer bargaining power with producers. In chapter 3, Bondorevsky and Petrecolla illustrate this problem in Argentina, where a single private producer sells more than 60 percent of its gas.[8] In chapter 4, García shows that, in Colombia, a single producer also controls the wholesale gas market, but unlike the Argentina case, this producer is a stated-owned company. The authors of both chapters recommend

---

[8] Since 1993, prices at the wellhead have increased by about 17 percent in real terms; as a result, ENARGAS is considering presenting the case before the Competition Commission.

BOX 3. PERU'S CHANGING MARKET STRUCTURE OF TELECOM PROVIDERS

When Peru's telecommunications sector was privatized in 1994, a seven-year contract was awarded to the monopoly Telefónica for fixed phone services. The goal was to force large investments to increase coverage and penetration and allow for a smooth restructuring of tariffs. In 1998, however, Telefónica and the Peruvian authorities renegotiated the contract, opening all services to competition.

---

measures to reduce dominant market share. For Argentina, divestment is suggested, while, for Colombia, less structural measures are proposed, including selling a portion of the gas managed by the state-owned company through public auctions.

Chapter 3 also considers the extent to which the natural gas industry structures of Brazil (controlled by a state-owned company) and Argentina (controlled by a private company) prevent effective regional integration of gas markets. To advance development of these markets and accelerate investment in new transport networks, the authors recommend four short-term measures. The first is to ensure that the producers' pledge to divest assets is completed. The second is to guarantee that large, dominant actors will not monopolize Bolivia's natural gas production market. The third is to have national and regional antitrust agencies closely examine the effects of alliances between dominant actors. The fourth is to ensure that gas producers in Bolivia and, in the future, Peru can supply the Argentinean and Brazilian markets and have open access to the gas pipelines that connect the national systems, regardless of who owns these lines.

Another question is how competitive the market structure should be for infrastructure users and competing infrastructure providers, given that the major problem for developing countries is attracting foreign capital (box 3).

Rules to Regulate Monopolies

In developing countries, regulating natural monopolies arbitrates between efficiency and the cost of the information rents relinquished to firms. High-powered incentive schemes, such as price caps, encourage cost-minimizing behavior, yielding large rents to the most efficient types of firms. Conversely, low-powered incentive schemes, such as cost-of-service regulation, control those profits but create weak incentives for minimizing costs. In chapter 5, Beato and Laffont analyze factors, summarized below, that determine the appropriate mechanism for regulating prices in developing countries.

High Cost of Public Funds

The high cost of public funds, which characterizes developing countries, clearly calls for higher-priced commodities produced by the natural monopoly, as well as high shares of cost reimbursement.

Monitoring and Incentives

The effect of monitoring on the power of incentives differs according to type. Monitoring of effort, for example, generally enables the regulator to reduce information rents and requires higher-powered incentive schemes. Less efficient monitoring technologies demand weaker incentive schemes. Indeed, inefficient technologies and weak incentives together substitute for extracting a firm's rent.

Hierarchical Regulation and Corruption

A major role of the regulatory agency is to bridge the information gap between the public decisionmaker and the regulated firm. Yet, this raises the issue of possible capture of the regulatory agency by the firm. This type of collusion is more likely to occur if the stakes (the information rent that an efficient firm obtains when the regulator hides the fact that it is efficient) are high, the costs of side transfers between the firm and the regulator are low, and no incentive mechanism is in place for the regulator.

Credibility of Commitment

Compared with governments of developed countries, those in developing countries often lack credibility of long-term commitment to regulatory rules, which puts the ratchet effect into motion. Faced with incentives during its initial period, a firm may fear that taking advantage of current incentive schemes (efficient firms make more money by having low costs) will lead to more demanding incentives in the future. Credibility of a government's commitment to not seize future rents may mean remaining ignorant of a firm's efficiency.

Weak Enforcement of Regulations

In developing countries, poor enforcement of regulations has several causes. First, the high cost of public funds decreases optimal enforcement. Second, the principal-agent paradigm, which attributes full bargaining power to the regulator, does not fit the reality of developing countries; however, weakness in the bargaining position during renegotiation calls for more investment in enforcement. Third, corruption of the enforcement or regulatory mechanism calls for less enforcement (Laffont 2001).

Financial Constraints

Financial constraints compound the difficulties of asymmetric information for regulation. The basic analysis involves simple moral hazard control problems with risk neutrality. In a delegated activity, moral hazard can be controlled without giving up rents to the agent if penalties can be imposed, even when accurate observance of performance is not possible. However, if limited liability constraints obstruct the imposition of such penalties, then only rewards for good performance can induce appropriate levels of effort.

Interface of Monopoly and Competition

Regulating the interface of monopoly and competition in infrastructure sectors must ensure that operators have access to the necessary infrastructure to operate their services and are treated equally. Issues of access and equity are especially important in cases of vertical integration, where an owner of an essential infrastructure is also an operator of services using that infrastructure. Nevertheless, problems may also arise with vertical disintegration, where the owner of the bottleneck infrastructure does not offer services in the competitive segment. In chapter 6, Wood discusses such an interface for transportation services within the context of the European Union. The sections below show how the problem of access changes with the structure of the industry.

Vertical Disintegration

In the simplest case, competitive industries produce final services at constant marginal costs, and one company is dedicated soley to providing bottleneck infrastructure services. Optimal pricing says that markup of the access price over the marginal cost of access for a given good, relative to the access price for this good, should be inversely proportional to its demand price elasticity. Such a pricing scheme can be decentralized with price caps on the regulated public utility, thus relying on the firm's demand information. Clearly, users of the infrastructure control the demand information. The utility can infer this information from the demand for access as long as users report truthfully on the type of final good for which they use the infrastructure. In developing countries, where inspection systems are easily corrupted, it may be difficult to foster truthful reporting. In addition, interest groups can manipulate the price discrimination that results from sophisticated Ramsey pricing (Laffont and Tirole 1993). Consequently, in developing countries, Ramsey pricing should be based on broad categories of use that do not raise complex inspection issues and should be decentralized through price caps.

In chapter 7, Beato, discusses one reason for rejecting Ramsey pricing and other types of price discrimination. Imperfectly implemented, such practices may lead overpriced consumers to abandon the regulated firm or force the exclusion of underpriced consumers. Overpriced consumers may realize that their payments to the regulated firm are higher than they would be under other arrangements. They also may notice that, by excluding underpriced consumer groups, they could reduce their payments to the regulated firm. Thus, overpriced consumers may force the splitting of the service, causing the community as a whole to lose the benefits of technologies with economies of scale.

Another reason to reject Ramsey pricing is that users of the infrastructure facility are treated differently. In chapter 6, Wood presents the case of pricing practices at Brussels National Airport, which shows the position of European competition authorities on price discrimination. The airport authority was found to hold a dominant market position in aircraft landing and takeoff services. It had not been demonstrated previously that handling takeoffs and landings by one airline versus another gives rise to economies of scale. The system of discounts on landing fees had the effect of applying dissimilar conditions to airlines for equivalent transactions linked to landing and takeoff services, thereby placing some airlines at a competitive disadvantage. In chapter 10, Cisnal de Ugarte discusses practices in energy markets that may contravene European Community competition rules. The author points out that a transmission price may be excessive within the rules of Article 82 of the Rome Treaty if price exceeds the value of the service provided. Therefore, Ramsey pricing may be denounced as anticompetitive. The process of assessing transmission tariffs might, however, be complicated; experience of Swedish regulators has shown how difficult and demanding the process is in terms of the time and resources required to determine a reasonable price for transmission.

In developing countries, another concern is the market power of infrastructure users, such as electricity producers. The regulation should not attempt to undo the monopoly power of infrastructure users by means of access pricing policy. Indeed, such a policy requires the regulator to have much knowledge and raises issues of favoritism. In the absence of long-term contracts, there is also a potential for expropriating the investments of large users, which negatively affects foreign capital.

One-way Access with Vertical Integration

If competitive users of the infrastructure supply an imperfect substitute for the service of the dominant provider (for example, mobile phone versus fixed-link telephony), then access should be regulated like end-user service. The dominant provider will be willing to provide access, thereby increasing its business and having little effect on its service market. For example, global price caps, including final and access goods, can be used.

The situation becomes more difficult when competitive users offer services that are close substitutes for those offered by the dominant provider. In such a case, the Ramsey rule says that the access price should be high enough to avoid inefficient business stealing and to balance the budget of the dominant provider. One is tempted to favor an access pricing rule that is generous to the dominant provider (such as the efficient component pricing rule) to avoid foreclosure and focus regulatory resources on implementing quick, high-quality interconnection. Alternatively, one can use a global price cap, supplemented by maximum prices determined via the efficient component pricing rule. This is a difficult case, requiring much regulatory expertise; therefore, this solution may not be easily implemented in developing countries. Examples from Colombia (box 4), China, Ghana, and other countries show that dominant telecom providers use various strategies, including exclusion, delays, and raising rivals' costs, to avoid competition.

Two-way Access for Competition

Competition in infrastructure services, particularly telecommunications, usually results in deregulation of final prices, and the issue becomes regula-

---

BOX 4. COLOMBIA'S TELECOM INDUSTRY: INCENTIVES FOR EXCLUSION

In Colombia, where the constitution prohibits monopolies—even public ones—several regional public companies offer local telephony: Bogotá Telecom (25 percent), Medellín (10 percent), and Cali (7 percent). The country also has four mobile phone companies. Setting interconnection charges for both long-distance and mobile services does not appear problematic. The services are sufficiently complementary so that both operators gain from quick interconnection. However, there is concern that access charges may be too high.

When Medellín and Cali attempted to enter Bogotá's local market, Bogotá Telecom denied them access. As a result, the three fixed-link companies in Bogotá are not fully interconnected. Indeed, access charges are not included in the price cap on final prices or determined by historical costs according to the fully-distributed method. Bogotá Telecom, which makes no money on access, has every incentive to behave in an exclusionary manner.

---

tion of access prices. The literature shows that access prices in telecommunications should be regulated because firms (at least for symmetrical networks) can use access charges to collude (high access charges result in high final prices) and block entry (Armstrong 1998; Laffont, Rey, and Tirole 1998a, 1998b). The bill-and-keep policy, which amounts to a zero access charge, is a simple solution that encourages competition in final prices. It is used between peering backbones in the Internet (Laffont, Rey, and Tirole 2001).

A more difficult situation occurs when networks are asymmetrical in size or traffic. In such cases, policymakers must ensure that network competition does not interfere with network development. The regulator may require negotiations for interconnection under the threat of arbitration by an international body. It is unlikely that the regulator will have the information needed to set access prices. In this area, it is not enough to declare that competition is possible or even to sell licenses for competition to occur. Inability to ensure fair competition may make it undesirable, in which case, a better option might be a regulated monopolist with a strict program for developing the network.

Competition Policy

Competition has several requirements. First, an industry must have a sufficient number of firms or potential entrants. Second, those firms must not
enter into collusive side contracts. Third, a firm that has developed a dominant position through innovation should not abuse this position.

In developing countries, lack of participants is a major problem, particularly in infrastructure industries where investments are held for long
periods. The goal is to attract local or foreign capital by creating the conditions that make investment attractive, but this is not a competition agency's
usual task. Unfortunately, most characteristics of developing countries cause
difficulties that are not easily solved. These include inefficient financial sectors; lack of institutional credibility, enforcement of laws, and consumer
information; and inefficient transportation and communications.

As Rey (1997) observes, collusion is facilitated by entry barriers, market
concentration, and capacity constraints. In addition, the transaction costs of
collusion are likely to be lower in developing countries, and predatory strategies may be particularly dangerous where credit markets are weak. Rey also
argues that the high entry barriers often found in developing countries give
more force to the market foreclosure argument when discussing the essential
facility doctrine; he also recommends a more cautious attitude toward vertical restraints.

In chapter 8, Tomiak and Millan illustrate that, in Central American
countries, lack of an enabling environment is a particular problem for power
sector infrastructure in which technologies favor high concentration. The
authors also point out that international trade cannot be relied on to create
competitive pressures.

In chapter 9, Fuente reviews competition policy in six Latin American
countries. The author's analysis emphasizes that competition policy should
apply to the competitive segments of the deregulated industry (for example,
generation for electricity, long distance for telephony, and operating services
for transportation). This is particularly important in countries where
attracting capital requires giving sizeable market share to investing firms.
Merger and acquisition rules in developing countries should emphasize simplicity, nondiscrimination, and adaptability to rapidly changing market
structures. One possibility is to have explicit market share constraints relinquishing efficiency defenses, which can be revised periodically.

More generally, the need to attract capital generates market structures
that are imperfectly competitive and call for more intrusive regulation than

classical competition policy can provide. It also creates conflicts between privatization committees or regulatory institutions, which are well aware of the constraints that attracting capital imposes on competition and competition authorities, which ex post facto tend to breach the explicit or implicit agreements to restrict competition obtained by investors.

In any case, United States-style competition policy is unaffordable and difficult to implement in developing countries. While designing simple, transparent rules for those countries remains a worthy task, particularly to prevent horizontal collusion and abuse of dominant position, benefits in the foreseeable future remain small. Lack of appropriately trained professionals to staff those agencies is acute, especially given that the economic analysis of such questions as predatory behavior and vertical restraints is both ambiguous and complex. Emerging industries, necessarily, will be highly monopolistic, and interest groups will have considerable potential for interference. Nonetheless, competition agencies should be established to educate the public on the social benefits of fair competition. These agencies should also focus on specific areas of concern, such as how poor communications systems and inefficient trading organizations weaken competition.

In chapter 10, Cisnal de Ugarte illustrates how European competition regulations apply to relevant sectors. Regarding the power sector, the author concludes that electricity has been determined to be a good that is subject to the rules on the free movement of goods. Moreover, European Community Treaty provisions on state aid are applicable to the energy sector. Furthermore, firms operating in the electricity sector are subject to all competition rules contained in the Treaty. Finally, general rules on free movement and competition are subject to exceptions in the Treaty, which, in certain cases, may mean that the electricity sector would not be subject to such rules.

Recommendations and Editors' Remarks

In the Epilogue, Fernández-Ordóñez presents the dual perspectives of competition and sector regulatory authorities on most issues discussed in this book. He recommends requiring structural and behavioral provisions for introducing competition into both conventional and network-based sectors. For conventional sectors, he recommends promoting competition by easing of regulations (market liberalization) and privatization, followed by enforcement of antitrust law. Structural measures, such as placing constraints on mergers or rulings on abuse of dominant position, may be taken to promote competition; however, these must always be a posteriori. For network-based sectors, structural measures must be taken a priori. For this reason, restructuring mechanisms must be adopted in advance to enable these sectors to begin operating under a competitive model. Pro-competition measures can only be effective when anti-competitive behavior is the natural result of the existing business structure.

In addition, Fernández-Ordóñez recommends that structural measures focus not only on the vertical side of the chart, but also seek to provide competitive businesses with a competition-friendly structure to solve competition difficulties. In order for competition to succeed, former monopolies must undergo a process of horizontal breakup. However, feasibility of implementation requires a case-by-case examination in each particular sector.

As editors of this book, we would like to conclude by highlighting two limitations of the analyses found herein, followed by a recommendation.

Liberalization, competition, and regulatory reform are recent in developing countries, especially the poorest ones. Empirical evidence is limited, difficult to access, and unavailable in a form that allows rigorous econometric tests. Case studies and theory, the only available tools, must be used cautiously because the economic theory relevant to developing countries requires further elaboration. In addition, although some government characteristics are discussed, a broader political economy of reform that considers historical characteristics and relevant political situations is needed.

Finally, we recommend that more empirical work be done to characterize the precise features of developing countries that are relevant to regulatory economics. Such research should lead to distinguishing among various stages of development and classifying countries that require different policies.

That said, we believe the chapters that follow will provide a useful framework for those who face the challenge of advising developing country authorities on implementing public services more efficiently.

References

Armstrong, M. 1998. "Network Interconnection." *Economic Journal* 108: 545–64.

Auriol, E., and J. J. Laffont. 1992. "Regulation by Duopoly." *Journal of Development and Management Strategy* 1: 503–33.

Beasley, T., and R. Burgess. "The Political Economy of Government Responsiveness: Theory and Evidence from India." London School of Economics, 2001. Mimeographed.

Laffont, J. J. "Enforcement, Regulation, and Development." ARQADE, Université de Toulouse, 2001. Mimeographed.

Laffont, J. J., and J. Tirole. 1993. *A Theory of Incentives in Regulation and Procurement.* Cambridge, MA: MIT Press.

Laffont, J. J., P. Rey, and J. Tirole. 1998a. "Network Competition I: Overview and Non Discriminatory Pricing." *Rand Journal of Economics* 29: 1–37.

———. 1998b. "Network Competition II: Price Discrimination." *Rand Journal of Economics* 29: 38–56.

Laffont, J. J., S. Marcus, P. Rey, and J. Tirole. 2001. "Internet Peering." American Economic *Review, Papers and Proceedings*: 287–91.

Mishkin, F. 1997. "Understanding Financial Crises: A Developing Country Perspective." In *Annual World Bank Conference on Development Economics*, eds. M. Bruno and B. Pleskovic. Washington D.C.: World Bank.

Ordover, J., R. Pittman, and P. Clyde. 1994. "Competition Policy for Natural Monopolies in a Developing Market Economy." *Economics of Transition* 2(3): 317–43.

Rey, P. "Competition Policy and Development." IDEI, 1997. Mimeographed.

Tirole, J. 1992. "Collusion and the Theory of Organizations." In *Advances in Economic Theory*, ed. J. J. Laffont. Cambridge, U.K.: Cambridge University Press.

Trebilcock, M. 1996. "What Makes Poor Countries Poor? The Role of Institutional Capital in Economic Development." In *The Law and Economics of Development*, eds. Buscaglia and Cooter. Stamford, CT: JAI Press.

Chapter 1

Designing Infrastructure Regulation in Developing Countries

Cécile Aubert and Jean-Jacques Laffont

In developing countries, designing regulation raises critical questions related to geographic decentralization, industrial scope of regulators, and functional dimensions. The first set of questions centers on the desirable balance of federal and decentralized regulation. For example, for telecommunications, should one recommend federal regulation, as in Brazil, or a two-tier system of state and federation regulations, as in the United States and the European Union? For water distribution, should one recommend regulation at the provincial level rather than the national level? To tackle such questions, one must clearly understand the trade-offs of decentralization.

The second set of questions focuses on the desirable number of industries that a regulator should supervise. Should one regulator supervise all industries, as in Panama and Jamaica, or should each industry have its own regulator, as in Mexico and Canada? Should the optimal design evolve over time, as the recent integration of gas and electricity regulations in the United Kingdom might suggest?

The third set of questions involves various functional dimensions of regulation, including price, quality, environmental effects, entry, and ex ante (as in traditional regulation) versus ex post (as in competition policy) regulation. Should a single national body deal with regulation and antitrust, as in Australia, or should separate regulators handle price, quality, and environmental effects, as in the United Kingdom's regulation of water? What are the respective responsibilities of ministries and independent regulators?

Such critical questions are as old as economics, as the following quotation attests:

> Public works of a local nature should be maintained by local revenue because the abuses which sometimes creep into the local and provincial administration of a local or provincial revenue, how enormous so ever they may appear, are in reality, however, almost always very trifling in comparison with those which commonly take place in the administration and expenditure of a great empire. (Adam Smith, *The Wealth of Nations*, 1776)

Even today, these questions are at the heart of political debate, as Boris Berezovsky expresses in his opposition to Vladimir Putin:

> On the whole, the horizontal and vertical division of power is a guarantee against arbitrary rule and the usurping of power... In other words, a bad elected leader is better than a good leader appointed from above because the system of appointing leaders is defective in principle. The point of a federal organization of Government lies in the rational balancing of real, objective contradictions between central and local interests. (*The Moscow Times*, January 6, 2000)

Three types of lessons must be considered when making recommendations on regulation: the long experiences of developed countries; the more recent, often partial experiences of developing countries; and economic theory. Given available technologies and resources, including human resources, the normative approach of economic theory seeks to design regulatory structures that maximize social welfare. A complementary viewpoint considers the political implementation of new institutions, including regulatory rules, which immediately leads to the historical viewpoint and the path dependence of institutional evolution.

Lessons from Industrial Countries: Historical Overview

In industrial countries, regulatory agencies were established in the late 19th and early 20th centuries according to each country's needs, without reference to a theoretical framework for optimal regulatory design. The degree to which agencies were centralized or specialized was decided without much reference to institutional theory. Looking back at the evolution of these institutions, a historical path-dependence emerges, whereby agencies were created in succession as firms and public pressure demanded them. European countries typically have dealt with strong political constraints, which have limited the efficiency of regulation. Their response to this inefficiency often has been to nationalize utilities, especially after World Wars I and II. The United States, on the other hand, has had a more innovative pattern of regulation, creating a complex system of overlapping responsibilities between agencies at various levels of government. It has outpaced other countries in terms of regulatory efficiency and reliance on market forces.

Typically, regulation emerged at the level of municipalities, before evolving toward state and federal levels. Since regulation entails giving up rents, control by political entities was necessary to ensure accountability. The allocation of regulatory authority, therefore, closely followed the political structure of the states. Regions of France and Germany assumed regulatory responsibilities when technical or coordination issues justified it. Intervention by upper levels of government was relatively extensive, depending on a country's degree of political and administrative centralization.

In the case of local services, such as bus transport or waste collection, regulation often remained at the local level, since centralized regulation had no possible economies of scope and therefore no justification for depriving municipalities of their regulatory power. A certain degree of centralized regulation of water stemmed from the necessity to coordinate extraction and distribution, as well as environmental concerns. Municipalities or regions, therefore, often maintained control of the design and allocation of concessions.

Nationalization in the United Kingdom: Telephony and Railways

In the United Kingdom, the first 30 years of telephony were characterized by formal competition. In 1880, the Postmaster General began issuing licenses to private and municipal suppliers. Yet network effects rapidly gave rise to unregulated regional monopolies. In response to public pressure, the service was nationalized in 1912. Statutory monopoly was granted to the British Post Office. However, telecommunications, unlike other utilities, remained privately owned until World War II. This stemmed from the perception that coordinating private networks would be more difficult for telecommunications than for other industries.

4 AUBERT AND LAFFONT

Although the British Parliament had discretion and frequently changed legislation, the Post Office retained autonomy. Regulation consisted merely of rate-of-return mechanisms, with government intervention on tariffs for macroeconomic control. Regulation rejected the will of the Treasury to use the industry as a revenue resource. This explains the lack of investment in the network and technological upgrading until the 1960s, at which time the industry was characterized by poor service and long waiting lists.

The British Telegraph and Post Office were nationalized in 1869. The Post Office retained monopoly over long-distance telephony lines in order to protect telegraph investments from too intensive competition. Since the Post Office was a government department, all of its expenses had to be approved by and revenues repaid to the Treasury.

While the Treasury had complete control of daily expenses, the Parliament could not distinguish between expenses incurred for telephony, telegraph, or postal services. Political control seems to have been only a formality; in reality, control belonged to the bureaucracy after 1911 (Hills 1986). The 1979 election of Margaret Thatcher led to the 1981 Telecommunications Act, which created British Telecom and opened telephony services to competition. British Telecom was privatized, and Oftel, the regulatory office of telecommunications, was established in 1984.

Regulation of the British railways was driven by the fear that competition could lead to firms' bankruptcy and to an eventual decrease in the number of competitors. After a laissez-faire period, which began in 1830, Parliament took measures to ensure that many producers would survive. It used price fixing as a way to stabilize profits, at the expense of competition, and encouraged cartels while preventing consolidations. At the end of the 19th century, Parliament issued a decision to outlaw price discrimination, prevent mergers, and enforce cartel agreements. In the 1920s, cartelization was again encouraged and imperiled firms were subsidized.

After World War II, most utilities were in public hands, but were autonomously managed. Subsidies, production quotas, and price fixing continued to protect firms from market pressure. Finally, until the Thatcher administration, an impressive program of regulatory reform of institutions and privatization was launched.

Nationalization in France: Railways

In France, state intervention in railways began in 1823; however, this represented a continuation of previous intervention in other transportation areas, such as canals. As Dobbin (1994) emphasized in his interesting comparison of U.S., British, and French railways of the 19th century, the primary concern of French politicians and officials was to develop a coherent and rational rail system, which translated into developing it under government planning.

The French government attracted private investment by guaranteeing a return on capital and by restricting entry into the industry through establishing six regional monopolies. The Ponts et Chaussees administrative body designed the routes that appeared most necessary, and exclusive concessions of 99 years were auctioned off. Under administrative oversight, civil servants with no legislative mandate granted concessions (Dobbin 1994). Unsolicited applications were systematically refused until 1833, when Parliament overruled the Ponts et Chaussees to grant a concession.

Regional and local governments were virtually excluded from the design of railway planning, which was considered to be of national interest. Railways were viewed as a way to achieve order and regional integration. Adolphe Thiers, then Minister of Commerce and Public Works, supported public planning on efficiency and political grounds. This strongly contrasts with the building of railways in the United States, where local governments were active, and where concessions were granted according to expected financial viability. In France, by contrast, the main criterion was optimal use of the nation's resources, given the existing roads and canals.

In 1837, a debate arose on whether railways should be public or private. The debate continued in parliamentary commissions, where it was recognized that the need for private funds had to be balanced with the central government's ability to preserve the public interest. A compromise was reached, whereby the government and private investors each provided half of the capital for construction, and operation was private, under a system of concessions and franchises. Ongoing corruption led to several scandals, to which the central government responded in 1880 by increasing state controls. This response corresponded to the prevailing belief that the central government was benevolent, not corrupt, and was acting in the public interest. Once again, this response contrasts with that of the United States, which, when faced with a similar situation at about the same time, limited state intervention to remove discretionary power from the hands of local politicians.

The debate over public versus private control arose again when the first concessions came to an end. Nationalization was decided in 1937, with the creation of the Société Nationale des Chemins de Fer (SNCF), which still operates today. When World War I broke out, France became a command economy, and increased state control persisted after the war ended. Then, after World War II, partially because of the role large industrial companies played in collaborating with the Nazis (for example, Renault), a series of nationalizations occurred.

A privatization program, begun in 1986, was halted and then resumed because of political changes. Today, privatization is a motto of all major political parties, but several utilities, including the SNCF, remain publicly owned.

Complexity of the U.S. Regulatory System

In the United States, states are highly autonomous, particularly regarding businesses that remain within their borders. This particular feature explains, in part, the regulatory system that has emerged in the 20th century. Reliance on market mechanisms for attaining efficiency, and distrust of state intervention have also conditioned the evolution of regulation over time.

Context of the Sherman Act

The Sherman Act, passed in 1890, provided a sound framework for fighting collusive agreements and abuse of dominant position, although, at the time, it was viewed as insufficient and was poorly enforced to control utilities. Specific regulatory agencies were created to answer firms' demands; indeed, firms requested a degree of regulation to protect them from local political extortion or abuse of power by clients and suppliers.

If judges with a strong conviction about the benefits of competition had enforced the Sherman Act, the tool could have been used more powerfully (Kovacic and Shapiro 2000). Interpreted broadly, the Act could even have been used to fight harmful mergers on monopolization grounds. The general doubt about the benefits and costs of competition may explain, in large part, its relatively weak enforcement until the 1910s, and the necessity of creating other judiciary tools.

Competition was viewed as potentially harmful for high-fixed-cost or sunk-costs industries, particularly railways and utilities. Indeed, fierce competition with little or no interconnection in the late 19th and early 20th centuries resulted in waste and frequent railway and telecommunications bankruptcies. Consolidation soon appeared as the widespread response because, without interconnection, club effects naturally led to concentration in a few networks.

In 1912, the courts reacted to this trend by imposing interconnection. Their decision in *United States versus Terminal Railroad Association of St.*

Louis (224 U.S. 383) obligated railways that controlled terminal facilities to offer rivals access on reasonable terms. The court also appealed to the Interstate Commerce Commission to set fair access prices. This decision led to the essential facilities doctrine. Moreover, it reinforced the legitimacy of utility regulators by calling for access regulation, in addition to more standard types of regulation. Yet, at that time, it was viewed as proving that the terms of the Sherman Act were too vague and subject to interpretation.

Competition Laws and Agencies

In 1914, Congress passed two laws enabling reduction of the power of judges: The Clayton Act and the Federal Trade Commission Act. The Clayton Act reduced the discretion of courts by specifying forbidden practices per se, such as exclusive dealing, interlocking directorates, and mergers resulting from purchasing stock.[1] The Federal Trade Commission Act created the Federal Trade Commission (FTC), an independent administrative agency in charge of promoting competition. Its mandate was similar to that of the Department of Justice (DOJ) with regard to enforcement of the Sherman Act. Creation of overlapping agencies was publicly motivated by the fact that the DOJ was overloaded with work. Yet, it seems reasonable to consider other motivations for creating the FTC since, in theory, a specialized bureau within the DOJ would have sufficed and would have made the separation of tasks easier (specialization need not imply separation). Moreover, that the FTC Act "ended the executive branch's monopoly on public enforcement of antitrust laws," a fact highlighted by Kovacic and Shapiro (2000), seems to indicate political motives.

Kovacic and Shapiro argue that this separation stems, at least in part, from the desire to better control antitrust enforcement after the much debated decision *Standard Oil versus United States* (221 U.S. 1 (1911)) and, to a lesser extent, the 1912 Terminal Railway decision. If one accepts this argument, then separation of regulators can be seen as a way of relying on competition between regulators to limit their discretion. As an administrative body, the FTC was easier for Congress to control than the DOJ.

---

[1] See Kovacic and Shapiro (2000) for an interesting survey of U.S. antitrust policy since 1890.

Federal Sector Agencies and State Multisector Commissions

After creating the FTC, the overlapping mandates and competition that arose with the DOJ seemed representative of the general U.S. regulatory structure. Overlapping mandates of agencies were also seen in the dual enforcement role of federal agencies and state utility commissions.

The first state Public Utility Commission (PUC) was set up to answer the expressed need of local firms for more regulation. The general tendency seems to have been to request regulation from the closest political body. Thus, municipalities were asked first, their regulatory power having resulted from their ability to sell and auction concessions for water, electricity, mining, and other services. When municipalities appeared corrupt, extortive, or unable to deal with firms located in multiple areas, state regulation began with the creation of PUCs. They have endured because of the structure of the country's political system.

The strong autonomy of U.S. states gave them the constitutional power to establish their own agencies to regulate intrastate issues. Politicians have viewed potential disagreement with federal rules as a strong reason for not relinquishing the possibility to regulate utilities. Because of the large size of U.S. states, the PUCs have remained multisector agencies; conversely, owing to the country's large size, it was more practical to set up sector specific or even industry specific federal regulatory agencies. The 1946 Administrative Procedures Act authorized the commissions to make industrywide rules. Most state commissions still use quasijudiciary proceedings, with adjudicatory processes, rather than rule-making. This follows the example of the Interstate Commerce Commission, which established a regulatory model in the 1880s that allowed for maintaining strong accountability of the regulators, even though they benefited from much discretion in the U.S. system.

Telecommunications: Competition and Regulatory History

The late 19th and early 20th centuries were characterized by strong competition between local exchange operators, usually with at least two—one of which was Bell—in each city. Since most companies did not interconnect, Bell used network effects to gain a competitive advantage over independent competitors and a larger consumer base. This advantage was further strengthened by AT&T denying interconnection with its intercity network to independent companies for long-distance calls. The DOJ challenged this behavior, and A. Kingsbury, then Head of AT&T, settled the dispute in 1913 by signing a commitment, later known as the Kingsbury Commitment, to follow certain rules, including offering interconnection to all. In 1921, much of this commitment became irrelevant after forceful lobbying of Congress resulted in adoption of the Willis-Graham Act, which exempted AT&T from antitrust laws when acquiring additional companies. An aggressive policy of consolidation followed, which led to creation of the 1934 Communications Act. This Act remained in effect for 62 years, when it was replaced by the Telecommunications Act of 1996.

The 1934 Communications Act established the Federal Communications Commission (FCC), empowering it to approve new services, compel interconnection, suspend rates, and allocate frequencies. The Act required rates to be "just and reasonable," but no precise definition of these terms was given. It also obligated common carriers to provide service to the public. Indeed, at that time, AT&T provided 90 percent of telecommunications network service but covered less than 50 percent of the country's land area.

Independence of the federal regulator. The 1934 Communications Act ensured independence of the federal regulatory agency through several provisions. First, the FCC was responsible to (and its budget was decided by) Congress, not the executive branch. Second, the five commissioners governing the FCC were nominated by the President and confirmed by the Senate. No more than three commissioners could represent the same political party, which constituted a balance-of-power mechanism and ensured insulation from political pressures. Third, to prevent capture by the industry, the commissioners were barred from having any financial interest in an industry related to the work of the FCC.

Regulatory problems. One of the main difficulties regulators faced was the complex set of relationships that linked AT&T, Bell operating companies, Bell Laboratories, and Western Electric. Regulation, therefore, consisted of a relatively simple rate of return. As early as 1938, the FCC reported (and later disproved) that the vertical monopoly allowed the company to escape regulation: that AT&T charged high rates to local operating companies, who then incorporated these prices into their costs and, therefore, into the regulator's rate base. After long, often heated debates, the controversy ended in the divestiture of AT&T in 1980.

Other difficulties linked to the regulatory framework involved lack of clear allocation of authority between regulators. The 1996 Telecommunications Act has strongly increased the FCC's authority, investing it with the power and duty to adopt detailed rules and standards.[2] This provision should not create much concern about excessive discretion of the Commission since the DOJ and state commissions can challenge its authority. The regulatory costs associated with the design and implementation of these rules are likely to be significant and would prevent giving enough attention to other issues.

Unclear allocation of tasks between state and federal commissions. As stated in Section 1 of the 1934 Communications Act, the FCC was responsible for regulating prices and mergers and acquisitions; these were limited to interstate services, while intrastate services remained under control of state commissions, who frequently granted monopoly licenses to operators (most of them were regional Bell operating companies). The 1996 Act modified this feature by allowing the FCC to intervene in the local exchange market. However, the provision lacks clarity regarding the precise allocation of authority between the FCC and the state commissions, thereby giving rise to judicial uncertainty and potential disputes.

Firms can use unclear allocation of authority opportunistically to delay implementation of regulatory rules or introduction of competition. The suit brought by incumbent local exchange carriers and state regulators against the FCC in 1996 illustrates this point. The FCC issued a first report and order, in which it prescribed the use of pricing based on total element, long-run incremental cost. This was challenged on the grounds that local competition provisions should be designed and implemented by the states, not by the FCC. In October 1996, the Court of Appeals for the Eighth Circuit asserted that the FCC lacked jurisdiction to issue pricing rules. Finally, in January 1999, the Supreme Court overturned this decision. This dispute has been costly, causing much delay in implementing the 1996 Act. Kerf and Geradin (1999) report that this case is thought to have discouraged entry into the local exchange market because of the perceived legal risks.

Allocation of power between the FCC and the DOJ. Under the 1996 Act, the FCC has to consult the DOJ before deciding whether to allow regional Bell operating companies to enter the long-distance market. The FCC and DOJ share responsibility in the area of mergers and acquisitions. Both can review

---

[2] See Kerf and Geradin (1999) for a detailed comparison of U.S., Australian, and New Zealand regulation of telecommunications.

mergers independently with different statutory authority. This system has both benefits and costs. The benefits stem from the possibility that the two agencies use different approaches, the DOJ focusing more on competition. The costs lie in duplicate expenses, delays in reaching a decision, and regulatory uncertainty. The overlapping of responsibilities risks inconsistency, particularly since the review process differs by agency. For example, in 1997, the DOJ unconditionally approved the Bell Atlantic/NYNEX merger, contrary to the FCC decision, which required measures to open markets before accepting the merger.

Summary of Historical Findings

Historical evidence shows that two main factors have affected the design of regulatory institutions: the technical characteristics of the industry and the political organization of the state.

Effects of Technical Characteristics

Regulation seems to have started at the local level, when municipalities first began to use their power of allocating licenses and concessions and of issuing price and safety regulations. Whether regulation has been taken over by higher levels of government has depended on the structure of the industry. When regulation had no economies of scale, municipalities retained power. Economies of scale arose with externalities in the operation of firms between neighboring areas, the need for regional coordination (for railway design or interconnection of telecommunications and electricity networks), or when regulation required specific skills and expertise.

Since regulation of local transportation and waste collection and treatment do not demand specific technical expertise, and because no externalities exist between municipalities, the local government has retained regulatory control over these industries. Similarly, regulation of water, with the exception of environmental concerns, has remained at the local level. Since water consumption at the level of a given municipality has little effect on other localities, it seemed natural for the municipalities to retain the power they had initially over the industry. Karhl (1982) also relates how financial constraints have affected the behavior of municipalities in U.S. water management. Though private investment achieved major projects during the 19th century, these were limited to ones that could use locally available water. When the need appeared to move water from one hydrologic basin to another, financial issues arose because firms were not willing to assume the risk of having two local regulatory authorities.

By contrast, railway, telecommunications, and electricity industries operate on a much larger geographic scale, requiring specific expertise to understand their functioning. Duplicating specific skills at lower levels of government would clearly have been wasteful, and the public could easily perceive the economies of scale in having a centralized regulation. Therefore, in Europe, national regulation emerged. Owing to their large size, U.S. states retained considerable regulatory powers, while federal regulators took charge only when interstate issues arose.

Effects of Government and Political Structures

A second factor that seems to have played a crucial role in the design of regulation in industrial countries is the general structure of the respective governments. Effective regulation needs both administrative bodies to execute it and political entities to ensure its legitimacy. Regulatory structures have therefore been closely linked to the organization of the state. When regulatory needs arose in Europe and the United States, it was natural to first use the existing structure to deal quickly with problems. In general, regulation has first been undertaken by local political entities (municipalities or regions) that had the required legislative legitimacy. The case of railways in France is an exception since an administrative body undertook to regulate the industry without any prior legislative mandate. However, this action reflects the informal authority of technocrats in the French state at that time.

Once an entity began to regulate an industry, the regulatory structure was slow to change. This is because regulation entails the power to create and distribute rents, and political and administrative bodies are reluctant to relinquish such power. Thus, removing authority from an existing structure has proven difficult. Nevertheless, it has been easier to do so when the public was aware of problems in the existing structures. Scandals linked to corruption, for example, have usually been followed by a change in the regulatory structure, either toward more centralized regulation, as in France, or less public intervention, as in the United States. Poor-quality service leading to widespread discontent has also helped to reform the regulatory structure.

The influence of a government's political structure on its regulatory system can be seen by comparing the approaches of France, the United Kingdom, and the United States. France, which has a centralized political system, quickly adopted national, centralized regulation, except for water and local transportation, which are still largely controlled by municipalities. The United Kingdom adopted centralized regulation, but with the participation of regional entities and monopolies with substantial power. This approach reflects the political autonomy of the regions and their will to assume sufficient regulatory power. United States states retained many regulatory powers because of their autonomy and large size.

Several observations can be drawn from the example of French railway design and management. First, cultural environment plays an important role in choosing regulatory structures. Given its culture of state intervention and benevolence, France reacted to regulatory issues by further increasing the government's role in economic life. This contrasts with the United States, where belief in market mechanisms led to very different outcomes. Second, expanding or reforming existing institutions is more common than creating new ones. The reason may be that economies were linked to avoid investing in a new structure or in existing institutions that strove to gain more power by obtaining broader mandates. In most countries where new agencies have been created, they have usually been patterned on existing ones. In the United Kingdom, for example, Parliament used the outline of the early factory inspectorates to design its railway regulatory agency. Similarly, the United States followed the model of state banking commissions to design its regulatory agencies. For example, the main structure of the Interstate Commerce Commission, established in 1887, was replicated, with few adjustments, in the Federal Reserve Board (1913), FTC (1914), Federal Power Commission (1930), and FCC (1934). Third, it should be noted that the notion of independent regulators dates back to the early 20th century in the United States, compared with only 20 years ago in Europe and other regions. This is because the answer to United States regulatory problems was independent regulation, while that of other countries was nationalization of infrastructure services.

Organization Theory

This section uses organization theory to analyze various trade-offs that affect choice of a single regulator versus multiregulators. Four stepwise analyses follow. The first maintains the myth of the benevolent, informed government and assumes bounded rationality in its decisionmaking. The second assumes decentralization of information and strategic behavior of the agents. The third maintains benevolence of the government, but assumes that lack of complete contracts limits the mechanisms that the government can implement. Finally, the fourth analysis eliminates the benevolent government assumption, and considers that interest groups influence governments. The effects of developing country characteristics on conclusions made along the way are also analyzed.

Bounded Rationality

Sah (1991) shows that the role of human fallibility or bounded rationality had not been studied in prior debates about diversification versus concentration of political authority. Even if one maintains that the government is a benevolent, informed principal, the assumption of its bounded rationality leads to insights into the structuring of power. Thus, multiple agencies in the United States (DOJ, FTC, state attorneys general, and private parties), which are authorized to contest mergers, might exemplify multiregulation, motivated by bounded rationality.

Centralization versus Decentralization

Sah and Stiglitz (1986) provide a model of bounded rationality that sheds light on the issue of centralization versus decentralization. A decisionmaker can make two types of errors when choosing a project, a manager, or a rule. The first type of error is accepting a bad project, manager, or rule; while the second type is rejecting a good project, manager, or rule.

If two decisionmakers are available in a given situation, the first question would be: Should decisionmaking be organized as a hierarchy, in which an acceptance decision must be made by both individuals, or as a polyarchy, in which one individual can make the decision and a project that is rejected by one is examined by the other?

In a hierarchy, the probability of accepting a good project is $(1 - p_2)^2$, while the probability of accepting a bad project is p_1^2 (where p_1 and p_2 equal the probability of making type one or type two errors, respectively). In a polyarchy, these probabilities are respectively $(1 - p_2)(1 + p_2)$ and $p_1(2 - p_1)$. If W and $-V$ equal the respective values of a good or bad decision and v equals the probability of a good project, then, in a hierarchy, expected social welfare would equal $v(1 - p_2)^2 W - (1 - v) p_1^2 V$; while, in a polyarchy, it would equal $v(1 - p_2^2) W - (1 - v)(2 - p_1) p_1 V$. Thus, a hierarchy is better if $(1 - v)(2 - p_1) p_1 V > (1 - p_2) p_2 W$.

A hierarchical decisionmaking process corresponds to centralization, while a polyarchical one corresponds to decentralization. When mistakes are costly and bad projects are common, centralization is a better approach. When good projects with high value are common, decentralization is preferable. Although the robustness of this conclusion should be checked in other bounded rationality models, the following recommendation can be derived: Centralization is favored for questions that involve threats to society, such as public health or security, while decentralization is favored for projects that have great potential value and weak downside effects.

If the two decisionmakers differ in their decisionmaking abilities and if decentralization is associated with a larger number of decisionmakers, then random selection of decisionmakers in a less centralized society has the advantage of diversifying performance. In more centralized societies, welfare will have the same mean, but higher volatility.

However, decisionmakers are not chosen randomly. To the extent that a single decisionmaker of a centralized system can be well chosen (through a sound, merit-based selection process), centralization is favored. This is particularly true for decisions that are well-identified ex ante and for which appropriate selection mechanisms can be designed. It is not necessarily true in a changing world where diversity of decisionmakers in a decentralized system might induce a greater ability to react to unanticipated events. Thus far, possible gains from coordination and economies of scale, which favor centralization, have not been considered. However, centralization requires communication, and, since communication is also fallible, limiting communication, and therefore centralization, also has value.

Lessons for Developing Economies

In many developing countries, more fallible decisionmaking, higher communication costs, and less efficient systems for selecting central authorities will favor decentralization. However, extreme lack of human resources in the regulatory area and the large opportunity cost of those resources will favor centralization to the extent that economies of scale exist. For these reasons, regional regulation that encompasses several countries, multisector regulators, and an integrated regulation and competition policy are envisioned for developing economies. The prospect of rapidly improving the expertise of a limited number of regulators with international support appears great. If new information technologies can be developed, lower communication costs also favor centralization (but not relative to developed countries). As important as these regulatory questions are, they do not threaten the survival of developing countries. So the added value of hierarchical systems, which mul-

TABLE 1-1. FACTORS RELEVANT TO REGULATORY SYSTEM CHOICE IN DEVELOPING ECONOMIES

Relevant factor	Preferable choice (relative to developed countries)
High cost of communication	Decentralization
High cost of regulators	Centralization
Fallibility of decisionmaking process	Decentralization
Poor quality of selection	Decentralization

tiply decisionmakers in a centralized way, seems limited. The results are conflicting, as summarized in table 1-1

Benevolent, Informed Government

The next analysis centers on the benevolent government, where regulated agents have private information. If all concerned parties are rational agents and the judicial system allows signing complete contracts, then the Revelation Principle provides a useful proposition: any form of regulation by the government can be replicated by a centralized mechanism whereby all agents transmit, in an incentive compatible way, their private information to the government, which, in turn, issues orders for verifiable variables and makes recommendations for moral hazard variables. According to the Revelation Principle, centralization remains optimal, despite the superior information of the periphery.[3] The government may behave more proactively with respect to its asymmetric information. It can use intermediaries to mitigate the extent of the asymmetric information. Regulatory agencies can be viewed as such intermediaries, and one can raise the question of optimal structuring of these agencies.

Trade-offs of Separating Regulators

In Dewatripont and Tirole (1999), the separation of two bodies is based on the notion of advocate. Two types of favorable information can be pursued.

---

[3] Some authors argue in favor of decentralization because information is decentralized. However, under the assumptions of the Revelation Principle, this argument is invalid. The desirability of decentralizing decisionmaking demands additional fallibilities, such as costly communication or other forms of bounded rationality.

The first type favors one decision (decision A), while the second type favors another (decision B). (No favorable information leads to no decision.) It is further assumed that rewards for information can only be provided if a decision is made. The two costly activities of searching for information create negative externalities. Indeed, after finding the first type of information for which the regulator can be rewarded by a payment conditional on decision A, the regulator has no incentive to search for the second type of information because this could only lead to no decision and therefore no reward. By having two regulators, each in charge of searching for only one type of information, and to the extent that these regulators do not collude, better incentives can be provided. Indeed, when searching for one type of information, one regulator does not internalize the fact that, if that regulator succeeds, a negative externality is created on the other regulator. The two moral hazard variables are the search for information and transmission of this information when the search is successful.

It is often thought that, when two activities, such gas and electricity, interact, a single regulator (as in the United Kingdom and soon in France) is preferred. However, two regulators may create better incentives. Similarly, it may be preferable to separate the ministry of finance, which seeks reasons not to spend on projects from the ministries of industry, transportation, agriculture, and other spending ministries. To what extent this argument compensates for loss of coordination resulting from separation is, of course, an empirical question.

Laffont and Martimort (1999) model the idea of separating regulators as follows. In their supervisory function, regulators generally have a certain degree of discretion. Rather than transmitting the acquired information to the government, which can then decrease the information rents of the agents, the regulators can be captured by the agents for not revealing this information and share the information rents with the agents (Laffont and Tirole 1991). Laffont and Martimort (1999) show that dividing the supervisory functions among several regulators often makes side contracting more difficult, and therefore distorts the government's regulatory response to collusion less. It is important to take the government's regulatory response into account because it makes use of the lack of coordination among regulators. Not considering its response may mislead one to think that centralized regulation is better for controlling corruption because decentralized corruption leads (with a free-rider argument) to excessive corruption (Shleifer and Vishny 1993).

TABLE 1-2. CHARACTERISTICS RELEVANT TO REGULATORY FRAMEWORK SELECTION IN DEVELOPING ECONOMIES

Relevant factor	Regulatory framework (relative to developed countries)
High cost of public funds	Several regulators
Transaction cost of collusions	One regulator
Large size of agency problem	Several regulators
High cost of regulators	One regulator
Costly enforcement of separation	One regulator

The major weakness of the above arguments is that they assume the separated regulators will not collude.[4] Indeed, most literature on mechanism design that uses the competition of agents to create incentives has made this naive assumption. Perfect collusion would mean a return to the single regulator framework. However, to the extent that the government controls the information technologies made available to agents, it can create asymmetries of information among them. As emphasized in Laffont and Martimort (1998, 2000), asymmetric information between colluding agents creates transaction costs, which are beneficial to the principals. So collusion will be imperfect and separation of powers can be designed to be collusion-proof between regulators. Of course, such considerations weaken the value of this institutional design. Finally, the dangers of reciprocal supervision, which favors reciprocal collusive activities at low transaction costs, should be noted (Laffont and Meleu 1997).

Insights for Developing Countries

Laffont and Meleu (2001) show that most characteristics of developing countries (such as cost of public funds, transaction costs of collusion, and size of asymmetric information) favor more separation, as described in Laffont and Martimort (1999). Unfortunately, those same parameters also increase the cost of implementing collusion-proof separation of powers (table 1-2).

---

[4] It is important that structural regulation discussions take collusive behavior into account. Faure-Grimaud, Laffont, and Martimort (2000) show, in a principal-supervision-one agent adverse selection problem, that the optimal collusion-proof contract is equivalent to decentralizing the supervisor's choice of the agent's contract. That is, if the principal cannot prevent collusion, the principal is as well off completely relinquishing control of the agent.

Benevolent Government with Contractual Constraints

Various types of contractual constraints affect the optimal structuring of regulation. Two major types—incomplete contracts and lack of commitment—are discussed below.

Incomplete Contracts

Laffont and Zantman (1999) argue that local politicians are better informed than the central government about local conditions. The authors' justification is that local politics creates the incentives for local politicians to acquire information. However, the constitution does not allow a complete contract that would enable the central government to remunerate local politicians for information transmission. Consequently, it may be better to decentralize certain collective decisions, rather than use a centralized process with no prior information. Gilbert and Picard (1996) study the same trade-off, where local decisionmakers are better informed, but their objectives are biased and unknown to the central government. The better information of local authorities is balanced by greater information rents (capture) that local authorities leave to regulated firms (Caillaud, Jullien, and Picard 1996).

Aghion and Tirole (1997) illustrate that information structures are endogenous. The choice to decentralize decisions creates more incentives to acquire information locally. However, the value of local information acquisition is limited by local preferences, which differ from those of the central government.

The Tiebout (1956) model of decentralization can also be interpreted as a response to incomplete contracts. Here, the difficulty is eliciting willingness to pay for local public goods to achieve appropriate partitioning of the population into communities and levels of local public goods within those communities. These objectives could be achieved through a mechanism that uses nonlinear, personalized transfers to elicit relevant information with the best rent-efficiency trade-off. Alternatively, if payments are constrained to uniformity within each community, then the next best mechanism for information revelation is decentralization of the level of public goods to communities within which agents vote for themselves.[5]

---

[5] Bardhan and Mookherjee (1999) suggest that the role of this mechanism may be less relevant in developing countries.

One can expect that, in developing countries, contracts between the center and periphery will be more incomplete than in developed countries, but there is no particular reason why local preferences should be more biased or coordination problems worse. This type of thinking favors decentralization when local information is good and explains the trend toward local decisionmaking for managing natural resources, such as water and forests. On the other hand, for health and specific environmental issues, local information may be weaker than that of the central government, which has better access to international information.

Lack of Commitment

Lack of commitment is also a form of contract incompleteness. Delegating decisionmaking authority to agents who have specific functions may solve commitment deficiency. For example, if a government cannot make the commitment to resist a merger, then delegating the right to decide to a competition agency may be optimal. However, delegation may tie the government to inefficient decisions. Thus, delegation, within the context of a benevolent government, requires incentives for agency members, which will lead them to favor competition.

Contract theory states that, under the assumption of repeated relationships, adverse selection, and perfectly, temporally correlated types, it is ex ante optimal to commit to use each period of the optimal static contract in the rent-efficiency trade-off. However, after the first period, this contract is not ex post optimal, and the contracting partners would likely renegotiate (see, for example, Baron and Besanko 1992).

Although efficiency demands that governments have the credibility to commit to not renegotiate, they often lack the ability to do so with regulated agents. Dewatripont (1989) first modeled this contractual opportunism, which was emphasized by Williamson (1985); however, the full characterization of optimal mechanisms when the government cannot commit to not renegotiate was achieved in Laffont and Tirole (1990). The first step of that analysis showed that the optimal mechanism is renegotiation-proof, since the principal can anticipate the outcome of renegotiation and mimic it. The optimal, renegotiation-proof mechanism leads to semi-separating equilibria, in which agents only partially reveal their types in the first period in order to maintain an information rent in the second period. By inducing a first-period equilibrium in which the principal remains uninformed, the principal commits to not extracting the information rent of tomorrow completely, since the optimal ex post, renegotiated contract entails an information rent for the agent. Therefore, the principal commits to some ex post inefficiency. A strong result can be achieved when the government has two lines of activities and commits to having a regulator for each. The noncooperative behavior of the regulators in the second period may lead to a higher rent awarded to the agent; that is, it indirectly yields a commitment to a greater inefficiency (Martimort 1999).

Problems of credibility in developing countries, which are likely worse than in developed countries, tend to favor decentralization and delegation. However, several characteristics of developing countries weaken the strength of this conclusion. First, delegating decisionmaking to overcome lack of commitment is more difficult to implement in developing countries. Second, the capacity of increasing efficiency through competition among agencies depends on each agency's ability to resist capture, which appears lower in developing countries because of lower transaction costs. Third, increasing commitment by establishing several agencies rests on the assumption that those agencies will not collude; however, collusion appears easier in developing countries.

Nonbenevolent Government

If the above assumption of a benevolent government that aims to maximize social welfare is dropped, then government accountability plays a crucial role in choosing between centralized and decentralized regulatory mechanisms. For Seabright (1996), the difference between centralized and decentralized government depends on which groups of electors are collectively empowered. He argues that local politicians have greater accountability because voters (through election mechanisms) have more influence over their reelection than do central government politicians. This gain may counterbalance any loss in coordination that decentralization entails.

Bardhan and Mookherjee (1999) use the Bernheim and Whinston (1986) political economy model of capture to compare centralization and decentralization. They argue that, contrary to a widely shared belief, decentralization is not necessarily worse from the point of view of capture.

Crémer and Palfrey (1996) show how voting procedures affect choice of centralization versus decentralization at the constitutional level. Their main assumptions are as follows: First, collective decisions are made by majority rule,[6] with the further constraint that centralization requires uniform rules,

---

[6] Majority rule yields decisions that generally do not maximize social welfare.

which favor policy moderation (Beasley and Coate 1998). Second, agents are risk averse. Third, voters must arbitrate between their forecasts about the identity of the median voter in their region or the entire country. Crémer and Palfrey show that a two-stage procedure, in which voter-elected representatives decide between centralization and decentralization with majority rule, is more favorable to centralization than direct voting by agents. Similarly, Bolton and Roland (1997) find that alternative mechanisms for assigning public goods within a region are more likely when the region's median income differs from the aggregate median income (political effect), when positive externalities between regions are low (efficiency effect), and when production levels differ between regions (tax effect).

Laffont and Pouyet (2002) show that competition between national regulators leads to excessively high-powered incentive schemes, as each regulator tries to reimburse less of the cost than others to induce a strategic allocation of costs. When this distortion is combined with a political system, decentralization, which induces incentive schemes from regulators but destroys the discretion of politicians, can dominate centralization, which internalizes externalities between regulators but suffers from excessive policy fluctuation caused by majority rule. The high cost of public funds associated with developing countries favors centralization.

Lack of confidence in government leads to limiting its mandate. Consequently, governments can only commit for a short period. In the context of an adverse selection principal agent, this leads to the ratchet effect. The agent hides behind a mixed strategy to maintain a future rent, knowing that future regulators will leave no rent if they are fully informed about the agent's type (Laffont and Tirole 1988). Olsen and Torsvick (1995) show that committing to have several regulators (who will leave more future rents to the agent through their noncooperative behavior if the regulated activities are complements) helps mitigate the ratchet effect. Less pooling is needed during the first period to indirectly commit to the same information rent during the second period.

Nonbenevolence at all levels poses a greater problem for developing countries than for developed countries because of lack of appropriate institutions and counterpowers. However, whether this tilts the choice toward centralization or decentralization is unclear. As Bardhan and Mookherjee (1999) state: "Simple generalizations about relative capture are therefore hazardous on the basis of theory alone."

Recent Experiences in Industrial Countries

The United Kingdom: Independent, Industry-specific Regulators

The United Kingdom's two-party political system, with majority control of both the executive and legislative branches, accords the government much discretion since it can modify regulatory rules whenever it deems necessary. This would be a factor of regulatory risk a priori. Yet, as Spiller and Vogelsang (1996) underscore, informal norms constitute a strong check on a government's discretionary power. They include permanency of bureaucracy, having most officials remain in office after majority changes, publication of intended government reforms in white papers, allowing concerned parties to react, and significant informal delegation of power from the minister to regulators.

Judiciary checks are more often effected through enforcement of contracts than through review of regulatory decisions. The country has long relied on regulation by contracts as a way to reassure investors. Detailed licenses, first issued in 1880 for telecommunications, are used to impose obligations on utilities and usually include maximum prices and a rate of return.

How the System Works

Design of the U.K. system—one of the clearest examples of independent, industry-specific regulation—reflects the government's strong will to ensure independence of regulators.[7] The system works as follows: The minister appoints one director general per sector. Their appointments can last for more than one term, and those appointed cannot be removed from office unless proven guilty of incompetence or misconduct. They are ultimately accountable to Parliament, and the Treasury votes on the budget of their office. Oversight is ensured by the Competition Commission, known as the Monopolies and Mergers Commission; the courts; and parliamentary committees. Firms can appeal to the Monopolies and Mergers Commission (Green and Rodriguez-Pardina 1999).

Although the country relies on industry-specific regulators, it has also recognized the need for closer cooperation across overlapping sectors. For example, in 1999, separate regulatory agencies for gas and electricity were

---

[7] The United Kingdom's regulatory system, fully designed in the 1980s, has served as a model for several developing countries, including Argentina.

merged into a new regulatory body, known as the Office of Gas and Electricity Markets or OFGEM.

Water Regulation Debate

The United Kingdom has chosen to have functional regulation within the water industry. Several distinct agencies have received specific, nonoverlapping mandates over the industry according to the regulatory function to be effected: economic regulation, quality oversight, or promotion of competition. The Office of Water Regulation is responsible for controlling prices and ensuring the viability of suppliers, the Drinking Water Inspectorate oversees the quality of tap water, and the Environment Agency maintains the quality of rivers and canals. This industry, like other utilities, is subject to the 1992 Competition and Services (Utilities) Act and the 1998 Competition Act.

This separation of regulatory functions into distinct entities contrasts with the structure chosen for other sectors. For example, the Office of the Rail Regulator is in charge of consumer protection; enforcing domestic competition laws concerning railroads; safety and health issues; and environmental effects of railroads. It may be argued that environmental concerns are less important for the rail industry than for the water industry, and therefore do not require specific supervision. Yet, experience of the water sector sheds light on the pros and cons of functional regulation. Since the definition of mandates has been quite clear, the issue does not involve as much overlap as it does in the United States or as do the externalities at the firms' level of specialized regulations.

This experiment of having multiple functional regulators has been criticized as the cause of several problems in the water industry. The Office of Water Regulation, in particular, has been cited for insufficiently considering the social and public costs and benefits of water sector investment programs. In addition, the investment incentives of the Office of Water Regulation and the environmental regulator have been described as conflicting and unclear.

New Zealand: Lessons from a Novel Approach

New Zealand's regulatory system is an exception to the general rule of separating competition regulations. Its novel approach, used to regulate first telecommunications and then power, is based on general competition laws and is enforced by courts and an industrywide competition authority.

Councils composed of industry participants introduced self-regulation, setting the main rules and access conditions. This form of regulation is consistent with the notion that these industries will become sufficiently competitive for regulation to be eliminated. However, relying on negotiated agreements between firms on interconnection pricing and related matters has proven unsatisfactory, and the country is returning to specific regulatory tools.

Telecommunications

Telecom is the dominant telecommunications provider. It is privately owned, has control over the local loop, and competes with other providers for most other services linked to telecommunications. As early as 1988, measures were taken to facilitate competition, including cost-based charges for interconnection, obligation to consult the industry to set up those charges, and operation of Telecom subsidiaries as separate profit centers. These obligations and others, linked in particular to universal service, are known as Kiwi share obligations.

Three features characterized New Zealand's approach. First, regulation relied only on the Kiwi obligations and on general competition rules, as written in the Commerce Act of 1986, without sector-specific regulation or legislation. The Commerce Commission oversaw not only mergers, but also pricing schedules and access terms related to the telecommunications sector. Second, Telecom was subject to information disclosure requirements. Third, the industry had to negotiate access and other measures without government intervention.

The number of cases brought to court since this type of regulation was put in place shows that specific characteristics of the telecommunications industry make it difficult to convict a firm of abuse of dominant position, as required by the Commerce Act.

The government has decided to modify competition rules so that they better apply to the telecommunications and electricity industries. Thus, the concept of taking advantage of a substantial degree of market power will replace that of abuse of dominant position. Similarly, the Commerce Act will prohibit acquisitions that would substantially reduce market competition, rather than those that would lead to strengthening of dominance.

Electricity

Following the experiment in the telecommunications sector, the electricity industry was similarly deregulated. The government's approach for this sector, as its approach for telecommunications, featured self-regulation and general competition rules to regulate contracts, rather than industry-specific rules and disclosure. Voluntary multilateral agreements were key to governing the wholesale electricity market.

A bill introduced in 1999 proposed that price controls be imposed on electricity line businesses, which would constitute a move toward more stringent regulation. The government will decide on this proposal after thoroughly studying results of the ministerial inquiry into the industry. Other laws that restrict private contracts include the following: the Resource Management Act, which concerns emissions from thermal plants and setting other environmental restrictions; the Electricity Act, passed in 1992, which removes statutory barriers to competition in retailing and line distribution; the Electricity Industry Reform Act of 1998, which requires separate ownership of line, generation, and retail companies and specifies that price controls can be applied to regulated charges for supply to domestic and rural customers; and the Electricity Information Disclosure Regulation of 1999, which requires transport and electricity line businesses to disclose financial statements, line charges, terms of contracts, and various performance measures.

The wholesale electricity market is governed by the New Zealand Electricity Market (NZEM), a self-regulated structure that resolves disputes between firms and sets rules on offers, dispatch, pricing, and clearing and settling transactions.

Return to Specific Regulations

A perception of deficiencies in the existing regulatory system led the ministries responsible for telecommunications and electricity to request ministerial inquiry into these industries. Reports of the two inquiries, published in 2000, concluded that specific regulation was needed to deal with particular issues.

The report of the Ministerial Inquiry into the Telecommunications Industry recommended creating an Electronic Communications Industry Forum. Funded by the industry and with compulsory membership, the Forum would be responsible for industry self-regulation. The Inquiry established that self-regulation should remain a major component of the regulatory system. Yet, it called for specific, designated electronic services, including pricing rules, to be subject to regulation. These services are interconnected with Telecom's fixed-wire network and its wholesaling of retail services. Other services, which would be subject to light regulation (without pricing regulation, for example), include interconnection between all networks, carrier preselection, co-location at mobile cell sites, and other services linked to cell telephony (but only for a limited time). The Inquiry recommended that the office of the Electronic Communications Commissioner, an industry-specific regulator, undertake regulation.

The Inquiry considered that the appropriate course of action would be to have a specialized, stand-alone industry regulator until the telecommunications markets could become fully competitive. This marked a shift away from the previous system, since it recognized that specialized oversight of the industry might be necessary, at least until the telecommunications sector could approach any standard industry. The general belief was that the sector should quickly shed any remaining natural monopoly characteristics, that oversight by competition authorities would soon suffice, and that specific regulation was needed to facilitate this transition.

It was recommended that industry-specific regulation contain a dispute resolution process, since disputes among telecommunications companies have shown that a general competition authority and nonspecialized courts are inappropriate for dealing with technical issues. The report of the Inquiry into Telecommunications stated that relying on courts and arbitration to solve disputes has led to significant delays and costs, and cannot provide consistent and clearly articulated guidelines with respect to access issues. Thus, the Inquiry not only recognized the need for a dispute resolution mechanism sufficiently specialized to be rapid and to have the necessary expertise. It also underscored the slowness of courts in establishing precedents to increase judicial security, as well as the lack of coherence and consistency of individual judgments.

The Inquiry still recommends setting up appeal rights, but only on matters of substance and with a provision that regulatory decisions apply until the appeal has been concluded. The regulatory agency's determination should, on the other hand, be subject to judicial review. Tests to determine which specific services should be regulated and when to stop regulation should also be set up to ensure that regulation be kept at a minimal level.

The report of the Ministerial Inquiry into the Electricity Industry also insisted on the need to provide a coherent, comprehensible pattern of regulation. In the wholesale, nonfinancial markets, it was recommended that regulation cover registration, pool rules, dispatch, security, constraint standards, settlement, transmission and distribution pricing methodology, and a mechanism for dispute resolution. Market participants should elect the market structure accountable for this regulation (referred to as the Board in the report), and a majority of its members should be independent from the industry. The report recommended that the Board be given the authority to impose price control on individual distribution companies and to choose the criteria and thresholds on which price control should be imposed.[8]

Limits of Self-regulation

The example of New Zealand shows that an innovative approach that uses only well-developed competition authorities to oversee a self-regulating industry may not be doomed to immediate failure. Yet, after some years, the government has recognized the need to retain regulatory control over certain industries because their transition from a protected monopoly to competition is not sufficiently advanced to abandon formal regulation. Relying solely on competition laws is inefficient during a transition period, even when those laws are well developed and enforced.

Australia: An Original Combination

Australia is a federation of largely autonomous states that are free to follow different policies. The country's current regulatory system has been designed to correct the problems perceived in New Zealand's system. In Australia, regulation is organized around the Australian Competition and Consumer Commission (ACCC), a federal multisectoral, multifunctional agency; several specialized agencies; and state regulation. The system is relatively complex, since some issues are resolved at the national level, while others are left to regional governments. The system is also innovative, given the important role accorded the ACCC.

Overview of Telecommunications

Until 1975, postal services operated domestic telecommunications, while overseas commissions operated international telecommunications services; both were public enterprises. Despite a move toward functioning more like private firms, a 1988 review showed that competition was nearly nonexistent. Then, in 1989, the Telecommunications Act liberalized markets and created the Australian Telecommunications Authority (AUSTEL) to separate regulatory and operational functions. For the next 16 years, the industry was

---

[8] New Zealand's prevailing structure contrasts with those of other countries; in Mexico, for example, the competition authority is the entity that decides when to impose and remove price controls.

under a traditional oversight structure, with AUSTEL in charge of industry-specific regulations and the Spectrum Management Agency (SMA) in charge of frequency allocation.

In 1993, the Himler Report recommended economywide regulation of all matters related to competition and access. Thus, AUSTEL and the SMA were eliminated. All former functions linked to competition (particularly interconnection) were taken over by the ACCC. The decision to create the Australian Communications Authority (ACA) reflected the recognized need for specialized expertise on technical issues, including frequency management.

The ACCC has mandate over the industry's most sensitive issues. Its oversight involves lighter regulation than a specialized regulatory agency would have effected. However, regulation still allows for more standard intervention (on pricing, for example) where needed. Thus, compared with New Zealand, Australia's institutional framework is more flexible. Under the law, consultative processes are included to facilitate coordination between the ACCC and the ACA.

Moreover, several industry associations have been established to encourage all members of the industry to participate in the regulatory process: The Telecommunications Access Forum deals with access issues, the Australian Communications Industry Forum develops technical and operational standards, and the Telecommunications Industry Ombudsman settles the unresolved complaints of small users, including residential and small business consumers (Kerf and Geradin 1999).

The telecommunications industry, like other sectors in Australia, is supervised by regional regulatory agencies. Regional regulators have substantial independence to oversee intraregional problems, while the ACC appears responsible for general oversight.

ACCC: A Multisector, Multifunctional Agency

Following recommendations of the 1993 Himler Report, the ACCC was created in 1995 by merging the Trade Practices Commission and the Price Surveillance Authority. The ACCC is in charge of competition promotion, safety, intellectual rights, access issues, and organizing coordination and information exchange between regulators. The Commission's integrated structure comprises sectoral and functional bureaus with coordination units that handle a range of issues (product safety, consumer protection, mergers and restrictive trade practices, and access) across sectors as diverse as telecommunications, electricity, gas, transport, and airports.

The ACCC comprises numerous, specialized commissions and offices, which are organized by sector and geographical area (for example, the Office of Water Regulation or the South Australian Independent Pricing and Access Regulation). Offices are located in all capital cities, as well as in Townsville and Tamworth.[9] The Utility Regulators Forum ensures coordination of the regulatory activities within the ACCC. Created in 1997, nearly two years after the ACCC, the Forum was established in recognition of the need for cooperation between state-based regulators in a federal system, in accordance with the ACCC's stated mission.

Justification for a Multisector, Multifunctional Agency

Creation of a comprehensive competition authority has given rise to debate about the range of problems that a single agency should tackle. The need for an agency with a broad mandate has been felt, particularly with respect to introducing competition in regulated utilities. Designing access regimes for electricity or tradable water rights are examples of issues in which regulation and competition are closely related.

Fels (1996) argues that traditional, narrow competition policy relies on independent nonpolitical agencies and courts. When moving to a comprehensive view of competition policy (including safety norms, trade policies, and regulation of public utilities), it is not possible to isolate the agency from political processes. In Australia, the ACCC is independent and nonpolitical, while legislators and governments determine major policy changes. In 1996, the state governments agreed to review all regulations likely to affect competition for the following five years. The National Competition Council was appointed to review this process and administer the access regime (Fels 1996; OECD 1999).

The Himler committee based its decision to favor a national authority, rather than state agencies, on three main arguments. The first argument was that markets were now more national than regional, particularly as advances in transport and communications permitted many firms to develop national trade networks (Fels 1996). Second, many goods and services within sectors governed by state or territorial laws were now protected from exposure to competition from other national firms because of constitutional and ownership limitations. Eventually, it was argued, a national competition policy would ensure consistency of pro-competitive reforms and avoid the costs

---

[9] Australia's large size appears to require local offices, despite recent advances in communications technology and transportation.

linked to industry-specific and subnational regulatory arrangements (Fels 1996). This argument seemed to express the defiance of state regulators, who may have favored regional firms at the expense of other competitors. The third argument highlighted the difficulty of coordinating the actions of state agencies and the costs of separation across sectors and states.

European Commission: New Decentralization Process

Until today, the European Competition Policy has functioned in a strongly centralized way. Notifications, in particular, have been handled at the continental level. The white paper on modernizing rules for implementing articles 85 and 86 of the European Commission Treaty (dated April 28, 1999) proposes to adapt the existing system to alleviate excessive administrative procedures, allow the European Community to focus on major torts, and develop and stimulate enforcement of competition laws at the national level. Nevertheless, the white paper recognizes that the centralized system, aside from ensuring firms' judicial security, has been used by them to counteract the actions of national courts and competition authorities.

The main recommendations for reform are to eliminate the current notification process and give national authorities responsibility for investigations that concern only national markets. If in doubt, national authorities can ask the European Community a preliminary question. The European Community could still intervene in any national procedure and remove a case from the national jurisdiction if there is risk of divergence. It is essential that decentralization does not result in incoherence in applying European competition laws. Therefore, national authorities should be obligated to avoid conflicts with the European Community.[10]

The European Parliament organized a public hearing for September 22, 1999, and a resolution was taken January 18, 2000. The European Parliament, Economic and Social Committee (ECOSOC), and all member states unanimously agreed to abolish the centralized system and increase involvement of member states in enforcement. Most memoranda submitted by lawyers tend toward this direction. However, with regard to decentralization, many firms show more concern about harmonization of procedures than do member states. Many companies fear inconsistency and lack of expertise and

---

[10] At the same time, it should be noted that, under the previous system (from 1962 to the present), parallel enforcement of European Community rules has not given rise to any significant conflict.

time on the part of national courts. Moreover, the companies are concerned that national authorities and courts may make decisions for industrial policy and political reasons. According to these companies, national authorities are less insulated from political pressures than is the European Community.

The general belief about the new European Community decentralization process is that it answers more practical questions of congestion and overload rather than representing any theoretical belief in the benefits of decentralization or the political will of governments. Yet, the process recalls the need to rely on local structures to access information at lower costs and to ensure enforcement of rules enacted at a central level.

Latin American Experiences

Multisector Agencies in Small Countries

Several countries—Bolivia, Jamaica, and Panama—have chosen a multisector regulatory agency over specialized entities. This choice seems particularly rational in small countries, where duplication of costs associated with establishing multiple sector-specific agencies would outweigh the benefits of focused regulation and where human capital and expertise are lacking.

Bolivia: Compromise between Coordination and Specialization

Bolivia has established a regulatory system that balances a multisector agency with specialized regulators. The system is composed of sector-specific branches supervised by a coordination entity. Thus, the structure approximates a multisector agency with specialized bureaus, yet it gives the branches more independence, thereby making the system more acceptable to officials otherwise reluctant to relinquish their regulatory power over an industry.

Regulation falls primarily under the Ministry of Economic Development, which is composed of four branches: transport, communications, and civil aeronautics; energy; minerals and steel; and domestic trade and industry. The Vice-Ministry of Sectoral Coordination (directly under the Ministry of Economic Development) supervises all four divisions.

This structure reflects a compromise between sector regulation, demanded by the former sector regulators, and multisector coordination, as requested by the upper echelons of government in 1996, when the Ministry was designed.

One drawback of this type of structure is that, if it helps reduce the threat of capture of regulators by the industry, it may not sufficiently insulate the agency from political interference. This may be costly since it increases the risk perceived by investors and therefore the return on capital they will demand before agreeing to invest in the country.

When a country's judiciary system is sufficiently reliable, one solution, which is subject to unilateral modifications by the government, is to rely on licenses that can be enforced more easily than other regulatory rules (as in Jamaica, for example). If a judiciary system is not well developed, making a commitment not to expropriate investors will, of course, be more difficult.

Jamaica: Multisector Response to Political and Resource Constraints

Early on, Jamaica chose to establish a multisector agency to regulate utilities. Created in 1966 by the Public Utilities Commission Act, this agency has remained nearly unchanged since then. Given the small size of the country, creating specialized agencies would have been extremely costly in terms of duplicated administrative, human resource, and material costs. In Jamaica, policy coordination is a less relevant justification for a multisector agency than are cost-benefit analysis and resource constraints.

The Jamaica Telephone Company, a protected monopoly, dominates the country's telecommunications industry. The company has a monopoly not only over basic telephony, but also over all associated services, including equipment supply. It is also guaranteed a high rate of return, which has been strongly criticized. Yet, according to Spiller and Sampson (1996), allowing such a rate-of-return contract with a monopoly may have been the best available regulation, given the country's political constraints.

Jamaica has a strong judiciary, with independent, reliable judges. Yet its parliamentary system accords the government administration sufficient power to change legislation whenever needed; therefore, the judiciary cannot guarantee enforcement of current regulatory rules. Although a strong judiciary system may seem, at first glance, to imply regulatory certainty for regulated firms, this is not the case because the executive branch can easily change laws and jurisdictions.

Moreover, the political system is composed of two parties that have alternately dominated for short periods of time. Frequent reversals of political majorities create an unstable environment for companies. This adds to the fear of regulatory expropriation, since its services are used mainly by middle and upper-class voters, who constitute the swing vote in Jamaica.

Thus, each party has strong incentive to maintain low prices in local telephony to strengthen its chances of winning the next election.

Within such a context, the main problem in designing regulatory institutions is finding commitment devices that reduce uncertainty and potential expropriation by the government. In Jamaica, the device used was contracts. Indeed, the government cannot unilaterally modify contracts between itself and the regulated firm. Furthermore, contracts are credible instruments that can be enforced by the country's sound judiciary. As underscored by Spiller and Sampson (1996), licenses are long-term contracts that constitute a commitment not to expropriate investors. Moreover, concessions can be granted for all cross-subsidized telephony services to maintain low prices for local calls; this approach can also attract investors by committing to high rents. The costs of this arrangement—in addition to high rents—include foregoing the benefits of competition over the period of time that the exclusive concession contract is valid.

Using a multisector agency and licenses that ensure large rates of return appear to be optimal choices for Jamaica, given the country's institutional and economic characteristics.

Panama: Multisector and Competition Agencies

In 1996, Panama enacted laws that defined the respective functions and structure of its regulatory and competition agencies. In January 1996, Law No. 26 created the Public Services Regulatory Entity as a legal body independent from Panama's central government. This regulatory entity administers its own budget, which is supported through an independent central government fund, and is subject to control by a court of auditors.

The Public Services Regulatory Entity is responsible for regulating and controlling public services across a range of sectors: potable water and sewerage systems, electricity, telecommunications, radio and television, and transmission and distribution of natural gas. Thus, the Regulatory Entity is a multisector agency. Its functions include promoting competition; regulating principles on methods for calculating public service fees; verifying that basic services, their improvement, and expansion goals comply with sectoral laws; and ensuring financial independence.

The regulatory entity is financed mainly by a tax that it fixes on public services. The annual tax rate for each public service is calculated on the basis of the cost of complying efficiently with its functions. The rate does not exceed one percent of the sector's net income from the preceding year. The public services are obligated to pay the tax, which is established in the contract for provision of services, and cannot transfer it to users through an additional fee.

A three-member board of directors, appointed for five-year terms by the government and ratified by Panama's Parliament, governs and administers the Regulatory Entity. Legal provisions ensure that the directors' five-year terms are staggered, ending at different times.

To be considered for membership on the board of directors, qualified candidates must be of Panamanian nationality, have a recognized university degree, and have a minimum of 10 years of public sector experience. An individual may not be appointed to the board if the individual is guilty of any offense against heritage, public administration, or public faith; is related to the President, Vice-President, Ministers of Health, Justice, Finance, Treasury or any other director of a Regulatory Entity; or has directly or indirectly been a shareholder in the public service firm.

The Regulatory Entity's annual budget must be balanced and attached to the state's general budget. However, the board of directors, in plenary session, is authorized, by reasoned decision and within the budget approved by Parliament, to transfer entries required to comply with its functions. Such transfers must not alter the total amount of the budget. Once the transfer of entries is authorized, the Regulatory Entity must register it with both the Ministry of Economy and Finance and the Court of Auditors.

All actions related to personnel—appointments, dismissals, salary revisions, promotions, and changes in the personnel structure of the entity—must be registered with the Ministry of Economy and Finance, Court of Auditors, and Budget Commission of the Parliament.

Argentina: Competition Authorities and Industrial Regulators

Argentina chose to create independent agencies to regulate electricity, gas, and telecommunications. All three agencies are financed by taxation on industry firms and consumers; yet their degree of autonomy varies, with the structure of appeal being a determining factor of regulators' credibility and independence. Study of the country's agencies shows that financial autonomy and nomination procedures are similar across sectors.

The regulatory agencies for both electricity and gas have independent and sufficient funding, skilled staffs, and autonomy. They are accountable to both the executive and legislative branches of government. Yet, their first appeal is to the secretariat, not the courts, which means the government may be able to reverse their regulatory decisions.

Regulation of electricity is divided between federal regulation of transmission and state regulation of distribution, even though this creates coordination problems for large consumers who can sign contracts with generators outside their respective states. However, regulation of gas—both transmission and distribution—is a federal responsibility. The most likely reason is that a federally-owned enterprise controlled the gas industry at the time of privatization and liberalization, so the federal government retained full regulatory powers.

Privatization of telecommunications, first undertaken by the government to show its commitment to reform, has failed in many respects, even though some initial difficulties have been resolved. Regulation of telecommunications is divided between the National Telecommunications Commission (CNT) and the Secretariat of Telecommunications. Creation of the CNT in 1990 did not result from legislative debate, making the agency accountable to the executive branch only and implying a lower level of independence. Since its inception, the CNT has changed ministries twice (because of a merger between the Ministry of Public Works and the Ministry of the Economy), and it lacks autonomy and expertise. Its first committee included former members of the Secretariat of Telecommunications, who had not supported privatization.

The first years of regulation proved unsatisfactory, and staff changed rapidly. Once the CNT's credibility was lost, it was difficult to regain. The Commission has remained slow in dealing with problems, and its accountability is limited. Regulatory separation between the CNT and the Secretariat has also proven costly. For example, it has been difficult to coordinate end-user and access rates, and controversies have arisen between the two regulators. Such costs of separation need to be weighed against the benefits of reduced capture and increased enforcement.

A new Competition Law (Law 25.156) was established to transfer the decision capacity from the public administration to the competition tribunal through creation of an antitrust body (an autonomous agency empowered to impose sanctions that can be appealed in the corresponding federal court). Formerly, the National Competition Commission was entitled only to issue nonbinding reports, whereas the Secretary for Competition Defense made the final resolution. However, under the new Competition Law, the official channel ends with the competition tribunal. Furthermore, the Competition Law revokes all other jurisdictional powers conferred on other government agencies regarding competition issues.

The competition tribunal is organized as a self-financing, independent agency. However, three years after approving this law, the tribunal is still not in place, remaining only a legal mandate.

Decentralization of Regulatory Responsibilities

Mexico: Specific Tasks in a Centralized Country

Mexico is a clear example of decentralization of selected tasks within a centralized country. Saleth and Dinar (1999) underscore that, although Mexico has a strongly centralized government, an emerging trend is to decentralize water supply functions to state and municipal governments. While the central government is responsible for water resource management, many tasks are managed at the local level. Saleth and Dinar, nonetheless, note that one of Mexico's main challenges regarding water is to make better use of local information. They suggest using the data available in the National Registry of Water Users to allocate water more efficiently between competing users. Institutions capable of allocating water across regions and sectors are still lacking, which suggests the need for a mechanism to transmit available local-level information.

The 1982 reform, which aimed to increase private participation in road freight, has succeeded (Dutz, Hayri, and Ibarra 2000). The reform not only authorized free entry into the industry and moved toward a system of market-based pricing; it also resulted in decentralization, much of it directed toward the private sector, as well as local authorities.

Recently, the Mexican government decided to introduce more decentralization into regulation of the seaport industry. Trujillo and Nombela (1999) emphasize the trend toward decentralization as an observable success factor for Latin America's seaport industry. In a general law enacted in 1992, the government chose to relinquish control over port administration, terminal operation, and provision of related services. Authority is decentralized to individual port authorities, who manage their respective ports according to the specifications of their concession contracts.

Regulation of Water Services:
Conflicts between Local and Central Authorities

In many Latin American countries, regulation of water distribution suffers from a conflict between local and central authorities. In most countries (with a few exceptions, such as Chile), general responsibility for water services relies on municipalities. Moreover, such responsibility often is established in a high-ranking law or even in a constitution. However, at the same time, central government regulatory agencies for water services are established through sector laws. The result is that, when central regulatory institutions set tariffs across an entire country, their regulations are often rejected, both politically and socially.

Several models for regulating water distribution can be found in Latin American countries. One model, found in Brazil, is characterized by lack of regulation at both local and central levels and by public enterprises that provide and regulate the service. In Brazil, efforts to establish water regulations and increase private participation give rise to conflicts between federal, state, and municipal governments. As such conflicts prevent large, private sector participation, the need for independent regulatory bodies to attract investment becomes a relevant issue.

In Argentina, water regulations rely on the central government in some cases and on provinces and municipalities in others. However, regulatory conflicts have not prevented private participation, and ad hoc solutions to regulatory questions have been established. In Buenos Aires, for example, the solution is an independent entity that must defend the interests of the national government, which owns water assets; the municipality of Buenos Aires; and the provinces. Since these three layers of government can be controlled by different political parties, strong tensions may arise. Provinces have followed different paths to structure regulation. Some states, such as Córdoba and Salta, have created multi-industry regulators for distribution of electricity, water, and transport; others, such as Buenos Aires and Tucumán, have created industry-specific regulators.

The models of Colombia and Peru are similar. While conflicts do not arise, regulatory agencies do not enforce the law. A central agency, created by a law that takes responsibility away from municipalities, supervises and regulates distribution of water supply. However, municipal companies continue to supply and distribute potable water, which limits the regulatory agency's capacity to enforce the law. For example, both countries established laws to set tariffs at levels to make services financially viable. Yet, most companies experience losses year after year, and the corresponding agencies are unable to enforce setting of appropriate tariffs.

Trade-offs between Investor Security and Excess Profit

Investors fear two types of regulatory behavior. The first is a regulator with no power, under direct government control, who uses pricing and investment requirements to extract excess profits from a firm. The second is an independent agency, which could easily be captured by the industry. Having relinquished control over the regulator, the government will be unable to reduce the rents the firms are allowed.

The first case will encourage little investment by regulated firms. In Chile's telecommunications industry, for example, changes in investment levels over time can be explained as a move from the first type of expropriation to a system more favorable to investors. The second case may lead to political difficulties, with consumers and voters frustrated by high prices and excess entrepreneurial profits, as in Mexico.

Chile: Regulation of Telecommunications

Chile was one of the first Latin American countries to promote competition among utilities and to introduce competition into power generation and long-distance telephony, following examples in the United States and the United Kingdom. In the late 1980s, following privatization of major telecommunications companies, Chile introduced competition into data and cable television services and private networks. Galal (1996) distinguishes three phases of telecommunications regulation in Chile. The first phase, from the 1930s to 1971, corresponded to regulation and private ownership. The second phase, from 1971 to 1982, was characterized by the nationalization of long-distance operators. Initiated by socialist president Salvador Allende after his 1971 election, nationalization was not challenged by Allende's successor, dictator Augusto Pinochet, after his 1974 military coup. The third phase started in 1982, when privatization and deregulation of telecommunications began.[11]

Chile's telecommunications experienced two opposite types of regulatory uncertainty over a brief period. The companies suffered from expropriation of investments during the early 1970s. At that time, Allende's socialist regime adjusted prices to a level lower than the inflation rate to increase consumer surplus. This happened despite the concession contract that guaranteed firms a 10-percent rate of return. When Pinochet seized power in 1974, a policy reversal occurred. A state holding company, CORFO, which became a joint owner of CTC and ENTEL, gained more influence in practice than the regulatory authorities.[12]

---

[11] Galal (1996) notes that, after privatization of long-distance operators CTC and ENTEL, the number of lines doubled over a four-year period.

[12] Interestingly, the general managers of CTC and ENTEL were generals, while the head of SUBTEL, the regulatory agency created in 1977, was only a colonel.

Competition regulation is one of the tools Chile uses to promote efficient resource allocation in its infrastructure sectors. Supervision of competition law is decentralized, and tasks are clearly allocated among levels. For cases in specific regions, regional commissions ensure compliance with competition law; a central commission intervenes in cases involving more than one region; and a resolution commission is invested with large investigatory powers. A representative of the Ministry of Economy chairs the regional and central commissions, each of which includes a representative of the Ministry of Finance; while a minister of the Supreme Court chairs the resolution commission. This structure takes into account the stakes of the concerned ministries, while defining the allocation of authority and preeminence rules. That different ministries have interests in the commissions appears as a credible way to ensure judiciary security. The allocation of tasks is relatively clear, and monitoring of regional agencies appears sound.

The will to design clear rules and decisionmaking processes can also be found in the organizational structure of Chile's sector regulatory agencies. A salient feature is that regulators have little discretion, since the rules they apply are precise. For example, regulators set prices on the basis of the estimated cost of a model operator. The Economics Ministry intervenes if a dispute arises, and the regulator is not ultimately responsible for tariffs. This increases the need for the regulator to explain and justify its decisions. Moreover, the rules are usually set in sector laws so that the legislative process reinforces their legitimacy. Thus, Chile has chosen to have more certainty in its regulatory environment, at the expense of flexibility.

Regulators also have little discretion in implementing redistribution policies. Aid is carefully targeted at low-income users through a comprehensive subsidy scheme. A special fund, created in 1994, facilitates access to public telephony in rural areas and in low-income, urban areas.[13] Such subsidy schemes and investment programs are more costly to set up than downward pressures on tariffs, but they avoid price distortions. Moreover, they have the advantage of reassuring investors since they constitute a (partial) commitment to cost-covering tariffs. With targeted aid, social motives cannot be used as a pretense for expropriating investments from firms. Firms operating in the country perceive the regulatory risk as lower than in neighboring countries and are therefore more willing to invest, even when rates of return are lower. An unstable regulatory system, in which regulators or ministries

---

[13] In 1997, 10 percent of Chile's population lived in areas without public telephony (Wellenius 1997).

have much discretion in modifying rules, translates into higher financing costs.

Nonetheless, the current system has its drawbacks. The boundaries between competitive and restricted segments are unclear, which explains why many suits have been filed against CTC and ENTEL on the grounds of anticompetitive behavior in providing interconnection. Lack of regulatory precision is costly in terms of judiciary disputes, but may be rationalized as the need to retain flexibility in a rapidly changing industry. Blurring the definition of segments can be viewed as an indirect way of retaining flexibility while giving discretionary powers to the courts, rather than to the regulators. This aspect can be better understood by recalling Chile's tradition of a strong, independent judiciary, as exemplified by Congress' refusal to allow Allende to expropriate shareholders during nationalization (Galal 1996).

Mexico: Telecommunications Regulations

Some five years after a public monopoly is privatized, public discontent and even political unrest are common in both developed and developing countries. Indeed, attracting private capital requires committing to high rents, either by granting a monopoly position or by setting a generous price cap or rate of return for the initial years that a privatized firm operates. But excessive profits are usually viewed as a failure of regulation or as a sign of regulatory capture. Regulation of telecommunications in Mexico exemplifies this problem.

Until 1990, Mexico's telecommunications services were operated by Telmex, a state-owned enterprise. Following its privatization in 1990, Telmex was largely unregulated. Two years after the 1995 Telecommunications Law was passed, telephony markets were opened to competition. Yet this action was more theoretical than real, since, in 1998, Telmex still enjoyed a dominant position in five markets, according to Mexico's competition commission. An OECD report on regulatory reform assessed the 1995 Telecommunications Law as a good tool, but emphasized that the regulator had inadequate powers, particularly over the dominant provider in markets where its power was substantial.

Discontent has grown among local residents because of the high cost and poor quality of service. For example, although regulation allows Telmex to charge high access rates to keep profits high enough to encourage network expansion, no new line was added in 1996 or 1997. Faced with harsh criticism, the telephony regulator has attempted to introduce more stringent obligations for Telmex. Yet the government fears that too severe regulations will negatively affect the stock market. In October 1997, for example, Minister Carlos Ruiz Sacristan responded to pressures to diminish Telmex's market power by asserting that one had to "take care not to negatively affect the stock market." Once again, the need not to discourage investment appears as a strong constraint on regulation. This argument can, of course, be used to mask other reasons for helping the firm make large profits. Attracting investors through excessive reduction in the effectiveness and scope of regulatory intervention may be politically costly and makes it difficult to introduce needed competition or adjust regulated prices after the "golden period" that follows privatization.

Conclusions

Decentralization or Centralization?

The main arguments regarding decentralization versus centralization fall into one of four groups (table 1-3).

Differentiation versus Coordination

According to Smith (2000), decentralization allows local conditions, priorities, and preferences to shape regulatory objectives and approaches. Yet, a priori, nothing prevents a centralized regulator from differentiating rules according to regional conditions. Two major arguments, nevertheless, may support this viewpoint: bounded rationality and capture. Regarding bounded rationality, if transmitting and processing information are costly, then the centralized regulator will be obligated to use uniform rules. Such costs depend on communication technologies and location of expertise. As for capture, the regulatory response of uniform rules is usually obligatory when the dangers of capture become too high. Thus, knowledge about the nature of the information required, as well as national and local political conditions, is needed to conclude whether centralized or decentralized institutions will be better adapted to design regulations suited to local conditions.

Smith also discusses the negative effects of lack of coordination between decentralized regulators. The major issues are potential misalignment between jurisdictional and industry boundaries, control of spillover effects, interjurisdictional trade, and concerns about destructive competition.

TABLE 1-3. FAVORABLE CHARACTERISTICS OF DECENTRALIZATION AND CENTRALIZATION

Pro decentralization	Pro centralization
Differentiation	Coordination
Local information	National expertise
Creative competition	. No destructive competition
Enforcement	Control over regions

Local Information versus National Expertise

As Smith points out, centralization enables one to address information asymmetries between firms and consumers. Regarding firms, a high degree of technical expertise is needed to evaluate available information; in most developing countries, only national regulators have this type of expertise. This is less true for information concerning consumers, even if reliable statistical information is not available locally. On the other hand, local accountability of politicians is greater when decisions are based on locally available information. This is because local electors can better judge the quality of regulation if they share information on which regulatory choices are based.

The argument that national expertise is better mobilized through centralized mechanisms strongly favors centralization, at least as a first step in development. This is an evolving criterion that must be assessed according to specific cases; in this regard, the international community can play an important role by transferring technical expertise to the countries in question.

Creative versus Destructive Competition

One argument frequently given in favor of decentralization is that it promotes creative competition among regulators. Such competition may reduce the discretion of politicians, improve accountability, and enable the efficiency of regulators to be assessed. Yet, competition may be excessive and lead to resource waste. One problem that may arise is "forum shopping;" that is, firms decide to settle in localities that have the most favorable legislation and regulations. While this encourages regulators to compete in order to attract firms, another consequence may be a too lax regulation that enables firms to earn excessive profits. The central government's ability to retain sufficient control to prevent this type of behavior among decentralized regulators is a criterion when considering decentralization.

Central Government: Better Enforcement versus Better Control

Decentralization allows better enforcement by local authorities, at the expense of a certain amount of control. Large countries, such as the United States, Brazil, and Russia, have turned over sufficient responsibilities to their states and regions to encourage more participation in local-level enforcement. Although this approach entails the federal state's loss of control in a world of incomplete contracts and asymmetric information, it may be less costly than establishing independent federal enforcement mechanisms.

Ambiguous Results on Corruption and Capture

Smith states that one drawback of the decentralized system is the potentially greater risk of political and industry capture. Even though greater proximity may decrease the transaction costs of capture, this is a debatable point, both empirically and theoretically. Sound knowledge of local politics is essential before one can assess the degree of risk of capture involved in decentralization.

Centralization versus Decentralization: Summary of Arguments

Striking a balance between the above arguments is complex, and general rules cannot apply. As Smith (2000) shows, size of jurisdiction, industry characteristics, nature of the regulatory issue, and regulatory capacity (including human resources, expertise, and vulnerability to capture) are relevant variables. Benefits and costs of decentralization have to be assessed for each country, keeping in mind that the institutional structure is important in defining the degree of control that the central government will have. Several Latin American countries have begun decentralizing responsibilities, yet the general consensus is that this decentralization is largely formal and has little effect on the functioning of the state. Thorough knowledge of a country's specific conditions is indispensable for evaluating the consequences of reforms.

Nevertheless, normative conclusions are clear in a few cases. For example, telecommunications, a network industry spanning an entire country and requiring a high degree of technical expertise, is a leading candidate for national regulation. The same is true for electricity transmission grids, gas transport, and railways. At the other extreme, price regulation of local distribution of water, electricity, and gas should be decentralized to benefit from

TABLE 1-4. ARGUMENTS FOR INDUSTRY-SPECIFIC VERSUS MULTISECTOR AGENCY REGULATION

Pro industry-specific	Pro multisector agency
Differentiation	Blurring industry boundaries
Specific expertise and focus	Sharing resources
Risk diversification	Better coordination
Creative competition	Avoidance of destructive competition

local information and better accountability. This recommendation is not incompatible with national or federal oversight of corruption issues or other dimensions of regulation that require specific expertise, such as regulation of quality or certification of operators.

At the implementation level as well, one must consider the initial responsibilities that have been allocated to political bodies. Even if reallocation of powers is within sight, the first priority may be to improve the regulations themselves—to favor horizontal or vertical cooperation of existing authorities—so that the ground is prepared for politically acceptable institutional reforms.

Industry-specific or Multisector Agency?

Similar to the decentralization versus centralization argument, those arguments that favor industry-specific and multisector agency regulation can be grouped (table 1-4).

Differentiation versus Blurring Industry Boundaries

Arguments in favor of differentiation (similar to those for decentralization) demand a specific sector agency. However, when communication and cooperation among regulators are problematic, multisector agencies can better deal with rapidly changing industries with loosely defined boundaries, such as telecommunications.

In New Zealand, for example, the Ministerial Inquiry into Telecommunications emphasizes this aspect of the industry. It prefers to use the term electronic communications to avoid restricting its analysis to only a portion of the economy (New Zealand Ministry of Economic Development 2000b).

Specific Expertise and Focus versus Sharing Resources

Only the bounded rationality of regulators may justify the advantage of industry-specific expertise, since nothing prevents an integrated regulatory agency from having specific departments that allow specialized expertise and differentiated treatments. But again, the issue of availability of regulatory resources is crucial for developing countries since regulatory activities appear to have sizeable economies of scope. Moreover, a multisector agency may foster expertise in crosscutting issues. (This was argued for Australia after publication of the Himler report, when creation of the ACCC was being considered.) This argument is linked to the idea that communication between regulators is imperfect; therefore, sharp competition between regulators may result in limited communication, which, in turn, may be exacerbated by separation of regulators across industries.

Risk Diversification versus Better Coordination

Industry-specific regulation, it may be argued, allows for more experimentation in regulatory design. Yet, this argument, like that of decentralization, is invalid in a world of benevolent, unconstrained, and rational regulators. Here again, bounded rationality may explain why a multisector agency may be unable to diversify regulation so as to decrease the risk of unadapted regulation (Sah and Stiglitz 1986). However, multisector agencies may be favored for reducing the risks of economic distortions (Smith 2000). Indeed, one of the benefits of better coordination is reduction of economywide risk.

Creative Competition versus Avoidance of Destructive Competition

The arguments in favor of creative competition are similar to those that assess the benefits of decentralization. However, the nature of specific industries limits the scope and criteria of such competition.

Industry-specific versus Multisector Agency: Summary of Arguments

In summary, bounded rationality and creating incentives for regulators favor specific regulation, while coordination and limited expertise favor integrated regulation. Capture and accountability are ambiguous. Therefore, as Smith (2000) concluded, no single approach is always superior. The best solution depends on the size of the economy, scope of regulatory responsibilities, nature of the industries, and regulatory capacity. Despite lack of general rules, conditions in the poorest developing countries argue in favor of integrated regulation.

Historically, the reform of utilities in most countries has proceeded industry by industry; thus, it is institutionally simpler to establish a new regulator for each industry. In this case, one must encourage cooperation between regulators. Eventually, where natural industry overlaps occur (for example, the massive production of electricity using gas turbines), greater interaction between industries will, in some cases, result in mergers.

Tentative Guidelines

Decentralization of regulation is relevant only for federal states (except in the case of water distribution). As a starting point, the following guidelines are recommended for allocating regulatory responsibilities by industry:

- *Electricity*—An initial approach may be to assign high-voltage transmission to a specific federal regulation, and enforce competition in generation through antitrust regulations and authorities. Distribution should be assigned to state regulation. However, several clarifications should be considered. First, when consumers are eligible for direct purchase of generation outside their state, appropriate coordination between state regulation of captive consumers' final prices, as well as regulation of transmission, is needed. Second, open access to distribution networks should be established across a country. Third, if final prices are regulated, federal regulation should be responsible for transmission and generation. These guidelines and clarifications also apply to the gas industry.
- *Telecommunications*—Local calls and Internet access should be assigned to state regulation, while long-distance and international calls should be assigned to federal and antitrust regulations. All final prices can be deregulated when competition is sufficient, but access prices must remain regulated. The technical nature of telecommunications regulation may call for federal regulation only, despite problems of accountability.
- *Water distribution*—Regulation of water quality and pricing can be regulated at the state, and even the municipal, level. However, when expertise is lacking, regulation of quality may be assigned to the federal level. Federal regulation should concentrate on minimal-quality, environmental, and resource management issues.

- *Transport*—Interurban transportation should be regulated at the state level, while interstate transportation should be regulated at the federal level.
- *Postal services and railways*—These should be federally regulated, except for local passenger traffic.

References

Aghion, P., and J. Tirole. 1997. "Formal and Real Authority in Organization." *Journal of Political Economy* 105: 1–29.

Bardhan, P., and D. Mookherjee. 1999. *Relative Capture of Local and Central Governments: An Essay in the Political Economy of Regulation.* Institute for Economic Development, Discussion Paper Series, No. 97. Boston: Boston University.

Baron, D., and D. Besanko. 1992. "Information, Control, and Organizational Structure." *Journal of Economics and Management Strategy* 1: 237–75.

Bernheim, D., and M. Whinston. 1986. "Menu Auctions, Resource Allocation and Economic Influence." *Quarterly Journal of Economics* 101: 1–31.

Beasley, T., and S. Coate. 1998. "Centralized versus Decentralized Provision of Local Public Goods: A Political Economy Analysis." Working Paper No. W7084. Cambridge, MA: National Bureau of Economic Research.

Bolton, P., and G. Roland. 1997. "The Breakup of Nations: A Political Economy Analysis." *Quarterly Journal of Economics* 62: 1057–090.

Caillaud, B., B. Jullien, and P. Picard. 1996. "National vs European Incentive Policies: Bargaining, Information and Coordination." *European Economic Review* 40: 91–111.

Crémer, J., and T. Palfrey. 1996. "In or Out? Centralization by Majority Vote." *European Economic Review* 40: 43–60.

Dewatripont, M. 1989. "Renegotiation and Information Revelation over Time." *Quarterly Journal of Economics* 103: 589–620.

Dewatripont, M., and J. Tirole. 1999. "Advocates." *Journal of Political Economy* 107: 1–39.

Dobbin, F. 1994. *Forging Industrial Policy: The United States, Britain and France in the Railway Age.* Cambridge, U.K.: Cambridge University Press.

Dutz, M., A. Hayri, and P. Ibarra. 2000. "Regulatory Reform, Competition and Innovation: A Case Study of the Mexican Road Freight Industry." Research Policy Working Paper No. 2318. The World Bank, Washington, D.C.

Faure-Grimaud, A., J. J. Laffont, and D. Martimort. "Collusion, Delegation and Supervision with Soft Information. IDEI, 2000. Mimeographed.

Fels, A. 1996. "Decision Making at the Centre." Speech presented at the workshop, Implementation of Antitrust Rules in a "Federal" Context, 19 April, at European University Institute, Florence. Speech available at http://www.accc.gov.au.

Galal, A. 1996. "Chile: Regulatory Specificity, Credibility of Commitment, and Distributional Demands." In *Regulation, Institutions, and Commitment: Comparative Studies of Telecommunications,* eds. Brian Levy and Pablo Spiller, 121–44. Cambridge, U.K.: Cambridge University Press.

Gilbert, G., and P. Picard. 1996. "Incentives and the Optimal Size of Local Jurisdictions." *European Economic Review* 40: 19–41.

Green, R., and M. Rodriguez-Pardina. 1999. *Resetting Price Controls for Privatized Utilities: A Manual for Regulators.* WBDS Report No. 19016. The World Bank, Washington, D.C.

Hills, J. 1986. *Deregulating Telecoms, Competition and Control in the United States, Japan and Britain.* Westport, CT: Quorum Books.

Karhl, W. L. 1982. *Water and Power: The Conflict over Los Angeles Water Supply in the Owens Valley.* Berkeley: University of California Press.

Kerf, M., and D. Geradin. 1999. "Market Power in Telecommunications." *Berkeley Technology Law Journal* 14: 919–1020.

Kovacic, W. E., and C. Shapiro. 2000. "Antitrust Policy: A Century of Economic and Legal Thinking." *Journal of Economic Perspectives* 14(1): 43–60.

Laffont, J. J., and D. Martimort. 1998. "Collusion and Delegation." *Rand Journal of Economics* 29: 280–305.

———. 1999. "Separation of Regulators Against Collusive Behavior." *Rand Journal of Economics* 30(2): 232–62.

———. 2000. "Mechanism Design with Collusion and Correlation." *Econometrica* 68(2): 309–42.

Laffont, J. J., and M. Meleu. 1997. "Reciprocal Supervision, Collusion and Organization Design." *The Scandinavian Journal of Economics* 99: 519–40.

———. 2001. "Separation of Powers and Development." *Journal of Development Economics* 64: 129–45.

Laffont, J. J., and J. Pouyet. 2002. "The Subsidiarity Bias in Regulation." *Journal of Public Economics.* Forthcoming.

Laffont, J. J., and J. Tirole. 1988. "The Dynamics of Incentive Contracts." *Econometrica* 56: 1153–175.

———. 1990. "Adverse Selection and Renegotiation in Procurement." *Review of Economic Studies* 75: 597–626.

———. 1991. "The Politics of Government Decision Making: A Theory of Regulatory Capture." *Quarterly Journal of Economics* 106: 1089–127.

Laffont, J. J., and W. Zantman. 1999. "Information Acquisition, Political Game and the Delegation of Authority." Working Paper GREMAQ, Université de Toulouse 1.

Martimort, D. 1999. "Renegotiation Design with Multiple Regulators." *Journal of Economic Theory* 88(2): 261–94.

New Zealand Ministery of Economic Development. 2000a. "Ministerial Inquiry into the Electricity Industry." Report available at http://www.electricityinquiry.govt.nz/reports/issues.

————. 2000b. "Ministerial Inquiry into Telecommunications." Report available at http://www.teleinquiry.govt.nz/reports/draft.

OECD. 1999. *OECD Review of Regulatory Reform in the United States*. Paris: Organisation for Economic Co-operation and Development.

Olsen T., and G. Torsvick. 1995. "Intertemporal Common Agency and Organizational Design: How Much Centralization." *European Economic Review* 39: 1405–428.

Sah, R. 1991. "Fallibility in Human Organizations and Political Systems." *Journal of Economic Perspectives* 5: 67–88.

Sah, R., and J. Stiglitz. 1986. "The Architecture of Economic Systems: Hierarchies and Polyarchies." *American Economic Review* 76: 716–27.

Saleth, R. M., and A. Dinar. 1999. "Water Challenge and Institutional Response: A Cross-country Perspective." Research Policy Working Paper No. 2161. The World Bank, Washington, D.C.

Seabright, P. 1996. "Accountability and Decentralization in Government: An Incomplete Contracts Model." *European Economic Review* 40.

Shleifer, A., and R. Vishny. 1993. "Corruption." *Quarterly Journal of Economics* 109: 599–617.

Smith, W. 2000. "Regulating Utilities: Thinking about Location Questions." Presented at the World Bank Summer Workshop on Market Institutions, July 2000, Washington, D.C.

Spiller, P., and C. Sampson. 1996. "Telecommunications Regulation in Jamaica." In *Regulation, Institutions, and Commitment: Comparative Studies of Telecommunications*, eds. Brian Levy and Pablo Spiller, 36–78. Cambridge, U.K.: Cambridge University Press.

Spiller, P., and I. Vogelsang. 1996. "The United Kingdom: A Pace-setter in Regulatory Incentives." In *Regulation, Institutions, and Commitment: Comparative Studies of Telecommunications*, eds. Brian Levy and Pablo Spiller, 79–120. Cambridge, U.K.: Cambridge University Press.

Tiebout, C. 1956. "A Pure Theory of Public Expenditure." *Journal of Political Economy* 64: 416–24.

Trujillo, L., and G. Nombela. 1999. "Privatization and Regulation of the Seaport Industry." Research Policy Working Paper No. 2181. The World Bank, Washington, D.C.

Wellenius, B. 1997. "Extending Telecommunications Services to Rural Areas: The Chilean Experience." *Viewpoint*, No. 105. The World Bank, Washington, D.C.

Williamson, O. 1985. *The Economic Institution of Capitalism*. New York: Free Press.

Chapter 2

Chile's Antitrust Legislation: Effects on Essential Facilities

Pablo Serra

Chile's antitrust law vaguely defines conduct that violates the law and situations that put efficient market development at risk; the law is equally ambiguous about which instruments antitrust institutions have at their disposal. To fully grasp the effect that Chilean antitrust legislation has had on development of the country's infrastructure services, it is first necessary to analyze the major rulings of these institutions and the consequences of their decisions. Therefore, this chapter focuses on how Chile's antitrust commissions—its advisory board, adjudicative body, and investigative/prosecutory body—have dealt with essential facilities.

Traits of Infrastructure Sectors

One common characteristic of infrastructure-based sectors is that competitive market segments coexist with natural monopoly segments. Firms that participate in competitive market segments usually need to access monopolistic segments, known as essential facilities or bottlenecks, in order to reach their clientele.[1] In such situations, sector regulations usually provide for and

---

[1] For example, the local telephone network is an essential facility to communications companies, just as the transmission system is to power generators. Economides (1998) provides the example of Microsoft, an essential facility that is not infrastructure. While Microsoft dominates the market for personal computer operating systems, it competes with other firms in the software applications market. The company has been accused of discriminating against its competitors by creating incompatibility or not revealing to them operating system capacity useful to applications.

determine the price of open access to the essential facility. Nonetheless, if the monopoly is vertically integrated into nonregulated segments, the monopolist may be tempted to provide its competitors poor quality service.[2]

Sabotage

Several economists have analyzed the potential anticompetitive effects of nonprice discrimination by the integrated monopoly, a practice known as *sabotage*. This issue is particularly consequential in Chile, whose policy has been to introduce competition wherever possible and to regulate noncompetitive industry segments.

Over the past few years, a much-debated topic has been whether the owner of an essential facility has sufficient incentive to sabotage its rivals in the competitive segment. Mandy (2000) states that such an incentive would be blurred at best, because any increase in earnings that may result from discrimination downstream may not offset the loss of profits upstream. He argues that sabotage raises the costs to rivals, who are forced to increase their prices. This price increase may reduce sales of downstream competitors, thereby lowering demand for the essential input. Nevertheless, if the integrated firm is as efficient as its rivals in providing the nonregulated service and can absorb additional demand while maintaining its marginal costs, then discrimination does not affect sales of the essential input. Determining whether owners of essential facilities have sufficient incentive to discriminate is an empirical question.

Other Risks to Competition

One must remember, however, that sabotage is not the only risk to competition when an essential facility is vertically integrated. In fact, competition may be adversely affected by the following factors:

- *Asymmetric information*—Information the integrated company has about its downstream competitors' business. For example, the local telephone company knows the customers of its long-distance service rivals.

---

[2] The monopolist may also delay negotiation with its competitors in order to determine the terms and conditions of using the essential facility, especially if interconnection is required; meanwhile, it attempts to steal its competitors' customers.

- *Strategic advantage*—Knowledge the integrated company gains of its rivals' plans because use of the essential asset requires that rivals reveal their plans to the company in advance. For example, power generation companies must negotiate energy transport with the transmission company in advance.

- *Regulated price of essential input exceeding marginal cost*—The regulator setting a price for the essential input above its marginal cost, giving the integrated company incentive to charge a price for the nonregulated service below its average cost—and even below its marginal cost. In fact, the integrated company compensates the fall in price of the nonregulated service with the increase in demand for the essential input, something that its rivals cannot do.[3] This pricing policy, sustainable in the long run, may even force competitors out of the market.

- *Cost transfer*—A ploy integrated monopolies use to raise a regulated rate by artificially transferring costs from nonregulated services to the regulated service.

According to the literature, monopolies have less incentive to sabotage when the costs of doing so are higher, when the monopoly faces more competition from providers of substitute inputs, and when the subsidiary that provides the nonregulated service is more autonomous (Mandy 2000). The cost of market sabotage can increase either by imposing harsher punishment or by intensifying oversight to increase the likelihood of detection, thereby rendering such an undertaking too costly. Often, two or more companies may offer the essential input or alternative providers may offer substitutes to the competition. In such cases, the regulatory agency may promote the creation of these options. Moreover, it may force the parent company to grant greater autonomy to the subsidiary. A totally independent subsidiary would have no incentive to reduce the price in order to boost sales of the essential input. Finally, greater transparency of information would help end the monopoly's advantage, making it less likely for the monopoly to transfer costs to the regulated service.

Services characterized by network externality are similar to those of essential facilities, where the dominant firm is positioned to sabotage competition (Spiller and Cardilli 1997).[4] For example, in local telephone service,

---

[3] The lower price for the nonregulated service expands consumption, which, in turn, increases demand for the essential input.

[4] Network externality occurs when connection of an additional user causes the service to take on a higher value for other customers.

a new carrier must be interconnected with the existing network so that subscribers of both carriers can communicate with each other.[5]

Evolution of Regulatory Changes

In the early 1980s, prior to privatization of state-owned enterprises, Chile's regulatory framework underwent changes in the electricity and telecommunications sectors. However, these changes did not adequately level the playing field for new operators who sought to compete with established companies in competitive market segments. During the process of privatization, industries experienced a high degree of horizontal concentration, unjustified in terms of economies of scale. Furthermore, regulations allowed for vertical integration between essential facilities and competitive market segments. Even more critical, regulation of technical conditions and economic terms for access to essential facilities and interconnection in industries with network economies was inadequate. In fact, parties were free to negotiate both electricity transmission rates and interconnection charges in telecommunications.[6]

The problems that ensued as a result of vertical and horizontal integration of privatized industries led antitrust institutions to analyze these markets and issue several rulings aimed at creating a climate in which markets could run more efficiently. In addition, these institutions had to settle many private litigation cases. Entry of new competitors into the market, coupled with a lack of regulations for essential inputs, gave rise to conflicts between private parties. Lawsuits pitted owners of essential facilities against competitors in other industry segments. In their complaints, the new companies charged that the integrated monopolies took predatory actions and discriminated against new companies gaining access to essential facilities.

During the 1990s, antitrust institutions played a different role in the privatization that occurred. The government administration, dissatisfied

---

[5] Laffont, Rey, and Tirole (1998a, b), for example, examine how to determine the most appropriate interconnection charge between the networks of two carriers that compete for the same subscribers. Armstrong (1998) analyzes what happens when two network carriers of comparable size negotiate the interconnection charge. He finds that, if their services differ sufficiently, these companies may use this negotiation as an opportunity for collusion.

[6] This can be explained by several factors: the inexperience of a country that was a pioneer in deregulation of public services, the overconfidence of the government at the time of developing private industry markets, and the ideological desire of government officials to minimize the state's role.

with regulation of privatized industries, took greater care regarding competition issues, as state-owned enterprises were transferred to the private sector.[7] Antitrust institutions were thereby given the opportunity to examine the conditions under which public services would be privatized and issue reports on aspects of their own competence or jurisdictional authority.[8]

In recent years, governments have awarded concessions for highways, airports, and seaports. These concessions have been publicly bid, generating ex ante competition on a playing field where no competition can exist. When the infrastructure bid has constituted an essential facility, antitrust institutions have been called on to issue an opinion on the bidding rules, which usually have included restrictions on vertical integration.

Looking closer at the rulings of these antitrust commissions, one can see that they have been particularly concerned about the risks vertically integrated monopolies may pose in discriminating against downstream competitors. This concern is perhaps most evident in the commissions' request that the government regulate rates of any essential facilities that remained unregulated. On the other hand, vertical integration came to be accepted by the commissions, as long as the integrated monopoly provided the competitive service through a subsidiary with an exclusive line of business.[9] Other requirements provided for greater transparency in information reporting, making it more difficult for integrated monopolies to gain a strategic advantage.

Over the past few years, the antitrust commissions have adopted a more drastic position with regard to vertical integration, recommending restrictions (such as gas pipelines in 1997 and port services in 1998). Although the

---

[7] Privatized public service companies increased their internal efficiency, but these gains are reflected only in prices of services for which a competitive offering was available. This situation led to a significant increase in profitability of electricity distribution and fixed telephone companies. Profits of the largest electricity distributor rose from 10.4 percent in 1987 to 31.8 percent in 1997, and the fixed telephone monopoly grew from 11.5 percent to 18.7 percent over the same period. However, firms that provided nonregulated services in the same industries showed different results. In 1997, profits of the main electricity generation company were 9.9 percent, after having attained rates higher than 15.7 percent in 1994, but still an improvement over the 5.2 percent recorded in 1987. Profits of the long-distance telephone monopoly fell dramatically after the sector was opened to competition in 1993 (from 37.4 percent in 1993 to 5.1 percent in 1997).

[8] The bidding rules for ownership of the state-owned electric utility company in northern Chile were submitted to the antitrust commissions for their opinion. These institutions also ruled on reform of the sanitation sector law, which was enacted prior to privatization.

[9] For example, the commissions allowed local telephone companies to participate in long-distance service through a subsidiary. They also allowed the northern electric utility company to maintain subsidiary ownership of the transmission system after it was privatized.

main generator for Chile's central zone has been allowed to maintain ownership of its transmission subsidiary, in 1997, the Antitrust Resolution Commission (the country's antitrust adjudicative body) forced this power generator to recharter its subsidiary as a public stock corporation and recommended opening its ownership to other shareholders.

Antitrust Legislation and Institutions

The first piece of antitrust legislation in Chile, dating back to 1959, was inconsequential until 1973, when a rapid process of deregulation began. In that year, issuance of Executive Order No. 211 defined the principal rules of promoting and protecting free competition.[10] The first two articles of this legal decree (which has the force of a parliamentary act) defined anticompetitive conduct to a certain extent. Article 1 establishes that anyone who carries out any act that may tend to impede free competition may be penalized with a maximum punishment of a term of incarceration. Article 2 provides examples of such acts, including setting production quotas, dividing geographic areas of exclusive sales among competitors, and price-fixing arrangements. Because of the law's general nature, learning how the antitrust commissions have dealt with fair competition issues related to essential facilities requires examining how these institutions have ruled and explained their decisions over time.

Institutional Composition and Constraints

Executive Order No. 211 also created the three institutions charged with enforcement of antitrust laws and regulations: Antitrust Prevention Commission (*Comisión Preventiva*), Antitrust Resolution Commission (*Comisión Resolutiva*), and Office of the National Economic Prosecutor (*Fiscalía Nacional Económica*).[11] The Antitrust Prevention Commission is primarily an advisory body, while the Antitrust Resolution Commission is a tribunal that has exclusive jurisdictional powers to punish anticompetitive conduct

---

[10] This law was subsequently revised in 1979 (Legal Decree No. 2,760), 1980 (Legal Decree No. 511), and 1999 (Law No. 19,610).

[11] All regions of the country have antitrust prevention commissions, whose jurisdiction is limited to their respective geographic areas.

and settle disputes related to competition jurisdiction. All representatives appointed to these two commissions serve voluntary, two-year terms. The National Economic Prosecutor, in turn, represents the economic interests of the society overall before the Antitrust Resolution Commission and courts of justice.

The Antitrust Prevention Commission consists of one representative from the Ministry of Economy, who chairs the body; one representative from the Ministry of the Treasury; two university professors appointed by the Council of University Rectors; one attorney; one economist; and one representative of the Neighborhood Boards (similar to U.S. civic associations).[12]

The Resolution Commission consists of one Associate Justice from the Supreme Court, who is appointed by members of the Court and who presides over the Commission; two Chiefs of Public Administration Services (one appointed by the Minister of Economy and the other by the Minister of the Treasury); and two deans of Santiago-based universities (one from the School of Economics and the other from the School of Law [selected through a random drawing]).

The membership prescribed for the three commissions was designed to balance the system's legal approach with an economics-based perspective. However, commission members are usually not experts in antitrust matters. For example, the legislation that chartered the commissions to provide for one representative of the Neighborhood Boards to sit on the Antitrust Prevention Commission was viewed as a way to give consumers a voice; however, this representative is usually not qualified to serve in a body whose functions are technical in nature. Furthermore, because members of the Antitrust Resolution Commission must be individuals who serve in specific offices, the pool of potential members is limited, and those selected are usually not well versed in antitrust matters.

Over the past few years, many private universities have been established throughout Chile; consequently, selecting two deans through a random drawing may run the risk that unqualified members will serve on this commission. Commission performance is further constrained by the short amount of time devoted to examining each case. Since seats on these commissions are unpaid positions, members must hold other offices or have other jobs, leaving little time for proper fulfillment of duties as commission-

---

[12] This representative is elected by presidents of the community union of Neighborhood Boards of the Metropolitan Region.

ers. For this reason, commission members depend heavily on reports prepared by the Office of the National Economic Prosecutor in rendering their decisions. Commissions are further constrained by their ties to the government, which only weaken their autonomy in issuing rulings.

The National Economic Prosecutor, head of the Office of the National Economic Prosecutor, is appointed by Chile's president. A lawyer by training, the Prosecutor usually has no prior experience in antitrust law.[13] This Office has been plagued by many public sector drawbacks, particularly low salaries, which prevent qualified professionals from applying and encourage current qualified staff to move into the private sector. Although Law No. 19,610, which strengthens the Office of the National Economic Prosecutor, was enacted in 1999, thereby partially solving the problem, the dilemma of unqualified staff remains. Out of 45 professionals and managers, only six are engineers or economists. Thus, reports of the prosecutory and investigative office, which form the basis for the commissioners' decisionmaking, are replete with legal arguments but lack supportive economics theory. This Office lacks the capacity to track markets, even when it suspects collusion.[14]

Powers of the Commissions

The National Economic Prosecutor is empowered to defend or challenge the Commission's judgments before the Supreme Court. The Prosecutor has several prerogatives available, including the exclusive right to call on antimonopoly commissions to fulfill their duties (particularly, to request that the Antitrust Resolution Commission sanction an entity or take precautionary measures), enforce rulings handed down by this Commission or the courts of justice in competition-related matters, and conduct any related investigation it considers appropriate. In turn, the Prosecutor is required to issue any reports that may be requested by the antitrust commissions.

---

[13] In 1992, one pharmaceutical company accused another of unfair practices because it had sent a letter to doctors claiming that the product of its competitor was less effective. It backed this claim with results of a scientific study conducted by a university. The complainant maintained, based on another report from the same university, that the claim was untrue. The Prevention Commission requested that the National Economic Prosecutor investigate the claim. At a subsequent Commission meeting, the Prosecutor joyously announced that the problem had been settled; thanks to his good offices, both companies had agreed to market the product jointly.

[14] This may explain why the Commissions more often function as a civil court for settling disputes between litigants, rather than fulfilling their more important role as a criminal court that punishes anticompetitive conduct.

This Office has a wide array of instruments available with which to exercise its prerogatives. One is the ability to request the courts to order that a suspect be held in custody for up to 15 days if it is believed that the suspect is obstructing the investigation. This request may only be made, however, after obtaining prior approval from the Antitrust Resolution Commission. A second instrument is the ability to use the human resources of Chile's Bureau of Investigation, with prior knowledge of the Chairman of the Antitrust Resolution Commission.

The Antitrust Prevention Commission is an administrative body whose functions are preventive and advisory in nature. It performs its advisory duties by providing private parties or the state the information they request about whether to enter into agreements or take actions that may adversely affect competition. This Commission is empowered to rule on two preventive measures that the National Economic Prosecutor may request: a 14-day suspension of any anticompetitive act or contract, and the temporary setting of maximum prices, which may remain in effect for up to 15 days (the Commission may extend the deadline, if needed). The Commission is also empowered to propose measures designed to correct situations that may adversely affect competition and prevent abuse of dominant market position (Executive Order No. 211, Article 8, Section c).[15] Opinions of the Antitrust Prevention Commission may only be appealed before the Antitrust Resolution Commission.

On the other hand, Executive Order No. 211 confers broad powers on the Antitrust Resolution Commission to hear cases, investigate alleged violations, and punish anticompetitive conduct. The Commission can modify or terminate contracts that violate the principles of free competition, order the modification or dissolution of corporations that have committed anticompetitive acts, impose fines of up to 10,000 UTM (1 UTM equals about 50 US$), and order the National Economic Prosecutor to file a criminal complaint against a defendant whose conduct hampers free competition.[16]

The Antitrust Resolution Commission has exclusive powers to rule on whether an act or conduct violates free competition rules and laws. Only

---

[15] The Antitrust Prevention Commission is not empowered to impose sanctions. Whenever it believes that a violation of fair competition practices has occurred, it calls on the Economic Prosecutor to file a request for action before the Resolution Commission; however, the Prosecutor is not obligated to heed the Prevention Commission's petition.

[16] The National Economic Prosecutor must file a request with the Court of Appeals to impose a jail term, in which case, the Court of Appeals acts as a trial court.

when its rulings order modification or dissolution of corporations (artificial entities) and impose fines can this Commission's decisions be appealed to the Supreme Court.[17] Under Article 17b of Executive Order No. 211, the Commission is empowered to "issue instructions of a general nature to which private individuals must conform in entering into acts and contracts that may go against free competition."

Powers of the antitrust commissions have been a source of controversy. Some jurists maintain that the commissions lack the legal authority to regulate markets, and only have the power to penalize conduct that violates free competition. In the view of these legal experts, market regulation would infringe on the civil rights and freedoms established under Chile's Constitution (Article 19) and can only come about by enacting a statute.[18]

Specifically, these jurists claim that market regulation would infringe on the right to exercise lawful business activities, right to the equal treatment that the state is obligated to afford all persons, freedom to acquire dominion over all types of property, and right of ownership. All of these rights are expressly protected by the Constitution. According to this logic, if the commissions intend to regulate markets by means of their opinions and rulings, this would violate Articles 6 and 7, which establish that agents of the State shall act in accordance with the Constitution, and that their actions are valid only if and when these agents have lawful jurisdiction to act and action is taken in a manner consistent with provisions of the law.

---

[17] Most decisions handed down by the Antitrust Resolution Commission are not of this nature; therefore, the parties affected by its decisions usually file a special appeal with the Supreme Court, known as a "petition in error," which relates to the procedural, rather than meritorious, aspects of the original Commission proceedings. If the appeal is accepted, the Court requires the Commission to amend the "mistake or abuse" committed when the Commission issued the decision challenged. Thus, by using petition in error, the substance of a decision can be modified, even though, in principle, this is not permitted.

[18] Article 19 of the Constitution ensures the right of all persons to conduct any business activity that does not go against public morals, law and order, or national security, while abiding by the particular statutes and regulations that govern the particular business activity (Article 21); the right to no arbitrary discrimination by the State and its agents in business matters (Article 22); the freedom to acquire dominion over any type of property, except that [property] which nature has made common to all men or which must wholly belong to the nation and is declared so by law (Article 23); and the right to ownership in its different forms over all types of tangible and nontangible assets (Article 24). Only the law can establish how property may be acquired, used, enjoyed, and disposed of, as well as the limitations and obligations that derive from its social function. Additionally, Article 26 guarantees that legal precepts that restrict, regulate, or supplement constitutionally guaranteed rights and freedoms will not affect the essence of rights or impose conditions, taxes, or requirements that impede free exercise of rights.

Conversely, a group of legal scholars holds that the commissions have broad discretionary powers to regulate markets. These jurists argue that, in conducting business activities, other legal precepts must also be respected, including provisions contained in Executive Order No. 211. In their view, Article 8 (Section c) and Article 17 (Section b) grant the antitrust commissions powers to regulate business activity. They claim that Executive Order No. 211 includes broad provisions that cover all potential ways in which individuals could conceivably impede competition. Moreover, these experts state that the antitrust commissions have the legal authority to prevent any act or event that may hinder free competition. Specifically, the commissions may prohibit vertical integration or the merger of companies when such events lead to business consolidation in a market, which could bar new companies from entry into the market.[19]

The crux of the debate is whether Executive Order No. 211 (especially Article 17, Section b) grants the Antitrust Resolution Commission the power to regulate business activity. According to one school of thought, this executive order has broad provisions that cover any potential situation. Therefore, decisions issued by the Antitrust Resolution Commission would constitute part of the public economic order by which everyone must abide. On the other hand, other legal scholars believe that the Antitrust Resolution Commission's decisions are not part of the established legal order and therefore cannot impinge on constitutional rights.

Commission Precedents

Rulings of the antitrust commissions have been setting precedents, not only with regard to rules governing the workings of the market, but also regarding its own legal authority. In fact, in many cases heard by the commissions, controversy has focused on the scope of their own authority. However, these precedents are not conclusive about whether commissions have the power to regulate market structures and whether it is appropriate to implement such regulation.

In earlier rulings, the Commissions claimed to lack the power to regulate markets. Resolution No. 349 (issued November 20, 1990), involving discounts

---

[19] According to Enrique Barros, if constitutional freedoms are not the subject of any statute or regulation designed to limit or prevent abuses in the exercise of constitutional freedoms or rights, [then] a legal system that makes the freedom to do business possible for others would be unworkable, according to the principle of public economic order that underlies the Constitution. According to this argument, respect for the rules of free competition ensures the freedom of anyone to do business.

given by pharmaceutical companies, established that it is not the job of antitrust institutions to regulate markets, but rather to achieve an appropriate degree of transparency so that the most efficient firms can prevail to consumers' benefit. Resolution No. 349 also warned against regulating markets. In fact, it stated that free competition cannot be protected by imposing arbitrary requirements or conditions on economic or business agents or by attaching a set of obligations to pricing freedom, rendering it meaningless under the pretext that end users will benefit. Moreover, Opinion 744 of the Antitrust Prevention Commission (issued September 21, 1990), involving the merger of soft drink companies, held that it is not critical to competition for company ownership to be in either one or several hands; rather, competition depends on the companies' behavior. In short, market regulation would be an unwise policy because it would set up roadblocks to competition, which is already adequately deterred through existing sanctions on abuse of dominance.

An opposing position can be found in Resolution No. 368 (issued in April 1992).[20] In the telecommunications sector, the government privatized two monopolistic enterprises: Compañía de Teléfonos de Chile (CTC) for local telephone services and Entel for long-distance telephone services. In January 1990, Telefónica de España, a Spanish telephone company, which already owned 20 percent of Entel shares, acquired 49.2 percent of CTC shares. Three months later, the Antitrust Prevention Commission ruled that Telefónica could have a presence in either Entel or CTC, but not both. Telefónica appealed this opinion, arguing that the Constitution does not permit competition agencies to regulate markets. In April 1992, the Antitrust Resolution Commission upheld the Prevention Commission's decision. In its ruling, members of the Antitrust Resolution Commission stated that consolidation of economic power per se may affect a sector's efficiency. The Resolution further stated: "For purposes of competition, especially with regard to possible barriers [for other companies] to enter [into the market] and to the subsistence [or survival] of the competitors of these companies, the circumstance that they [these companies] act with absolute independence from one another or that they act with any degree of joint ownership, whether in their management [administration], business policy or other policy setting, cannot be immaterial."

Regarding the Antitrust Resolution Commission's authority of scope, the decision stated that, although the Constitution guarantees freedom to

---

[20] All appeals filed with the Supreme Court against Resolution No. 368 were rejected by final rulings issued in April 1993.

conduct any type of business activity, this must be done while respecting legal provisions that regulate those activities. It also stated that one of the most important provisions that regulates this constitutionally guaranteed freedom and that is part of the Public Economic Order is Executive Order No. 211, since its purpose is to prevent economic distortions that can lead to manipulating market supply and demand. Since the intent of Executive Order No. 211 could be violated in various ways, its drafters included broad provisions to cover all potential situations and, in turn, conferred vast authority on the antitrust commissions to prevent, correct, and punish events or acts that might restrict free competition.

The current trend maintains that antimonopoly commissions have the power to establish structural regulations after following proper legal procedures in which evidence of the facts is offered and an opportunity for proper legal defense is provided. Resolution No. 445 (issued in August 1995) involves a request filed by Chile's two main domestic airlines, who sought approval for creating a partnership. The Resolution begins by stating that the opening section of Executive Order No. 211 does not sanction or prohibit the existence of companies that occupy a dominant position, but rather sanctions and prohibits any conduct that these companies may have engaged in that constitutes an abuse of dominant position. This Resolution adds that the chartering legislation of the antitrust commissions empowers these bodies to prevent the occurrence of such conduct. In fact, this ruling states that the commissions must determine whether an association or merger of companies constitutes an act that may impede or lead to restricting free competition, and must not rule on the legality of the particular conduct.[21]

---

[21] Following this analysis, the Antitrust Resolution Commission approved the association of both companies. It gave three main reasons for approval. First, the Commission believed that this association would create economies of scale, which, in turn, would reduce costs that could eventually benefit passengers. Second, it considered that this association would not limit or restrict competition in the domestic airline market. Third, if the association were to affect competition negatively, the Commission believed that the antitrust institutions could apply appropriate corrective measures.

It should be noted that the Commission was unconvinced of its own arguments since, in the same decision, it called on the government to introduce a change in the law, giving the Commission discretion to set rates for air transport services when market conditions called for such action. It also ordered the companies to submit a self-regulation rate scheme to the Prevention Commission for approval within a 90-day period.

The airline companies' argument (although not documented in the Commission's decision, it finally swayed members) was that domestic airlines needed to be of minimum size in order to compete internationally.

The antitrust commissions have asserted their authority to order restrictions on vertical integration in cases involving the bidding of public infrastructure that constitutes essential facilities to private companies. For example, in 1996, the government awarded airports a concession after having first consulted the Antitrust Prevention Commission regarding bidding rules. According to these rules, the maximum voting shares of stock that air transport companies could own in the concessionaire were restricted to 15 percent. In April 1997, the Commission raised this limit to 20 percent (Opinion 1,014).[22]

Vertical Integration in Telecommunications

Overview of the Problem

Ambiguity in Chile's telecommunications law created a legal monopoly in long-distance telephone services, and poor rate regulation enabled Entel to achieve annual profits of more than 40 percent over equity. As a result, many companies grew interested in providing this service; several firms, including CTC, applied to the Subsecretariat of Telecommunications (Subtel), the sector's regulatory agency, for operating licenses in long-distance service. Although a consensus had been reached on the need to end monopolies in long-distance service, doubts emerged about whether local telephone companies should be allowed to participate in the long-distance business. It was feared that local telephone companies would tend to favor their own business in long-distance services, for example, by giving their competitors poor interconnections. It was generally thought that it would be too difficult to put a regulatory scheme in place that was capable of preventing discrimination entirely. Three factors contributed to this belief: it would be too difficult to enforce technical standards, the regulatory system was not sophisticated enough, and the legal system did not facilitate conflict resolution.

The regulators, on the other hand, were aware that vertical integration has its advantages. For example, it makes it possible for telecommunications companies to use existing economies of scope in providing services and for

---

[22] The Commission originally prohibited vertical integration, stating that it would permit airline companies to discriminate against competitors not participating in the concession. As a result of a request for clarification from the government, the Commission took a more flexible position, arguing that changes in the bidding rules, including minimum operational standards, which would be subject to government oversight and inspection, would provide greater guarantee of equal access to concessionaire services.

consumers to sign up with a single company for all services. Although it would be ideal for integrated companies to compete in offering a wide array of services, the nature of a natural monopoly in basic telephone services, coupled with a highly concentrated market share of these services in a single company (nearly 95 percent of Chile's subscribers were with CTC at the time) made this option difficult to achieve.

Proceedings before the Antitrust Commissions

In June 1989, Subtel consulted the Antitrust Prevention Commission to inquire whether entry of local telephone companies into the long-distance business would clash with the provisions of Executive Order No. 211, especially in the case of CTC. In October of that year, the Antitrust Prevention Commission, through Opinion No. 718, recommended maintaining vertical disintegration in the sector. CTC appealed that opinion, and, in November, the Antitrust Resolution Commission, through Resolution No. 332, reversed the opinion. The Resolution Commission decided that, by adopting measures and precautions set forth in the ruling, local telephone companies could provide long-distance services. These measures limited local telephone companies' long-distance participation to a multicarrier dialing system that enabled users to select a long-distance carrier for individual calls by dialing a certain number of digits.

The Resolution Commission also directed local telephone companies to provide all long-distance operators equal opportunity to interconnect with the local network, with access fees approved by Subtel. Moreover, the companies that became vertically integrated were required to undergo this process by means of subsidiaries chartered as publicly traded stock corporations that forced transactions between the parent company and subsidiary to mimic market conditions. Resolution No. 332 also made it mandatory for local telephone companies to provide carriers all information related to long-distance traffic (for example, subscriber number, type of traffic, billing amount, and carrier used) and to offer the long-distance companies metering, appraisal, and billing and collection services, abiding by nondiscriminatory rates pre-approved by Subtel.

In response, Entel filed an appeal, known as "petition in error"[23] with the Supreme Court, which, in May 1990, nullified the earlier decision and sent the case back to the Resolution Commission. In formulating its ruling,

---

[23] See footnote 17.

the Court said that the Resolution Commission failed to include in its argument all relevant technical information needed to establish that, with currently available technology, it would be possible to ensure compliance with conditions essential to establishing a competitive long-distance market. In addition, the Court ordered the Resolution Commission to carefully decide which technical conditions would guarantee fairmarket conditions, including supervision of interconnection quality. Consequently, this was the central focus of the rehearing before the Resolution Commission.

Positions of the Parties Involved

The rest of the telecommunications companies claimed that CTC's integration into long-distance services would make it possible for that company to extend its monopoly from local to long-distance service, despite installation of a multicarrier dialing system. From these companies' perspective, CTC could provide different levels of quality in the interconnection, thereby adversely affecting service quality of potential long-distance competitors, since the technical, financial, and legal means to implement all required monitoring or oversight to guarantee nondiscrimination were not in place.[24] Furthermore, CTC would have incentive to transfer profits from the regulated market to the competitive market. Being the only company in direct contact with users, CTC would have a commercial advantage. Finally, having prior access to information related to long-distance service would make it possible for CTC to offer different service plans.

For its part, CTC argued that the Resolution Commission did not have the legal authority to prohibit market access in the absence of an unlawful act or event to justify its intervention, since the function of the antitrust commissions was to sanction unlawful acts classified as such in Articles 1 and 2 of Executive Order No. 211. It also asserted that installation of a multicarrier dialing system would prevent nontariff discrimination. Furthermore, it claimed that operating its long-distance service through a subsidiary subject to supervision of the Office of the Superintendent of Securities, Stocks, and Insurance of the sector would be sufficient guarantee that no cross subsidies between CTC and its long-distance affiliate would occur. Lastly, CTC offered to set aside a minimum of 10 percent of the capital shares of its long-distance subsidiary for another telecommunications company, also giving it the right to appoint at least one member to the subsidiary's board of directors.

---

[24] These companies argued that quality discrimination does not have to be ongoing to be effective.

Opinion of the Antitrust Resolution Commission

The Resolution Commission issued its new ruling in April 1993 (Resolution No. 389).[25] As a preliminary matter, the Commission addressed the issue of its scope of authority. It maintained that, contrary to the CTC's claim, the Commission had the discretionary power to rule on the matter submitted by Subtel, even though the case did not involve an offense or crime as such. Thus, it rejected allegations regarding its lack of jurisdiction to establish regulations. Regarding the merit of the case, the Commission held that it was improper to divide up the telecommunications market into segments, citing that technological advancements in this sector made it difficult to differentiate between services. Nevertheless, it warned that vertical integration posed a risk to fair competition, which made it necessary to establish an efficient, strictly controlled, regulatory framework with drastic sanctions for offenders. In its ruling, the Commission reiterated the measures that must be adopted before deregulating the long-distance market, giving the government 18 months in which to implement them.[26] In addition, Subtel was ordered to regulate direct connection of users to long-distance companies.[27]

Consequences of the Ruling

Law 19,302, which paved the way for deregulating long-distance services, was approved in March 1994. This law encompassed all of the requirements imposed by the Resolution Commission and included a constraint on participation of all companies in the long-distance market over the subsequent five years. These constraints were most stringent for carriers affiliated with local phone companies. The multicarrier system became operational in October 1994. Deregulation of the long-distance market met expectations.[28]

---

[25] Some companies filed an appeal against the decision of the Resolution Commission with the Supreme Court, alleging that the Commission was not empowered to regulate situations that are properly governed by law. In its 1994 decision, the Court denied the appeal, declaring that the Resolution Commission has the power to issue resolutions of a general nature to which private parties must adhere.

[26] Perhaps the only difference between Resolutions Nos. 332 and 389 is that the latter allowed service contracts and multidial service to coexist, while the former only accepted the dialing multicarrier.

[27] Direct connections are those that bypass the network of local companies, which, prior to that time, had not been permitted.

[28] Opinions Nos. 826 and 887 of the Antitrust Prevention Commission were also significant, as they recommended incorporating the new long-distance companies as signatories of INTELSAT in representation of Chile. Until that time, Entel was the only signatory of the convention, which gave it preferential access to INTELSAT's satellites, the main path for international transmission at the time.

TABLE 2-1. COMPANIES' PARTICIPATION IN THE LONG-DISTANCE SERVICE MARKET

Company	Domestic traffic (%)		Outgoing international traffic (%)	
	1997	1994	1998	1995
Entel	40.9	37.4	34.0	40.5
CTC-Mundo	34.4	28.9	19.6	20.7
Telex Chile	14.6	21.9	18.5	19.4
Bell South Chile	1.4	1.6	10.7	7.0
VTR	3.7	7.9	10.1	10.2
Transam	5.0		3.1	
Manquehue			1.6	
Iusatel			1.6	
Others	0.0	2.3	0.8	2.2

Source: Subtel.

New firms, including CTC-Mundo (CTC's subsidiary), entered into the long-distance service market, and its power was swiftly dispersed. The volume of international calls handled by Entel, which had held a monopoly position until 1994, dropped to less than 41 percent of total volume by 1995, and its market share in this sector continued to decrease (table 2-1). Entel's market share drop was even more dramatic in domestic long-distance service, where it fell to 37.4 percent by the end of 1994.[29]

Long-distance rates dropped dramatically, as evidenced by the change in the cost of a one-minute phone call from Chile to the United States, a route that represents 42 percent of total international traffic. During peak hours, the regulated rate had been US$2.40 per minute, while today, the same call costs less than US$0.18 per minute.[30] The total number of outgoing and incoming international and domestic long-distance calls using the local CTC network nearly tripled over the five-year period, increasing from 159 million minutes in 1993 to 476 million minutes in 1997 (approximately 93 percent of this traffic uses the CTC network).

Giving subscribers the ability to select a particular carrier by simply dialing two digits for each call made it easier for competition to thrive in this

---

[29] However, domestic long-distance services later became more concentrated, largely because only three companies (CTC-Mundo, Entel, and Telex Chile) had fiber optic networks that covered the entire country; thus, other carriers has to lease use of networks from these companies.

[30] This dramatic price decrease can be attributed, in part, to technological changes and elimination of cross subsidies.

TABLE 2-2. PROFITS OF TELECOMMUNICATIONS FIRMS
(Return on equity)

Year	CTC	Entel	Telex	Bell South Chile
1992	19.4	49.7	28.3	
1993	23.0	37.4	58.9	
1994	18.7	17.2	16.5	0.0
1995	17.3	8.4	10.2	-70.4
1996	20.9	2.4	5.6	-250.3
1997	18.7	5.1	-29.9	-1.0
1998	10.8	-3.8	-41.5	62.6

Source: Company annual reports.

sector. In countries with less competition than Chile, multicarrier systems require that users call through the company with which they have a service contract. This explains why the Antitrust Prevention Commission prohibited cutting off multidialing service to subscribers under a service contract. In 1996, CTC-Mundo offered appealing discounts to any users who requested that CTC, the parent company, disconnect the multicarrier dialing, leaving active service contract dialing through that company. The Prevention Commission admonished CTC-Mundo to discontinue the offer.[31]

With the exception of CTC-Mundo, the financial health of long-distance companies has been poor (table 2-2). After losing money over a three-year period, Iusatel changed ownership. VTR sold its long-distance subsidiary to CTC in 1998, after suffering annual losses since its inception in 1994.[32] Telex Chile experienced several periods of financial hardship, which caused the price of its American Depository Receipts to drop from a high of $11.75 in January 1995 to $2.90 in March 2000, compelling its former owners to transfer control of the company.

The troubles experienced by many long-distance telephone companies during 1994–98 stemmed from the high local network access fees they were charged during that period. Although introduction of the multicarrier system eliminated the need to set long-distance rates, regulating the charge for access-

---

[31] Permitting users to eliminate the multidialing capability would generate the well-known prisoner's dilemma. If no one accepted eliminating the capability, everyone would be better off; however, not accepting it is risky because one does not obtain the initial benefits and then suffers the effects of a less competitive industry.

[32] The Antitrust Resolution Commission, through Resolution No. 525 (August 1998), approved VTR's request to authorize selling its long-distance subsidiary to CTC.

ing the local network became critical. During the rate-setting process in 1994, it was established that the access charge for incoming and outgoing domestic long-distance calls and outgoing international calls would equal 0.63 times the charge of a local call, which was higher than the cost of providing the service. However, one charge that was totally unjustifiable was the access charge for incoming international calls, which was computed at 14 times the local rate during peak hours and 84 times the local rate during off-peak hours.

In April 1998, within the context of the rate-setting process conducted every five years, the Antitrust Resolution Commission further clarified, through Resolution No. 515, the concept of a local segment or leg, which fixed telephone subscribers must pay when making calls to receivers on other companies' local networks in the same primary zone, a long-distance company, or a mobile phone company. In addition, the Resolution made domestic long-distance telephone transmission or exchange services provided by Entel, CTC-Mundo, and Telex Chile subject to regulation. It also recommended to government regulators that the maximum unbundling technically feasible for local services be subject to price setting. Partly in response to this Resolution, during the rate-setting process of 1999, Subtel reduced local access charges by 62.7 percent for outgoing international and domestic calls. The charge for incoming international calls was reduced 97.5 percent during peak hours and 99.6 percent during off-peak hours.

Conflicts also emerged as a result of integrating the dominant company into fixed mobile phone service. These conflicts were compounded by poorly regulated service, whereby subscribers to mobile services were charged for use of the mobile network on both incoming and outgoing calls. The telecom law was amended in 1998 to establish the calling-party-pays rule (entered into force in February 1999). Under this rule, only the person placing a call to or from a mobile phone, not the receiver of the call, is charged. Users of basic service who call a mobile telephone pay a regulated access charge to the mobile phone company.

As of October 1995, CTC offered an option to its subscribers of fixed telephone services who entered into contract for cellular services through CTC Cellular (CTC's affiliate in mobile telephony): call forwarding to the cellular phone, with no charge for any calls made to the fixed number when a caller receives no answer at the other number. Although CTC did not charge its customers to transfer from the fixed to the mobile phone, it did pay its subsidiary for this traffic. Another mobile phone company, however, eventually reported this promotional ploy to the Antitrust Resolution Commission. The Commission determined that CTC had indeed discriminated by not extending the same terms and conditions to other mobile phone companies that had requested to participate in this arrangement. Moreover, the Commission considered that the parent company had subsidized the subsidiary company;[33] for these reasons, it ordered CTC to pay a fine of 5,000 UTM (Resolution No. 483, April 1997).

In the same ruling, the Commission called on the government to introduce an amendment to the telecommunications law to prevent such incidents in the future. The Commission sought to require any firm that wished to operate in the mobile phone market, while simultaneously offering other telecommunication services, to do so through publicly traded stock corporations subject to oversight and enforcement by the Superintendent of Stocks, Securities, and Insurance. This principle was applied across the board to all telecommunications services through Resolution No. 515, issued in 1998.

In February 1998, CTC Cellular began offering plans, whereby subscribers of mobile phone services would pay only for outgoing calls at the existing rate. Therefore, no one paid for use of the mobile network on calls from fixed telephones to mobile units. In August 1999, at the request of the National Economic Prosecutor, the Resolution Commission declared that this plan could distort free competition in these services; therefore, it ordered CTC Cellular to pay a fine of 10,000 UTM. The Commission characterized the offer as predatory conduct because, after computing the estimated loss of income the company would have had to endure, it was concluded that, in the long term, the losses would make such a scheme unworkable. The situation was even more dramatic for other mobile phone companies, whose losses in mobile business could not be offset by the extraordinary profits that increased fixed-to-mobile phone traffic would generate for CTC Cellular's parent company.

Market Power and Vertical Integration in the Electricity Sector

Overview of the Problem

Chile has two electricity systems, the more important of which is the Interconnected Central System (*Sistema Interconectado Central*), known as the

---

[33] CTC alleged that the charge for said traffic had been made in error. That claim, however, was not accepted by the Commission. The Commission further ruled that the introduction cost of the promotional arrangement as well, which had been absorbed by the parent company, constituted a subsidy, since this action directly benefited the subsidiary.

SIC. In 1997, the SIC system was responsible for 78 percent of all electricity generated and consumed in the country. That year, SIC market power was heavily concentrated in a single company, Endesa, which was vertically integrated. Endesa and its subsidiaries owned 54.8 percent of installed power generation in the system, while the second largest, Gener, and its affiliate companies held 28.1 percent, and the third largest, Colbún, had only 10 percent. Endesa also held water rights to build hydroelectric plants, which were appealing in a system where hydroelectric power was the least expensive source of electricity.[34] Endesa owned the main transmission system, which was managed by Transelec, a subsidiary.[35] Enersis, the electricity holding company that owned Chilectra and Río Maipo distributors, which together supplied 44.4 percent of all customers in the SIC in 1997, had a controlling interest in Endesa.[36]

Legislation in the electricity sector, dating back to 1982, distinguishes between large and small customers. Large customers freely negotiate the terms of supply with generating companies, while small customers acquire electricity from distribution companies at a regulated price. The price for small customers consists of two components: the nodal price (the price at which distributors purchase electricity from the generators) and the value-added distribution price (compensation for distribution services).[37] The nodal price must fall within 10 percent of the average contract price that large-volume consumers freely negotiate with companies. Generators have free access to transmission and distribution lines, but must pay a fee for their use. The fee is negotiated between the owner of the lines and individual gen-

---

[34] The cost of hydroelectric generation was $US1.87 per kilowatt hour (kWh), while the cost of producing electricity at coal-burning plants was $3.60 per kWh. Endesa holds 60 percent of all nonconsumptive water rights that have been assigned to date and has only developed 13 percent of this potential. In 1996, it applied for an additional 20 percent of these rights. This prompted the Presiding Commissioner of the National Energy Commission to request the opinion from the Preventive Commission whether the additional concession that Endesa was applying for would adversely affect free competition in the electricity market. In November 1996, the Antitrust Prevention Commission recommended that new water rights not be assigned unless applications involved specific projects (Opinion No. 992).

[35] This company owned 100 percent of the 500 kilovolt (kV) lines.

[36] In the late 1980s, Enersis began to acquire shares of Endesa, and, by April 1990, it owned 12.3 percent. However, because other shareholders represented different companies and because of the support of pension funds, Enersis chose four members of Endesa's nine-member board of directors. As of 1992, the general manager of Enersis was chairman of Endesa's board. In November 1995, Enersis bought a stock package that enabled it to reach 25.3 percent of total capital shares in Endesa, thereby becoming a legal controller of Endesa.

[37] Distributors also purchase capacity from generators at a regulated price.

erators; when they cannot reach an agreement, they must resort to commission arbitration.

Horizontal concentration in distribution, as well as vertical integration, has caused litigation between companies in this industry. Historically, the nodal price at which distributors purchased power to supply regulated customers has been, on average, above the spot price.[38] This differential is significant because generators without contracts must sell to other generators at the spot price. Moreover, the spot price, which equals the variable cost of the last dispatched unit, fluctuates significantly over the course of a day and seasonally. Also, because of the way it is computed, the nodal price is set for six-month periods and varies minimally from one period to another.[39] Distributors purchase power in blocks in order to adapt to hourly and seasonal fluctuations in demand; therefore, a distributor can discriminate against a generator by only purchasing blocks when the spot price is high. In March 1992, Colbún reported Chilectra and Endesa to the Antitrust Resolution Commission for abuse of monopolistic position and abusive discrimination by Chilectra in negotiating supply contracts with generators.

Inadequate regulation of the transmission network also hampers competition in generation. Currently, the cost of developing transmission networks involves heavy economies of scale, making such a business a natural monopoly. For this reason, the transmission rate has two components: marginal cost of transmission and a fixed charge. The marginal cost of transmission between two nodes is the difference between energy and power prices in both nodes. The owner of the transmission line receives the marginal cost, but this income is insufficient to amortize the network. The fixed charge, a basic toll, is added to the marginal cost to finance the system. Regulations provide certain guidelines for negotiating this toll. Nevertheless, Rudnick, Soto, and Palma (1999) show that the guidelines are general, allowing for a wide range of criteria. In simulations conducted for the SIC, the fraction of the fixed cost of the transmission system assigned to a specific plant fluctuated between 0.7 percent and 13 percent of the total, depending on which criteria were used.

Vertical integration between generation and transmission has led to sector problems. Direct negotiations between Transelec and generators other than Endesa have never succeeded and have given rise to lengthy and costly arbitration. Paredes (1995) points out that, even four years after the legal

---

[38] Between May 1986 and September 1996, the nodal price was an average of 11.5 percent higher than the spot price.

[39] Entering into a contract to sell at the nodal price helps reduce price uncertainty.

change specifying how to calculate transmission tolls went into effect, only temporary contracts for use of lines were being entered into. Paredes adds that analysis of the terms and conditions of contracts between Colbún and Transelec revealed that, in every case, reaching agreement on a temporary contract took the maximum length of time permitted by law (280 days) and, on the average, the final cost of transmission had been 50 percent lower than the amount that Transelec originally sought.

In addition, results of arbitration in transmission are unpredictable because no solid legal theory exists to back up decisions. Endesa remains unaffected by the costs and uncertainty associated with the arbitration process. Moreover, if a generator wishes to supply a new client, Transelec can delay calculation of the corresponding toll, thus making it easier for Endesa to negotiate with the client. Colbún has complained that, on several occasions, after requesting a quote from Transelec, Endesa contacted the client to make an offer, essentially stealing the client from Colbún and, at other times, forced the company to lower its prices.

Owners of the transmission system are under no obligation to expand; therefore, existing capacity constrains open access to the system. If a generator wishes to have additional capacity at its disposal on a congested line, it must make a request to the owner of the transmission system, who, in turn, determines the amount the generator must invest. Because no arbitration procedure is used to determine the amount of this payment, the monopoly is free to dominate the market. Furthermore, the law does not indicate how future income resulting from the new investment should be prorated between the parties involved.

Colbún built a new plant and requested that Transelec expand existing transmission capacity. The transmission toll originally sought by Transelec was so high that, despite the heavy economy of scale involved in transmission, Colbún decided to build a line. In light of this decision, Transelec reduced the toll it sought considerably; nevertheless, Colbún, retained its original decision to lay its own transmission line next to the one managed by Transelec.

Supplying unregulated customers located in the concession area of distributors also posed problems.[40] The toll for using distribution lines, like

---

[40] Lack of competition in supplying nonregulated customers is also important to regulated customers, since the nodal price must remain within a range that hovers about the average of nonregulated prices. Until 1997, however, binding limits were imposed on only two occasions. In 1991, the regulated price was raised 4.6 percent and, in April 1993, it was lowered 2.1 percent.

transmission lines, must be negotiated between the parties, and, when disagreements arise, parties must resort to arbitration. It is difficult for a generator to participate in the bidding to supply a potential unregulated customer while unclear about the price that should be paid for transporting power. Furthermore, because distributors are generators' main customers, it would be foolish to take customers away from them. In fact, this issue was the main focus of a September 1996 complaint filed with the Antitrust Resolution Commission. Colbún filed the complaint against Chilectra, after having been awarded a contract to supply electricity to the greater metropolitan area of Santiago, which until then had been supplied by Chilectra.

Request for Commission Intervention

The question of whether integrated companies have abused their dominant position, as their competitors have repeatedly claimed, is a matter of debate. Nonetheless, consolidation of market power and vertical integration, within the context of an inadequate regulatory framework, considerably increased the risk to potential market entrants.[41] In January 1994, this situation led the National Economic Prosecutor to file a request with the Resolution Commission (against Transelec, Chilectra, Endesa, and subsequently Enersis) to proceed to disintegrate the generation, transmission, and distribution business at SIC by creating separate companies with independent assets and management.[42, 43]

In his submission, the Prosecutor maintained that, in any business activity with market imperfections, vertical integration must be prevented in order to maintain competitive conditions in other market segments. In the Prosecutor's opinion, when only a few companies control distribution, these distributors are positioned to give preferential treatment to their associated generation companies. Thus, the Prosecutor considered it appropriate to break up the generation and distribution business. He also asserted that competition in electricity generation would be possible only to the extent

---

[41] Government authorities stated that companies originally interested in bidding in the privatization of Colbún in 1994 backed down because of the heavy vertical integration in SIC.

[42] This was the second vertical integration case in the electricity sector that the Antitrust Resolution Commission examined. When Enersis chose four of Endesa's nine-member board of directors in 1990, a lawyer filed a complaint with the Office of the National Economic Prosecutor. In 1991, the Prosecutor requested that the Resolution Commission prevent Enersis from increasing its capital shares in Endesa beyond what it held in April 1990, alleging that vertical integration of generation and distribution activities would have a detrimental effect on market transparency and free competition.

that the natural monopoly of the transmission system did not bar entry or operation in the generation business. Therefore, it would be necessary for generation companies to have equal access to transmission networks, requiring that transmission companies be independent of generation companies, as well as transparent, nondiscriminatory, and efficient in charging for system use.

The Prosecutor's submission was backed by a report that the Ministries of Energy and Economy filed in 1996. Both ministries stated that the regulatory framework did not prescribe a clear way to compute transmission tolls and that, in potential arbitration proceedings, the generator would not have the same information at its disposal that the transmitter would to support its positions. They also pointed out that the owner of the transmission lines could delay toll negotiations, thereby enabling an associated generator to make an offer to the customer. The ministries' report further stated that lack of objective criteria to determine whether capacity is sufficient to justify granting a request for a toll, creates a potential bias of the owner toward certain generators. Moreover, the ministries asserted that the distribution monopoly created competition problems in supplying nonregulated customers within the concession zone, since the distribution company could give preferential treatment in awarding contracts to any generators that waived their right to compete for these customers.

In its view, this increase in capital shares could lead to discrimination and other abuses at the cost of users and third-party competitors. The Resolution Commission denied the Prosecutor's request in 1992 (Resolution No. 372), stating that the law established adequate safeguards for protection of users and that no proof had been introduced showing that the parties against whom the complaint was filed had abused dominant position.

The Prosecutor then filed an appeal ("petition in error") with the Supreme Court against the Resolution Commission. In September 1992, the Court denied the appeal, claiming that the alleged evidence was insufficient to prove that Enersis had a controlling interest in Endesa, either solely or through an agreement with other parties. The Court did state, however, that the fact that an Endesa representative would have been elected chairman of Endesa's board in 1992, coupled with the potential increase in stock share ownership of Enersis, established a precedent that could negatively affect transparency in the electricity market, leading to decisions that could restrict free competition in the sector. Therefore, the Court instructed the antitrust bodies to monitor the conduct of the companies involved and to adopt, at the appropriate time, any measures they believed necessary to ensure and restore market transparency.

[43] When Enersis purchased a stock package, thus gaining control of Endesa, the National Economic Prosecutor requested the Antitrust Resolution Commission to stay this transaction until a final ruling was handed down on the Prosecutor's request for disintegration, which the Commission eventually denied. Enersis justified the purchase, stating that, in the United States, companies whose main income source is investment in other companies in which they own less than 25 percent of all shares, do not get more favorable tax treatment, which raises the cost of capital.

For these reasons, the ministries proposed the following measures: make it mandatory for distributors to contract out their supply in a competitive manner; gradually reduce the size limits of customers who can freely negotiate their electricity supply; establish a clear, precise method for calculating tolls paid to owners of transmission and distribution lines; require transmission companies, within a reasonable time period, to reincorporate as publicly traded stock corporations, have a single line of business, have sole ownership of transmission assets, and be open to third-party, stock-share ownership; and restrict vertical integration between generation and distribution companies by limiting the percentage of voting rights that an individual or a group of individuals who have agreed to act jointly may hold in a single generating company, when the individual or group has a controlling interest or holds sway or tie-breaking power in a distribution company of the same interconnected system.

Positions of the Companies Involved

Enersis argued that the Commission lacked the legal authority to order the breakup and vertical disintegration. In its view, in order for the Commission to apply a sanction, an offense must have been committed and the sanction must have been expressly stated in the law as a potential penalty for violating free competition established in Executive Order No. 211. Since neither vertical integration nor horizontal concentration are listed in any of this law's provisions, Enersis argued that forced disintegration would infringe on a constitutionally guaranteed economic freedom, inasmuch as it would make conducting a business activity contingent on changing company structure. This would violate the essential powers that right to ownership involves, such as the power to use, enjoy, and freely dispose of assets. Moreover, the company cited precedents of the Resolution Commission, which stated that the law does not sanction mere expectation of monopoly, but rather concrete acts and conduct that constitute violation of free competition.

Companies targeted by the Prosecutor's complaint also gave reasons why sectoral disintegration was both unnecessary and unwise. First, they argued that, because most industry activity and pricing are regulated, sufficient safeguards are in place to prevent abuse of dominant position, even in monopoly segments. Second, any conduct that would violate free competition could be investigated and sanctioned by the oversight bodies. Third, arrival of natural gas from Argentina in August 1997 would make it possible to build power plants near centers of consumption, thereby detracting from the importance of a transportation monopoly and facilitating entry of new players into the generation business.[44] Fourth, breaking up the monopoly by creating a subsidiary (as had been done with Endesa and Transelec) would suffice in protecting sector competition, as the antitrust commissions had earlier established.[45] Fifth, because of the economies of scope involved, vertical disintegration would increase costs by about 17 percent.[46]

Chilectra maintained that power generation companies were not discriminated against and that such incentive was nonexistent. It further argued that the power distribution companies are legally obligated to provide service within their concession area. These companies cannot afford to risk having a single supplier; therefore, they must maintain contracts with all available generators. Chilectra also expressed disagreement with mandatory bidding of electricity power among generators. In its view, this mechanism would make it harder to spread out supply risks; that is, diversify supply to reduce risk. Chilectra also stated that it did not believe bidding would make it possible for distributors to purchase power at a lower price and pass on the benefits to consumers because no generator had ever offered to sell Chilectra power for regulated customers at a price lower than nodal price.

The distributor also opposed measures proposed by the ministries to regulate fees for using distribution networks and lower the threshold for nonregulated customers. It maintained that open access to lines, as well as arbitration guidelines for setting fee rates when disagreements arise between parties, would ensure fair access to the distribution network. It also asserted that its high degree of participation in supplying unregulated customers located in its own concession area resulted from its additional services, which gave it a competitive edge. These services included 24-hour-a-day operators, continuous handling of emergencies, an operations center that enabled the company to monitor conditions of the entire network, and good communi-

---

[44] The gas pipeline would reduce the advantage of hydroelectric plants since the cost of generation in a combined-cycle, gas turbine was $2.05 per kWh. Furthermore, the risk associated with hydroelectric power generation, coupled with more stringent environmental rules for constructing dams, is leading to a more balanced stock of Chilean generators. Initiation of operations of a Colbún-owned transmission line in 1997 also helped break up the transmission monopoly.

[45] In September 1993, the Antitrust Prevention Commission ruled, through Opinion No. 874, that a transmission subsidiary created by a generation company that owned the transmission lines ensured effective separation of electricity generation and transmission business activities in the Interconnected System of the Greater North.

[46] The companies supported this claim with a report prepared by university economists; however, the data used to run the regressions were not made available to the public. In addition, the companies failed to explain why costs did not fall when they vertically integrated.

cation lines with customers. Furthermore, the distributor claimed it would be unnecessary to lower the threshold for a customer to qualify as nonregulated because the nodal price is related to the average of freely negotiated prices; consequently, regulated customers also benefit from decreases in nonregulated rates. In any case, the distributor believed this measure would require a change in the law.

Decision of the Antitrust Resolution Commission

In July 1997, the Antitrust Resolution Commission issued Resolution No. 488, which stated that the Prosecutor had failed to offer any proof that the companies charged had abused their market power, inasmuch as the arguments merely hypothesized the potential risk of anticompetitive behavior. Despite the above ruling and availing itself of the powers invested in it by law, the Commission decided to conduct a detailed examination of the arguments set forth by the parties. It held that a basic role conferred on the antitrust commissions by law is to prevent companies from taking strategic actions that could create, increase, or maintain market power that significantly alters the efficiency of market structure.

Based on its examination of the facts, the Resolution Commission did not grant the Prosecutor's request because, in its view, compulsory breaking up of monopolies in the electricity sector was not the appropriate way to solve the sector's problems. The Commission argued that the current ownership structure was not a significant factor in adversely affecting current or potential competition. Notwithstanding, the Commission used its legal authority (conferred on it by Executive Order No. 211, Article 17, Section b) to outline several requirements. First, the regulatory agency was called on to introduce amendments to the law, as soon as possible, to clarify existing ambiguities regarding usage, rates, and fees of transmission and distribution networks. Second, within a reasonable period of time, Transelec would assume ownership of transmission assets and become a publicly traded stock corporation with a single line of business open to third-party shareholders. Third, distributors were required to put up supply of electric energy for bidding.

Consequences of the Ruling

In December 1998, the government enacted an electricity regulation that included the requirements of the Resolution Commission. Although progress was made in tightening room for negotiating the calculation of transmission fees, this was done by granting the regulator discretionary powers to decide on aspects that bear directly on this calculation. The question of what effect the new regulations will have on the industry remains unanswered. To date, the most significant event related to regulatory changes has been Endesa's transfer of ownership of Transelec to end vertical integration between transmission and generation. However, the Resolution did not differentiate between marketing electricity and providing distribution lines for medium and small-volume customers. Rather, it left vertical integration in the area of greatest regulatory problems virtually untouched.[47]

Gas Pipelines

Overview of the Problem

In December 1994, two consortia applied to the Office of the Superintendent of Electricity and Fuels for concessions to build gas pipelines to transport natural gas from Argentina to Chile's central region for distribution. In January 1995, the Superintendent requested a ruling from the Antitrust Prevention Commission regarding conditions under which such concessions should be granted. In his submission, the Superintendent made it clear that, for economic reasons, it would only be possible for one of the two consortium projects to be implemented in the short term. Therefore, gas transport service would be considered an essential facility for all of Chile's natural gas consumers.

Perhaps the regulatory agency's main concern was the close link between the gas transport and electricity sectors; in each consortia, a significant participant was one of the two main electricity generators. Demand for gas-powered electricity generation justified construction of the gas pipeline and, with the arrival of natural gas, most new generation plants would use this fuel. Consequently, if a generator were permitted to control the gas pipeline, the electricity sector would experience considerable consolidation of market power. On the other hand, if all potential users had equal access to gas transport, competition in electricity power generation would increase, while the importance of holding water rights for construction of hydroelectric plants would decrease.

---

[47] It should be noted that this issue was not addressed in the Prosecutor's request to the Commission.

Opinion of the Antitrust Prevention Commission

In April 1995, the Commission filed a report requested by the Superintendent (through Opinion No. 933), listing the requirements concessions must fulfill to prevent abuse of dominant position in the sector. The Commission's main recommendations were to:

- Grant nonexclusive concessions and establish mandatory interconnection of networks when the regulatory agency so requests.
- Grant transport and distribution concessions to companies whose sole line of business is one of these activities and who must also be subject to oversight of the Office of the Superintendent of Securities and Exchanges.
- Restrict participation of large-scale gas purchasers, including gas distributors, to a maximum of 15 percent of capital in the gas transport company. This same restriction applies to the holdings of gas transport companies in distribution companies.
- Institute an open-access policy in gas transport; that is, establish an obligation to provide nondiscriminatory service to anyone who requests it.
- Make it mandatory for gas transport companies to publicly disclose pricing structure and information on available transport capacity.
- Grant distribution concessions by geographic zone, limiting each distributor's ownership in other distribution companies to a maximum of 15 percent.

Regulation of gas transport rates was not considered necessary because it was believed that the ex ante competition between the two consortia that would emerge to attract customers would ensure that prices would be determined by market conditions. The reasoning was that, because of the heavy economies of scale involved in gas transport, construction of only one gas pipeline would be justified. And, because of the project's high cost, the financial system would require the consortia to have signed contracts with high-volume consumers prior to approval of financing. Since users would award their contract for gas transport to whichever supplier offered the best conditions, the gas pipeline project that offered the lowest rates would be the one built. With regard to distribution, competition would be between distributors of liquefied gas. Despite this reasoning and the fact that future conditions are subject to unpredictable changes, the Commission recommended vesting the government regulatory agency with the legal authority to set rates when and if the Antitrust Resolution Commission directed it to do so.

Appeals Against the Opinion

One of the two consortia that had applied for a concession appealed to the Antitrust Resolution Commission, requesting that it overturn the Opinion of the Antitrust Prevention Commission. The consortium argued that allowing the opinion to stand would violate the Constitution (Articles 6, 7, and 19) and Executive Order No. 211 (Article 8) because the Antitrust Prevention Commission lacked legal authority to regulate markets and establish requirements in conducting activities that do not violate public morals, public safety, or national security, since this is the exclusive province of legislators. For its part, the Ministry of Energy issued a technical analysis of the Commission's Opinion, stating that it had drafted a bill for introduction in Congress that contained most of the requirements of the Opinion. But the Ministry considered the horizontal restrictions inappropriate because they would force the drawing of arbitrary geographic zones. Furthermore, the Ministry stated that the 15-percent limit on vertical integration between owners of the gas pipeline and large-scale consumers seemed restrictive because it could jeopardize project financing.

The Antitrust Resolution Commission rejected the appeal, stating that the Opinion of the Prevention Commission expressly recognized that some of its recommendations were subject to legislative change; therefore, the requirements listed in the Opinion constituted recommendations to the houses of the legislature. In fact, Opinion No. 933 of the Prevention Commission stated that any requirements designed to ensure proper observance of the principles of free competition must be considered within the context of the legal system under the appropriate hierarchy and applicable laws.

Consequences of the Opinion

Prior to the Resolution Commission's issuance of its July decision, the government had laid out rules regarding concessions for gas transport and distribution, stipulating that these concessions are not exclusive in nature. Gas transport must operate under an arrangement of open access, and gas transport and distribution services must be provided on a nondiscriminatory basis.

Meanwhile, the two consortia tendered their bids, which included a tentative initial price that allowed potential customers to provide the consortia their specific transport requirements. After being fully apprised of customers' specific requirements, the consortia would offer a final price and provide a brief period of time during which prospective customers could accept the conditions and establish guarantees. GasAndes, a consortium that included Gener, won the bid to build the pipeline because this group's project was less expensive and could therefore offer the lowest rates. It was extremely important that Endesa, the main generator in SIC, participate in this bidding process. The other consortium that bid for the concession to build the gas pipeline included Enersis (the company with controlling interest in Endesa). Independent members of the board of directors exerted great influence in ensuring Endesa's participation in the GasAndes bid. Because of the magnitude of the investment, the GasAndes bid would have failed without Endesa's participation.

Concessions for Port Management and Operation

Overview of the Problem

In the mid 1990s, it became evident that rapid growth in foreign trade would, in the short term, render cargo transfer capacity in state-owned ports inadequate. This was particularly true of ports located in the country's central zone, which has few natural and protected bays and inlets, making development of new ports difficult. Moreover, constructing new docking sites in existing ports would be too expensive, given the region's steep coastline. In addition to these stumbling blocks, the ports have a dearth of stacking and storage facilities because urban growth and sprawl have severely limited their ability to expand.

These ports serve as an essential facility for maritime cargo transport. Port activity is essential to the well-being of Chile's economy because of the critical role foreign trade plays in the country and the overwhelming preference for shipping by sea as the primary means of transporting goods. For these reasons, port services are vulnerable to being misused to obtain a competitive edge in other lines of business. Furthermore, the relatively low cost of port services in the overall cargo transport chain makes such abuses appealing. Mandy (2000) shows that there is greater incentive to discriminate when potential benefits in the competitive segment are higher than potential profits from the essential facility. During 1997, the free on board cost of foreign trade in Chile's three major state-owned ports (Valparaíso, San Antonio, and

San Vicente) was US$14.329 billion, while related freight costs totaled $1.324 billion, and billing of port services totaled only $55 million.

The government estimated that it was possible to increase transfer capacity of the state-owned ports by increasing private participation in port administration and operation. Based on its assessment, a bill was introduced in Congress to modernize the state-owned port sector, which was enacted in December 1997 after undergoing the normal legislative process. The law led to creating 10 port authorities or enterprises, one for each state-owned port, which were empowered to award private companies concessions for administering and operating port infrastructure. Port authorities could put a comprehensive concession up for bid, in which case the concessionaire would take charge of all longshoreman duties, including loading and unloading cargo onto and off ships docked in the port and hauling services, as well as managing port infrastructure; alternatively, port authorities could put a concession up for public bidding, involving only port administration, while maintaining the infrastructure system of unrestricted, nondiscriminatory access for loading, unloading, and hauling.

Granting concessions for state-owned port administration and operations posed certain risks to sectoral competition. Only three ports are operative in Chile's central zone (Region V), where the highest volume of cargo passes into and out of the country. Two of these ports (Valparaíso and San Antonio) are state owned and one (Ventanas) is privately owned. Together, these three ports are equipped with seven terminals,[48] although not all are capable of handling the same maximum vessel capacity.[49] It should be noted that some terminals are built especially for transfer of containers, others for solid bulk cargo, and others for standard cargo (table 2-3).

In other countries, large-scale port users, mainly shipping companies, own their cargo terminals because this arrangement provides operational advantages. In Chile, however, where few piers or docking areas are available, only a few users can own their own terminals, placing other users at a great disadvantage. Although regulations make it mandatory for prices to be made public and set on a nondiscriminatory basis, concessionaires can use subtle methods of discrimination that are difficult to prove and, therefore, to penalize. Such methods include assigning choice spaces in the holding areas to one

---

[48] A terminal is an autonomous operational unit consisting of side-by-side berthing spaces and their associated support service areas, thereby making it possible to bid out each one separately.

[49] Maximum vessel capacity refers to the ship of greatest length and maximum draught and displacement when fully loaded that can operate in a berthing pier.

TABLE 2-3. CARGO TRANSFER IN CHILEAN PORTS OF REGION V, 1997

Port	Terminal	No. of piers	Cargo type (TM)			Total cargo (TM)
			Container	Solid bulk	Standard	
	For bid					
Valparaíso	1	5	2,219		1,201	3,420
San Antonio	1	3	2,746	556	557	3,859
San Antonio	2	1		796	13	809
			4,965	1,352	1,771	8,088
	Not for bid					
Valparaíso	2 and 3	5	469	--	779	1,248
San Antonio	3	5	996	524	425	1,945
Ventanas	1		--	2,280	20	2,300
Subtotal			1,465	2,804	1,224	5,493
Total			6,430	4,156	2,995	13,581
Percentage of capacity set for bid			77	33	59	60

Source: Emporchi.

company rather than another, providing higher-quality service to one company compared with others, using insider information, and manipulating reserves of available spaces.

In drafting the port modernization law (Law 19.542), legislators considered the above-mentioned problems and wrote specific clauses to safeguard sector competition. First, the law requires that concessions be awarded through public bidding and be valid for up to 30 years. Second, concessionaires must incorporate as publicly-owned stock companies engaged in a single line of business. Third, the rates concessionaires set must be made public and established on a nondiscriminatory basis. Fourth, proposed by-laws and internal regulations for terminals are required as an integral part of the bidding rules. They must conform to objective technical and nondiscriminatory standards, especially with regard to assignment of spaces and reserve capacity.

Additionally, the law establishes three instances in which port authorities must obtain a preliminary report from the Antitrust Prevention Commission to be able to award the concession for a docking area. These instances are as follows:

• When no other terminal exists in the region capable of accommodating the maximum vessel capacity in the terminal that is the subject of the concession.

- When concessionaires of terminals in the same port are associated with each other.
- When an integrated operating system (both management and operations) is opted for in the terminal that is the subject of the concession and no other terminal in the region that is operated under the open-access system is capable of accommodating maximum vessel capacity in the terminal being bid out.

Antitrust Commission's Opinion

The two port authorities of Region V decided to simultaneously put up for public bidding three of the six docking areas they owned between them, which together represent 60 percent of available capacity (table 2-3). These docking areas were capable of accommodating maximum vessel capacity in each port, as well as the bulk terminal of San Antonio. These port authorities also opted to use the integrated operation scheme because several studies they had commissioned showed that this was the most efficient system since it helped solve problems of coordination in port activities and facilitated investment in cargo transfer equipment. These decisions obligated port authorities to request an opinion from the Antitrust Prevention Commission regarding general requirements for bidding rules.

Position of the Parties Involved

In addition to filing the request for an opinion, the port authorities attached proposed general requirements for the rules of bidding that these authorities considered necessary to prevent risks of abuse of dominance, as provided for by the law. Their proposed requirements included ceilings on horizontal integration; restrictions on vertical integration; additional rules of transparency; and reserving the right to set maximum prices and, indirectly, quality standards.

The port authorities proposed that the bidding rules establish that shareholders in the concessionaire who, either individually or jointly, own more than 25 percent of the capital, voting capital (capital with the right to vote), or profits, may not own, either directly or indirectly, more than 16.7 percent of the capital, capital with voting rights, or rights to profits of another concessionaire or owner or operator of a private port in the same region. An analogous restriction was included for shareholders of companies that own or operate private ports in the region.[50] In addition, port authorities proposed that higher-volume users as a whole should not possess more than 40 percent of the capital, more than 40 percent of capital with voting rights, or rights to more than 40 percent of the profits of the concessionaire of a terminal.[51] According to the port authorities, it was necessary to limit overall ownership of significant users to 40 percent, given the incidents of collusive behavior that have occurred in the past between the country's major shipping companies.

The port companies also suggested that concessionaires ought to grant any interested party open and expeditious access to any information listed on forms that would be compiled by the bidding port authority, such as cargo contracts, service priorities, type of cargo, and consignees, so that all interested parties would have the same information. It was also proposed that concession contracts empower port authorities to request necessary information from the concessionaire in order to enforce the law. Moreover, port authorities proposed that they be empowered to set maximum bidding rates in order to prevent low bidder turnout. The proposal also included fines for concessionaires, in the event that a docking area's occupancy threshold would be exceeded, as defined in the rules. These rules aimed to control quality of service during congested periods when ships must wait their turn to be serviced. In the view of port authorities, a certain amount of idle capacity would be optimal in terms of overall cargo movement.

The Commission passed on the port authorities' submission to the agents involved in maritime transport. The Maritime and Port Chamber of Chile, the national association of shipping companies, was opposed to the general requirements of the bidding rules proposed by port authorities. The Chamber argued that these rules were unnecessary because it would be impossible for any concessionaire of port infrastructure to discriminate against users. Furthermore, the Chamber claimed that the port authorities' proposals contained several provisions that constituted a form of market regulation not addressed in Law 19.542 or Executive Order No. 211; therefore, these provisions were illegal and unconstitutional, since this subject

---

[50] The ban on vertical and horizontal integration is not absolute insofar as port authorities believed that, as long as opposing interests existed among shareholders of the concessionaire, this would suffice to allow the concession to be managed as an independent business.

[51] The term higher-volume user refers to shipping companies, importers, exporters, and freight companies that hold more than 15 percent of the tonnage of maritime cargo mobilized in the respective region or more than 25 percent in the port that is the subject of bidding.

may only be regulated by law. The Chamber's specific argument was that neither the Prevention Commission nor the port authorities had discretionary power to limit, restrict, or regulate property of the concessionaires, much less property of owners or operators of private ports.[52]

The Chamber argued that restrictions on vertical and horizontal integration violate the right to exercise a lawful business activity and right to ownership, which the Constitution guarantees all. Freedom to dispose of one's own property, including its pricing, and freedom to determine how to market or commercialize one's property are essential components of right of ownership. The Chamber further argued that imposing a maximum rate in the bidding rules infringes on right of ownership, which may only be curtailed or enhanced by law. In addition, the proposal's focus on ensuring access to information that may appear on forms drawn up by the port authority adversely affects the constitutionally guaranteed right to privacy and secrecy for all. In the Chamber's view, port authorities may not request information, other than data contained in the port sector statistical reporting system, as established in the law of sector modernization.

In its response to the Chamber's submission, port authorities argued that, if the Constitution supported the Chamber's claim, it would lead to the absurdity of regarding the entire antitrust law (Executive Order No. 211) as unconstitutional. Moreover, port authorities opined that it is ludicrous for the Chamber to insist that details of the bidding rules be determined by the law, inasmuch as it would be unwise to expect that such tasks would be in legislators' domain. The law establishes criteria for public bidding and grants other bodies the legal authority to issue general supplementary requirements. Specifically, it empowers the Antitrust Prevention Commission to establish the terms under which bidding must be conducted. In addition, it is self-evident that port authorities, in their capacity as owners of public ports, are qualified to specifically define the rules of public bidding that they are authorized by law to call for by setting the ex ante rules for participants in the bidding process.

Rulings of the Antitrust Commissions

The Antitrust Prevention Commission sided with port authorities, adopting their proposals with a few changes, and rejected the Chamber's argument of

---

[52] In the Chamber's view, that this matter involves a concession is immaterial because, according to modern-day administrative law philosophy, the right of a concessionaire over its concession is a right over real property or right in rem (jus in re).

illegality and unconstitutionality. In its opinion, the Commission stated that Law 19.542 grants a far-reaching mandate for the Commission to determine which conditions must be fulfilled to ensure competition in situations established by the law, and this mandate is not subject to any constraints. The Commission also stated that, in its view, Executive Order No. 211 grants extensive powers of general application, not only to fulfill its mission of preventing anticompetitive acts or conduct, but also to rule on market structures—the only way to ensure that economic power does not accumulate in the hands of a few, that market distortions are prevented, and that the goal of healthy competition is attained.

The Chamber appealed this opinion to the Resolution Commission, arguing that the Prevention Commission lacked discretionary power to regulate markets. The Resolution Commission, through Resolution No. 529, denied the appeal because, in its view, the Prevention Commission's Opinion No. 1,045 of 1988 was not issued to exercise powers conferred upon it by Executive Order No. 211; rather, it was issued to exercise the exclusive, specific mission with which the legislature, through Law 19.542, entrusted it.[53]

Consequences of the Rulings

The concessions were awarded in July 1999. In principle, each one was to be awarded to the bidder that offered the lowest maximum rate index, an average of four rates. Nonetheless, in fairness to private port competitors, the bidding rules for each docking front specified a minimum rate floor index. In the event that more than one bidder offered the minimum rate index established in the rules, a tie-breaking payment was to be offered. This payment was over and above the leasing payment established in the bidding rules for port infrastructure, and was calculated on the basis of the property's economic value. The bidding attracted much interest, with a total of 21 bids tendered by consortia consisting of leading domestic and foreign companies, of which 19 included the minimum rate index, plus the additional

---

[53] The Chamber filed an appeal (petition in error) with the Supreme Court against the Resolution Commission's decision to deny appeal because, in its view, the appeal before the Commission was admissible, and because it believed that the decisions were unconstitutional and illegal. In its report to the Supreme Court, the Commission argued that the appeal to the Supreme Court was inadmissible because it was only appropriate with regard to jurisdictional decisions, and Resolution No. 529 did not involve such an issue since it was not rendered in a dispute between parties involved in an administrative procedure. The Supreme Court denied the appeal because it believed the antitrust commissions had acted within the limits of their powers.

tie-breaking payment. All terminals were awarded on the basis of the tie-breaking payment amount. Consequently, an average rate reduction of more than 10 percent was generated in port services for fronts that were awarded in concession, and the government was also able to take in revenue totaling US$267 million (three times the expected amount).

Results of the first years of operation have also satisfied the government's expectations, as the data for Port of Valparaíso illustrates. The time required to load and unload a eurosall vessel with 1,150 cargo movements decreased from 45 hours to 21 hours. In the Valparaíso concession, investment in new cranes, computer software, and other equipment during 2001 topped US$8 million, with another $27.5 million expected by 2006.

Vertical Integration in Solid Waste Processing

Overview of the Problem

The solid waste processing chain can be divided into three stages: home and street collection and transport or hauling to a transfer center, compacting and transfer to a refuse dump, and final disposal at the refuse dump. For environmental reasons, few sites qualify for use as refuse dumps; thus, these sites have become essential facilities. Although concessions for refuse dumps are awarded on the basis of price, a vertically integrated concessionaire might discriminate against downstream competitors (for example, by giving preferential treatment in unloading to its own vehicles).

During the 1980s, many municipalities in Santiago began transferring the first two stages in the chain to private companies, while maintaining ownership of the dumps. In the early 1990s, solid waste from districts in the city of Santiago was deposited at one of three dumps. Refuse from 21 municipal districts was deposited in Lo Errázuriz, located in the southern part of the city. This refuse dump was administrated by Emeres, a company composed of the municipalities in these districts. Garbage from the 16 northern districts was deposited at Cerros de Renca, a refuse dump owned by the municipality of Colina and managed by a private firm. Lepanto, a privately-owned dump, received solid waste from two western districts of the city.

An assessment conducted by the regional sanitation authority in the early 1990s showed that the two main dumps were collapsing (they were closed down in 1996). This forced the municipalities to search for new dumping sites. In 1995, the northern districts' council of mayors awarded a concession to

KDM, the company that tendered the lowest bid, to construct and operate a sold waste dump. That same year, KDM obtained approval from the Regional Commission of the Environment (COREMA) after submitting an environmental impact study (EIS), which cleared the way for creating Las Bateas refuse dump. The following year, this refuse dump became operational. Emeres, for its part, considered several alternatives, including a plot of land located across from KDM, but COREMA rejected the sites on the basis of the EIS.

At the end of 1995, with the closing of Lo Errázuriz dump, Las Bateaswas site was the only remaining site for dumping solid waste. Although this was not necessarily a problem, since prices had been determined in the bidding process, the effect of closing down other dumps on links in the refuse processing chain was cause for concern. KDM not only performed transport functions; it also handled collection of 97 percent of the solid waste of the 16 northern municipalities through its associate companies (DeMarco and Starco). This led to a request for the Office of the National Economic Prosecutor to open an investigation. In addition, one of the requesting parties claimed that, during the bidding process that municipalities in the northern zone had called for, KDM purchased Starco, one of its major rivals, thereby stifling competition to an even greater degree.

Opinion of the Antitrust Prevention Commission

The Prosecutor's Office conducted an investigation that led to various recommendations being incorporated into Opinion No. 995 of the Prevention Commission. The Opinion addressed four issues. First, it warned government regulators about increased market power in the sector.[54] Second, it stated that KDM must grant equal terms to anyone who wished to use the Las Bateas dump.[55] Third, it recommended that the environmental commission consider approval of new dump sites. Fourth, it recommended that municipalities request an opinion from the Commission on rules of the new bidding process.

---

[54] In 1998, the Mayor of Rancagua charged that a person who claimed to be a representative of DeMarco offered him money in exchange for being awarded the concession contract for garbage collection in the district of that company. DeMarco denied any dealings with this person.

[55] KDM charges nonmunicipal clients who dump solid waste in Las Bateas a significantly higher rate than that charged municipalities.

Appeals Against the Opinion

KDM appealed the opinion of the Prevention Commission to the Resolution Commission, stating that the Prevention Commission lacked the legal authority to regulate an ongoing business activity. Additionally, it maintained that the antitrust commissions have the discretionary power to sanction abuses of a dominant market position, but not a monopolistic position per se, which, in this case, was the result of greater efficiency. It stated that, for this reason, ruling against KDM would amount to punishing a company for being more efficient than its competitors. Lastly, it claimed that the Prevention Commission was impinging on the powers of the environmental regulatory agency. The Resolution Commission decided that the Prevention Commission had sufficient power to rule on market structures and potential risk of anticompetitive conduct stemming from a dominant position.

KDM filed a motion for economic protection with the Court of Appeals, stating that its right to equality under the law would be adversely affected should it be precluded from participating in the new bidding process. In its report to the Court of Appeals, the Resolution Commission stated that the preventive nature of the measures proposed by the Prevention Commission did not threaten exercise of those rights and guarantees, but merely constituted expectations, not a vested right. The Court denied the motion, stating that the Resolution Commission is not an administrative body, but rather a jurisdictional tribunal—an adjudicatory body whose decisions may not be the subject of motions for protection. KDM filed an appeal with the Supreme Court, which denied the motion without further comment.

Outcome of the Ruling

The most important consequence of this ruling was that Emeres enlisted the opinion of the commissions regarding rules of the bidding process it was about to conduct. Specifically, Emeres inquired whether KDM was eligible to participate in the bidding. After several consultations with the Commission, Emeres eventually issued the invitation to bid. The concession was awarded to another company, but the Regional Environmental Commission did not approve the EIS filed by the winning company. Meanwhile, Lo Errázuriz was shut down, and southern municipalities began dumping their solid waste in Lepanto. However, this site, which should have been shut down earlier, has since collapsed. Lepanto was finally closed in May 2002 after a new refuse dump (Santa Marta), whose EIS was approved, became operational.

Conclusions

This chapter has analyzed how Chile's antitrust commissions have dealt with essential facilities by examining their rulings in five cases across various sectors of the Chilean economy. The first three cases—external telecommunications network, electricity transmission system, and gas pipelines—are natural monopolies resulting from the heavy economies of scale involved in their development. The last two cases—maritime ports and solid waste processing—illustrate how the essential facility status can result from geographic conditions. In Chile, maritime ports are an essential facility because of the scarcity of natural bays; in the solid waste management sector, restrictions imposed by environmental protection agencies, coupled with opposition from neighboring communities, have blocked construction of new refuse dumps, thereby converting existing refuse dumps into essential facilities.

Measures to Prevent Sabotage

Examination of the antitrust commissions' rulings shows that these bodies concur that vertically integrated monopolies pose a risk to competition in services where this is possible. Therefore, the commissions have called upon appropriate government agencies to regulate the rates of essential facilities.[56] To reduce the likelihood of sabotage by integrated monopolies, the antitrust commissions have arbitrated five major measures, which are discussed below.

Investigate and Penalize Anticompetitive Conduct

The antitrust commissions have investigated, either on their own initiative or as a result of charges by others, anticompetitive practices in infrastructure services. In some cases, the commissions have succeeded in proving and sanctioning anticompetitive practices. Nevertheless, lack of capacity to technically scrutinize and legally prove acts of discrimination has limited the ability to penalize such conduct.[57]

---

[56] Electricity transmission, access to the local telecommunications network, and gas transport.

[57] For example, long-distance telephone companies have historically complained about the interconnection services of local phone companies, but regulators lack sufficient resources to effectively oversee the technical conditions of interconnections.

Therefore, the government introduced a bill in Congress to strengthen the Office of the National Economic Prosecutor. Enacted in December 1999, the bill increased the number of trained professionals involved in oversight duties, raised the salaries of these positions, and created a team of full-time inspectors. One weakness of the bill, however, was that it failed to increase resources at the disposal of the antitrust commissions, which increased the likelihood that these bodies would have to depend on reports prepared by the Office of the National Economic Prosecutor.

Promote Entry of New Providers of the Essential Input

The second mechanism antitrust commissions have used to prevent sabotage is to promote having multiple providers of the essential input whenever possible. For example, the Resolution Commission required that the legislature amend the telecommunications law to enable long-distance companies to establish direct connections to users bypassing local companies' networks. In the case of bidding on port concessions, the Prevention Commission placed more stringent restrictions on horizontal integration than those the government proposed. This policy usually has its costs and must be weighed against the benefits that enhanced competition can bring about. In the case of refuse dumps, the Prevention Commission requested that environmental regulators consider approving new dumping sites, even though, from an environmental point of view, it would be better to oversee only one refuse dump.

Impose Standards of Transparency on Integrated Monopolies

Another requirement the antitrust commissions have imposed on vertically integrated monopolies is achieving the greatest transparency possible. In the telecommunications sector, for example, the Resolution Commission required local telephone companies that wanted to operate in long-distance markets to provide carriers with all information concerning long-distance traffic. In the electricity sector, distribution companies were obligated to auction power supply. In the port sector, the Prevention Commission backed the government's proposal to make public all information pertaining to port management. In these cases, the commissions believed that, if all operators had access to the same market information at the monopoly's disposal, the strategic advantage of vertical integration would be mitigated, and the likelihood of nonprice discrimination would be reduced.

The commissions also required monopolies that wished to engage in nonregulated services to do so through affiliates or subsidiaries with a single line of business, thereby forcing them to maintain separate books in the nonregulated business.[58] Moreover, the commissions have opined that the subsidiary must be a public stock corporation, or at least subject to oversight by the Superintendent of Securities and Insurance. This distinction is important because corporate law establishes that transactions between a parent company and its subsidiaries must observe the same rules of fairness as those that usually apply to the market.

Demand Autonomy of the Business Unit That Provides the Nonregulated Service

Another method the commissions have used to reduce the likelihood of nonprice discrimination is to enhance the autonomy of the business unit that provides the nonregulated service. Mandy (2000) shows that when the subsidiary is managed independently, there is less incentive to discriminate.

This goal can be variously achieved. In the vertical integration of the electricity sector, the Resolution Commission chose to recommend incorporation of new ownership on the subsidiary. The reasoning was that participation of other owners creates opposing interests and, consequently, the subsidiary company makes decisions with greater autonomy. Another option is to demand independence of the board of directors and independent management of the subsidiaries. The commissions have not yet applied this option, despite the fact that CTC suggested that this be done in seeking authorization to enter the long-distance telephone market.

Restrict Vertical Integration

A more radical option is to demand that the company providing the essential input not participate in the industry's competitive segments.[59] In the case of privatized public services, the antitrust commissions have rarely called for taking such a measure.[60] In certain rulings, the commissions believed that the

---

[58] Laffont and Tirole (2000) believe that it is difficult to measure and prevent cross subsidies.

[59] This rule could be less restrictive and merely set a ceiling on how many shares owners of the monopoly may hold in the company that provides the nonregulated service.

[60] Perhaps the only significant example was the Resolution Commission's decision to order Telefónica de España to sell its shares of either CTC or Entel.

mechanisms described above were sufficient to ensure equal access to the essential facility, making vertical disintegration unnecessary. In other cases, they stated their strong belief that the merger of companies would make it possible to take advantage of economies of scope and scale (Resolution No. 445 of 1995 involved association between airlines, and Resolution No. 389 of 1993 concerned vertical integration in telecommunications).[61] In these cases, however, price reduction was not appended as a condition, and the costs of integration were not weighed. If economies of scale and scope indeed existed, then downstream competitors could not survive without the benefits of integration. This situation would make it necessary to regulate vertically integrated monopolies, which involves significant cost, considering that regulation is a poor substitute for competition.

However, it appears that the Resolution Commission's main reason not to force the vertical disintegration of monopolies has been to avoid infringing on vested rights.[62] Although the antitrust law (Executive Order No. 211), in principle, grants broad discretionary powers to the antitrust commissions, some jurists hold that these institutions only have the legal authority to punish anticompetitive conduct. In these experts' judgment, structural regulation affects essential rights protected by the Constitution, which may only be regulated by statute. Others jurists, however, believe that the antitrust law grants the commissions legal authority to prevent acts that may put competition at risk, including the power to regulate market structure. The commissions' decisions have not been consistent on whether they have the legal power to establish structural regulations in situations that pose a risk to free competition.

On this issue, the commissions have been determined in proposing that the bidding rules for public infrastructure concessions contain restrictions on vertical integration. That such concessions do not involve vested rights may explain their seemingly contradictory view. Some jurists have argued that any right stemming from a concession is an in rem right (administrative right over something); therefore, a concession should be treated no differ-

---

[61] Those opposed to forced vertical disintegration have also argued that the monopoly may enter into an under-the-counter arrangement with a nonrelated company of a nonregulated segment to discriminate against other competitors. But the antitrust commissions have not resorted to that argument. In any case, when two parties need to enter into such an agreement, detection and transaction costs are likely to increase.

[62] The integrated companies are usually worth more than the sum of their parts because they could wield market power, enjoy economies of scope, and reduce transaction costs; this explains why the forced breakup of vertical integration adversely affects ownership rights.

ently than private property.[63] Since no ownership rights existed prior to granting the concession, it is difficult to argue that these rights are being infringed on. Therefore, opponents of horizontal and vertical restrictions on concessions have argued that such restrictions would involve arbitrary discrimination by the state and its agents in matters of economic freedom, essentially nullifying the freedom to acquire ownership or dominion over any type of property; in so doing, it would violate rights contained in the Constitution. Even so, the antitrust commissions have favored the rights of the infrastructure owner (the state), allowing it to determine the conditions of concession.

Far-reaching Effects of the Rulings

Despite the above-mentioned arguments, antitrust law has facilitated the introduction of changes in regulating public infrastructure. Prior to infrastructure privatization, detailed regulations had been incorporated into the laws to reassure and guarantee investors that property would not be administratively expropriated. Even the slightest attempt at modifying the regulations caused owners of the privatized companies to complain that the rules were being changed in midstream, thereby slowing the pace of urgently needed changes in the regulatory regime.[64]

Since enactment of Executive Order No. 211 predates the privatization process, it cannot be claimed that changes have been made to the regulations when it is the rulings of the antitrust commissions that have been responsible for increasing industry competition. The Antitrust Resolution Commission has the legal authority to request that the government amend or repeal provisions of laws or regulations it considers anticompetitive (Executive Order No. 211, Article 5). For this reason, the government has consulted the commissions before introducing changes in the law or regulations of several sectors.

---

[63] A concession is an authorization in which the administration confers on a private entity temporary use of a government-owned property, including rights and responsibilities benefiting both the concessionaire and society as a whole.

[64] Fischer and Serra (2000) believe that private sector opposition to changes delayed implementation of changes in the electricity law, which would have helped to prevent the severe power shortages that occurred in 1998 and 1999. The companies feared the changes being made in the law, in part because of the uncertainty involved in a highly politicized legislative process with little technical input. The energy crisis finally led to changes in laws and regulations; unfortunately, these changes, introduced hastily and in a politically charged atmosphere, were ill-conceived.

Opinions of the Antitrust Prevention Commission have been similarly far-reaching in exercising advisory and preventive functions, at the request of regulatory agencies. Two particularly relevant cases are natural gas pipelines (Opinion No. 933 of 1995) and water rights (Opinion No. 992 of 1996). In both cases, appeals filed with the Resolution Commission claimed that the Prevention Commission lacked the legal authority to regulate markets. The Resolution Commission declared, however, that the Prevention Commission had exercised its legitimate powers in a manner consistent with the law. Moreover, given that the Prevention Commission's opinions are nonbinding, recommendations to the Resolution Commission stated that it was not called on to rule on the substance or merits of the cases (Resolutions No. 448 of October 1995 and No. 480 of January 1997, respectively).

Final Thoughts

Given the general nature of Chile's antitrust legislation, the rulings of the antitrust commissions have been essential in establishing public economic order and in providing guidance on which behaviors or actions, in their view, constitute a violation of free competition principles. Nevertheless, the actions of the antitrust commissions have not been without their problems or uncertainties in interpreting the law. Lack of a clear definition of the commissions' legal authority to regulate market structures has given rise to debates in most cases of vertical disintegration or breakup of market power. These debates, however, have focused more on the commissions' powers than on the true merits or substance of the measures in question. The current trend is leaning toward recognizing the antitrust commissions' power to establish structural regulations, following legal proceedings in which evidence is introduced and ample opportunity is given to mount a defense.

References

Armstrong, Mark. 1998. "Network Interconnection in Telecommunications." *Economic Journal* 108(448): 545–64.

Economides, Nicholas. 1998. "The Incentive for Nonprice Discrimination by an Input Monopolist." *International Journal of Industrial Organization* 16: 271–84.

Fischer, R., and P. Serra. 2000. "Regulation of the Electricity Sector." *Economía* 1(1): 155–218.

Laffont, Jean-Jacques, and Jean Tirole. 2000. *Competition in Telecommunications.* Cambridge, MA: MIT Press.

Laffont, Jean-Jacques, Patrick Rey, and Jean Tirole. 1998a. "Network Competition I: Overview and Nondiscriminatory Pricing." *Rand Journal of Economics* 29(1): 1–37.

———. 1998b. "Network Competition II: Price Discrimination." *Rand Journal of Economics* 29(1): 38–56.

Mandy, M. D. 2000. "Killing the Goose That May Have Laid the Golden Egg: Only the Data Know Whether Sabotage Pays." *Journal of Regulatory Economics* 17(2): 157–72.

Paredes, Ricardo. 1995. "Evaluating the Cost of Bad Regulation in Newly Privatized Sectors: The Chilean Case. *Análisis Económico* 10(2): 63–88.

Rudnick, H., M. Soto, and R. Palma. 1999. "Use of System Approaches for Transmission Open Access Pricing." *International Journal of Electrical Power and Energy Systems* 21(2): 125–35.

Spiller, Pablo, and Carlo G. Cardilli. 1997. "The Frontier of Telecommunications Deregulation: Small Countries Leading the Pack." *Journal of Economic Perspectives* 11(4): 127–38.

Chapter 3

Argentina's Natural Gas Markets: Antitrust and Regional Integration Issues

Diego Bondorevsky and Diego Petrecolla

In the Southern Cone of South America, natural gas basins are located far from consumption and production centers, most of which are connected by point-to-point networks rather than an interconnecting grid. This type of network configuration has led to market segmentation, whereby the outputs and transport capacity of individual markets differ, with few available exchange nodes. As a result, gas prices are independently set in local markets and are not based on an international benchmark price, as are other commodity markets. Novara (1997) remarks that, even in trade between the United States and Canada, no evidence points to a representative or marker price, either for natural gas production areas or entry points into large urban population centers.[1]

Regional Integration: A Global Trend

Despite independent price-setting, integration of natural gas markets is spreading throughout the world.[2] The European market, for example, is

---

[1] Novara (1997) further states that, contrary to what one would expect, prices in different spot markets are not co-integrated and are not merged into a single net price of transportation cost differentials.

[2] Compared with other transport fuels, natural gas is relatively inefficient because of its high volume on a caloric potential, per-unit basis. For example, one million BTUs of natural gas occupy approximately one square meter under normal atmospheric conditions and temperatures, while only 7.5 gallons of gasoline contain the same amount of energy.

highly integrated. Europe's major exporting countries are Norway, the Netherlands, and Russia (which has the most extensive natural gas reserves in the world); while its major importing countries are Germany, Italy, and Spain. As Osmundsen (2000) points out, a key factor contributing to market integration is that gas-importing countries seek to diversify supply—that is, promote competition in gas supply to ensure that energy is provided in flexible amounts, rather than search for the lowest possible prices. In Asia, moreover, the number of natural gas pipelines between producer and importing countries is on the rise. In China, for example, many transportation projects are meeting growing demands of energy markets by importing gas from the basins of Russia and Indonesia.

Overview of Argentina's Market

Regional integration of Argentina's gas market began in the 1970s, when an agreement was signed to construct a gas pipeline between Bolivia and Argentina. Through this agreement, Gas del Estado (Argentina's state-owned gas transport and distribution company) purchased natural gas produced by Yacimientos Petrolíferos Fiscales Bolivianos (Bolivia's state-owned oil company, widely known by its Spanish abbreviation, YPFB). The agreement assured Bolivia of a certain volume of gas exports to Argentina, amounting to 5 percent of Bolivia's gross national product. Argentina secured a steady flow of nonrenewable fuel at a low price, making it possible to satisfy the country's fast-growing domestic need, while maintaining reserves. Over the past few years, Gas del Estado and YPF have been privatized, and construction of a gas pipeline between Bolivia and Brazil has led Bolivia to redirect its gas output to the Brazilian market.

Between 1995 and 2000, significant progress was made toward integrating Argentina's energy with that of neighboring countries. However, contrary to its original integration experience with Bolivia, Argentina has become a net exporter of energy products. Furthermore, state-owned enterprises are no longer the motivation behind integration; rather, the private sector has taken the lead in this effort. In fact, private companies began to lay the first gas and oil pipelines and establish the first electrical transmission networks in 1995 (between Argentina and Chile). Jadresic (1999) states that several factors contributed to the development of these networks. First, deregulation of the energy sector in both Argentina and Chile enabled the private sector to invest in markets traditionally controlled by the public sector. Second, the two countries achieved political integration, having settled longstanding border disputes.

Third, they adopted new technologies in electricity power generation, such as the combined-cycle generator, which provided critical mass for construction of infrastructure works. In addition, private companies, such as Enersis and Transcanada, have played a major role in developing electricity and gas transport networks between Argentina and Chile.

Why Consider Market Integration?

Throughout South America's Southern Cone, consumption of natural gas is on the rise as a result of countries having developed combined-cycle electricity power plants. In addition, research on market integration can provide insight into how the structure of Argentina's gas sector has barred competition from Bolivia, leading Argentina toward higher prices than other countries in the region, even though it has significant reserves and is the main producer in the Southern Cone. Because YPF controls the gas pipeline between Bolivia and Argentina and most of Argentina's gas reserves, it is virtually impossible to diversify sources of supply. Such diversification would make it possible to expand market supply in Argentina, making it easier for distributors and major users to find prices other than those offered by YPF.

This chapter takes a close look at the infrastructure and performance of Argentina's natural gas sector, the effects this sector has had on market integration in the Southern Cone region, and the resulting regulatory and antitrust issues that have arisen.

Restructuring and Privatization: Transport and Distribution

Until 1992, Gas del Estado handled all purchases, transport, distribution, and trading (of mainly YPF-produced gas) in the Argentinean gas basins of Neuquén, Noroeste, San Jorge, and Austral. Law 24,076, enacted in 1992, ordered the unbundling of these activities, which were horizontally divided by geographic zone. The law established a regulatory framework for the transport and distribution segments, which, in turn, gave rise to concessionaires who were awarded a contract through a process of international tender in December 1992.[3] Thus, the structure of that part of the industry con-

---

[3] US$2.077 billion in revenue was collected from privatization of Gas del Estado; of this amount, US$680 million was paid in cash, while the remainder was funded using internal and external debt instruments.

trolled by Gas del Estado was divided into two transport companies, to which existing gas pipelines were assigned, and nine low-pressure distributors to serve the retail market.[4] Consequently, over a seven-year period beginning in December 1992, transport network capacity rose from 74.7 to 149.9 cubic meters (cu m) per day (at a winter utilization rate of 95 percent). With regard to the distribution network, 66,765 kilometers (km) of pipeline had been laid by December 1992. Currently, the total length of pipeline has reached 101,569 km, representing an increase of more than 52 percent.[5]

Increase in the system's transport capacity made it possible to markedly reduce gas consumption restrictions that had been placed on major users during times of peak demand. For example, in 1993, such constraints applied to more than 34 percent of all gas injected into the system; in 1996, the percentage decreased to 12.6 percent; and, in 1999, these restrictions affected only 1.2 percent of the total amount of gas.[6] Moreover, price controls on gas transport and distribution increased between December 1992 and May 2000 by only 3 percent for residential users. Additionally, price controls on industrial rates fell by more than 13 percent over this period as a result of discounts granted by transport companies on the maximum regulated rate.

Unbundling

Law 24,076 established the regulatory framework for concessionaires of natural monopolies of gas transport and distribution.[7] Article 33 established a separation between gas transport and sales to prevent carriers from distorting competition in the trading segment. This unbundling helped to eliminate the incentive to discriminate in providing transport services between producers and users as a function of or in conjunction with trading activities.

The law specifically states that "carriers may not purchase or sell gas, except for acquisitions that may be carried out for their own consumption and for the natural gas required to maintain operability of the transmission system, the volume of which shall be determined by the [regulatory] entity on a case-by-case basis."

---

[4] There were eight low-pressure distributors until July 1998, when Gasnea was added. It should be noted that, in some cases, these distributors also handle medium and high-pressure service.

[5] ENARGAS (1994–1999).

[6] Ibid.

[7] A natural monopoly occurs when a single firm can offer a good at a lower total cost than can two or more firms.

The trader (*comercializador*) category is defined in Article 14 of Law 24,076 as "someone who purchases and sells natural gas on [behalf] of third parties." These traders, who bring large consumers and producers together, play a key role in competition by stimulating better downstream prices. To broker such transactions, the right of open access to the networks and physical bypass must be guaranteed.

Open Access to Networks and Consumer Choice

Article 26 of Law 24,076 states that "carriers and distributors are obligated to permit indiscriminate access of third parties to any transportation and distribution capacity of their respective systems that may not be under a commitment to the supply of contracted demand."

The law establishes consumers' freedom to choose a trader. Users requiring more than 5,000 cu m per day may refrain from using the distributor's services and directly acquire energy from producers or traders.[8]

In order for freedom of consumer choice to be viable, regulations allow for construction of lines that physically bypass existing networks. Thus, Article 49 of Law 24076 establishes that "... Consumers who contract directly with the producer may build, at their own cost, their own feeder branch lines to meet their own consumption needs." Article 13 further provides for commercial bypass, stipulating that "Notwithstanding the rights granted to distributors for their qualification [eligibility], any consumer may agree to the purchase of natural gas directly with producers or traders, by freely negotiating the terms and conditions of the transaction."

In 1993, four companies opted to use a supplier other than the local distributor in their geographic zone (who together represented only 3 percent of the total gas delivered). This number rose to 60 companies in 1996 (23 percent of total gas delivered), and to 149 companies in 1999 (33 percent of the total gas delivered).

Rate Regulation

Transport and distribution rates or tariffs are determined by the regulatory agency of the sector, which sets maximum prices. During the international tender, tariff ceilings were written into the terms of bidding for gas transport

---

[8] Until 2000, the requirement was 10,000 cu m.

and distribution services, and these prices are subject to review every five years. Biannual rate adjustments are based on the formula RPI − X + K, where RPI equals the retail price index in the United States, X is a factor designed to stimulate allocation efficiency, and K is a factor aimed at promoting investment in the service.

The rate charged to end users consists of three price components: transport, distribution, and gas at the point of entry into the transport system.[9] This arrangement means that users who purchase through a distributor absorb the price of gas negotiated by the distributor, while those who negotiate directly with a trader or producer absorb the agreed price.

Performance-based Regulation

Even though Law 24,076 does not mention comparison of efficiency between companies as a regulatory mechanism, the horizontal breakup of the transport and distribution segments makes it possible for regulators to compare companies' performance. Nevertheless, the regulatory agency, as yet, has not conducted such comparisons in determining rates, even though regulators could readily gain access to each company's records and information.

Wholesale Market

Major Players

The wholesale market for natural gas at the wellhead or point of pipeline injection has various players: gas producers and importers on the supply side and distribution companies, traders, and customers (whose requirements exceed 5,000 cu m per day) on the distribution side.

Distributors act as exclusive purchase agents for consumers who require less than 5,000 cu m per day and whose demand is highly inflexible. Electricity, liquefied petroleum gas (LPG), and other fuels mainly used for home heating are alternatives to natural gas.[10] Industrial consumers and electricity

---

[9] These prices differ from the wellhead price, since they are added to the cost of gas treatment, processing, and transport. The processing stages determine gas quality and the appropriate price based on caloric efficiency, degree of purity, and content of pollutants and other harmful substances.

[10] In Argentina, the technology that allows consumers to switch immediately between gas and electricity is not widely used.

power generators may carry out physical or commercial bypass and are characterized by having more flexible demand.

If the price consumers are willing to pay for natural gas at the point of entry into the transport system or if the net back value (the price at the point of consumption minus the transport cost up to that point) is greater than the cost of production in the gas field, then agents will be interested in gas extraction. Otherwise, natural gas will simply not be extracted. In Argentina, the wellhead price of natural gas is lower than that of other countries, but transport costs to consumption centers, particularly Buenos Aires, tend to drive up the price. Nevertheless, it is noteworthy that the net back value in Argentina, as of 1998, was higher than the wellhead price. In Brazil, by contrast, the net back value was lower than the wellhead cost of gas. This is because, on the one hand, transport costs and caloric requirements are high; on the other hand, the price of fuel oil (the benchmark of natural gas value) is relatively low since it is subsidized (Visintini 1993).

Removal of Price Controls

In Argentina, gas extraction and production are governed by Law 17,319, known as the Law of Hydrocarbons (in addition to amendments to this law and decrees or executive orders emanating from it). Nonetheless, all price controls on wellhead prices were totally removed as of the beginning of 1994, under decree 2,731.

Balzarotti (1999) states that, because of growing marginal costs of the fields and because the minimum scale of gas extraction platforms (the point of production where economies of scale are exhausted) is not too large in relation to the size of the markets supplied, opening up the gas market to more competition leads to higher efficiency in resource allocation. In Argentina, however, removal of market restrictions and wellhead price controls occurred in an environment unsuitable for building a competitive market. That environment was characterized by several circumstances that blocked promotion of competition in gas supply.[11] First and foremost, a single company, YPF, controlled 60 percent of all sales. Second, heavy investment in exploration of reserves was required, which kept new suppliers from entering the market, since exploration involves high sunk production costs.

---

[11] The characteristics that prevented emergence of a competitive market are listed in ENARGAS, file 4,943 (August 1999).

TABLE 3-1. YPF'S SHARE IN THE NATURAL GAS MARKET, 1994–99
(Percent)

YPF share	1994	1995	1996	1997	1998	1999
Own gas	40	39	34	34	34	40
Own gas plus third-party gas	63	58	60	62	59	51

Source: ENARGAS (2000).

(This means it will take a company a long time to produce enough to recover the initial investment.) Third, legal barriers to entry exist as a result of the way ownership rights are acquired in this industry. Specifically, companies are required to obtain permits for exploration and, subsequently, a concession for operating from the Secretariat of Energy. These circumstances, where a high level of reserves is in the hands of one company or an associated group, act as a barrier to the entry of potential competitors or prevent existing competitors from increasing their share of sales by lowering prices.

Supply Structure

When Gas del Estado was privatized in December 1992, it purchased 90 percent of its gas from YPF, while the remaining 10 percent was either imported from Bolivia (7 percent) or purchased from other private, domestic producers (3 percent). As table 3-1 shows, between 1994 and 1998, YPF posted a decrease in sales of the gas it produced, which was offset by an increase in sales of third parties controlled by YPF.[12] In 1999, YPF market share was significantly reduced, mainly as a result of a drop in third-party gas traded by YPF. Implicitly, the company recognized its anticompetitive practices and pledged to gradually reduce trading in third-party produced gas.[13]

Market Power Indexes

The Herfindahal-Hirschman index of market power, which ENARGAS conducted for 1998 and 1999, also shows a decrease in market power for this

---

[12] When REPSOL took control of YPF in September 1999, the merged company became known as REPSOL-YPF; for convenience, this chapter refers to the company as YPF for all periods after September 1999.

[13] ENARGAS, file 4,943 (pp. 467–69).

TABLE 3-2. THE MARKET POWER INDEX OF MAJOR ARGENTINEAN GAS BASINS, 1998-99

Index	Gas-producing basin			Country total
	Neuquén	Austral	Noroeste	
Herfindhal-Hirschman				
1998	3,703	3,271	5,772	3,725
1999	3,493	2,587	2,978	2,841
Top four producers (%)				
1998	84.7	89.5	96.9	80.2
1999	86.7	91.9	92.2	74.9

Source: ENARGAS (2000).

period in all basins included in the study, particularly the Noroeste Basin. These variations may result from YPF's policy of gradually abandoning the trading of third-party produced gas. Nevertheless, as table 3-2 shows, indexes of the top four gas-producing basins have not varied substantially.

Distributors' Anticompetitive Behavior: Causes and Cures

Understanding Consumer Types

To examine the potential for gas distributors to engage in anticompetitive behavior, it is helpful to divide their clientele into two groups: customers who are free to choose a supplier, and "captive" customers or those without freedom to choose who are served by the distributor. Distribution companies that serve these two consumer groups usually subsidize freedom-of-choice customers at the expense of captive consumers to prevent noncaptive consumers from switching to other suppliers. Distributors have few incentives to reduce the acquisition costs of gas for captive customers as long as they can pass these costs on to consumers. Distributors may even have an incentive to acquire gas at high prices for these customers, if the trading margin is a percentage of the acquisition costs. This type of behavior has been considered anticompetitive by some U.S. court cases, such as *Illinois Brick* and *Illinois versus Panhandle Eastern Pipeline Company* (Stewart 1990).

In the *Illinois Brick* case, the New Mexico court authorized consumers to file suit, based on their claim that the wholesale gas price passed on to end-users by the distributor resulted from an agreement between producers and distributors outside of the market. In the case *Illinois versus Panhandle Eastern Pipeline Company,* the court only ruled in favor of a complaint filed by residential, not industrial, consumers of natural gas. In this ruling, the judge distinguished between two types of transactions in order to examine agreements between distributors and producers. One type consisted of gas sales to the distributor for subsequent resale to residential captive customers. In such cases, the surcharge stemming from an agreement between producers and distributors was passed on entirely to the consumer.

The other type was sales to distributors for subsequent resale to industrial consumers who were free to switch suppliers. In these cases, the surcharge was not passed on to the customer because the option to switch suppliers was available. When this type of transaction occurred, the distributor lost, as a result of the anticompetitive behavior between distributor and producer. If the result were loss of industrial sales, the distributor would have had greater incentive to report such anticompetitive behavior in the wholesale market. However, since most of its customers were residential (those with inflexible demand who would absorb all or most of the costs), the distributor had less incentive to file a complaint.

Effects of the Wholesale Market

In ENARGAS file 4,943, which was prepared as part of an examination of a price increase in the nonregulated component for residential and industrial customers, it is stated that distributors in Argentina engage in discriminatory practices in the treatment of industrial vis-à-vis residential customers. This behavior is caused by the need to make heavily discounted rates available to freedom-of-choice customers as a result of the practices of suppliers.[14]

The evidence cited in this file shows that distributors, facing the likelihood of losing customers who were free to chose a supplier—namely, thermal-powered electric generator plants and large industry—were forced to further discount prices and cut into their distribution margin.

---

[14] According to ENARGAS data, from December 1992 to May 1999, residential and industrial rates increased, respectively, by 7.67 percent (74 percent of which was caused by a rise in gas prices on the wholesale market) and 11.53 percent (82 percent of which was caused by the same rise). Predictably, the increase stemming from the regulated component was less significant for industrial than for residential customers.

TABLE 3-3. YPF'S PHASE-OUT SCHEDULE FOR THIRD-PARTY GAS TRADING

Year	Trading of third-party produced natural gas (million m per day)
1998	14
1999	14
2000	10
2001	9-8
2002	8-7
2003 (through April)	6-5
2003 (from May on)	0

Source: ENARGAS (file 4,943).

Third-party Gas Trading

When the natural gas industry was privatized in 1993, gas purchase contracts from other producers were transferred to YPF. In addition to receiving contracts as a result of such transfers, YPF continued to sign new contracts with other domestic and foreign producers. A contract entered into between Petrobas Internacional S.A., Braspetro, and YPF, S.A. in 1994 is particularly noteworthy because it represents failed attempts to open the natural gas supply to diverse players in the Noreste Basin for the distributors Litoral Gas and Gas del Centro.

YPF had pledged to pay the price that it stipulated in its contracts with distributors or major customers for natural gas it acquired from Petrobras; in so doing, it inexorably restricted competition in the Noreste Basin. Moreover, the time limit on YPF's right to trade up to 15 percent of the production of Bridas, Pluspetrol, and Tecpetrol in the Ramos field was extended. In fact, 15 percent of the total volume produced by these companies was transferred to YPF for trading at the time of privatization. Subsequent to the date of original transfer, YPF filed a request for the national government to extend its concession for 10 more years and maintain YPF's option to trade up to 15 percent of gas production from those companies. The government granted the request and issued Administrative Decision 92/96, which provided for these terms.

As a result of a public hearing, YPF signed a letter of commitment on October 7, 1999, pledging to gradually phase out trading in natural gas produced by third parties (table 3-3).[15]

---

[15] ENARGAS, file 4,943 (pp. 467–69).

Benchmark Prices: Incentive to Reduce Wholesale Prices

In July 1995, Administrative Decree 1,020 introduced an optional system to provide an incentive for natural gas distributors to minimize the high cost of gas acquisition for captive users resulting from pass-through. This measure was intended to provide incentive for the purchase of inexpensive gas on the spot market by introducing a benchmark price that acted as the minimum price and an average basin price that acted as the maximum price.

In the event a distributor acquired natural gas at a price lower than the reference price, it was rewarded by being allowed to pass on 50 percent of the difference between the purchase and reference prices. However, if the purchase price came in higher than the average basin price, then the distributor was punished by being allowed to pass on only 50 percent of the difference between the purchase and average basin price to the consumer. When prices came in between the ceiling and the floor, a distributor was neither rewarded nor punished, but rather permitted to pass on the purchase price to customers (a classic pass-through).

As a result of poor development of Argentina's natural gas spot market, compared with its contract market, the average number of distributors that used the benchmark price system between October 1995 and April 2001 was only four.

YPF's Effort toward Price Stability

YPF controls the trading market, single-handedly brokering more than 50 percent of natural gas sales. The remaining suppliers are smaller companies that separately represent an insignificant percentage of market share. Consequently, the dominant company pays little or no attention to smaller companies in designing pricing and volume strategies because the smaller companies are not in a position to increase sales by lowering prices. These companies follow YPF's lead in setting prices since, in the end, a policy of price decreases would be ineffective in boosting sales because of YPF's most-favored-customer policy.[16]

The most-favored-customer clause, which YPF used to include in its business contracts with distributors and other consumers, ensured YPF cus-

---

[16] ENARGAS file 4,943 highlights the close correlation between YPF price performance from 1994 to 1998 and prices of Pluspetrol, Petololera San Jorge, and Perez Companc in the Austral basin, which 97 percent of the time matched YPF's prices.

tomers a price as low as the lowest price offered by its competitors. In implementing such a practice, YPF made it virtually impossible for competition to increase market share by lowering prices, since YPF's most-favored customers were in a contractual position to demand the same price from their supplier. The most-favored-customer clause thus facilitated tacit collusion between the dominant company and its allies and barred entry to new competitors. YPF acknowledged that use of such a clause was an unfair practice and, in its October 1999 letter of commitment, pledged to discontinue inserting such provisions into new contracts.

Regional Integration

Importer versus Exporter Requirements

Importers of natural gas require volume and price flexibility in order to adapt to changes in end users' needs. Exporters, on the other hand, often face heavy sunk costs for exploration and even gas pipeline construction in some cases; thus, they require long-term contracts with little or no variation in price or volume (Osmusden, Asche, and Tveteras 2000).

The most common type of trading contract is a fixed amount agreement, known as a "take-or-pay" contract, which has a pricing structure with both fixed and variable components. The variable part is a function of the price of substitute fuels, while the fixed amount portion is designed to cover gas producers' fixed costs. Under such contracts, the seller runs the partial risk of price fluctuations, while the purchaser runs the risk that prices of alternative fuels may be lower than the fixed price component.

Differences between Domestic and Export Prices

Mounting evidence over the past decade shows that producers are selling natural gas on foreign markets, particularly in Chile, at lower prices than the domestic market (Novara 1997).[17] The price differential is the result of sellers' behavior and the demand requirements in the purchasing country, even though the selling company sets the price. Thus, the peculiarities of domestic demand in a given market for natural gas account for price differences.

---

[17] See also ENARGAS, file 4,943 (p. 422, quote from Ministry of Economy, file 750.681).

In the energy mix of Argentina, natural gas represents one of the highest percentages in the world, at 47 percent of total output. In Chile, natural gas accounted for only 7 percent of the total energy mix in 1994, and in Brazil, the current estimate is 3 percent. The biggest difference, however, are the requirements of natural gas consumers in each country. In Argentina, residential users, the main consumers, are relatively inflexible with regard to demand and are supplied by distribution companies. The distributors, who pass along the cost of acquiring gas to the residential end users, lack incentive to minimize costs. In Chile, by contrast, natural gas is mainly used by companies to generate electric power. These companies have the ability to substitute natural gas for alternative fuels or sources, such as hydroelectric power, in the process of generating electric power. Consequently, Chile tends to have greater flexibility in gas pricing than does Argentina.

Prices differ widely between domestic and foreign markets in this region for two additional reasons. The first is Chile's policy on purchasing natural gas. Novara (1998) states that, when the process of international tender was held for construction of gas pipelines and gas supply from Argentina to Chile, the criteria used for selecting the winning bid was the price of natural gas, as well as the cost of transport. Therefore, in order for a construction company to be awarded the contract, it was essential to minimize both the transport cost and the wellhead price of gas acquisition. This competition helped to spur negotiations between gas pipeline-building consortia and Argentinean natural gas producers, thereby enabling better prices to be obtained than those offered to domestic distributors.

The second reason for price differences between foreign and domestic markets is a clause in export contracts that prohibits resale of gas on the domestic market. These provisions, for the most part, make it impossible for traders to engage in arbitrage. YPF recognized the use of these clauses in its October 1999 letter of commitment, in which it states, "We would propose to our customers the elimination of the clauses that prevent unconditional resale and/or re-importation of gas, but with the proper safeguard over fiscal responsibility in export operations."[18]

---

[18] Bogo (2000) states that these types of clauses are prohibited in Japan, the United States and the European Community. The author maintains that the ability to engage in arbitration has been considered a basic tool for building and sustaining a common European market.

Business Strategies and Obstacles to Open Access

The regional energy market shapes the strategies that distributors, carriers, and producers follow. Nevertheless, these strategies are developed on the basis of the regulations that are in effect in different countries, which sometimes hamper development of a competitive market and, at other times, serve to promote competition.

The process of integrating Argentina's market with those of neighboring countries illustrates the role that business strategies and regulations play in shaping regional markets. This integration would make it possible to open up supply to a diversity of players, thus increasing competition in the Argentinean market by importing gas from Bolivia. Moreover, as a logical corollary to integration, market size would increase; consequently, exports to Chile and Brazil would rise, enabling absorption of the sunk costs of raising the level of proven reserves. Nevertheless, increased natural gas exports from Argentina to Brazil via Bolivia would require a higher capacity connection with the neighboring country. This expansion is also the key to hemispheric integration of the market, since it would make it possible for potential gas exporting countries, such as Peru, Ecuador, and Venezuela, to trade through Bolivia.

Argentina-Bolivia Pipeline

Argentina's ability to import gas from Bolivia is predicated on the gas pipeline connecting northern Argentina and Bolivia. Over the past few years, the capacity of this pipeline has been 6,000 cu m per day, accounting for only 7 percent of Argentina's domestic consumption. Even with this limited capacity, the pipeline has not been used to import gas from Bolivia to Argentina since 1998. The reason is that the strategy the producing companies devised, following YPF's leadership, uses the capacity of this pipeline (as well as another that connects Bolivia and Brazil) to export Argentina's natural gas output to Brazil.

When YPF was privatized, two events occurred during the bidding process that placed the company at an advantage to effectively control the market of the northwest basin. First, YPF was given the option to sell Bolivian gas under a purchase contract to Gas del Estado of Argentina. Second, YPF was given majority ownership in Refinor, where Bolivian gas is refined before being injected into the pipeline of Transportadora de Gas del Norte

(TGN). Refinor is also the owner of the gas pipeline that connects the Bolivian pipeline with the refinery.[19]

As an example of business strategies aimed at holding up imports, it is worth mentioning that, in 1993, a group of distributors sought an alternative supplier to YPF in Bolivia.[20] However, the offer that these distributors received from Refinor for gas imported from Bolivia was extremely high.[21]

Change seems to loom on the horizon regarding this situation, as an Argentinean company, Pluspetrol, announced in April 2001 that it will construct another gas pipeline between the two countries and that importation of natural gas from Bolivia for electric power generation in its combined-cycle plant in northwest Argentina shall begin thereafter. Furthermore, British Gas plans to lay a new pipeline between Tarija (Bolivia) and Uruguayana (Brazil), which will stretch through northeastern Argentina, supplementing the installed capacity of TGN.

Bolivia-Brazil Pipeline

The length of the gas pipeline that runs from Santa Cruz de las Sierras to San Pablo and Porto Alegre surpasses 3,000 km, ranking as one of South America's greatest energy infrastructure feats. Petrobras was the main force behind this project, despite Bolivia's proven gas reserves being far below the level of transport capacity required to make the project viable and Brazil's low demand for natural gas. The investment of about US$2 billion was partially financed by a loan from the Inter-American Development Bank (US$240 million) and the World Bank (US$310 million).

Two companies were created for constructing and operating the gas pipeline. On the Bolivian side, the company was chartered as Gas Transboliviano S.A. (GTB), and was composed of the subsidiary of Petrobras, Gaspetro (with 9 percent of shares), together with Enron (30 percent), Shell

---

[19] The collection and transport lines in the upstream segment remained in the hands of the producers without any restrictions. Stock share ownership was broken down as follows: YPF (30 percent), Perez Companc (28 percent), Pluspetrol (21 percent), Astra (10.5 percent), and Isaura (10.5 percent). Furthermore, the conditions for open access to the gas pipeline between Bolivia and Argentina were stipulated in Law 17,319.

[20] Litoral Gas, a group that included Gasnor S.A., Distribuidora de Gas del Centro S.A., and Gas Natural Ban S.A.

[21] These attempts culminated in a note from the distributor, Litoral Gas, to the Argentinean regulatory body, ENARGAS, stating that it had no other choice than to accept YPF's price for domestically produced or traded gas (ENARGAS, file 4,943).

(30 percent), Bolivian pension funds (25 percent), and BBPP (6 percent) (a holding company headed by El Paso Energy, British Gas, and the Australian company BHP). On the Brazilian side, Transportadora Brasileira Gasoduto Bolivia-Brasil (TBG) was created, which consisted of Gaspetro (51 percent), Enron (7 percent), Shell (7 percent), and Bolivian pension funds (6 percent). Law and Franco (1998) state that, during project development, the World Bank, in its capacity as financier, negotiated with the Brazilian government and TBG (the controlling company of the Brazilian side of the gas pipeline in which Petrobras is majority shareholder) certain policies to be followed once the project became operational. These policies involved nondiscriminatory access of third parties to the network; unbundling of functions; adoption of transport rates for noncommitted capacity on the basis of length of pipeline to be used; and the requirement that TBG act only as a carrier or transport company and not as a trader of its own upstream reserves.

Nevertheless, negotiations between the national oil companies of Bolivia and Brazil were predicated on the Brazilian government's good intentions. The true basis for the project was the contract signed in 1993 by Petrobras and YPFB for the Brazilian company's purchase of natural gas from the Bolivian oil company over a 20-year period. The contract also included a provision stipulating a maximum volume of 8 million cu m per day, which would subsequently be increased to 16 million cu m per day. Moreover, the contract contained an option for purchase of additional amounts of gas, not to exceed 30 million cu m per day, provided that these amounts were available and not required to supply the Bolivian market.

A transmission capacity option (TCO) was created as part of the funding structure of the project, whereby the purchaser could transport up to 6 million cu m per day above the amount stipulated in the contract by paying in advance for the operational costs of transport.[22] This option was available to all participants until construction of the gas pipeline began, at which time Petrobras took advantage of the option, thereby excluding others.

In September 2000, following negotiations with Agencia Nacional de Petróleo de Brasil (ANP), Enron signed a contract with Petrobras, whereby the company was granted the right to transport natural gas (1 million cu m per day) from Bolivia to Brazil via the gas pipeline connecting the two countries. Thus, eight years after the project began, the principle of open access to

---

[22] Additional capacity above the volume handled by TCO until maximum pipeline capacity was reached was known by the project as "extra transmission capacity" or "TCX."

independent traders not associated with Petrobras was implemented for the first time.

During that same year, Enron was eventually authorized by the regulatory agency of the Brazilian electricity sector to import 150 megawatts (MW) of electricity from Bolivia. Consequently, Enron plans to construct a thermal electric generation plant in Porto Suarez, a town located on the Bolivian-Brazilian border. Since the price of natural gas in Bolivia is US0.90¢ per million BTU, while, in Brazil, the lowest price is US$2.26 for the same quantity, Enron will sell the electricity produced at the Porto Suarez plant to Electro, the subsidiary distributor of San Pablo. According to reports published by *Brasil Energía* magazine, Enron expects to complete both the Porto Suarez project and the Cuiaba combined-cycle plant in 2003. This combined-cycle generating plant, which is the property of Enron,[23] is located close to a node in the Bolivia-Brazil gas pipeline. The plant is slated for natural gas supplied by Argentina, where Enron is a shareholder in Transportadora Gas del Sur, which owns the segment of the gas pipeline running within Argentina's borders.

Enron's conduct clearly exemplified the trend toward horizontal integration of Argentinean and Bolivian basins with Brazilian centers of consumption, as well as vertical integration between natural gas and electric power generation.[24]

Mercosur Countries

In December 1999, full members of Mercosur—Argentina, Brazil, Paraguay, and Uruguay—signed a memorandum of understanding (MOU) on gas exchange between the state parties of the region. As part of this agreement, the countries pledged to "develop a competitive gas supply market in the short and long term, by offering to the agents of supply and demand of the sector in each state party, conditions of nondiscriminatory treatment and the possibility of access to the market of the region."

Article 9 of the MOU specifies that access to remaining capacity of transport and distribution facilities must be respected, including access to international interconnections. The Article further states that companies may not discriminate on the basis of nationality, destination (internal or

---

[23] Statements of the President of Enron for South America, Michel Guerriero, to Buenos Aires Económico (BAE), January 13, 2000.

[24] Given the recent Enron debacle, the trend is likely to change.

external) of natural gas, or public or private ownership; in addition, companies must respect regulated usage rates and contracts currently in force. In addition, Article 14 establishes protection against monopolistic practices and abuse of dominant position for all users of natural gas.

This MOU has been critical since it was designed to ensure that the mistakes made in Bolivia, Argentina, and Brazil were not repeated. In that earlier experience, two companies—YPF and Petrobras—either prevented or hindered the participation of rival companies in shaping a competitive energy market.

More companies have begun participating in the market as a result of agreements that ensure unrestricted entry and participation. Gas integration between Argentina and Bolivia became viable because the TGN network was extended to the Brazilian border.[25] Afterward, it became interconnected with Transportadora de Gas del Mercosur (TGM) within Brazil's borders. It is noteworthy that AES is building a 600-MW, combined-cycle plant in Uruguayana (Brazil) that will be fed by gas produced and transported from the Neuquén Basin by TGN, whose shareholders include TotalfinaElf.[26]

Moreover, construction of the Santa Cruz gas pipeline, which links Punta Lara in Argentina to Colonia and Montevideo in Uruguay, is now under way. The contract for pipeline construction was awarded to a consortium comprising Pan American Energy (40 percent), British Gas (40 percent), and Ancap (20 percent). Eventually, Transportadora Gas del Sur will complete the extension in Argentina to Punta Lara.

Plans are being made to extend the pipeline to Porto Alegre so that the connection between the Neuquén and Austral fields will meet Brazil's demand. This project is viable only because of the extraordinarily high demand found between these two points in the cities of Buenos Aires and Montevideo. Consumption rates in both cities are so high that it will help cover the sunk costs of extending the connections.

---

[25] Export of electricity has also been significant as a result of Enersis' major role in Yacilec.

[26] In 2000, Gener (currently owned by AES) and TotalfinaElf formed a strategic alliance. Even though voided a month later, it was symbolic of these companies' intent to integrate the natural gas production business. TotalfinaElf has a significant share in Bolivia, is the second-largest producer in Argentina, and has a share in the main gas pipelines (Gas Andes, TGN, Transportadora de Gas del Mercosur), with the electric power generation business, in which AES is the top regional producer.

Argentina-Chile Agreement

In July 1955, Argentina and Chile signed a joint economic agreement, known as the "complementary economic agreement," whereby standards regulating natural gas interconnection and supply between the two countries were set forth. Article 2 of this agreement provides that "the parties shall not place restrictions on producers and other users of natural gas from Argentina and from Chile to export gas to the neighboring country on the basis of their properly certified reserves and availability, for which exporters and importers make a commitment." Article 6 further specifies that operation of the gas pipelines will be governed by a system of open access.

Energy integration between Argentina and Chile has been extensive and diverse, as a result of this agreement. Completed infrastructure works include the gas pipelines of Magallenes (methanol exporter) in the southern zone; Gas Pacífico and Gas Andes, which transport natural gas from the Neuquén and Mendocina basins to the Central Interconnected of Chile (SIC), where the main generators (Enersis, Gener, and Colbún) have built combined-cycle power plants. In northern Argentina, the Norandino and Gas Atacama gas pipelines provide natural gas from the Noreste Basin for the Northern Inter-connected System (SING) of Chile, where increasing energy demand, fueled by the mining sector, is expected to rise 15-20 percent over the coming years.

It should also be noted that the Termoandes combined-cycle plant was built near the wellheads of the Noroeste basin, and electricity is being exported to Chile via Interandes high-tension lines into the SING. These examples show that integration can be achieved using high-tension line networks that transmit gas-produced electricity instead of transporting the fuel to the consumer country and generating electricity at the final destination.

Bolivia-Peru: Expanding the Regional Market

Producer countries, such as Peru, could provide another alternative in the quest for diversification of supply in a market whose integration is planned by incumbent companies.

Carlos Salinas, President of YPFB, stated that plans are under way to build a gas pipeline from the Bolivian gas reserves site to the Peruvian port of Ilo for export of LPG. Salinas further commented that plans are being developed for constructing a larger gas pipeline connecting the gas fields of Camisea in Peru with Bolivia and for subsequent distribution to the Brazilian transport network via the Bolivia-Brazil gas pipeline.

Bringing Peruvian gas into Bolivia would also make it possible to supply the Argentinean and Chilean market. This could be achieved by using the pipeline that connects Bolivia to Argentina and the Norandino and Gas Atacama pipelines, which connect Argentina to Chile.

Looking Ahead

It is hoped that further development of natural gas pipelines in the Southern Cone region of South America will come about as use of natural gas in the overall energy mix of Chile and Brazil, as well as Argentina, increases. By 2010, it is estimated that natural gas use in Brazil will rise to 12 percent.[27] By 2005, use in Chile will account for 23 percent of the country's energy mix, compared with only 7 percent in 1994 (Jadresic 1999). Construction of the pipeline extension between Buenos Aires and Montevideo to Porto Alegre, which recently began, illustrates the rapid pace of development, since this project was not even in the planning stages as recently as 1996.[28]

Natural gas pipelines can facilitate development of a competitive, integrated gas market to the extent that two requirements are met. First, national governments must eliminate economic and administrative roadblocks to pipeline development. This can be accomplished through economic integration agreements, like those of Mercosur and the Andean Group. Such agreements can avoid unnecessary delays, such as the recent incident of Camisea, where the Peruvian government postponed construction for several years.

Second, countries in the region must guarantee competition between producers of natural gas by setting clear regulations regarding open access to networks. The cases presented in this chapter—YPF in Argentina and Petrobras in Brazil—illustrate the danger of dominant producers abusing their position and the regulatory roadblocks their potential competitors face as a result of the dominant producers' privileged arrangements with national governments.

Even though YPF has pledged to cut down on trading in third-party produced gas and to phase out most-favored-customer clauses in its contracts, these steps alone cannot increase competition in the natural gas market of the Southern Cone. Similarly, the authorization granted to Enron to

---

[27] Information provided by Carta Petrolera (October 1997).

[28] See Revista CIER (September 1996).

sell gas using the pipeline between Bolivia and Brazil does not suffice. To progress in developing these markets and accelerate investment in new transport networks, it is essential to ensure that:

- YPF's 1999 pledge to divest its assets is completed.
- YPF and its contractual agreements with Petrobras do not monopolize Bolivia's natural gas production market.
- National and regional antitrust agencies examine the effects of alliances between dominant regional actors on how integrated markets work (such as the recent agreements between Petrobras and YPF for participating in joint ventures in Venezuela and Trinidad and Tobago and the exchange of assets in Argentina and Brazil).
- Natural gas producers in Bolivia and, in the future, Peru, can supply Argentinean and Brazilian markets and have open access to the pipelines that connect the national systems, regardless of who owns these lines.

References

Balzaorotti, N. 1999. *Antitrust en el mercado de gas natural.* Serie Textos de la Discusión No. 10. Buenos Aires: Centro de Estudios Económicos de la Regulación.

Bogo, J. 2000. "La privatización de un campeón nacional: El caso de YPF en Argentina." *Boletín Latinoamericano de Competencia* 10(1): 34.

Buenos Aires Económico, January 13, 2000.

ENARGAS. 1994–1999. *Annual Reports,* Buenos Aires: Ente Nacional Regulador del Gas.

————. 1999. "Actualización tarifaria por cambios en el precio del gas en boca de pozo." File 4,943. Buenos Aires: Ente Nacional Regulador del Gas.

————. 2000. "Competencia y monopolio en los mercados de gas y electricidad." Course presented by Héctor Formica at Ceare, October 2000.

Jadresic, A. 1999. "Investment in Natural Gas Pipelines in the Southern Cone of Latin America." Working Paper No. 2,315. World Bank, Washington, D.C.

Law, P., and N. de Franco. 1998. "International Gas Trade: The Bolivian-Brazil Gas Pipeline." Private Sector and Infrastructure Network, Note 144. World Bank, Washington, D.C.

Novara, J. 1997. "Precios internos y de exportación de gas natural y gas licuado de petróleo: ¿Diferenciación o discriminación de precios en el mercado interno?" *Estudios* XX: 83.

————. 1998. "Las reservas de gas natural ante los crecientes requerimientos de los mercados internos y de exportación." *Estudios* XXI: 85.

Osmusden, P., F. Asche, and R. Tveteras. 2000. "European Market Integration for Gas?: Volume Flexibility and Political Risk." Working Paper No. 358. Munich: Center for Economic Studies and Institute for Economic Research.

Stewart, M. 1990. "Antitrust and the Economics of Natural Gas." Working Paper No. 5. White Plains, NY: National Economic Research Associates.

Visintini, A. 1993. Integración gasífera entre Argentina, Brasil, y Bolivia. ENARGAS, Buenos Aires. Mimeographed.

Chapter 4

Colombia's Natural Gas Industry: A Competition Failure

Alfredo García

Development of the natural gas sector in Colombia began in the early 1980s when Ecopetrol, the country's gas monopoly, implemented an aggressive fuel substitution strategy. Initially, the gas industry was vertically integrated to ensure coordination of investments and operations (production, transport, distribution, and retail). In the early 1990s, the gas sector—along with the water, electricity, and telecommunications sectors—was restructured. The reforms had three main components. First, the state took on a new role as regulator, delegating provision and management of services to the private sector. Second, competition was enabled in those segments where a natural monopoly no longer existed; consequently, the natural gas industry underwent a vertical separation of businesses, and new restrictions were imposed on horizontal and vertical integration. Third, an independent regulatory agency was created for the industry.

Overview of the Institutional Structure

Within the new institutional structure, the Energy and Gas Regulatory Commission (CREG) assumed functions previously assigned to the Petrol and Natural Gas Prices Commission (CPCGN) and the National Tariff Board. Compared with its previous mode of operation, the CREG is now reasonably independent from the executive power. Fixed terms have been established for its members, and it has a degree of budgetary autonomy. On the other hand, the Ministry of Mining and Energy (MEM) and its dependent entities, including the Mining-Energy Planning Unit (UPME), are in charge of defining the energy sector's policies. The subtle differences between policy and regulatory-making processes have frequently caused controversies between institutions. The Minister of MEM presides over CREG sessions and approves all new resolutions, and serves as the de facto chairman of the board of many state-owned natural gas firms. The result is a weak separation between industry regulation and the management concerns of state-owned enterprises.

The Colombian natural gas market is composed of gas producers—mainly oil companies—who produce and commercialize gas through their association contracts with Ecopetrol, which has traditionally been viewed as a complement to oil commercialization; distribution and commercialization companies; and large users—mainly gas-fired power plants—that were attracted to the market by deregulation of the electricity sector, coupled with a history of low gas prices.

Although increasing competition was a goal of the reforms undertaken in the 1990s, competition in Colombia's gas sector remains largely ineffective. Understanding why requires critiquing the industry's regulatory framework, ownership structure, and legal framework—the primary focus of this chapter.

Regulatory Framework

Constructing the regulatory framework for Colombia's natural gas industry is a work in progress. The core body of regulations governing the operation of pipelines and secondary market transactions associated with short-term trading have just recently been implemented. The National Council on Natural Gas Operation, the institution charged with oversight of implementation, was created only recently. A scheme for rationing demand in times of shortage has not yet been defined. Once completed, this scheme will surely affect the contractual nature of potential gas exports to neighboring countries, which may radically alter the industry's structure. Finally, in the area of energy policy, no measures have been taken to eliminate subsidies for other fuels, such as propane, that compete unfairly with natural gas. Such fuel substitutes may explain, at least in part, the relatively low penetration of natural gas into new markets.

Structural Definitions

The legal foundation for CREG's regulatory role is derived from Public Service Law (Law 142/94), which includes specific articles that address natural gas as a public service. Based on the electricity sector model, the functional structure of the natural gas industry is defined as follows:

- *Producer*—A firm that extracts or produces natural gas of a quality that conforms to regulated standards.
- *Retailer*—A firm whose activity is the commercialization of combustible gas (a retailer may or may not be a producer).
- *Transporter*—A firm that provides the service of transporting natural gas by pipelines through specified points of entry and delivery.
- *Gas distributor by networks*—A firm that provides the public service of distributing natural gas through mid or low-pressure pipeline networks.
- *Nonregulated Customer*—Consumer of more than 500,000 cubic feet per day (cfd) (effective through December 31, 2001), of more than 300,000 cfd (effective through December 31, 2004), and of more than 100,000 cfd (beginning January 1, 2005). Demand is measured at only one delivery point.

Limits to Structural Integration

Restrictions on horizontal integration of the gas industry follow those of the electricity sector. Nevertheless, while the electricity sector has reached a high degree of market saturation, the gas industry still has many economies of scale to attain, and many areas of the country remain in the initial stages of market penetration and consolidation.

Lack of institutional ability to monitor, detect, and punish potential abuses has justified horizontal restrictions to date. In fact, many resolutions emphasize the need to prevent establishment, rather than control abuse, of dominant positions. No mention is made of the possible deadweight losses derived from potential economies of scale and scope that are consequentially neglected.

The formal limitations to vertical and horizontal integration are as follows:

- No retailer, acting alone or through a company, can sell more than 25 percent of the total national volume of transactions. Nevertheless, the selling of natural gas to electricity generation firms is excluded from this limitation.

- Producers cannot own more than 25 percent of total shares of any gas-fired electricity generation firm. During the transition period, however, they are allowed to own up to 50 percent of those plants that became operational prior to November 2, 2000, provided they decrease their ownership to 25 percent within five years of operating the respective plants. Transporters have the same 25-percent ownership requirement if the power plants in question are located in the service area.

- Transporters cannot retain more than 25 percent of the shares of a distributor, retailer, or nonregulated customer. In addition, they cannot participate in contracts with distributors or retailers for utility sharing, cost reduction, or risk mitigation.

- Producers, distributors, and retailers cannot own more than 25 percent of transporter shares; they cannot agree in statute or through contractual mechanisms to anything that would give them influence over price-fixing and other transport service conditions. Moreover, they cannot grant credits to affiliates under more favorable conditions than those of the market. Finally, no producer can own more than 20 percent of a distributor; if several producers are shareholders, they cannot collectively own more than the 30 percent of shares.

- Beginning in 2005, no distributor will be allowed to service more than 30 percent of the consumers connected to the country's local networks. Any company that exceeds that limit will not be permitted to acquire shares or control existing or new distribution companies, and divestiture may be mandated.

These restrictions do not apply to companies formed before Law 142 was enacted. Nonetheless, these companies are subject to the accounting unbundling of business activities. For example, Ecopetrol was ordered to divest its shares from distributors and retailers by December 31, 1997 (this process was successfully completed). Finally, gas producers and retailers must sell their gas separately. This rule applies to gas extracted under association, as well as to other types of contracts.

Price Regulation

On October 7, 1975, the CPCGN enacted Resolution 039, which regulated natural gas prices for Guajira fields.[1] These prices were indexed bi-annually with fuel oil prices (free on board Cartagena). On July 22, 1983, through Resolution 061, CPCGN issued price regulations for other fields (including offshore fields) along the Caribbean coast and in the Magdalena valley, using the same indexing scheme.

Since 1995, CREG has issued a series of resolutions that regulate transport and distribution pipeline rates and wholesale retailing margins. Enacted July 30, 1996, Resolution 057 incorporated all relevant regulations to date. Together, Resolutions 029 (enacted in 1995) and 059 (enacted in 1996) established a program to liberalize wholesale gas prices progressively. These two resolutions defined four natural gas categories and determined that, from 2005 on:

- Prices will be freely determined for exploration and exploitation contracts signed after September 11, 1995.
- Prices will be freely set from September 10, 2005 for reserves discovered during the contractual periods for exploration and exploitation signed before September 11, 1995.
- Differences in the regulatory treatment of free and associated gas may have been justified in light of the common cost nature of investments for oil and gas production.

The announced commitment to price liberalization, which aimed to encourage new explorations, has largely failed. One possible explanation is that the scale of the Colombian market may not have been sufficiently large to justify investment in gas exploration on a stand-alone basis. The risky nature of investing in exploration is a peculiar aspect of the gas market, which is shared, not surprisingly, by the oil market. The proposed unconditional liberalization did not consider the increasing monopolization of the activity. Unlike other industries, entry of new agents in the gas industry depends not only on the attractiveness of the business, but also on the effectiveness of uncertain exploration efforts. Such idiosyncratic risk is particularly high in Colombia, with its few oil and gas basins.

---

[1] US$0.80 per Kcf (nonelectric use); US$0.50 per Kcf (electric use only).

TABLE 4-1. CONTROL OF COLOMBIA'S NATURAL GAS RESERVES, 1999

Production field	Proven reserves Gas production capacity	%	Ecopetrol %	State royalties %	Texaco %	BP %
Opon	45-90	0.7-1.4	40	20		24
Others	316	4.6	40	20		
Piedemonte	390	5.7	40	20		
Cuisiana	3,004	44.2	40	20		15.2
Guajira	2,995	44.0	40	20	40	
Total	6,800	100	40	20	17.6	7.5

Source: Ecopetrol.

Ownership Structure

Concentration of Ownership

Ecopetrol controls, either directly or indirectly, a large proportion of Colombia's overall natural gas production capacity. Special legal features help explain this fact. First, constitutional law requires that exploration activities be implemented through association contracts (similar to joint venture contracts, whereby parties agree ex ante on cost and revenue allocation) between Ecopetrol and private companies. Second, Ecopetrol effectively commercializes the natural gas associated with royalties due to the Colombian state (20 percent of all discovered fields). As a result, Ecopetrol controls (directly and indirectly) 60 percent of available production capacity (table 4-1).

The value of the Herfindahl-Hirshmann index, including the special status of royalty gas, is 4,014, a much higher figure than traditional standards used to evaluate the competitiveness in a given market.[2] For example, if a retailer independent of Ecopetrol were given the task of commercializing the gas royalty, the value of the index would fall to 2,414, a figure more consistent with international standards in assuring a reasonably competitive market.

Distribution and commercialization for retail users is less concentrated and has an index of 2,128 (table 4-2). However, in practice, only three investment holdings effectively control nearly all distribution companies.

---

[2] For example, in its regular screening of mergers, FERC uses a figure of 2,500 as a proxy for potential problems.

TABLE 4-2. STRUCTURE OF GAS DISTRIBUTION, 1999

Company	Number of users	Participation (%)
Madigas engineers	397	0.03
Public companies in Medellin	228	0.01
Gas from Cuisiana	5,703	0.36
Alcanos from Colombia	73,197	4.63
Occident Gas Company	25,174	1.59
Natural gas of the Caesar	6,797	0.43
Metrogas	41,272	2.61
Gas from the Quindio	2,702	0.17
Gas from Risaralda	2,409	0.15
Gas from La Guajira	27,817	1.76
Gas from north of valley	4,196	0.27
Natural gas from the Center	4,318	0.27
Gas from Llano	59,271	3.75
Gas from Barrancabermeja	36,433	2.31
Orient Natural Gas	137,895	8.73
Natural Gas	573,664	36.31
Caribbean Gas Provider	254,482	16.11
Gas from the Caribbean	324,033	20.51
Total	1,579,988	

Source: CREG.

Evaluation of Integration Restrictions

The strict limitations imposed on vertical and horizontal integration appear justified by the general perception of institutional weaknesses regarding enforcement of competition law. Thus, it is feared that violations of competition law will not be detected, which may effectively undermine political support for the restructuring process. This preventive approach to competition policy may carry a social cost associated with the latent economies of scale and coordination that could emerge with more flexible regulations. Despite this conceptual justification, there are serious concerns about CREG's implementation of this preventive approach.

Relevant Markets

Analysis of competition in a given market starts with defining the term relevant market. This involves the concept of substitution in the line of products under consideration. It also includes the geographic component associated with transport costs and logistics necessary to deliver products to the location of demand. This means that the geographic extent of a relevant market is determined by the arbitraging possibilities limited by the economics of logistics.

The international application of competition law has traditionally used two lines of reference to define relevant market: the specific product and geographic extent. An estimation of cross-elasticity of demand among potential substitutes is the basis for analyzing specific product features. As stated above, the geographic extent of the market is determined by arbitraging costs. In defining the limits to vertical and horizontal integration, CREG resolutions only marginally consider the possible substitution of natural gas for other fuels. No mention is made of the geographic extent of the relevant markets considered.

Not considering the substitute products for natural gas (liquefied petroleum gas [LPG], electricity, and coal) when defining the limits to vertical and horizontal integration is a significant error in methodology, considering that many distribution firms are still in the process of market penetration and consolidation. Setting a horizontal limit as a maximum share of the total number of customers nationwide appears as a disincentive for newer firms to increase market penetration. On the other hand, not accounting for the demand of thermoelectric plants and petrochemical industries for natural gas when the limits to horizontal integration are calculated for retailing appears to contradict the entire "preventive" strategy. In essence, most demand concentrates on these two types of users. Not accounting for them simply exempts Ecopetrol, the larger retailer, from the restrictions.

Need for Flexible Approach to Vertical Integration

Given that most of the framework for pricing access to pipelines and ensuring nondiscriminatory service is already in place, the existing restrictions to vertical integration, which were justified initially to ensure open and fair access, may be obsolete. Recently, a decentralized institutional structure for governance was put in place. The National Gas Operational Council will have representatives of all activities in the natural gas supply chain that will vote to adopt changes to the pipeline operational rules, including short-term capacity trading.

Regarding the vertical relationships between natural gas transport and distribution companies, participants have many opportunities to engage in opportunistic behavior. Vertical integration is often cited as a means to avoid such behavior, particularly when there are sunk or irreversible investments. For example, in the absence of vertical integration, a distribution company may choose a strategy of "high margins, low volume," which may be attractive under an average-revenue regulatory scheme. The strategy will not be profitable for the pipeline, which would do better with higher capacity utilization. The strategy is facilitated by the flexibility implicit in an average-revenue regulation scheme for the distribution company; in turn, the distribution company may abuse the sunk or irreversible investment in transport pipelines.

Interestingly, an example along Colombia's Caribbean coast illustrates the benefits of a more flexible approach to vertical integration. This market has, by far, the fastest, most consolidated growth in natural gas demand, and its transport and distribution businesses have always been vertically integrated. Without vertical integration, joint marketing efforts, such as an aggressive campaign to promote use of gas-fueled household appliances, would have been impossible.

Another interesting case is the relationship between thermoelectric power generation companies and gas producers. Opportunism is provoked by lack of a competitive gas market; this is an inappropriate regulation, given the market's structure and strict vertical restrictions. Such opportunism may have emerged in high "take-or-pay" contract clauses. These clauses may have led to operational problems in the electricity market (such as water spillage in hydroelectric plants resulting from thermal plants bidding zero marginal costs), creating an inefficient use of the system's energy resources.

In this case, the issue is the socially efficient allocation of risk associated with infrastructure investments. Gas producers claim that high take-or-pay clauses are needed to save them from volatile thermal plant consumption (which, in turn, is caused by the country's high dependency on hydroelectric power). Merchant power plants, on the other hand, claim that they lose financial viability under such contracts. Clearly, this is an obstacle to one of the promises of deregulation: in an open electricity market, small players, such as small-scale merchant plants, would control wholesale electricity prices. In short, restructuring has created the need to rethink the efficient allocation of risks. Under the former regime, risks were fully internalized through cost-of-service regulation; now, they are re-allocated in a vertically disintegrated world in potentially inefficient ways.

Association Contract to Increase Market Concentration

Natural gas production in Colombia is carried out through association contracts. These contracts generally result from competitive tenders, in which Ecopetrol awards exclusivity over certain geographic areas for exploration of potential production. Owing to its special state-owned status, Ecopetrol automatically obtains property rights over 40 percent of the gas reserves to be discovered. Under the current royalty scheme, the nation is the claimant of 20 percent of these undiscovered reserves.

Historically, Ecopetrol traded the gas produced under these contracts on behalf of the associated company. This scheme helped ensure market penetration and other fuel substitution goals that were pursued in the early years of market consolidation. Within the context of the new regulatory framework, however, the association contract perpetuates Ecopetrol's dominant position in natural gas production. Another drawback of this arrangement is that price coordination, in the event of full price liberalization, is highly possible, given the commercial information flow between all market producers and Ecopetrol.[3]

Ecopetrol's current president has publicly expressed that concern about consolidation of its dominant position without any regulation in place is unwarranted, given that the company belongs to all Colombians (*El Tiempo* 2000). In other words, in this president's view, a public monopoly is not bad per se. It can adversely affect consumer welfare, as can a private monopoly. Although a form of political control of potential abuses exists, this also lends itself to corruption. This possibility must not be underestimated in developing countries, such as Colombia. With weak institutions, state-owned companies always have "owners," much like shareholders, with well-defined rights and obligations. They usually take the form of political barons with clientele or labor unions that wield disproportionate influence on the company's decisionmaking.

Competition Law and Sector Institutions

Article 333 of Colombia's 1991 political constitution ends by stating: "The State upon legal mandate will impede the obstruction or the restriction of the economic freedom and will prevent or control any abuse by persons or companies regarding their dominant position in the National market." The final words of this key article were the subject of great controversy during discussions that led up to the final drafting of the new political act in Colombia. Hernando Agudelo Villa (1999) states that the initial wording was as follows: "The State upon legal mandate will impede the obstruction or the restriction

---

[3] This structure was inherent in the oil exploration contract system. The first contract whose sole purpose was gas (not oil) exploration was signed in 1998.

of the economic freedom and competition or will end monopolies, and will control any kind of market dominance that adversely affects consumers."

The not so subtle differences between the two texts suggest the ideological struggle that occurred. The prevailing view was that, in small-economy countries, exploitation of economies of scale must prevail over the need for more competition; therefore, allowing a certain degree of market concentration was considered socially efficient. Dominant positions were to be tolerated, and the state's role was to focus on the effective ex post control of potential abuses. Nonetheless, the final text clearly gave the state ample room for taking measures to prevent abuses.

Applying Competition Law to the Gas Industry

Law 155 and Decree 2,153

Colombia's first important competition law, Law 155, was enacted in 1959 (one year after the Treaty of Rome was signed). The first article of this law forbids agreements that, directly or indirectly, imply limitations to production, supply, and distribution of domestic and/or foreign raw materials or inputs to any business.

In accordance with the Sherman Act and Article 85 of the Treaty of Rome, Law 155 outlawed all practices that restricted competition. The second article of this law established that companies with the capacity to fix market prices owing to their high market share were subject to monitoring by the relevant government agency. The third article compelled companies of a certain size to inform the government when merging, consolidating, or integrating their financial and commercial operations. Under this article, the government had to object to these operations when they tended to restrict competition unnecessarily. The fifth article established a set of rules to determine potential conflicts of interest between members of the governing boards and company managers.

In 1964, Law 155 was quickly neutralized by Regulatory Decree 1,302, which exempted sectors considered strategically important to the country (such as metal-mechanic; textiles; and state-owned companies, which, at that time, provided nearly all residential public services) from adhering to the rule. Therefore, in general, Law 155 had a limited application, particularly in the natural gas sector.

Chapter 5 of Decree 2,153 of 1992 described various business practices that may hinder competition. (This compendium was more precise and broader in scope than Law 155.) In Article 45 of the decree, the concept of dominant market position is developed at great length, and is succinctly defined as the "possibility to determine, directly or indirectly, the conditions for a given market, such as price, quality, and quantities."

Although Law 155 and Decree 2,153 established, in principle, a reasonably modern legal framework for competition law in Colombia, their enforcement has been the subject of debate. Previous government administrations carefully avoided the effective enforcement of these pieces of legislation on the grounds that substantial economies of scale needed to be exploited in order to provide public services—electricity, gas, and telecommunications—which, at that time, were the state's direct responsibility. Whether these exemptions should be transferred to new private investors that have since assumed control of state-owned public service companies is also a matter of debate.

The Minister of Mining and Energy exemplifies the practices tolerated under these exemptions. This individual can concurrently serve as president of those companies' boards of administration and, in the capacity of CREG chairman, their regulator.

Law 142 and Decree 1,165

Law 142 of 1994, which restructured provision of public services, delegated the monitoring and prevention of potential abuses to each sector-specific regulatory commission. Article 73 lays out these functions as follows:

> The regulatory commissions regulate the provision of public services by monopolies, when competition is not, in fact, possible; and, in the other cases, will promote the competition between public service providers. The purpose of these commissions is to ensure the economically efficient operation of providers, preventing the abuse of dominant position, and ensuring quality of service. (Article 73, Law 142)

This law designated the office of the Public Service Superintendent as the institution responsible for monitoring and enforcing compliance with the regulatory compact of public service providers. In particular, this office supervised compliance with sector-specific norms on competition in electricity and gas markets. Nevertheless, Decree 1,165, enacted in 1999, returned all legal responsibility to the office of the Industry and Commerce Superintendent, presumably to avoid duplicated efforts.

Article 7 of Decree 1,165 describes functions related to restrictive commercial practices as follows:

> In cases relevant to dispositions related to the promotion of competition and restrictive commercial practices contemplated in Law 155 in 1959, in Decree 2153 in 1992, and also for those related to restrictive business practices, as described in the present legislation and other competition norms, the Industry and Commerce Superintendent shall act as the Public Service Superintendent. (Article 7, Decree 1,165)

This back and forth between government agency duties reflects the debate between these agencies on whether enforcement of competition law should reside in a single entity for all economic activities or be decentralized in sector-specific agencies.

In 1999, the constitutional court declared Decree 1,165 unconstitutional because it exceeded certain temporary special powers conferred on the president. Currently, there is much confusion about which institution has immediate jurisdiction to enforce competition law in providing public services.

An Example of Institutional Conflict

As of October 2000, Ecopetrol, which is subject to CREG regulations, had not paid the fees it owes CREG. (CREG has an independent budget financed by relatively small fees charged to all regulated companies.) Following Ecopetrol's example, another gas production company, Texaco, refrained from paying its mandatory fees. Both Ecopetrol and Texaco argued that, because gas production was not subject to CREG regulation, they were entitled to an exemption. Recently, CREG initiated a judicial process to enforce Ecopetrol's payment of the fee (Texaco finally agreed to pay).

The apparent controversy about the validity of the assessed fees is based on Law 142, which outlines the scope and jurisdiction of sector-specific regulatory commissions. This law applies to the provision of water, sewage services, electricity, gas transportation, distribution and retail, local telephony, and local mobile telephony in the rural sector, all of which are considered residential public services; it also applies to other activities performed by public service providers as listed in Article 15 of the present law, and to complementary activities defined in chapter 2 of the present title and to other services provided in special norms of this law. (Article 1, Law 142)

Ecopetrol and Texaco argued that gas production was not mentioned in this wording. In response, CREG stated that gas production fits perfectly into what the law defines as "a complementary activity" to the gas distribution public service:

> These are the activities that are referred to in this law when defining each public service. When public services are mentioned in this law, without specifying which public service, we understand that such activities are included. (Article 14.2, Law 142)

Although it may seem rather trivial, this incident illustrates the overall dismissive attitude of established, dominant production players toward regulation.

Potential for Abusive Contractual Practices

Within the context of restructuring, the vertical relationship between the gas and electricity sectors has motivated many debates on the optimal risk allocation between industries.

Under the previous cost-of-service regulatory scheme, electric companies were generally assigned all risks in the production chain; they accepted take-or-pay clauses because they could easily transfer these fixed obligations to consumers. Under the vertical disintegration that ensued, restructuring this automatic transfer of obligations was no longer possible. In particular, it seemed that take-or-pay clauses did not fit the need for diversifying business risks along the supply chain. Nevertheless, Colombia's gas providers have continued to impose exorbitant take-or-pay clauses on gas-fired thermal plants.

A monopoly in natural gas production will extract all rents from downstream power plants. It does so by setting a variable charge equal to the marginal production cost and a fixed charge equal to the net benefit of downstream power plants. It is noteworthy that the utilization factor for different technologies is a function of the wholesale price of electricity. Interestingly, this "perfect" discrimination by the upstream gas monopoly does not affect operative efficiency in the dispatch of plants because a monopoly will impose higher charges on plants, depending on the economic merit (marginal cost ranking for electricity production), to maximize rents.

It follows that base-load plants will be subject to higher fixed payments than peaking plants. On the contrary, if a perfectly competitive market for providing gas existed, the fixed charge payment would equal the expected value of the plant's use, multiplied by the average cost of gas production. Any higher charge would be controlled through competition; any smaller charge would imply that the gas producer assumed a higher volume risk, which would be compensated by a premium in the variable charge. In both cases—an upstream monopoly and a perfectly competitive market—the downstream dispatch of plants would be efficient under the two-part pricing schemes discussed. Distribution of income and risks along the supply chain, however, would differ.

This rather theoretical discussion puts the current status of gas procurement by thermal plants in perspective. A sample of the contracts in force in 1999 shows that power generation companies are obligated to buy a fixed quantity of gas equivalent to 70 percent of the plants' maximum production capacity.[4] Moreover, the long-term utilization factors of these plants do not even equal 50 percent of plant capacity. This implies that electric companies are obligated to pay a gas surplus that they do not use. Existence of such contracts is explained by the market power of the country's gas producers.

Imposing high take-or-pay clauses in contracts that provide gas does not follow the rationale of similar clauses in gas transport contracts. Nontransported gas implies foregone revenues for the pipeline, while nonconsumed gas implies a change in the interim consumption pattern and is not necessarily a change in the present value of income associated with its retail. While gas can be stored, transport capacity cannot. There is, however, a financial cost associated with different interim consumption patterns.

These contract schemes have prompted distortions in the electricity market's normal operations. Thermal plants with high take-or-pay contracts have repeatedly been dispatched before hydraulic plants that, on many occasions, have had to spill water.[5] Such socially inefficient use of natural resources is caused by the artificially low marginal cost of providing gas for thermal plants, in view of the take-or-pay obligations that exceed their long-term utilization factors.

---

[4] CREG filing to the office of the Superintendent of Industry and Commerce, February 2000.

[5] The hourly dispatch of electricity is made according to merit order; that is, ranking of bids ($ per MWh) by power plants.

Wholesale Price Liberalization and Concentration: Open Debate

Recently, a congressional block, with the consent of Colombia's Minister of Mines and Energy, proposed legislation (Law Project 308, year 2000) that would end CREG's price regulation authority and allow natural gas prices to be set in a free market.

Defenders of this measure argue that price liberalization will make exploitation of the Cuisiana reserves (property of Ecopetrol, BP, Total, and Triton) financially viable. Such exploitation is needed to cover long-term market needs (particularly in the country's interior region). Given that gas from this wellhead is mixed with oil, it has been argued that, only through price liberalization could partners of the Cuisiana association contract earn the fair opportunity cost associated with black oil losses.

Weakness in the Institutional Framework

Initiated in 2000, the price liberalization process has uncovered weaknesses in the natural gas industry's institutional framework because Law Project 308 contradicts valid CREG resolutions. Both the Minister of Mining and Energy and the Ecopetrol board of directors have defended this Law Project as the only way to avoid potential natural gas shortages projected to occur by 2003. Nevertheless, the Minister of Mining and Energy, in his role as CREG chairman, recently signed Resolution 23-2000, which modified the current price regulation scheme by limiting use of take-or-pay clauses and setting a condition for liberalizing gas prices, in the form of a minimum increment in production capacity at the Cuisiana wellhead.

The Law Project reveals a contradiction between government and CREG decisions, made worse by the dubious role played by the Minister. Apparently, the government and Ecopetrol (the dominant producer) turned to the legislature to overrule the regulation CREG drafted using valid institutional rules, including veto power of government ministers who participate in the CPCGN decisionmaking process.[6]

Support for price liberalization, even in the presence of Ecopetrol's dominant position, has been justified on grounds of social and political feasibility; since Ecopetrol is a state-owned company, any abuse will be subject to political control. Nevertheless, this vision of an entrepreneurial state con-

---

[6] Three CREG ministers represent the government, and approval of any resolution requires the consent of at least two government representatives.

tradicts that of a modern regulatory state, with well-defined limits, which characterized the spirit of Law 142.

Wellhead Pricing Problem

CREG's long-term equilibrium price estimates for Colombia's interior region show that, after geographically aggregating gas demand in a predetermined delivery point (Barrancas) through the net back difference and transport cost, the marginal producer in most future scenarios is Cuisiana (Betancour and Ramírez 1999). This means that Cuisiana gas has market power because its output is essential for supplying demand.

CREG's estimates of Cuisiana gas production costs were performed amid much uncertainty about the total amount of oil losses generated (because of the inability to re-inject gas). The value of US$1.10/MmBtu, which was adopted by the CPCGN, differs substantially from the $1.40/MmBtu used by the firms that own Cuisiana reserves. Such a discrepancy makes CREG price regulation extremely complex. Setting a regulated price for gas carries considerable risk for error. An alternative would be deregulating prices; however, given the potential for market power abuse, price deregulation must be made conditional in order to protect consumers.

One basic concern regarding unconditional price liberalization is the potential for price discrimination. Producers could capture a disproportionate amount of consumer surplus (the area below the demand curve based on equilibrium price). The aggregated demand curve varies when consumers have substitution facilities or have not incurred substantial sunk costs for natural gas use. In this sense, consumers who have already incurred conversion costs for natural gas consumption would be captive and easily subject to price discrimination. Such considerations have prompted CREG to openly oppose price liberalization (Portafolio 2000).

Conditional Price Deregulation as an Alternative

CREG Resolution 23-2000 proposed implementing an auction process for selling all or a portion of Ecopetrol gas in a deregulated price setting. These auctions would warrant greater transparency and avoid potential abuse. If new independent retailers were to trade the gas associated with royalties, then the Herfindahl Hirshmann index would fall within internationally acceptable limits. On the other hand, to guarantee a fair sale price, restrictions on the minimum number of auction offers could be imposed. Nevertheless, designing such auctions would involve such complex issues as separating financial from physical rights in wellheads of joint ownership and developing an adequate format for price and quantity bids.

Toward Effective Competition: Obstacles and Needs

Despite substantive, pro-market reforms undertaken during the 1990s, effective competition in Colombia's natural gas sector does not yet exist. Moreover, complete liberalization of wholesale prices, recently proposed, is unlikely to increase competitiveness, although it could consolidate established dominant positions in the market. Development of effective competition in this sector is restricted by the four mechanisms described below.

Obstacles

First, there is confusion about the functions and jurisdiction of institutions in the sector, particularly regarding enforcement of competition law and market liberalization. Even if general competition legislation establishes this jurisdiction within the office of the Superintendent of Industry and Commerce, the Public Service Law delegates enforcement of sector-specific competition norms to the Superintendent of Public Service.

Second, limits to vertical integration that can be characterized as excessive are apparently justified by perceived institutional weakness, coupled with lack of confidence in these institutions. It is probable that limits to vertical integration, originating in the inability of agents (producers, transporters, distributors, and large consumers) to coordinate their actions, may be causing severe inefficiencies. Given that substantial progress has been made to ensure nondiscriminatory access to pipelines, it would be desirable to alleviate certain restrictions, which would require competition authorities to play a larger role.

Third, the country's natural gas production market is highly concentrated because entry of new agents depends not only on the attractiveness of the business (as dictated by market prices), but also on the uncertain results of exploration efforts. Such idiosyncratic risk is critical in the Colombian context, where few gas basins exist.

Fourth, Ecopetrol's dominant position has not been won through the merits of efficiency or innovation, but through its special legal status, which the traditional practice of association contracts has perpetuated. Potential abuses, in the form of high take-or-pay clauses and reluctance to recognize CREG's jurisdiction as a regulatory entity, clearly demonstrate that Ecopetrol has held an extraordinary—and probably harmful—dominant market position.

Needed Measures

To achieve effective mid-term competitiveness in the wholesale gas sector, reducing Ecopetrol's market share appears as a necessary condition. Accomplishing this goal without resorting to extreme measures, such as divestiture, could take two forms. The first measure relates to the existing agreement for retailing of royalty gas. This gas could be sold through long-term public auctions that ensure transparency, competitiveness, and stable prices for market participants. The second measure would be to modify the association contract scheme that assigns Ecopetrol a major role in production of all new exploitable wells in Colombian territory. If the main concern is to guarantee that benefits of natural resource exploitation are translated into social well-being, then many alternative approaches can be used without necessarily awarding Ecopetrol an automatic dominant position in the market.

References

Agudelo Villa, Hernando. 1999. *De los Monopolios a la Democracia Económica*. Barcelona: Editorial Ariel.

Betancour, Felix, and M. Ramírez. 1999. *Consultant for the Regulatory Wellhead Price Revision*. Bogotá: Energy and Gas Regulatory Commission (CREG).

Coase, R. 1937. "The Nature of the Firm." *Economica* 4(13-16): 386–405.

El Tiempo. 2000. Ecopetrol Defends Gas Prices Liberalization Projects. *El Tiempo*, October 2.

Portafolio. 2000. Gas Price Freedom Confronts Ministry of Mining with the CREG. *Portafolio*, September 7.

Williamson, O. 1975. *Markets and Hierarchies: Analysis and Antitrust Implications*. New York: Free Press.

Chapter 5

Pricing Monopoly Segments of Regulated Industries in Developing Countries

Paulina Beato and Jean-Jacques Laffont

Traditionally, the organization of infrastructure sectors has been based on tightly regulated, integrated monopolies, without room for market forces. The model for this type of organization has been the natural monopoly, whereby infrastructure services are less costly because they are performed by a single, integrated firm rather than by several firms. This means that economies of scale and scope have supported the organization of infrastructure sectors around franchised, vertically integrated utilities.

In the mid 1980s, a consensus emerged in industrial countries that questioned the natural monopoly character of infrastructure sectors. It was thought that increasing returns might favor having one firm provide some, but not all, consumer services. For example, power services include transmission, distribution, and generation; while the first two services are considered natural monopolies, the latter is not. The reduced optimum size of power generating plants allows various firms to participate without losing profits derived from scale economies. As for scope economies among the segments of an infrastructure sector, the new consensus stated that, because of technological developments, transaction costs arising from unbundling of segments are minor compared with the efficiency costs of an integrated monopoly.

Market Structure Options

Three types of market structures can be envisioned for infrastructure industries: vertical disintegration, vertical integration, and competition. In vertical
disintegration, the firm controlling the bottleneck (the natural monopoly
segment) is not allowed to compete in the services that use the bottleneck as
an input. For example, the local telephone company, which owns the local
loop, is not allowed to compete in long-distance service, which requires the
local loop to access consumers. In vertical integration, the firm controlling
the bottleneck is one among many competitors that provide services using
the bottleneck as an input. In the competition structure, multiple, vertically
integrated firms control a bottleneck and provide the service. In all three
cases, regulation ensures open access to the bottleneck facilities.

The proper pricing of the monopoly segment is a necessary condition
for effective open access to bottleneck facilities. This is a difficult task because
such pricing schemes must arbitrate between many goals, including efficient
pricing, no bypass, and cost recovery. Regarding the incentive structure of
final price schemes, two options, at opposite extremes, are available. One
option is high-powered incentive schemes (such as price caps), which
encourage cost minimizing behavior, require less data from individual firms,
and yield large rents to the most efficient types of firms. The other option is
low-powered incentive schemes (such as cost-of-service regulation), which
control profits of efficient firms, require much internal information from
firms, and create weak incentives for minimizing costs.

Comparing the costs and benefits of various schemes depends on the
technological features of the infrastructure sector, as well as the sociopoliti-
cal environment in which the infrastructure services are provided. Although
general recommendations that are valid for each environment cannot be
made, certain rules for analyzing the cost-benefit implications of environmental features can be given. This chapter illustrates how, in developing
countries, the features of a country and sector conform to the relative advantages of various cost-regulation schemes.

Regulation and Development

Regulation of natural monopolies requires striking a balance between efficiency and cost of the information rents. High-powered incentive schemes (such as
price caps), which create cost-minimizing behavior, yield large rents to the

most efficient firms. Low-powered incentive schemes (such as cost-of-service regulation) control those rents but create weak incentives for minimizing costs.

High Cost of Public Funds

A major characteristic of developing countries is the high cost of public funds. Clearly, this high cost calls for higher prices of the commodities produced by the natural monopoly and lower-powered incentive schemes (high shares of cost reimbursement). Before presenting the intuitive reasoning behind these results, it is important to emphasize that perfect cost observability and the regulator's full commitment are assumed.

Intuitively, one knows that higher cost of public funds means higher cost of relinquishing rents and higher inefficiency cost. However, the relative cost of rents increases faster because, when an additional rent is relinquished to a particular firm to support an efficiency improvement, the same incentive must be provided to all of the more efficient firms. The optimal regulation sacrifices some efficiency in order to decrease such rents. Thus, this argument favors cost-plus schemes over fixed-price schemes or, in the language of regulatory theory, rate-of-return regulation over price caps.

In addition, higher cost of funds means that it is more valuable to price above marginal cost—to use public utility prices to finance fixed costs and the government's budget. It is a mistake, particularly in developing countries, to advocate marginal cost pricing for public utilities.

The implied pricing difference between developed and developing countries can be substantial, since a move in the cost of funds from 0.3 to 1 translates into a relative deviation from marginal cost, which is double in the second case. Since levels of effort also decrease as cost reimbursement rules are tilted toward cost-plus schemes, marginal costs are higher and, therefore, prices in developing countries should be even higher.

To illustrate this point, one can suppose three units of production, with costs $\beta_1 < \beta_2 < \beta_3$ at the zero level of effort induced by cost-plus regulation. As costs are fully reimbursed, no rent is relinquished to the firm and the consumers' bill is $\beta_1 + \beta_2 + \beta_3$ (figure 5-1, gray area). In each production unit, price-cap regulation induces an effort e^*, which decreases monetary cost by e^* at a disutility cost of $\psi(e^*)$ for the firm. Total costs are then $\tilde{\beta}_1 = \beta_1 - e^* + \psi(e^*)$, $\tilde{\beta}_2 = \beta_2 - e^* + \psi(e^*)$, and $\tilde{\beta}_3 = \beta_3 - e^* + \psi(e^*)$. Production of the less efficient unit calls for a price of $\tilde{\beta}_3$, hence a consumer bill of $3\tilde{\beta}_3$ (figure 5-1, dotted area).

If the firm's rent is not taken into account, the comparison between cost-plus and price-cap regulations is reduced to the difference of con-

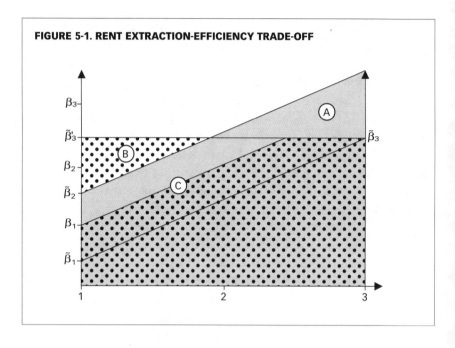

FIGURE 5-1. RENT EXTRACTION-EFFICIENCY TRADE-OFF

sumers' bills,[1] (the difference between the triangles A and B). If A > B (resp. A < B), then price cap (resp. cost plus) dominates. However, if the firm's rent (triangle $\tilde{\beta}_1\tilde{\beta}_3'\tilde{\beta}_3$ [figure 5-1, C]) enters the regulator's objective function with a weight, then price cap dominates if A - B < αC (that is, if the consumers' bill differential is less that the social valuation of the firm's rent). If the regulator does not care whether the rent is relinquished to the firm (α=1), then price cap always dominates (since C > B). However, when relinquishing a rent is socially costly, cost-plus regulation may dominate.

In such industries as rail and bus transport, where transfers of public money are possible, the cost of relinquishing a rent to the firm increases with the cost of public funds.[2] Accordingly, in developing countries with a high cost of public funds, the trade-off is tilted toward cost-plus regulation. However, in such industries as telecommunications and energy, where transfers are not allowed, the social weight attributed to the firm's profit does not bear any direct relationship to the cost of public funds, and the optimal trade-off

---

[1] For simplicity, it is assumed that the indivisibility is such that, under both types of regulation, all three units are operative.

[2] The reason is that each unit of account taken from the firm allows a decrease of the deadweight loss of the tax needed to raise one unit of account (Laffont and Tirole 1993).

between rent extraction and efficiency is not necessarily affected by the cost of public funds.[3]

If cost differences across units are larger—that is, if asymmetric information carries more weight, as is likely in developing countries—for example, if the cost spread increases with a constant mean, then it increases B - A and favors cost plus. However, taking C into account weakens this effect. Figure 5-2 shows consumers surplus under two cost schedules with different cost spread. Low cost spread is represented by dotted triangles, while large cost spread is represented by gray triangles. If the cost differences in one industry are higher than in another (for example, telecommunications versus power transmission), then price cap is relatively favored in the industry with lower spread (power transmission).

Monitoring

The effect of monitoring on the power of incentives differs, depending on which type of monitoring is used. For example, monitoring of effort generally enables the regulator to reduce the information rents and calls for higher-powered incentive schemes. A less efficient monitoring technology usually calls for less powerful incentive schemes. Indeed, low incentives and monitoring are substitute instruments used to extract the firm's rent. Decreased use of one instrument causes the other instrument to appear more attractive. As a result, an increase in the cost of public funds demands low-incentive schemes because of the decrease, both direct and indirect, in monitoring cost.

Thus far, perfect cost observability has been assumed. In practice, however, costs are not perfectly observable. One must consider potential cost padding—the many ways in which a firm can divert money—such as extra charges that benefit a firm's management and workers. Analysis of Laffont and Tirole (1993) shows that the imperfect auditing of cost padding calls for a shift toward higher-powered incentive schemes. In the extreme case of no auditing, only fixed-price contracts would be possible. Indeed, they would be the only contracts preventing unlimited cost padding by making firms residual claimants of their costs. Obviously, poor auditing technology, found in many developing countries, will call for an even greater shift toward fixed-price mechanisms. This effect is reinforced by the savings in auditing costs

---

[3] However, with higher prices, service disconnections are more likely; hence, balancing this negative effect may call for social funds.

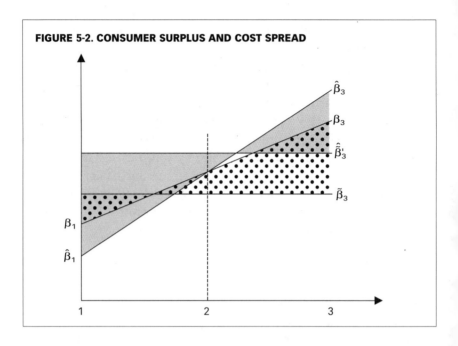

FIGURE 5-2. CONSUMER SURPLUS AND COST SPREAD

resulting from fixed-price mechanisms in countries with a high cost of public funds.[4]

Hierarchical Regulation and Corruption

The next issue to consider is the need to devolve regulation to the regulatory agencies or ministries. A major role of these institutions is to help bridge the information gap between public decisionmakers and the regulated firm. However, this gives rise to the possible capture of the regulatory agency by the firm. Such collusion is more likely to occur if stakes are high, the cost of side transfers between the firm and the regulator are low, or no incentive mechanism is in place for the regulators.

The stake of collusion amounts to the information rent that an efficient firm obtains when the regulator hides the fact that it is efficient. The above

---

[4] In the absence of auditing, the only answer is price-cap regulation; only through price-cap reviews can certain cost elements be brought in, leading to a degree of cost-plus shift through the ratchet effect. Making cost information public may help the regulator to improve the quality of accounting by fostering more truthful disclosure of information by the firm, establishing its reputation for honest behavior.

BOX 5-1. REGULATORY RESPONSE TO CAPTURE

Faced with a procurement problem, suppose the regulator hides, with probability ρ, the fact that the firm has an efficiency parameter β, when this parameter can be either $\underline{\beta}$ or $\bar{\beta} > \underline{\beta}$, with $\Delta\beta = \bar{\beta} - \underline{\beta}$.

If the government offers a price-cap regulation of $p = \bar{\beta} - e^*$, corresponding to the cost of an inefficient firm exerting the cost-decreasing, efficient level of effort e^*, then the rent of the $\underline{\beta}$ firm is $p - (\underline{\beta} - e^*) = \Delta\beta$, with an expected social cost (with respect to first-best regulation) of $\rho\lambda v\Delta\beta$, if λ is the deadweight loss of social funds and v is the probability that the firm is efficient.

Suppose, instead, that the regulator offers a cost-plus scheme. In this case, the cost is $\underline{\beta}$ (resp. $\bar{\beta}$) for an efficient (resp. inefficient) firm, since the level of effort is zero in both cases. The social cost of this regulation (with respect to first-best regulation) would be $(1 + \lambda)e^*$, and no corruption occurs.

The move to low-powered incentives is better than corrupt, high powered regulation if $(1 + \lambda)e^* < \rho\lambda v\Delta\beta$ or $e^* < \rho v\Delta\beta$ if the firm's profit in the social welfare function is not included. The higher the level ρ of corruption, the more likely it is worth switching to the cost-plus scheme (a low-powered incentive scheme that destroys the stake of corruption). Note, however, that this example assumes that the auditing of cost is not corrupt.

---

analysis shows that it increases with the level of effort chosen by the less efficient firm (since it is equivalent to the gain obtained by an efficient firm when it mimics an inefficient one). The maximum bribe that a firm is willing to offer the agency is this stake. However, it should be discounted by the price of internal transfers, which includes the cost of being discovered, as well as the need to use indirect transfers that are less efficient than monetary ones. Capture is avoided if the agency is paid an amount larger than the discounted value of the stake of collusion when it reveals that the firm is efficient (referred to as the collusion-proof constraint).

In the simplest cases, the regulatory response to the fear of capture is to satisfy the collusion-proof constraint at the lowest possible cost. This includes shifting optimal regulation toward cost-plus schemes to decrease the stake of collusion and improving monitoring to increase the cost of side transfers (see box 5-1).

Three features of developing countries call for even higher shifts toward cost-plus mechanisms. First, one can expect a lower cost of internal transfers because of less stringent monitoring of illegal activities. Second, incentive payments to the agency are more costly because of the higher cost of public funds. Third, it may be politically more difficult to create such strong incentive payments.

In the case presented above, the optimal regulatory response entails no corruption. However, if the framework is extended to a case in which regulators are relatively susceptible to corruption (some requiring low bribes, others requiring higher ones), it may be optimal to allow a degree of corruption if the proportion of regulators requiring low bribes is sufficiently small. Creating incentive payments that suppress the corruption of this type of regulator would be too costly because high payments required to fight corruption would have to be incurred, even for the other type of regulator (for whom it is unnecessary). Then, the same features of developing countries, which favor low-powered incentive schemes (high cost of public funds and poor auditing technologies), suggest that it is optimal to allow more corruption to occur at equilibrium.[5]

Thus, the effect of corruption is complex. Corruption of cost auditing will call for higher-powered incentive schemes, while corruption in information reporting will require lower-powered incentives.

Commitment

In developing countries, governments' commitment to long-term regulatory rules is less credible than that of developed countries. Lack of government commitment puts the ratchet effect into motion. In their initial period, firms fear that taking advantage of incentives (efficient firms make more money by having low costs) will lead to more demanding incentive schemes in the future. The way to commit credibly to not expropriating future rents reveals nothing about a firm's current efficiency. Instead of offering, as in the static case, a menu of contracts with variable sharing of overruns, which induces self-selection, the extreme attitude is to offer a single contract, which induces undereffort of the good type and higher-than-first-best effort of the bad type. The inefficiency created by the lack of commitment is an inappropriate provision of effort levels over the various periods, which cannot be simply interpreted in terms of the power of incentive schemes. In the case of linear schemes, it can be shown that the ratchet effect pushes toward high-powered schemes, which create higher rents in the initial period to induce the revelation of types (Freixas, Guesnerie, and Tirole 1985). More generally, the less

---

[5] See Laffont and Meleu (2001) for an analysis of how the separation of regulatory powers may help fight corruption.

BOX 5-2. ENFORCEMENT FAILURES IN TELECOMMUNICATIONS: EXAMPLES FROM AFRICA

In **Ghana**, the incumbent monopoly for fixed telephony, which was denied entry into the mobile business, eventually entered the market, using various tactics to delay interconnection.

In **Tanzania**, the regulator attempted to enforce the requirement of regional mobile licenses. However, Mobitel, the dominant operator, argued that its license was national in scope and launched service in an area where the regulator had attempted to shut down the operator. After a crisis involving the country's court and president, all cellular licenses were declared national in scope.

In **Côte d'Ivoire**, the incumbent monopolist priced access for competing public phones so that entry was blocked. In 1998, the regulator intervened, setting a minimum for the incumbent's prices at its own call boxes in order to allow entry. However, until recently, the incumbent refused to adjust its prices.

---

commitment ability there is, the less the regulator should try to separate types, particularly if the cost of public funds is high.

Lack of regulators' ability to make commitments can be mitigated by repeated interaction with the firms and by building a reputation of not expropriating the rents derived from future efficiency improvements.[6] It can be expected that this substitute for institutional commitment will be more difficult for developing countries to achieve.

No general analysis exists on ease of commitment according to regulatory regimes. Regulatory institutions, particularly in developing countries, must be scrutinized in terms of their ability to provide long-term incentives through their power of commitment, since a major goal is to attract foreign investment. For example, setting price caps has been advocated in Western countries as a way to provide high-powered incentives. However, price caps are regularly renegotiated, while a commitment to a fair rate of return might be less prone to costly renegotiations (Greenwald 1984).[7]

Weakness in Rule of Law

In developing countries, enforcement of regulatory rules is poor (box 5-2). Enforcement is costly, and optimal enforcement decreases with the cost of

---

[6] Gilbert and Newbery (1988) present a model of infinitely repeated contracting, whereby certain collusive equilibria do not exhibit the trading inefficiencies associated with shorter time horizons.

[7] However, one can also commit to a fair renegotiation of price caps.

public funds. Moreover, the principal-agent paradigm, in which full bargaining power is attributed to the regulator, does not fit the reality of developing countries. However, weakness in the bargaining position at the renegotiation stage calls for increased investment in enforcement. Finally, corruption of the enforcement or regulatory mechanism calls for less enforcement. In short, in developing countries, weakness in the rule of law is caused not only by poor human resources; it is part of an optimal regulatory response (Laffont 2001).

Financial Constraints

Financial constraints, in many cases, compound the difficulties of asymmetric information. The basic intuition can be stated simply in moral hazard control problems with risk neutrality. Moral hazard in a delegated activity can be controlled without relinquishing a rent to the agent if penalties·are possible, even when the observable performance is problematic. However, if such penalties are not possible because of limited liability constraints, only rewards for good performance can induce appropriate levels of effort; that is, information rents must be relinquished.

The greater the financial constraints, the higher the rents. Both the strength of financial constraints and the high cost of public funds favor a shift toward less powerful incentive schemes in developing countries. The irony is that, although developing countries should make more effort to emerge from underdevelopment, inducing such effort in these countries is more difficult.

Stages of Regulatory Development

Many arguments favor a move toward less powerful incentive schemes (and, therefore, a move toward less efficiency) in developing countries. However, using performance evaluation to improve the fundamental trade-offs between efficiency and rent extraction presumes a perfect (or at least unbiased) auditing of that performance. The main counterarguments, which favor fixed-price mechanisms that eliminate all auditing costs, are the effects of cost padding and corrupt cost audits.

One may distinguish three stages of regulatory development. In the first stage, poor auditing mechanisms call for advocating powerful incentive schemes that promote short-term efficiency in activities immune to ratchet effects. However, these schemes strongly favor ex post inequality and provoke social rejection because the more efficient firms (usually controlled by foreign investors with more transparent financial statements) make more money than inefficient ones. Moreover, the schemes encourage corruption of regulatory and political institutions and are costly for the rest of the economy because they create a money drain toward the regulated monopolies.

During this first stage, a sound auditing system should be developed. Once in place, a move can be made toward the second stage of promoting less powerful incentive schemes for the reasons explained above. Then, as development continues, gradual progress can be made toward the third stage, the optimal solution of more powerful incentive schemes. Success at each stage depends critically on the government's ability to make a credible, long-term commitment to implementing the resolutions.

Price Incentives in Selected Infrastructure Services

Power Transmission: High-powered Schemes

Setting transmission prices involves two steps. The first is to determine the revenues that the company that owns the network should receive for allowing market agents to use it. The second step assigns payments to market agents. As this chapter focuses on the trade-off between relinquishing a firm's rent and reducing production costs, only the first step is considered.

This first step requires that a distinction be made between the existing network and new additions. In most Latin American countries, traditional methods are used to estimate the existing network's operational cost (excluding power losses) and capital cost for a specific period of time (usually one year). Regulations in most of these countries include a standardized cost for avoiding the company incentive to exaggerate cost estimates. The case of Peru illustrates this process (box 5-3).

In Colombia, revenues of new transmission lines are determined through a public bidding process. The winning proposal is the one requiring the smallest payments, which may be established in terms of a price per unit of transported power, annual fees, or a combination thereof. If several proposals are submitted, competition for the line causes bidders to minimize cost. This procedure keeps regulators from having to calculate operational capital costs every year because company revenues are included in the proposals. Thus, the regulator's role in actualizing such prices is restricted by the concession contracts.

BOX 5-3. TRANSMISSION TARIFFS IN PERU'S PRIMARY SYSTEM

In Peru, all generators connected to the National Interconnected System pay a monthly tariff to the owners of transmission lines belonging to the primary transmission system (PTS). This tariff covers the transmission cost (established by the Electricity Tariff Commission), which equals annual investment in the line according to standard costs by investment type, plus standard costs of system operation and maintenance. Annual investment is calculated as the annuity corresponding to the VNR (in US$) of the transmission facilities over a 30-year period and is discounted at an annual 12-percent rate for the first 10 years. Total transmission consists of transmission costs plus costs of power losses, calculated by the Economic System Operation Committee (COES), which coordinates the economic operations of electricity systems and concessionaires.

Compensation for total transmission cost is made through the tariff income and connection toll (the total equals total transmission cost). Generators must make monthly payments to the transmission companies within seven days of the COES calculation of monthly energy flow.

COES sets the tariff income (the value added to the energy and capacity transported from one point in the system to another). The tariff income estimates transmission system efficiency (actual versus standard losses). The tariff income generators pay is a function of volume of energy, capacity, and distance transported; it is calculated by subtracting the value of actual losses from standard losses. In most cases, the value of tariff income is negative because actual transmission losses are higher than the standard losses considered.

The connection toll equals the total cost of transmission, minus the tariff income (pursuant to the values provided by COES). The connection toll is divided among the generators on a pro-rata basis, based on the actual energy provided to the system by each generator and calculated at the peak period of the month.

Once calculated in April of each year, the PTS connection toll is converted into 12 fixed, monthly payments. Each year, the Commission establishes a formula for monthly tariff adjustment, which is triggered by an adjustment indicator (of about 5 percent) that incorporates foreign exchange, import taxes, and Peruvian inflation. As a result, the foreign exchange exposure during a given year is capped to a maximum value, beyond which tariffs are automatically adjusted.

Retail Consumers: Low-powered Scheme for Buying Power

In most Latin American countries, the tariff of regulated users consists of two types of components: pass-through and standard components. The pass-through components are the transmission and energy costs, while the standard component is the added value of distribution (AVD). Since energy is the largest cost of servicing power to final consumers and is a pass-through component, final prices of regulated consumers have a strong cost-plus feature. Full rent extraction is achieved, but efforts of distributors to reduce the cost of buying energy are low. The willingness of regulatory institutions to extract rents of distribution companies, distributors' unwillingness to take the risk of uncovered power costs, and the weak regulatory capacity of auditing the cost of acquiring power explain the broad use of these schemes throughout the region.

Although most Latin American schemes for setting the price for final consumers have the above-mentioned features, standard costs for distribution and transmission and full costs for energy differ by country. For example, in the Dominican Republic, distributors must buy electricity through public bidding, while, in Argentina, energy must be bought through organized markets. The standard rules for cost distribution also vary widely among countries. In Chile and Peru, for example, the AVD is based on a cost model for an enterprise operating in a similar zone—that is, its density and other features are similar—established for four-year periods through authorized consultant studies. The AVD incorporates the fixed costs of administration, billing, and customer services; investment, operation and maintenance costs, and peak power losses over the distribution system; and energy losses in the distribution system. The global rate of return is set to a level of 6-14 percent. In Argentina, on the other hand, the AVD is based on the effective cost of the company. However, the company has incentives to minimize this cost since it is the criterion for selecting a proposal in the process of granting a concession for a distribution area.

Distribution and Retail: Low-powered Scheme for Gas Purchase

Gas prices for regulated consumers in Argentina, Colombia, and Mexico have both standard and pass-through components. The standard components are the elements of distribution costs. The pass-through component is the price of gas paid by the distribution companies; thus, distributors do not

---

**BOX 5-4. CALCULATING GAS PRICES FOR ARGENTINA'S
REGULATED CONSUMERS**

Calculating the gas prices of regulated consumers involves three factors: price at point of entry into the transport system, transport charges, and distribution rates.

Transport charges are based on cost of service, plus a reasonable rate of return on assets. They also consider the degree of efficiency that companies can achieve.

Distribution rates are based on distance from production centers, whether service is continuous or interrupted (continuous services are more expensive), and volume of gas consumed (cost per m3 decreases as consumption increases).

Transport and distribution rates are adjusted every six months to account for inflation. This adjustment is based on changes in the U.S. producer price index for industrial commodities.

Efficiency improvements are factored into the rates and remain fixed for five years; they serve as a mechanism whereby consumers and producers share efficiency gains.

The price is also adjusted by a factor, fixed for five years, that compensates companies for planned investments over the subsequent five years. In addition to these adjustments, ENARGAS can make rate changes to reflect unusual costs, such as tax changes.

Traditionally, gas costs were considered pass-through components. In 1995, however, to promote development of the short-term natural gas market, an optional regime for calculating prices was introduced. The new system is based on a reference price fixed by regulators. If the actual prices distributors pay are below reference prices, rate caps are not modified and distribution companies may profit from buying gas at favorable prices.

---

have incentives to reduce the costs of acquiring gas in wholesale markets. However, since 1995, distribution companies in Argentina may choose between two systems with different incentive structures: the pass-through scheme and a system with reference prices. In the latter system, the regulatory commission establishes a reference price; if the price paid by distributors is higher than the reference price, only half of the difference can be transferred to final consumers through pricing. If the price paid by distributors is lower than the reference price, the reference price is passed on to consumers. The remainder is a benefit for the distribution company (box 5-4).

BOX 5-5. PRICING WATER AND SEWERAGE SERVICES IN ARGENTINA

In 1993, a 30-year concession was awarded to Aguas Argentinas, a consortium led by Lyonnaise des Eaux to provide water and sanitation services to the population of Buenos Aires. (Prior to awarding this concession, services were provided by Obras Sanitarias de la Nación [OSN], a public company.) The concession contract specified performance targets, requiring a total investment of $4 billion over the 30-year period. The regulator is a tripartite body of federal, state, and municipal government representatives. It has an $8 million annual budget, financed by a 2.7 percent tariff surcharge collected by the concessionaire.

Tariff levels are formally reviewed at five-year intervals, using K factors in a price-capping system similar to that used in the United Kingdom. However, since winning the contract, the concessionaire has negotiated tariffs (denominated in dollars) to protect investments against local inflation rates. An additional 13-percent increase on the initial tariff has been negotiated with the regulator to meet unforeseen investment requirements associated with an accelerated program of meter installation. The original OSN tariff was raised by 8 percent just prior to privatization to attract bidders; it remains at about 17 percent below its pre-privatization level, despite these changes.

Water and Sanitation: A Mixed Scheme

Most Latin American countries have chosen to price water and sewerage services through a system that provides companies incentives for improving their efficiency over time. The system fixes prices based on company information over a four or five-year period. Such a system allows companies to profit from efficiency gains over the period; however, efficiency gains over a given period are included in the price calculations for the subsequent period. In Argentina and Colombia, average tariff prices are based on a firm's own costs, with some rules that prevent passing certain inefficiencies on to consumers (box 5-5). For example, the water losses used in calculating costs are theoretical, rather than actual.

In Chile, the regulatory agency fixes the prices of each water company, based on the firm's own costs, as in cost-plus schemes; however, the costs of each firm are not actual but are the theoretical costs that would result in a firm with technical and commercial features; while similar to the actual costs, they reflect optimal design of assets and management. A high degree of discretion is used to define a theoretical firm. It involves an arduous, costly effort, which, in the past, often called for third-party arbitration, resulting in a compromise of the prices proposed by the firm and the regulator.

Final Remarks

This chapter has summarized key factors that determine, on the basis of economic theory, whether high or low-powered incentive schemes should be used in developing countries. It was concluded that cost-plus pricing schemes are favored when perfect or unbiased auditing is expected. The key reasons are social rejection of the large rents of private regulated firms and the higher costs of public funds.[8] The main arguments against cost-plus schemes are the effects of cost padding and corruption of cost audits. These arguments favor fixed-price mechanisms, which also reduce spending by eliminating auditing costs.

The chapter advocates three stages of regulatory development: The first stage uses powerful incentive schemes to create a sound auditing system. Once the system is in place, the second stage shifts toward less powerful incentive schemes. As development progresses, a gradual move can be made toward more powerful incentive schemes. Success in all three stages depends on the government's ability to commit itself to their implementation.

Two caveats of the above analyses should be emphasized. The first is that, although certain government features have been discussed, a broader political economy of reform, which considers historical characteristics and relevant political contexts, is needed. The second is that liberalization, competition, and regulatory reform are recent in countries of Latin America and the Caribbean, particularly those of Central America. Available empirical evidence is limited, difficult to access, and not in a form that allows for rigorous econometric testing.

---

[8] The high cost of public funds is not a justification for selecting cost-plus schemes since most private companies that provide infrastructure services do not receive public transfers. Preference for cost-plus schemes is better explained as a social rejection of relinquishing rents, and because, in most private companies of the infrastructure sector, auditing reports are available.

References

Freixas, X., R. Guesnerie, and J. Tirole. 1985. "Planning under Incomplete Information and the Ratchet Effect." *The Review of Economic Studies* 52(2): 173–92.

Gilbert, R., and D. Newbery. 1988. "Regulation Games," Working Paper No. 8,879. Berkeley, CA: University of California at Berkeley.

Greenwald, B. 1984. "Rate Base Selection and the Structure of Regulation." *Rand Journal of Economics* 15(1): 85–95.

Laffont, J. J. 2001. "Enforcement, Regulation, and Development." ARQADE, Université de Toulouse. Mimeographed.

Laffont, J. J., and M. Meleu. 2001. "Separation of Powers and Development." *Journal of Development Economics* 64(1): 129–45.

Laffont, J. J., and J. Tirole. 1993. *A Theory of Incentives in Regulation and Procurement.* Cambridge, MA: MIT Press.

Chapter 6

Competition and Networks in the European Transport Sector

David Wood

In 1996, public or commercial transport activities in the European Union were valued at 270 billion ECU; private transport activities accounted for another 200 billion ECU. These represented 4 and 3 percent, respectively, of total gross domestic product (GDP). Six million people are employed in the transport service sector, representing 4 percent of total employment. In addition, two million people are employed in the transport equipment industry and more than six million in transport-related industries. Since 1970, growth in the transport of goods in European Union countries has been over 75 percent, while growth in the transport of passengers has exceeded 110 percent. There is every reason to believe that this growth will continue and that transport services, as other services, will remain a major dynamic force in the European economy.

Treaty Policy Principles

The transport chapter of the Treaty (Articles 70-80) sets out the principles for the European Community common transport policy, one of only three common policies in the Treaty—the others being agriculture and commerce.[1] The common transport policy focuses on railways, roads, and inland waterways, reflecting the concerns of the six original members of the Euro-

---

[1] All references to the "Treaty" are to the Treaty that established the European Community. The original Treaty of Rome of 1957 has been amended numerous times, most recently by the Treaty of Amsterdam, which entered into force on May 1, 1999.

pean Community.[2] At the time the Treaty was debated and adopted, no consensus had been reached on whether transport services were to be considered public services or an economic activity governed by commercial principles. In terms of the legal interpretation of the Treaty, the question of applicability of competition rules to the transport sector was effectively laid to rest by the Court of Justice in the French Seamens' case.[3] The Court ruled that economic sectors could only be excluded from the competition rules by express provision in the Treaty, as is the case for agriculture. Accordingly, Articles 81 and 82 of the Treaty are fully applicable to the transport sector.

Article 81 prohibits as unlawful agreements and concerted practices that may affect trade between member states whose objectives or effects are prevention, restriction, or distortion of competition. Such agreements may, nonetheless, be exempted if their benefits outweigh their harmful effects. Article 82 prohibits any abuse of a dominant position within the common market (or in a substantial part of it) insofar as it may affect trade between member states. No exemption is possible in Article 82.

Regulation 4,064/89, related to the vetting of mergers "with a Community dimension," states that mergers between companies with a turnover above a certain threshold that, in practice, affect three or more member states may not be put into effect without prior authorization of the Commission.[4] The main test is whether the merger creates or strengthens a dominant position in the European Community, the result of which would likely impede competition significantly.

Scheduled transport services have certain characteristics that, although not specific to transport, are seldom found together in other industries. High entry barriers, scheduled services requiring some reserve capacity or cyclical demands, strategic ramifications, and low participation of operating costs on total service costs are among the specificities the Commission must consider when applying the competition rules. Moreover, such specificities have led

---

[2] In practice, road transport does not fall within the scope of the European Community's competition rules because most scheduled road transport services are national in scope, and, with regard to non-scheduled services, both supply and demand are sufficiently fragmented as to make competition problems unlikely.

[3] Case 167/73, the French Seamens' Case, [1974] ECR 359 at paragraph 32: "Whilst under Article [80](2), therefore, sea and air transport, so long as the Council has not decided otherwise, is excluded from the rules of Title IV of Part Two of the Treaty relating to the Common Transport Policy, it remains on the same basis as the other modes of transport, subject to the general rules of the Treaty."

[4] Council Regulation (EEC) No. 4,064/89 of December 21, 1989, on the control of concentrations between undertakings, OJ 1989 L 395/1, as amended.

some transport undertakings to seek distinction between "fair" and "destructive" competition. Although not new,[5] this approach has not yet been accepted by the European Court of Justice (ECJ).[6]

This chapter analyzes competition regulations of the European Union's transport sector and the ways in which the Commission and the Court have interpreted them. It discusses the paths of liberalization for the liner shipping, rail, and air transport sectors; analyzes how the term relevant service market is defined to determine whether companies have dominant position; and reviews the European Community's competition regulations for inland, maritime, and air transport sectors, as well as problems of access and discrimination. Following the conclusion, which recognizes the need for both traditional competition tools and appropriate regulations, an annex presents summaries of 11 relevant cases.

Liberalization Process

Historically, most transport sectors have been characterized by supply-side monopoly or oligopoly, high prices, price fixing, limitations on market access, and little choice. These sectors have formed the essential infrastructure of countries, and it has been difficult to gauge their profitability.

Although the transport liberalization process has developed differently by sector, all agree on several key principles: First, price regulation should be left to the market, or at least should not be regulated by governments. Second, discrimination between operators of different nationalities should be eliminated. Third, discrimination on the basis of the country of origin or destination should be avoided.

Liner Shipping

In liner shipping, national carriers and liner conferences often have decided together with governments whether to allow competitors to have market

---

[5] See, for example, Case T-29/94 SPO versus Commission [1995] ECR II-289, at point 294, where the Court of First Instance considered that no distinction could be made between normal and destructive competition. The appeal was rejected as manifestly inadmissible by Order of the Court of March 25, 1996 (Case C-137/95 P [1996] ELR I-1611).

[6] The European Court of Justice is responsible for ensuring the interpretation and application of the Treaty, while the Court of First Instance deals primarily with competition cases.

access. For a long period of time, this highly unusual sector has enjoyed the privilege of self-regulation, meaning that economic control of maritime markets has been left in the hands of private companies. This contrasts markedly with air and rail transport markets, where government regulation has been considered customary.

Adoption of the Brussels Package in 1979 was the key to developing European Community policy for the maritime sector.[7] From a competition policy point of view, the most important aspects of the Package were that it centered on the UNCTAD Code of Conduct for Liner Conferences and accepted that international liner shipping services should be provided on the basis of the conference system.

This led to adoption of the Council Regulation in 1986, which applied the principle of freedom to provide services to international maritime transport, excluding transport between ports of a single member state.[8] The effect of this Regulation was to require elimination of restrictions on the carriage of certain types of cargo and removal of clauses from bilateral agreements between individual member states and third countries related to national flag reservations and other cargo-sharing arrangements. At the same time, the Council adopted Regulation 4,056/86.[9]

Air Transport

European air transport markets have been characterized by a system of inter-governmental agreements and cooperation between airline companies within the framework of the Chicago Convention on International Civil Aviation.[10]

The turning point for the application of European Community competition law was the Nouvelles Frontières case.[11] The Court made clear that, notwithstanding the absence of a common transport policy in the air transport sector, national competition authorities and the Commission could take

---

[7] Council Regulation (EEC) No. 954/79 of May 15, 1979, concerning the ratification by member states of, or their accession to, the United Nations Convention on a Code of Conduct for Liner Conferences, OJ 1979 L 121/1.

[8] Council Regulation (EEC) No. 4,055/86 of December 22, 1986, applying the principle of freedom to provide services to maritime transport between member states and between member states and third countries, OJ 1986 L 378/1.

[9] Council Regulation (EEC) No. 4,056/86 of December 22, 1986, laying out detailed rules for application of Articles 81 and 82 of the Treaty to maritime transport, OJ 1986L 378/4.

[10] Chicago, December 7, 1944.

[11] Joined Cases C- 209-213/84, Ministère Public versus Asjes et al., [1986] ECR 1425.

action with respect to infringements of competition rules included in Articles 81 and 82 of the Treaty. This case encouraged the Commission's efforts to liberalize intra-European Community air transport and to establish detailed rules for applying Articles 81 and 82 in the air transport sector.

In December 1987, the first package of aviation measures was adopted. From the point of view of freedom to provide services, the essential element of this package was establishment of third, fourth, and fifth freedom rights. The third freedom establishes the right to off-load, in another state, the passengers, freight, and mail loaded in the state in which the carrier is registered. The fourth freedom establishes the right to load, in another state, the passengers, freight, and mail for off-loading in the state in which the carrier is registered. The fifth freedom establishes the right to commercially transport passengers, freight, and mail between two states, other than the state in which the carrier is registered.

From a competition policy perspective, the essential element of the first package was the adoption of Regulation No. 3,975/87.[12] An enabling regulation, also adopted by the Council, gave the Commission the means to adopt group exemptions in the air transport sector.[13] In 1988, the Commission adopted three group exemptions: Commission Regulation No. 2,671/88,[14] related to the joint planning and coordination of capacities, sharing of revenue, tariff consultations on scheduled air services, and slot allocations at airports; Commission Regulation No. 2,672/88,[15] related to computer reservations systems; and Commission Regulation No. 2,673/88,[16] related to ground handling at airports.

---

[12] Council Regulation (EEC) No. 3,975/87 of December 14, 1987, lays out the procedure for applying competition rules to undertakings in the air transport sector, OJ L 1987 374/1.

[13] Council Regulation (EEC) No. 3,976/87 of December 14, 1987, on the application of Article 81(3) of the Treaty to certain categories of agreements and concerted practices in the air transport sector, OJ 1987 L 374/9.

[14] Commission Regulation (EEC) No. 2,671/88 of July 26, 1988, on the application of Article 81(3) of the Treaty to certain categories of agreements between undertakings, decisions of associations of undertakings and concerted practices concerning joint planning and coordination of capacity, sharing of revenue and consultations on tariffs on scheduled air services, and slot allocation at airports, OJ 1988 L 239/9.

[15] Commission Regulation (EEC) No. 2,672/88 of July 26, 1988, on the application of Article 81(3) of the Treaty to certain categories of agreements between undertakings related to computer reservation systems for air transport services, OJ 1988 L 239/13.

[16] Commission Regulation (EEC) No. 2,673/88 of July 26, 1988, on the application of Article 81(3) of the Treaty to certain categories of agreements between undertakings, decisions of associations of undertakings, and concerted practices concerning ground handling services, OJ 1988 L 239/17.

In June 1990, the second liberalization package was adopted. It was designed to establish a transitional regime that would allow carriers to adapt to the more competitive environment that would result from the anticipated third package. Adopted by the Council in December 1992, the third package consisted primarily of regulations related to operating licenses, market access, and tariffs.

Rail

Traditionally, domestic companies have enjoyed exclusive rights to all or most national railway activities. Governments have hesitated to liberalize the railway sector and have imposed public service obligations without fully compensating railway operators for the costs involved.

Although the Commission has had detailed rules for applying competition rules to railways since 1968,[17] isolation from competition has prevented these activities from benefiting from the positive effects of open market conditions: cost reduction, improved services, and development of new products and markets. As a result, the railways' share of the transport market has declined substantially. In those countries where railways formerly held a large share of the freight market, market share fell about 50 percent between the 1970s and the mid 1990s. Railways have continued to lose traffic to road transport, not only because road operators have successfully reduced their real costs and improved their quality, but also because road operators have not been confronted with the full costs of their activities.

Recently, this situation has started to change. Over the past six or seven years, to help European Community railways adapt to single market conditions and increase their efficiency, the Commission has taken initial steps toward full liberalization of railway services. However, given the special characteristics of the railways, these measures have fallen short of the liberalization measures in other transport sectors, such as air transport. Under the first package of liberalization measures, adopted in 1991[18] and supplemented in 1995,[19]

---

[17] Council Regulation (EEC) No. 1,017/68 of July 19, 1968, applying rules of competition to transport by rail, road, and inland waterway, OJ 1968 L 175/1.

[18] Council Directive 91/440/EEC of July 29, 1991, on the development of Eutopean Community railways, OJ 1991 L 237&25.

[19] Council Directive 95/18/EC of June 19, 1995, on the licensing of railway undertakings, OJ 1995 L 143/7. Council Directive 95/19/EC of June 19, 1995, on the allocation of railway infrastructure capacity and the charging of infrastructure fees, OJ 1995 L 143/75.

member states are required to ensure the independence of management of railway activities by separating management of railway infrastructure from provision of railway transport services. Furthermore, competition has been made possible by allowing access to railway infrastructure for international services offered by international groupings of railway activities and railway activities engaged in international combined transport of goods throughout the European Community.[20]

Market Definition

The general definition of the term *market* for the purpose of applying European competition law included in the Commission's 1997 Notice is also applicable to the transport sector.[21]

The standard approach to defining relevant markets in the transport sector is to consider the individual routes concerned and determine whether other routes, including those using different modes of transport, can be substituted.[22] Thus, for international transport services, *relevant market* would be defined as a particular route or, more likely, as in the transport of goods, a bundle of routes. Common practice in the three main transport sectors (air, maritime, and railway), as in other sectors,[23] is to focus on demand substitution, rather than supply substitution.[24] Thus, the Commission reviews the physical and technical characteristics of a transport service to determine whether it is functionally interchangeable with another transport service at a given price.[25] As the speed of conversion of the transport medium (airplane,

---

[20] Council Directive 75/130/EEC of February 17, 1975, on the establishment of common rules for certain types of combined road/rail carriage of goods between member states, OJ 1975 L 48/31.

[21] Commission Notice on the definition of the relevant market for the purposes of European Community competition law, OJ 1997 C 372.

[22] See Case 66/86, Ahmed Saeed [1989], ECR 803, at paragraph 40; and Commission decisions 96/180/EC of January 16, 1996, relating to a proceeding under Article 81 of the EC Treaty and Article 53 of the EEA Agreement (IV/35.545, LH/SAS) OJ 1996 L 54, paragraph 31; and 94/894/EC of December 13, 1994, relating to a proceeding under Article 81 of the EC Treaty and Article 53 of the EEA Agreement (IV/32.490, Eurotunnel) OJ L 1994 354, paragraphs 62-63.

[23] For example, Case T-30/89, Hilti AG versus Commission ECR [1991] II-1439, paragraph 70.

[24] Commission decision 94/985/EC of December 21, 1994, relating to a proceeding pursuant to Article 81 of the EC Treaty (IV/33.218, Far Eastern Freight Conference) OJ 1994 L 378, paragraphs 25-29.

[25] Commission decision 94/980/EC of October 19, 1994, relating to a proceeding pursuant to Article 81 of the EC Treaty (IV/34.446, Trans-Atlantic Agreement) OJ 1994 L 376, paragraphs 35-58.

vessel, or train) to provide a different service may be relevant, the supply sub-stitutability cannot be ignored.[26]

In some service markets, including transport, the geographic location of service provision needs to be considered to determine whether other serv-ices can substitute for the given service and to arrive at a definition of the term *relevant service market*. Thus, a relevant service market includes its own geographic element. However, the location of the purchaser of the service may differ from that where service is provided. Since the notion of a geo-graphic market is used to delineate the area in which market power is exer-cised, it follows that, in some service markets, the geographic market is the place where the consumer is located. This is not necessarily the location of service supply. The geographic market, in fact, identifies those consumers against whom market power is exercised.

Thus, a shipper in Australia may telephone a shipping line in Singapore to arrange the transport of a container from Munich to Pittsburgh. The mar-ket power of the service supplier is exercised in Australia, not Munich, Pitts-burgh, or Singapore. The same is true if an individual in Brussels telephones a travel agent in Manchester to purchase a plane ticket on Air India from London to New York. In both cases, the number of customers outside the usual "catchment" area may be statistically insignificant. In neither case does the location of the consumer affect the service market definition.

In Ahmed Saeed,[27] the ECJ's starting point for market definition in air transport is the particular route at issue. Once identified, the ECJ would look at possible substitutes, including other routes and other forms of transport to determine the relevant market. The ECJ stated:

> In that regard, two possible approaches emerged during the hearings before the Court: the first is that the sector of scheduled flights consti-tutes a separate market; the second that alternative possibilities, such as charter flights, the railways and road transport, should be taken into account, as well as scheduled flights on other routes which might serve as substitutes.

---

[26] In a report related to the agreement between British Airways and American Airlines, a distinction has been made between time sensitive and other passengers on certain specified transatlantic routes. A draft proposal (unpublished) was adopted on July 8, 1998.

[27] Case No. 66/86, Ahmed Saeed, ECR [1989] 803.

The test to be employed is wheth+er the scheduled flight on a particular route can be distinguished from the possible alternatives, by virtue of specific characteristics as a result of which it is not interchangeable with those alternatives and is affected only to an insignificant degree by competition from them. (Saeed 1989)

Finally, an essential part of the transport sector analysis is to consider the potential for market entry and, consequently, to assess the barriers to entry and exit.[28] Although potential market entry is often exaggerated by incumbents in a market with high market shares, in certain transport markets, entry can be accomplished relatively quickly, although it may be costly.

Application of Substantive Rules: Inland Sectors

Substantive Rules

Regulation 1017/68 lays out detailed rules for applying Articles 81 and 82 to the field of transport (by rail, road, and inland waterway), to horizontal and vertical agreements, and abuse of dominant position. Thus, the regulation applies to all agreements, decisions, and concerted practices that have as their objective or effect the fixing of inland transport rates and conditions, limitation or control of supply of inland transport, and sharing of inland transport markets.

The regulation also applies to the application of technical improvements or technical cooperation, or the joint financing or acquisition of transport equipment or supplies, where such operations are directly related to providing inland transport services and are necessary for the joint operation of services.

It should be noted that Articles 2 and 5 of Regulation 1,017/68 restate Article 81 of the Treaty, but with some minor differences. Article 8 of Regulation 1017/68 contains provisions that are identical to those contained in Article 82, except that they have been re-written to refer expressly to transport services.

In the context of Article 82 of the Treaty, it is obviously relevant that railway infrastructure providers are in a monopoly position. As with seaports

---

[28] Trans-Atlantic Agreement (n. 25 above).

and airports, it is essential to ensure that this position is not abused if competition in providing rail services is to exist. In particular, access rights need to be backed up by provisions on charging and capacity allocation to ensure that applicants for access are treated in a fair, nondiscriminatory manner. Furthermore, most national railway providers still enjoy monopoly power over traction and, consequently, operators who want to make use of access rights must purchase traction from a national monopoly. Under these circumstances, the traction providers enjoy a dominant position and must be prevented from putting into place abusive practices, such as discrimination or refusal to supply traction.

Relevant Decisions

The annex to this chapter contains summaries of 11 relevant transport cases, including several leading railway cases: Eurotunnel (case 1), European Night Services (case 2), and Deutsche Bahn (case 3). The Eurotunnel case demonstrates the importance of ensuring that access to infrastructure (in this case, the railway tunnel between England and France) is not blocked by long-term contracts favoring incumbents.[29] Some scope must be given to allow new entrants into the market. Somewhat similarly, in the European Night Services case, the Commission sought to ensure that a joint venture of national monopolies, which was set up to offer international services, did not prevent third parties from offering new international services. In the Deutsche Bahn case, the Commission imposed fines with respect to excessive pricing and price discrimination.[30]

In addition, the Commission has adopted guidelines for applying competition rules in the context of the trans-European networks. The Treaty states that:

> ...to enable citizens of the Union, economic operators, and regional and local communities to derive full benefit from the setting-up of an area without internal frontiers, the Community shall contribute to the establishment and development of trans-Euro-

---

[29] Joint cases T-79/95 and T-80/95, Société nationale des chemins de fer français and British Railways Board versus Commission ECR [1996] II-1491.

[30] Commission Decision 94/210/EC of March 29, 1994, relating to a proceeding pursuant to Articles 81 and 82 of the EC Treaty (IV/33.941, HOV SVZ/MCN), OJ 1994 L 104/4.

pean networks in the areas of transport, telecommunications, and energy infrastructures.

Within the framework of a system of open and competitive markets, action by the Community shall aim at promoting the interconnection and interoperability of national networks, as well as access to such networks. It shall take account in particular of the need to link island, landlocked, and peripheral regions with the central regions of the Community. (Article 154)

The trans-European rail freight freeways will be a series of railway corridors on which railway operators will be granted open access on a nondiscriminatory basis. These corridors will connect the main European economic centers with high-density freight traffic. Competition issues arise since rail infrastructure managers must cooperate in their organization. In assessing the trans-European network transport projects under European Community competition rules, the Commission has said that it will apply the following basic principles:[31]

- Where the infrastructure manager wishes to allow transport providers to reserve capacity, as from the launch of the project, all European Community providers that might be interested should be given the chance to compete.
- The capacity reserved to a provider should be proportionate to its direct or indirect financial commitments and should be in line with planned operational requirements over a reasonable period.
- As new infrastructure is usually not congested at the outset of an operation, a single provider should not be able to reserve all available capacity. Some should remain available so that other providers can operate competing services.
- The period covered by capacity reservation agreements must not exceed a reasonable amount of time, and should be determined on a case-by-case basis.

According to the Commission, these principles are intended to reconcile the need to maximize financial viability of rail infrastructure projects with the provision of free, nondiscriminatory access to infrastructure. By

---

[31] Clarification of the Commission's recommendations on the application of the competition rules to new infrastructure projects, OJ C 298 30/9/97, paragraph 5. Publication of a new notice is forthcoming.

clarifying the application of the competition rules, the Commission's intention has been to provide legal guidance, thereby facilitating creation of the trans-European networks.

Application of Substantive Rules: Maritime Sector

Regulation Scope

Regulation 4,056/86 sets out detailed rules for applying Articles 81 and 82 of the Treaty to international maritime transport services from or to one or more European Community ports, other than tramp vessel services. Therefore, the scope of the regulation also excludes cabotage services. Since its adoption in 1986, the biggest controversy surrounding this regulation has been whether its scope is limited to maritime transport services or whether it also covers multimodal transport services, including a maritime leg.

In the Far Eastern Freight Conference (FEFC) decision, the Commission concluded that the scope of the exemption contained in Article 3 of Regulation No. 4,056/86 cannot be wider than the scope of the regulation, which says that "it shall apply only to international maritime transport services from or to one or more Community ports."[32] Notwithstanding this apparently clear wording, the Commission's interpretation of the scope of the group exemption is still disputed, and the Court of First Instance (CFI) has not ruled on the application or annulled the decision.[33] Related to this point, another issue not yet fully addressed is defining the boundaries between maritime transport and land transport services. The Commission expressly avoided taking a position on this question.

Liner Shipping Conferences

The most distinctive feature of Regulation 4,056/86 is the group exemption that Article 3 contains with respect to horizontal price-fixing by liner shipping conferences. Exemption is also granted to the following activities (if one or more are carried out by members of a liner conference in addition to fixing prices and conditions of carriage for maritime transport services):

---

[32] Far Eastern Freight Conference (n. 24 above).

[33] The Court of First Instance deals primarily with competition cases.

coordination of shipping timetables, sailing dates, or dates of calls; determination of the frequency of sailings or calls; coordination or allocation of sailings or calls among members of the conference; regulation of the carrying capacity offered by each member; and allocation of cargo or revenue among members.

This is, without question, the most generous exemption that exists in European Community competition law, especially as it is unlimited in time and is granted regardless of market share. In accordance with general principles and influenced by the broad scope of the group exemption, the Commission has sought to interpret Article 3 narrowly.[34] This general approach was endorsed by the CFI in the Associated Central West Africa Lines (CEWAL) case (see Annex, case 4).[35]

Inland Price-fixing by Conferences

The Commission takes the view that the group exemption in Regulation 4,056/86 does not allow ship owners to jointly fix prices for the inland leg of a multimodal transport operation (such as from factory to port) or door-to-door prices (such as from Munich to Pittsburgh). Conferences that fix such rates do so unlawfully and, if they have not notified the Commission of their agreements, they remain potentially liable to fines.

The Commission has adopted two formal decisions prohibiting inland price-fixing: Trans-Atlantic Agreement (TAA)[36] and FEFC, both of which have been appealed to the CFI.[37]

If, as the Commission believes, the group exemption does not extend to agreements fixing prices for inland transport, then any such agreements must benefit from an individual exemption under Article 81(3). Inland

---

[34] See Case C-70/93, BMW versus ALD [1995] ECR I-3439, paragraph 28 and Case C-266/93, Bundeskartellamt versus Volkswagen and VAG, [1995] ECR I-3477, paragraph 33 "... having regard to the general principle prohibiting anticompetitive agreements laid down in Article 85(1) of the Treaty, provisions in a block exemption which derogate from that principle cannot be interpreted widely and cannot be construed in such a way as to extend the effects of the regulation beyond what is necessary to protect the interests which they are intended to safeguard."

[35] Joint cases T-24-26/93 and T-28/93, Compagnie maritime belge transports SA and Compagnie maritime belge SA, Dafra-Lines A/S, Deutsche Afrika-Linien GmbH & Co. and Nedlloyd Lijnen BV versus Commission, ECR [1996] II-1201.

[36] Trans-Atlantic Agreement (n. 25 above).

[37] Case T-395/94 ACL and others versus Commission, Case T-86/95 CGM and others versus Commission.

price-fixing would have to be shown to be genuinely indispensable for the improvement of services or in bringing about cost reductions. That ship owners are offering door-to-door services or that they wish to fix prices for door-to-door services to prevent price competition is not inherently sufficient reason to justify exemption.

To assist it in assessing applications for exemption of inland price-fixing, the Commission established a so-called "Committee of Wise Men" known as the Multimodal Group. The Group's final report, issued in December 1997, confirmed their interim report of February 1996, concluding that there was no reason to grant an exemption to collective inland price-fixing by conferences.[38]

In the Trans-Atlantic Conference Agreement (TACA) decision on immunity from fines, the Commission also confirmed its earlier position that inland price-fixing by liner shipping conferences neither fell within the scope of Article 3 nor qualified for individual exemption.[39]

Discrimination

Article 4 of Regulation 4,056/86 states that the exemption contained in Article 3 is conditional on the fact that differentiated rates and conditions of carriage, which cause detriment to ports, transport users, or carriers, must be "economically justified." The regulation appears to assume that discrimination without economic justification causes detriment, both to the completion of the internal market and to particular ports and regions. This provision is based on Article 79(1) of the Treaty and would therefore appear to be included in Regulation 4,056/86 for transport policy, rather than competition policy, reasons.

Article 4 contains a severance clause that expressly states that, if it can be severed, only that part of any agreement or decision not complying with the nondiscrimination provision shall automatically be void pursuant to Article 81(2) of the Treaty. The question of whether severance applies to other nonexempt behavior remains open.

---

[38] Office for Official Publications of the European Community, 1998, ISBN 92-828-2934-0.

[39] Commission Decision of September 16, 1998, relating to a proceeding pursuant to Articles 81 and 82 of the European Community Treaty (Case No. IV/35.134 Trans-Atlantic Conference Agreement), OJ 1999 L 42. Regulation 1017/68 is silent as to whether notification of an agreement falling within the scope of application of the regulation confers immunity from fines; the Commission has taken the view that it does not.

Dominant Position

Article 8 of Regulation 4,056/86 states that the abuse of dominant position within the meaning of Article 82 of the Treaty shall be prohibited. It also gives the Commission power to withdraw the benefit of the block exemption where it finds that the group exemption brings about effects that are incompatible with Article 82 of the Treaty.

In the CEWAL case, the CFI agreed with the Commission that members of the CEWAL liner conference presented themselves to the market as one and the same entity. The CFI also observed that the practices described in the decision revealed an intention to adopt together the same conduct in order to react unilaterally to a change, deemed a threat, in the competitive market conditions in which they operated. Consequently, the CFI considered that the Commission had sufficiently shown that it was necessary to assess the collective position of CEWAL members in relation to the relevant market.

In the TACA decision, the Commission found that TACA parties had abused their joint dominant position by inducing potential competitors to join TACA, thereby altering the competitive structure of the market. The TACA parties did this in various ways, particularly by agreeing that shipping lines that were not traditionally conference members could charge a lower price in service contracts than that charged by the conference members. Furthermore, the conference members did not compete for certain contracts, thereby leaving that part of the market open to the shipping lines that were not traditionally conference members.

Group Exemption for Consortia

At the time of the adoption of Regulation 4,056/86, the Council invited the Commission to study the situation regarding liner shipping consortia and consider whether submitting new proposals was needed. The Commission presented a communication and report to the Council in June 1990, in which it favored the adoption of a new group exemption for consortia agreements.[40] The objective of consortia agreements (joint ventures between two or more vessel operating carriers) is to facilitate cooperation between the parties to improve productivity and quality of liner shipping service and encourage greater, more efficient use of vessel capacity.

---

[40] COM 90 (260) final of 18/6/90.

On April 20, 1995, the Commission adopted Regulation 870/95 on the application of Article 81(3) of the Treaty to certain categories of agreements, decisions, and concerted practices between liner shipping companies.[41] Revised in 2000, this regulation exempts consortia from the prohibition contained in Article 81, provided that various conditions related to market share of the consortium as a whole are respected.

Mergers

In late 1996, the Commission approved the creation of P&O Nedlloyd Container Line Ltd., pursuant to Regulation 4,064/89.[42] The Commission concluded that the P&O Nedlloyd joint venture would not create or strengthen a position of dominance. The Commission reached this conclusion after examining the effect of the merger on the main trade routes to and from Europe along which both parent companies carried containerized cargo on liner shipping services. The Commission also considered the effects of the liner conferences and consortia that operated along those routes.

In the light of the CEWAL case, in which the CFI held that members of a liner conference could, under certain circumstances, be jointly dominant within the meaning of Article 82, the Commission also considered whether the P&O Nedlloyd merger could strengthen cohesiveness within existing conferences or consortia to create or reinforce an existing dominance. In 1999, the Commission approved the largest ever merger in the liner shipping sector when it unconditionally approved the merger between Maersk and Sea-Land.[43]

In its merger decisions, the Commission has followed its earlier practice of defining the relevant markets on the basis of "trades," the bundle of substitutable ports at each end of a major trade route. In most cases and on most major trade routes, the Commission has found that other forms of services are not substitutable for containerized liner shipping. However, it is clear that, on short sea routes, there is a greater possibility for substituting road for sea transport. Relevant factors to be considered include cost, time, and security.

---

[41] Commission Regulation (EC) No. 870/95 of April 20, 1995, on the application of Article 81(3) of the Treaty to certain categories of agreements, decisions, and concerted practices between liner shipping companies (consortia) pursuant to Council Regulation (EEC) No. 479/92, OJ 1995 L 89.

[42] Commission Decision of December 19, 1996, declaring a concentration compatible with the common market (Case No. IV/M.831, P&O / Royal Nedlloyd), according to Council Regulation (EEC) No. 4,064/89, OJ 1997 C 110.

[43] Case Comp/M1,651.

Application of Substantive Rules: Air Transport Sector

Substantive Rules

Council Regulation 3,975/87 lays out the procedure for applying Articles 81 and 82 to the air transport sector and grants the Commission power to adopt group exemptions related to specific, stated activities.

The geographic scope of Regulations 3,975 and 3,976 is limited to air transport services between European Community airports, including those located within the same member state, provided there is the necessary effect on trade between member states.[44] Regulations 3,975 and 3,976 apply to all forms of air transport, including passenger and freight, whether scheduled or charter, but do not apply to air transport services between the European Community and third countries, with the exception of the remaining EFTA states.

Block Exemptions: Air Transport

As part of the third package of air transport liberalization, the Commission adopted Regulation 1,617/93 on June 25, 1993. Article 1 grants group exemptions to agreements between operators in the air transport sector, decisions by associations of such operators, and concerted practices between such operators that have, as their purpose, one or more of the following: joint planning and coordination of the scheduling of air service between European Community airports; joint operation of a scheduled air service on a new or low-density route between European Community airports; holding of consultations on tariffs for the carriage of passengers, with their baggage, and freight on scheduled air services between European Community airports; and slot allocation and scheduling for air services between European Community airports.

In 1996, the Commission adopted Regulation 1,523/96, which amended Regulation 1,617/93 by removing tariff consultations for cargo rates from the scope of the group exemption.[45] The Commission is currently examining

---

[44] This results from Council Regulation No. 2,410/92 of July 23, 1992, Article 1, which provided for the deletion of the word international from Article 1(2) of Regulation (EEC) No. 3,975/87.

[45] Commission Regulation (EC) No. 1,523/96 of July 24, 1996, amending Regulation (EEC) No. 1,671/93 on the application of Article 81(3) of the Treaty to certain categories of agreements and concerted practices concerning joint planning and coordination of schedules, joint operations, consultations on passenger and cargo tariffs on scheduled air services, and slot allocation at airports, OJ 1996 L 190.

a request for individual exemption made by the International Air Transport Association (IATA) in relation to the same activities. This regulation expired in 1998 and was renewed with some modifications.

Block Exemption: Computer Reservation Systems

Regulation 2,672/88 contains a block exemption that allows airlines to set up and operate jointly-owned computer reservation systems under conditions that aim to ensure that all interested airlines have access to these systems and not discriminate against other airlines.[46]

Air Transport Mergers

None of the air transport cases that the Commission has handled under the merger regulation has been opposed. These merger cases are as follows:

- *Air France/Sabena.* This case concerned the acquisition of joint control and a minority shareholding in Sabena by Air France. One reason given for approving this arrangement was that the French government tried to allow a competitor of Air France to create a hub-and-spoke system in northern France, comparable to a system planned by Air France and Sabena for Brussels. These companies also gave undertakings to facilitate the entry of competitors onto a number of routes and to limit the number of slots they controlled at Brussels airport.
- *Swissair/Sabena.* The cooperation of these airlines created a monopoly on routes between Belgium and Switzerland for which the European Community's internal regime for market liberalization did not apply. In addition, a number of airports were congested, thereby increasing the difficulties for potential new entrants. To remove the Commission's serious doubts about the compatibility of this arrangement with the common market, the Belgian and Swiss governments declared they would mitigate existing regulatory barriers to entry onto the routes "to the extent required to generate sufficient competition to Swissair and Sabena." Moreover, Swissair and Sabena gave a number of undertakings to the Commission aimed at facilitating new entry.

---

[46] See Council Regulation 95/93 on common rules for the allocation of slots at European Community airports, OJ 1993 L 14; this regulation applies only to congested airports.

- *United Airlines/U.S. Airways.*[47] This merger raised concerns that competition would be substantially reduced on several routes between Germany and the United States. To address these concerns, United Airlines agreed to allot a number of slots at Frankfurt and Munich airports to allow new entrants to offer services on routes where problems had been identified.

Abuses of Dominant Position

The importance of Article 82 in the air transport sector is linked to the fact that "flag carriers" have inherited strong positions in their traditional home markets and often have considerable power to impede the development of competition, particularly from new entrants. The Commission has applied Article 82 to two air transport cases: London European versus Sabena,[48] which involved a refusal to supply computer reservation, and British Midland versus Aer Lingus,[49] which concerned a refusal to interline (see annex case 6).

Cases examined by the Commission concerning possible breaches of Article 82 have included the following:

- Frequent flier programs
- Override commissions (additional commissions over and above the standard commission to travel agents)[50]
- Excessive capacity or frequency (particularly when it aims to exclude new entrants).

Transport Infrastructure: Access and Discrimination

Two main issues relate to transport infrastructure: ensuring that operators have access to the infrastructure needed to operate their services, and ensur-

---

[47] Case Comp/M2,041.

[48] Commission Decision 88/589/EEC of November 4, 1988, relating to a proceeding under Article 82 of the EEC Treaty (IV/32.318, London European, Sabena), OJ 1988 L 317.

[49] Commission Decision 92/213/EEC of February 26, 1992, relating to a procedure pursuant to Articles 81 and 82 of the EEC Treaty (IV/33.544, British Midland versus Aer Lingus), OJ 1992 L 96.

[50] Commission Decision 2000/74/EEC of July 14, 1999, relating to a proceeding under Article 82 of the EC Treaty (IV/D-2/34.780, Virgin/British Airways), OJ 2000 L 30.

ing *nondiscriminatory treatment* of operators. This is especially important when an owner of essential infrastructure also operates services using that infrastructure. Problems may also arise when the owner of the infrastructure is a monopoly supplier of services to operators that use the infrastructure.

Airports

The Commission's main concerns in airport cases have been to ensure nondiscriminatory access, particularly at the level of airport charges, and to enable carriers to benefit from good-quality, reasonably priced airport services, such as handling of luggage or registration of passengers.

Nondiscriminatory Access

Discrimination cases arise when airports grant larger discounts from tariffs for landing fees to particular airlines or when landing fees are cheaper for domestic flights than for cross-border flights within the European Union. Since an airport is in a monopoly position regarding the design and maintenance of runways, such discrimination is unlawful unless it can be objectively justified. Such behavior may also be contrary to the principle of the single market. The *Zaventem* case illustrates landing fee discrimination and the Commission's position (see annex case 7).[51]

This case concerned a complaint by British Midland (BM) about the system of discounts granted on landing fees at Brussels National Airport. BM considered that the step system of discounts, which increase in line with an airline's volume of traffic, favored high-volume carriers, thereby placing small, competing carriers at a disadvantage. Moreover, according to BM, there was no objective justification for granting such discounts because the services that an arriving or departing aircraft requires are the same, however many times they are supplied. The Commission found that the Airways Authority held a dominant market position in aircraft landing and take-off services. The Commission also found that the system of discounts on landing fees had the effect of applying dissimilar conditions to airlines for equivalent transactions.

All Community airports, with the exception of those in Portugal (which have appealed to the Community Courts in Luxembourg), have now complied with the Commission's position and changed their charging practices.

---

[51] Commission Decision 95/364/EC of June 28, 1995, relating to a proceeding pursuant to Article 86(3) of the Treaty (Zaventem), OJ 1995 L 216.

Ground Handling Services

Ground handling services comprise all activities performed during an aircraft stopover, with respect to the aircraft, passengers, and cargo. In general, ground handling services may be provided for airlines by the airport operator; another airline; or an independent, specialized ground handling company (third-party handling). Air carriers may also provide their own handling services, either individually (self-handling) or pooled (joint handling).

Council Directive 96/67 on access to the ground handling market at European Community airports, dated October 15, 1996, stated that, for airports whose annual traffic is not less than three million passenger movements that have certain categories of services, member states are required to take necessary measures to ensure free market access by third-party suppliers, effective January 1, 1999.[52] However, they could limit the number of authorized suppliers to no fewer than two. Similarly, as of January 1, 1998, member states were required to take necessary measures to ensure the freedom to self-handle; however, they could reserve this right to no fewer than two airport users, self-handling being narrowly defined.

Where specific constraints imposed by the availability of space or capacity make it impossible to open up the market or implement self-handling, the member state in question may, subject to Commission approval, decide to limit provision of ground handling services to one supplier (for a once renewable two-year period) and to ban self-handling or restrict it to a single airport user (for a renewable three-year period). Member states must notify the Commission, at least three months before they enter into force, of any exemptions they grant.

The Commission has received many complaints concerning the supply by monopolies of poor quality, exorbitantly priced ground handling services. The Commission's approach has been to take steps to ensure that the monopoly is broken and that second operators are allowed entry on a nondiscriminatory basis. The Commission's decisions in the Flughafen Frankfurt Main AG (FAG)[53] and Alpha Flight Services[54] cases demonstrate how it has applied Article 82 to cases involving ground handling services (see annex cases 8 and 9).

---

[52] OJ L 272, 25.10.1996, paragraph 36.

[53] Commission Decision 98/190/EC of January 14, 1998, relating to a proceeding under Article 82 of the EC Treaty, Flughafen Frankfurt/Main AG, OJ 1998 L 72.

[54] Commission Decision 98/513/EC of June 11, 1998, relating to a proceeding under Article 82 of the EC Treaty, Alpha Flight Services/Aéroports de Paris, OJ 1998 L 230.

These cases are among the most difficult the Commission must handle. Often, there is substantial local political interest in the outcome of these cases. Moreover, they raise significant questions about the technical feasibility of allowing competing operators to provide services where safety is of paramount concern and space is limited.

Ports

Ports generate the same problems of access and discrimination as those found in airports. This is especially significant for the introduction of new ferry services, but also is relevant to other maritime transport services. With regard to access to ports, the general principle is that the owner of an infrastructure abuses a dominant position by refusing access to a port and thereby impeding the start-up of new service.

In its port cases (Holyhead[55] and Roscoff[56]), the Commission established the following principles. First, a company in a dominant position that sells services must have a valid reason for refusing to sell them to a willing buyer, particularly when the company in a dominant position controls access to an essential facility. Second, a company that both owns and uses an essential facility should not grant its competitors access on terms less favorable than those it gives its own services and may be obligated to alter temporarily some of its own sailing times (see annex cases 10 and 11).

In the Genoa pilots decision, the Commission required Italian authorities to modify a discount system on the piloting tariffs that amounted to discrimination between maritime shipping companies for the same service.[57] In addition, two merger cases involved port services, neither of which was opposed. The first, Pakhoed/van Ommeren, concerned various markets for storage facilities and was approved, subject to divestiture of two terminals in Rotterdam and one in Antwerp.[58] The second, Maersk/ECT, involved container terminal services and was approved unconditionally.[59]

---

[55] Commission Decision of June 11, 1992, relating to a proceeding under Article 82 of the EC Treaty (IV/34.174, Sealink/B&I, Interim Measures), unpublished.

[56] Commission Decision of May 16, 1995, relating to a proceeding under Article 82 of the EC Treaty (Irish Continental Group/CCI Morlaix, Port of Roscoff), unpublished.

[57] Commission Decision 97/745/EC of October 21, 1997, relating to a proceeding pursuant to Article 86(3) of the EC Treaty regarding the tariffs for piloting in the Port of Genoa, OJ 1997 L 301.

[58] Case Comp/M1621.

[59] Case Comp/M1674.

Conclusion: Achievements and Challenges

Competition and liberalization policies play a fundamental role in ensuring the creation of a single European Community market that is nondiscriminatory on the grounds of nationality. Transport, an industry that serves other industries, rather than being an end in its own right, is a key element in constructing this market.

For competition authorities, the key issue is to ensure that consumers of transport services can obtain the best quality services at the lowest possible prices. The tools used to realize this goal are those designed to prohibit anticompetitive agreements, abuse of market power, and emergence of monopoly power as a result of merger.

Liberalization policies also play a significant role in the transport sector. Their purpose is to ensure that infrastructure is used efficiently and that access and prices are fair and nondiscriminatory.

Railway liberalization appears to have stalled in the face of persistent doubts at the level of the Council of Ministers.[60] Thus, individual member states are proceeding with liberalization at different speeds and with differing degrees of success. Overall, railways are likely to continue declining, losing out to road transport.

In theory, this situation would suggest that the impetus for change would come from applying competition rules, as in the Deutsche Bahn case (see annex case 3), since the Commission can act independently of the Council in this area. However, applying competition rules to railway activities is complicated by the ambiguous scope of Regulation 1,017/68 and by national monopolies, which limit the scope of applying Article 81. This means that each national monopoly is unlikely to compete with other national monopolies and any agreement between them is unlikely to restrict competition. It also seems clear that national monopolies prefer doing business with other national monopolies rather than with new entrants.

Regarding liner shipping, every major position taken by the Commission concerning the scope of the group exemption has been challenged before the European Community Courts in Luxembourg. While some cases are reasonably far along, others remain at an early stage, and legal uncertainty persists. Many issues related to the scope of the group exemption have not yet been tackled, even by the Commission. The liner shipping industry

---

[60] The Council of Ministers is the body that represents the governments of the member states.

remains wedded to the idea that it is somehow different from other industries and that competition rules should be applied differently or not at all. Given the history of cartels in this sector, the problems of illegal price fixing and output restrictions are likely to continue.

The air transport sector has a comprehensive regulatory framework despite the fact that, other than in merger cases, the Commission cannot directly apply Articles 81 and 82 to routes between the European Community and third countries. In cases where the Commission has approved cooperative arrangements between airlines (for example, Lufthansa/SAS [see annex case 5] or Swissair/Sabena), it is not readily apparent that those activities have facilitated new entry. Indeed, many consider that airline fares for most city pair routes within the European Community remain high.

With regard to seaports and airports, significant progress has been made in both competition and liberalization. Clear case law exists concerning access conditions, although scarce facilities always raise the problem of rationing—an issue that spills over into liberalization, since the tendency is to protect incumbents. In the airport sector, this problem may arise because the incumbents tend to be of the same nationality as the owner of the infrastructure; in the seaport sector, on the other hand, the problem is that the port owner also operates the transport services.

Despite the progress that remains to be achieved, the Commission's competition policy for cases in the transport sector has been considerably advanced, especially since the adoption of Regulation 4,056 in 1986 and Regulation 3,975 the following year. The Commission's decisions, especially those in liner shipping and infrastructure cases, have been highly detailed and provide a substantial basis for future Commission activity.

Annex. Relevant Cases

Case 1. Eurotunnel

The Eurotunnel case concerned the individual exemption that the Commission granted Eurotunnel, the Société Nationale des Chemins de Fer Français (SNCF), and British Rail (BR) on December 13, 1994, with respect to their agreement on the use of the Channel Tunnel. This usage contract gave SNCF/BR 50 percent of the per-hour capacity in each direction of the fixed link, and Eurotunnel the remaining 50 percent. The usage contract was exempted for a 30-year period, effective November 16, 1991.

The decision identified relevant markets as those markets that provide hourly paths for rail transport in the tunnel and various markets in the international transport of passengers and freight between the United Kingdom and the Continent.

The Commission considered that the arrangement restricted competition in two ways. First, it restricted competition between Eurotunnel and BR/SNCF on the transport markets since the contract provided for dividing the markets: Eurotunnel operated shuttles, while SNCF/BR operated international trains carrying passengers and freight. Second, SNCF and BR were effectively given a monopoly of those hourly paths available for international passenger and freight trains. Accordingly, other railway companies could not obtain from Eurotunnel the hourly paths necessary to operate international passenger or freight trains in competition with SNCF and BR.

The Commission's exemption was subject to the condition that SNCF and BR should not withhold sales to other railway companies of at least 25 percent of the hourly capacity of the tunnel in each direction in order to run international passenger and freight trains.

On appeal, the CFI found that statements in the Commission's decision to reserve half of tunnel capacity for shuttle services and half for international trains and entitling SNCF/BR to all capacity reserved for international trains were wrong and that the contract's restrictive effects on competition were founded on errors in those statements. Thus, in evaluating those effects on other railway companies, the Commission failed to consider the possibility that Eurotunnel might still cede some of its own capacity to other companies wishing to run international trains through the tunnel.

The CFI held that, if the Commission had correctly assessed the opportunities available to other railway companies to obtain the hourly paths necessary to run international trains through the tunnel, it might not have deemed it necessary to impose conditions on the applicants.

Case 2. European Night Services

The Commission authorized the European Night Services (ENS) agreement between BR, Deutsche Bahn (DB), Nederlandse Spoorwegen (NS), SNCF, and Société Nationale des Chemins de Fer Belges (SNCB) concerning running night passenger trains between the United Kingdom and the Continent.

BR, DB, NS, SNCF, and SNCB had set up a specialized subsidiary, European Night Services, Ltd. (ENS), to organize and run night rail services. The Commission held that this agreement was likely to restrict competition between these parties and between them and other operators, who would face the obstacle of entering the market in question. Such an agreement also has advantages for consumers. Therefore, the Commission decided to authorize the agreement for eight years. However, to allow other operators to offer similar services, it required the railway companies to sell to them those rail services they had agreed to sell their subsidiary, under the same terms.

In October 1998, the CFI annulled the ENS decision on the grounds that the Commission's finding that the arrangements brought about a material restriction of competition was not supported by the evidence put forward in the decision.[61]

Case 3. Deutsche Bahn

On April 1, 1988, DB, SNCB, NS, Intercontainer, and Transfracht concluded the Maritime Container Network (MCN) agreement, which related to rail carriage of maritime containers to or from Germany that passed through a German, Belgian, or Netherlands port. Among the German ports that the MCN agreement referred to as "northern" were Hamburg, Bremen, and Bremerhaven. The Belgian and Netherlands ports, known as the "western" ports, included Antwerp and Rotterdam.

The Commission found that, in view of its statutory monopoly, DB held a dominant market position for the supply of rail transport services in

---

[61] Joint cases T-374/94, T-375/94, T-384/94, and T-388/94; European Night Services, Ltd., Eurostar (U.K.) Ltd., formerly European Passenger Services, Ltd. (EPS), Union internationale des chemins de fer (UIC), NV Nederlandse Spoorwegen, and Société nationale des chemins de fer français versus Commission, Judgment of the Court of First Instance of September 15, 1998, not yet reported.

Germany. DB had abused its dominant position such that tariffs for carriage between a Belgian or Netherlands port and Germany were appreciably and unjustifiably higher than for carriage between points within Germany and the German ports. In response, the Commission fined DB 11 million ECU. The CFI upheld the Commission's decision in October 1997.[62]

Case 4. Associated Central West Africa Lines

The Associated Central West Africa Lines (CEWAL) case arose out of the Commission's inquiries into the practices of the shipping conferences operating on routes between Europe and West Africa. On December 23, 1992, the Commission adopted a decision that found three liner shipping conferences had infringed Article 81 and that members of CEWAL, a liner shipping conference, had infringed Article 82. The CFI upheld the Commission's decision in all respects except duration of the infringement.

The CFI stressed that group exemptions, such as that found in Regulation 4,056/86, must be strictly interpreted. In particular, the CFI said that, while the aim of a shipping conference has been recognized as beneficial and therefore justifies the granting of a group exemption, it cannot be that every impairment of competition brought about by shipping conferences falls outside the prohibition laid out, in principle, in Article 81(1) of the Treaty.

This approach has led the Commission to adopt various decisions in which it has found that certain practices engaged in by members of a liner shipping conference neither fell within the scope of the group exemption nor qualified for individual exemption.

Case 5. Lufthansa/SAS

In May 1995, Lufthansa and SAS applied to the Commission for exemption of a general cooperation agreement providing for the establishment of an integrated air transport system between the two airlines.[63] In particular, they wished to set up a joint venture for traffic between Germany and Scandinavia that would be their exclusive vehicle for operating services on those routes, but each party would, nevertheless, retain its own commercial brand identity.

---

[62] Deutsche Bahn versus Commission, [1997] ECR II-1689, at paragraph 77.

[63] LH/SAS (n. 22 above).

On eight routes, Lufthansa and SAS were the only operative airlines, except for one frequency per day that Singapore Airlines operated between Frankfurt and Copenhagen. In terms of the number of passengers carried, these eight routes accounted for 66 percent of all traffic between Scandinavia and Germany. Furthermore, at least one of the two airlines was operating on 12 routes between Scandinavia and Germany. The new entity being set up would thus operate on 20 of the 25 routes between Scandinavia and Germany.

The Commission concluded that conditions needed to be imposed to ensure that the restrictions of competition remained within the bounds of what was necessary to safeguard the market presence of competing airlines and to ensure that opportunities for market entry were available to new entrants. The Commission considered that Lufthansa and SAS should freeze the number of daily frequencies they operated along a route when a new entrant decided to serve that route. This condition was designed to prevent the operating airlines from substantially increasing their number of frequencies aimed at squeezing out new entrants from the market.

New entrants' access to routes between Scandinavia and Germany was conditioned on the availability of slots at Scandinavian and German airports. Frankfurt, Dusseldorf, Stockholm, and Oslo airports were, however, saturated at certain hours of the day, and obtaining slots through the usual allocation procedures was virtually impossible. Lufthansa and SAS were therefore required to relinquish, as the need arose, a sufficient number of slots at each of these airports to enable other airlines to operate competing services on certain routes. This would be called for only when the new entrant had been unable to obtain slots through the usual allocation procedure in force at each airport.

Case 6. Aer Lingus

Aer Lingus was the dominant provider for the London-Dublin route. After British Midland announced its intention in 1989 to start its own service along that route, in competition with Aer Lingus, Aer Lingus terminated its interlining relationship with British Midland. As a result of that action, passengers holding British Midland tickets could no longer, as a right, change flights to Aer Lingus services, and travel agents could no longer issue tickets combining flights of both airlines.

Withdrawal of interlining facilities made British Midland's flights less attractive to travelers—particularly business travelers, who preferred higher-priced, fully flexible tickets—and travel agents. By terminating its interlining relationship, Aer Lingus made it more difficult for British Midland to compete. British Midland was deprived of significant revenue and forced to incur higher costs in order to overcome the handicap imposed on it.

Finding that Aer Lingus had abused its dominant position by terminating its interlining agreement with British Midland, the Commission fined Aer Lingus 750,000 ECU and ordered it to resume its interlining relationship with British Midland. However, it agreed that new entrants should not rely indefinitely on the frequencies and services provided by their competitors, but should be encouraged to develop their own. Therefore, the duration of the duty to interline could be limited to the time period that was objectively necessary for a competitor to become established in the market. Considering that three years had elapsed since British Midland started its new services, the duty to interline imposed by the decision was limited to two years, subject to review in light of competition development on the relevant route.

Case 7. Zaventem

The Zaventem decision concerned a complaint by BM about the system of discounts granted on landing fees at Brussels National Airport (Zaventem). BM considered that the stepwise discounts, which increased in line with an airline's volume of traffic, favored high-volume carriers, thereby placing smaller competing carriers at a disadvantage. Moreover, according to BM, granting such discounts had no objective justification since the services that an arriving or departing aircraft required were identical, however many times they were supplied.

The Commission said that the Airways Authority was a public undertaking within the meaning of Article 86(1) and that the Royal Decree stating the fees payable for the use of Zaventem, which established a system of discounts on landing fees, was a State measure within the meaning of Article 86(1). In 1992, Sabena received final step discounts (30 percent) equivalent to an overall reduction of 18 percent on its fees, whereas the other qualifying airlines (Sobelair and BA) were eligible for only a first step discount (7.5 percent). No other airline operating at Brussels National Airport qualified for a reduction in its landing fees, which placed BM at a competitive disadvantage.

The Commission found that the Airways Authority held a dominant market position in its capacity in aircraft landing and take-off services. It had not been demonstrated that handling the take-off or landing of an aircraft belonging to one airline rather than to another gives rise to economies of scale. The system of discounts on landing fees had the effect of applying dissimilar conditions to airlines for equivalent transactions linked to landing and take-off services, thereby placing some arlines at a competitive disadvantage. This constituted abuse of dominant position within the meaning of Article 82(c). Since this system had been established by a member state by way of an administrative act, it constituted an infringement of Article 86, read in conjunction with Article 82 of the Treaty.

The Commission noted that Article 82 also applies to cases in which a company in a dominant position discriminates against its partners for reasons other than its own interest. This may involve, for example, giving preference to another company from the same state or one that pursues the same general policy.

Case 8. Flughafen Frankfurt Main AG

Flughafen Frankfurt Main AG (FAG) is the company that owns and operates Frankfurt Airport. Overall airport capacity is dictated by three types of capacity: runway, stands, and terminal buildings. FAG has one runway, an additional take-off only runway, and two terminals.

On the land side, FAG allowed air carriers the right of self-handling and/or third-party handling. Regarding passengers, air carriers were allowed to self-handle their land side activities, and all airlines had the right to handle passengers of other airlines. FAG also supplied these services. It did not allow independent handling operators to provide passenger handling services. Regarding certain ramp side activities, FAG refused to allow self-handling or to admit third party handlers. Consequently, FAG was the sole provider of those services at Frankfurt Airport.

The scope of the FAG decision was limited to the ramp side activities for which FAG neither allowed self-handling nor admitted independent third-party service suppliers. The Commission considered that, as sole supplier of the services concerned, FAG held a dominant market position on providing ramp handling services at Frankfurt Airport. Potential alternative suppliers were not in a position to assail FAG's monopoly, as long as the airport operator continued to deny them access to the ramp where these services were provided.

In deciding to retain the market for ramp handling services at Frankfurt Airport, FAG extended its dominant market position to provide airport landing and take-off facilities to the neighboring separate market for ramp handling services. Furthermore, FAG used its power as exclusive provider of airport facilities to deny airlines the right to self-handle. This obligated users of FAG airport facilities to also purchase its ramp handling services.

FAG argued that its refusal to authorize self-handling and independent ramp handlers was objectively justified by lack of airport space. However, the Commission concluded that FAG's argument was not well founded. The experts' technical reports showed that the space constraints at Frankfurt Airport did not prevent authorization of self-handling or admission of independent ramp handlers. Moreover, even if such constraints existed, they would not be insurmountable.

The Commission therefore found that FAG had abused its dominant position in breach of Article 82 by denying, without objective justification, potential third-party handlers access to the ramp and airport users the right to self-handle, thereby reserving for itself the market for providing ramp handling services at Frankfurt Airport. The Commission ordered FAG to bring the infringement to an end, giving it three months in which to develop a reorganization plan that would give air carriers and independent providers of ramp handling services market access.

Case 9. Alpha Flight Services

The Alpha Flight Services (AFS) versus Aéroports de Paris (ADP) decision concerned the system of commercial fees charged by ADP in exchange for the operating license issued to suppliers of certain categories of ground handling services at Orly and Roissy-Charles de Gaulle airports (CDG).

AFS complained to the Commission about the discrepancy in the commercial fees that ADP charged AFS versus Orly Air Traiteur (OAT), a subsidiary of Groupe Air France and competitor for the supply of catering services at Orly. AFS considered that, if it were charged at the same rate as OAT, then its annual fees would be reduced by about 3.5 million FRF.

The Commission found that, because of ADP's dominant position, the payment of a commercial fee must not create dissimilar conditions for equivalent transactions, thus placing suppliers or users engaged in the same ground handling activity at a competitive disadvantage.

It further found that, in 1995, the commercial fee AFS paid was considerably higher than the amount OAT paid. On the basis of the turnover achieved by caterers and cleaners within the same airport, a rate lowered by only a few percent would reduce annual fees by several million FRF.

In addition, the Commission considered that the zero or low rates ADP applied to self-handling by airlines resulted from the cost of management services ADP supplied to all ground handlers, including self-handlers, being passed on to suppliers of services for third parties. Ground handling services for third parties were therefore more expensive than self-handling services.

The Commission considered that not imposing a fee on airlines licensed only to self-handle gave them an unfair cost advantage with regard to self-handling activities and, therefore, air transport.

The Commission concluded that the commercial fees charged by ADP for certain types of ground handling service at Orly and CDG airports, particularly catering, aircraft cleaning, and cargo services, were applied at discriminatory rates that affected competition between the suppliers of the handling services concerned and, indirectly, between European Community airlines that use Orly and CDG airports. This amounted to a breach of Article 82. No fines were imposed. An appeal against the Commission's decision was rejected by the CFI on December 12, 2000.[64]

Case 10. Sealink/B&I

The Commission found that Sealink (a British ferry operator that is also the port authority at Holyhead, Wales) had, prime facie, abused its dominant position, breaching Article 82 EC.

In its capacity as port authority at Holyhead, Sealink permitted changes to its own ferry sailing times, which involved movement of an additional ship past the B&I (an Irish ferry operator) vessel while it was in its berth in the mouth of the harbor. Because of the port's limitations, whenever a Sealink vessel passed a moored B&I ship, the water level in the harbor rose. As a result, the ramp of the B&I ship had to be disconnected for safety reasons, which interrupted loading and unloading of the vessel.

B&I asked the Commission to adopt interim measures to prevent Sealink from implementing its schedule on the grounds that B&I services would be seriously disrupted because of the reduced time available in which to carry out its loading and unloading operations.

The Commission stated that any company that both owns and uses an essential facility should not grant its competitors access on terms less favorable than those that it gives its own services. This decision obligated Sealink to alter its sailing schedule temporarily.

---

[64] Case T-128/98, Aéroports de Paris.

Case 11. Roscoff

In the Port of Roscoff decision, the Commission granted interim measures, at the request of Irish Continental Group (ICG), against the Chamber de Commerce et d'Industrie de Morlaix (CCI Morlaix), on the grounds of its having breached Article 82 EC. ICG complained to the Commission that CCI Morlaix had abused its dominant position as port authority at Roscoff by refusing ICG access to the facilities.

CCI Morlaix manages the port of Roscoff (Port de Bloscon) and also is a shareholder (of about 5 percent) in Brittany Ferries, the principal user of the port of Roscoff. Brittany Ferries operates ferry services between the Irish port of Cork and the French ports of Roscoff and St. Malo, as well as between certain U.K. ports and Brittany, and between Spain and Brittany.

In its decision, the Commission concluded that Roscoff was the only port that provided facilities for transport services between Brittany and Ireland, under conditions acceptable to ICG (Lorient being located too far away and St. Malo not having the technical facilities needed for large ferries). Consequently, CCI Morlaix, in its capacity as port authority, had a dominant market position for providing port facilities for passenger and auto ferry services between Brittany and Ireland.

CCI Morlaix occupied a dominant position in providing an essential facility—without access to which competitors could not provide services to their customers. Its refusal, without objective justification, to grant a company (wishing to compete with another company active in a secondary market) access to its facilities constituted an abuse of its dominant position, aside from any economic interest CCI Morlaix had in Brittany Ferries.

A company in a dominant position that sells services must have a valid reason for refusing to sell them to a willing buyer, particularly when the dominant company controls access to an essential facility. Furthermore, a company that occupies a dominant position in providing an essential facility is obligated to provide access, on nondiscriminatory terms, if its refusal would significantly affect competition.

The Commission considered CCI Morlaix's behavior as unjustified and inconsistent with its obligations as a company in a dominant position with regard to an essential facility. Therefore, the Commission ordered CCI Morlaix to grant ICG access to the port of Roscoff for a temporary period. In addition, in accordance with Article 5 of the European Community Treaty, it required all competent French authorities to take appropriate measures to ensure fulfillment of the obligations resulting from its decision.

Chapter 7

Cross-subsidy Prices in Public Utilities

Paulina Beato

During the past decade, many industries that historically have operated under heavy government control have undergone substantial reform. A new model of infrastructure provision has emerged and has been extended worldwide. Three features characterize the new model. First, the property, financing, and management of infrastructure assets rest, at least to some extent, on private sector firms. Second, the public sector plays a regulatory role that should complement, not substitute for, the market. Third, consumer prices should cover total costs. Multilateral institutions have made recommendations for providing infrastructure services, using the new model, that cover a range of topics—from selection of the private sector firm to organization of the regulatory institutions, from pricing policy to entry and exit control, and from financing policies to the role of markets.

Principles of Pricing Policies

Pricing policy recommendations are based on two principles. One is that prices should cover the total cost of service. The other is that cross-subsidy schemes should be avoided.[1] Although both principles may appear simple,

---

[1] The economic literature variously defines cross-subsidy schemes; four definitions are discussed in this chapter. Simply stated, a price scheme has cross subsidies if prices for some consumer groups are below average costs, while prices for other consumer groups are above average costs.

their application to real-world infrastructure services may be complex. The reason is that, among the several notions of free cross-subsidy prices, only one is fully compatible with both covering total cost and welfare goals when technologies have increasing returns.[2]

This chapter explores the economic literature for rules on applying these principles to real-world infrastructure services. Discussion is based on a partial equilibrium approach that uses market surplus as a proxy for social welfare and efficiency.[3] Although equity issues are important and are related to cross-subsidy pricing, they are not addressed because they require a different analytical framework. For efficiency issues, market surplus suffices, while for equity issues, social welfare functions and income distribution goals are needed. Therefore, a partial equilibrium analysis is appropriate for the former and a general equilibrium framework is best suited to the latter.

Three main conclusions are reached. First, if a uniform price schedule is established and prices diverge from marginal cost, then social welfare can be increased by establishing appropriate price discrimination schemes that have cross subsidies. This does not mean that all schemes with cross subsidies increase welfare, but some do. For example, cross-subsidy schemes where prices are lower than marginal cost are inappropriate from the welfare standpoint, whereas cross-subsidy schemes with prices below average cost may be welfare optimal. Second, from a voluntary sustainability standpoint,[4] some cross-subsidy schemes are not suitable, whereas others are appropriate. Third, occasionally, optimal and voluntary sustainable price schedules are incompatible. In these cases, a trade-off between what is optimal and sustainable is often necessary. The regulator's choice should be based on a comparison between efficiency losses and the cost of maintaining a price schedule that drives some consumers away from the regulated firm or forces the exclusion of other consumers.

---

[2] Although increasing returns are not always equivalent to decreasing average cost functions, for reasons of simplicity, this chapter considers the terms equivalent. The chapter assumes that the conditions for such equivalence hold. See Panzar (1989).

[3] The terms *social welfare* and *efficiency* are used synonymously.

[4] The section "Can Cross Subsidies Destroy Markets?" provides a thorough definition of the term *voluntary sustainability*. The idea is that a public service is voluntarily sustainable if consumers are unwilling to change suppliers; that is, all consumer groups are better off if the regulated firm continues providing the service.

Cross Subsidies and Consumer Separation: An Example

To illustrate the main issues discussed in this chapter, let us assume that a profit-regulated firm provides water to two neighborhoods, *a* and *b*. Water supply requires two types of investments: the first type, distribution pipelines, is specific to each neighborhood, while the second type, storage tanks and pumps, can be used by both neighborhoods. The regulated firm's total costs equal the capital cost of investments, plus the cost of electricity for pumping water from the river to the neighborhoods. The regulator sets the same price for both neighborhoods, which equals total average cost.[5]

The manager of the regulated firm notices that the company may increase its profit by providing water to a new neighborhood, *c*, at a lower price than that charged neighborhoods *a* and *b*. The manager sets prices in neighborhood *c* so that revenues are slightly above that neighborhood's costs, as well as the pipeline distribution and electricity cost. Nevertheless, the manager does not charge for the cost of the storage tank and pumps. After initiating the new policy, the firm profits and total consumption increases.

The regulator then imposes a penalty on the manager because, by setting lower prices in the new neighborhood, the manager is in noncompliance with existing regulations. The manager claims that the new pricing policy increases social welfare, arguing that, if consumers pay voluntarily, then consumer welfare should be larger than consumer payments. The manager also says that, if revenues from new consumers are greater than incremental cost, the welfare gains are larger than the increase in social costs; that is, a net increase in social welfare occurs.

Despite the manager's claims, the regulator forces the manager to distribute the cost of the tank and pumps uniformly among the three neighborhoods. The new pricing policy means an insignificant reduction in the prices paid by the consumers in neighborhoods *a* and *b*, and a large increase in the prices paid by neighborhood *c*. The results of this regulatory policy are a dramatic fall in consumption in neighborhood *c*, while consumption in neighborhoods *a* and *b* remains approximately at prior levels.

While the manager's arguments do not convince the regulator, real-life facts make the regulator reconsider the proposal. Thus, the regulator con-

---

[5] For a multiproduct firm, the average cost may be ambiguous because of the assignment of the common cost among products. In this example, the regulator defines the average cost of servicing water as follows: pump cost plus storage tank cost plus distribution cost to neighborhoods *a* and *b* plus electricity cost for neighborhoods a and b, divided by the amount of water service in both neighborhoods.

tracts a consultant to evaluate the manager's pricing policy. The consultant agrees that the manager's proposal increases social welfare, and points out that further increases in welfare can be brought to the community if a full-price discrimination scheme is set across the three neighborhoods. The consultant recommends increasing prices in neighborhood *a*, decreasing prices in neighborhood *b*, and maintaining the manager's pricing proposal in neighborhood *c*. The consultant supports the manager's recommendations with the following argument: Prices should be increased in neighborhood *a* because the area only has tourist hotels and the volume of water consumed by tourists is not sensitive to price increases.[6] Thus, prices can be increased in neighborhood *a* to include the entire cost of the storage tank and pumps, in addition to distribution costs, without resulting in a decline in water consumption. Prices can then be lowered in neighborhood *b*, where consumers are sensitive to prices and the regulated firm would not incur any losses. The increase in consumption in neighborhood *b*, is higher than the decrease in neighborhood *a*, and total consumption and social welfare increase.

The regulator carries out the consultant's recommendations. During the initial period, the new measures are popular. After six months, however, company revenues drop because of a decrease in consumption in neighborhood *a*, despite the sharp increase in the number of tourists. Further investigations reveal that each hotel has its own well-water system. Tourists may have low price elasticity, but hotels do not. The results are higher social costs for communities and large losses for the regulated firm. The regulator tries to forbid the use of well water, but is unsuccessful.

Price Schemes with Cross Subsidies

Are the proposals of the regulator, the manager, and the consultant free of cross subsidies? The answer depends on how a price scheme free of cross subsidies is defined. The notion of cross subsidies has been developed for dealing with the relation between service payments from a group of consumers and the costs associated with providing that group a service or related services. However, various definitions have been used for price schemes free of cross subsidies. The following four definitions are used in this chapter.

---

[6] The consultant is unable to estimate demand functions for each neighborhood because of a lack of price variation during the last period. However, the consultant calculates the demand of neighborhood *a* based on the demand for tourists. By doing so, the consultant does not mention in the analysis that the hotels can use well water as a source of supply.

Definition 1: Marginal Cost Criterion

Using this criterion, a price scheme is said to have cross subsidies if some consumer prices are lower than the marginal cost. Otherwise, if all consumer prices are equal to or above marginal costs, then the price scheme is subsidy free. According to this criterion, a price scheme in which all consumer prices exactly equal marginal cost is cross-subsidy free. However, such a scheme may not raise enough revenue to cover the total cost of service. In the previous section, the proposals made by the regulator, the manager, and the consultant are free of cross subsidies according to this criterion because the prices proposed by each cover neighborhood electricity costs in all three neighborhoods.

Definition 2: Average Cost Criterion

Using this criterion, a price scheme is said to have cross subsidies if some consumer prices are below and others are above average costs. This criterion may be difficult to apply to multiproduct firms because their average cost schedules may not be well defined. In particular, when some costs are shared among products, the average cost schedule cannot be precisely defined. For example, the regulated firm in the above example may be considered a multiproduct firm if providing water to neighborhoods a and b is viewed as two products. Therefore, an average cost schedule for each neighborhood cannot be precisely defined because of the different ways common costs are distributed. Nevertheless, for purposes of illustrating the average cost criterion, average cost is defined as the sum of all costs (pumps, storage, distribution, and electricity) in both neighborhoods, divided by the amount of water delivered to both neighborhoods. That is, water provision is considered a unique product, regardless of where it is delivered. According to this definition of average cost, the manager's proposal has cross subsidies since the price for neighborhood c is below average cost, while prices in neighborhoods a and b are above average costs.

Definition 3: Incremental Cost Criterion

Using this criterion, a price scheme is said to have cross subsidies if revenues from a consumer or a group of consumers are less than the incremental cost of providing services to that consumer or consumer group. In the above example, the incremental cost for neighborhood c is the cost of electricity for pumping (marginal cost) plus the cost of pipelines in neighborhood c. The incremental costs for the other neighborhoods are similarly defined. Therefore, according to the incremental cost criterion, the manager's price schedule is subsidy free since all neighborhood revenues cover variable and distribution costs for each neighborhood.

Definition 4: Stand-alone Criterion

Using this criterion, a price scheme is said to have subsidies if the revenues from a consumer or consumer group are larger than the cost of providing service alone to this consumer or consumer group. In the example, the price scheme proposed by the consultant is not subsidy free because revenues from neighborhood *a* are higher than the cost of producing the service for this neighborhood using wells.

Observations

First, definitions 1 and 2 compare prices with the actual costs of providing services, whereas definitions 3 and 4 compare prices with the costs of other alternatives for providing the service. This means that, for assessing price schedules according to criteria 1 and 2, only knowledge of the regulated firm's cost schedule is required, while, to assess price schedules according to criteria 3 and 4, information about other technologies is needed. Second, it is necessary to examine all groups of consumers to establish that a price scheme is subsidy free under definitions 3 and 4. It is not enough to test some individuals or groups. Thus, definition 3 requires that all consumers and consumer groups pay the incremental costs that correspond with the technology used by the regulated firm and any other available technologies. Definition 4 requires that all consumers and consumer groups prefer the service of the regulated firm to all other alternatives.

Third, with increasing returns, a price scheme that is free of cross subsidies according to the average cost criterion will also be subsidy free according to the marginal cost criterion since marginal costs will be below average costs when average costs are decreasing (figure 7-1). Finally, if the profit of the firm is zero, then a price scheme is subsidy free according to definition 3 only if it is subsidy free according to definition 4.[7]

---

[7] For a proof, see Braeutigam (1989).

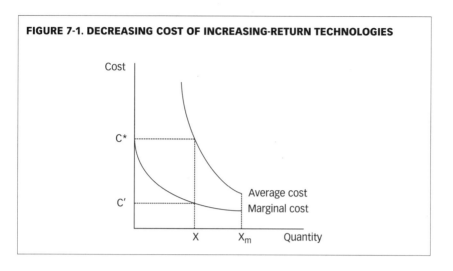

FIGURE 7-1. DECREASING COST OF INCREASING-RETURN TECHNOLOGIES

Cross Subsidies and Market Efficiency

In the previous example, the proposal of the manager of the regulated company is supported by well-known theoretical results that state: any uniform price schedule different from marginal cost can be welfare dominated by a nonuniform price schedule if consumers have different price elasticities. These findings are relevant for setting discriminatory prices in infrastructure services because marginal cost pricing does not cover total cost in the presence of increasing returns, a common feature of infrastructure. Therefore, if revenues from infrastructure services cover total costs, then prices must diverge from marginal cost. From a welfare standpoint, this means that price discrimination schedules may be better than a uniform price when the uniform price does not equal marginal cost and price elasticities differ among consumers.

However, price discrimination may or may not imply cross subsidies. If regulators set prices to cover costs exactly, without yielding extraordinary profits, then any price discrimination scheme has implicit cross subsidies according to the average cost criterion. The reason is that consumers who pay higher prices are paying more than average costs, while consumers who pay lower prices are paying less than average costs. In these cases, the allocations resulting from pricing with cross subsidies according to the average cost criterion may dominate, from an efficiency standpoint, allocations resulting from uniform prices. It may occur that a pricing scheme that

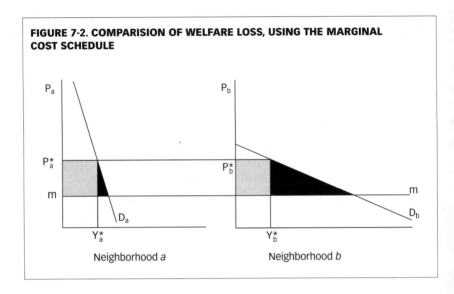

FIGURE 7-2. COMPARISION OF WELFARE LOSS, USING THE MARGINAL COST SCHEDULE

increases welfare with respect to uniform prices has cross subsidies according to the average cost criterion and does not have them according to the stand-alone or incremental criterion. However, it may also be that a pricing scheme appropriate for welfare purposes has cross subsidies according to the average cost, stand-alone, and incremental cost definitions. Nevertheless, as discussed below, prices must be free of cross subsidy according to the marginal cost criterion for welfare goals.

To better understand the above example, the following arguments may be useful. It should be noted that, if the price is above marginal cost and if consumers have different price elasticities, then welfare may be increased by reducing prices to consumers with a high price elasticity of demand and increasing prices to consumers with a low price elasticity of demand. This is so because the former group's increase in consumption and consumer surplus would compensate for the latter group's decreased consumption and consumer surplus.

In figure 7-2, m is the marginal cost schedule of providing an infrastructure service. Demand functions for neighborhoods a and b are represented by D_a and D_b, respectively. The price elasticity of demand for neighborhood b is larger than that for neighborhood a. Prices are equal in both neighborhoods and higher than marginal costs to cover fixed costs. The gray areas in figure 7-2 represent revenues over variable costs that can be used to cover fixed costs. The black areas represent the welfare loss, with respect to the maximum welfare that could be achieved if prices equaled

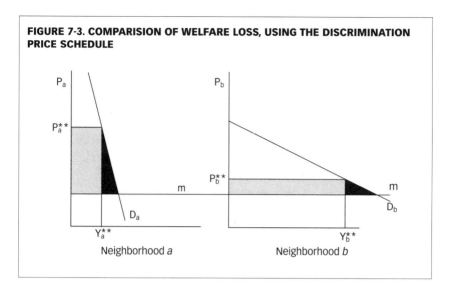

FIGURE 7-3. COMPARISION OF WELFARE LOSS, USING THE DISCRIMINATION PRICE SCHEDULE

marginal costs). The welfare loss is larger in neighborhood b than in neighborhood a because, given the difference in price elasticity of demand between the two neighborhoods, consumption in neighborhood b diminishes more than in neighborhood a as prices increase from marginal cost to P_a^*.

Figure 7-3 shows what happens when a discriminatory price schedule is established. In neighborhood a, prices are now higher than in the previous example (figure 7-2); that is, P_a^{**} is higher than P_a^*, while in neighborhood b, prices are lower; that is, P_b^{**} is lower than P_b^*. The new prices in both neighborhoods are above marginal costs. The difference between revenue and variable cost (shaded areas) is larger in figure 7-3 than in figure 7-2. The measure of welfare loss, with respect to maximum welfare (the black areas) is smaller in figure 7-3 than in figure 7-2. Thus, from a welfare standpoint, the price discrimination schedule is better than the marginal cost schedule.

Prices and Coverage of Marginal Costs

The previous sections show that price discrimination and cross subsidies may increase social welfare, when restricted by increasing returns and no losses. Yet, they fall short of demonstrating that all price discrimination schemes are appropriate for improving social welfare. This section discusses three key factors to consider when analyzing the social welfare implications of schemes that use price discrimination and cross subsidies.

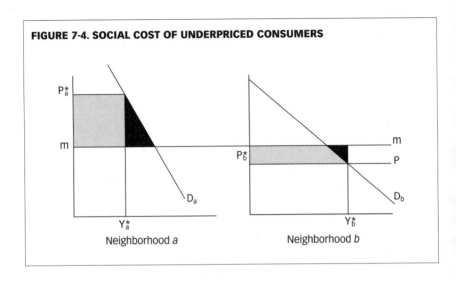

FIGURE 7-4. SOCIAL COST OF UNDERPRICED CONSUMERS

Neighborhood *a*

Neighborhood *b*

First, schemes in which prices are lower than marginal costs are inappropriate from an efficiency standpoint. The reason is simple: If the price a consumer pays is lower than marginal cost, then the social cost of this consumer service is larger than the benefit to the consumer, as measured by the price (figure 7-4). If there are no externalities,[8] social welfare is increased by reducing production in the amount corresponding to the underpriced consumer (figure 7-5). Therefore, a first rule is that consumer prices should be greater than marginal cost. This rule sets a lower bound for price schedules.

Comparison of figures 7-4 and 7-5 shows that social welfare increases simply by increasing prices in neighborhood *b* and retaining the pricing level in neighborhood *a*. The price increase, in turn, reduces consumption and losses, while improving social welfare; thus, the black areas (welfare losses) in figure 7-5 are smaller than in figure 7-4.

Second, schemes with cross subsidies and price discrimination increase welfare only if they increase the level of consumption, since price discrimination and cross subsidies cause marginal rates of substitution to differ among consumers. Therefore, for a given amount of consumption, they are socially inferior to uniform prices. However, if a cross-subsidy scheme suc-

---

[8] If there are externalities, subsidy schemes may need to be implemented to increase consumption. Direct subsidies, as in Chile, are preferable from an efficiency standpoint. Nonetheless, the administrative cost of direct subsidies is usually large.

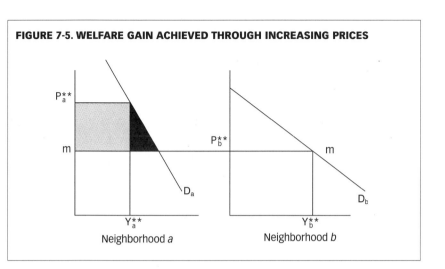

FIGURE 7-5. WELFARE GAIN ACHIEVED THROUGH INCREASING PRICES

cessfully increases the consumption level, the welfare improvement from greater consumption may be larger than the welfare loss from the difference in marginal rates of substitution. It should be clear that, if some prices are below marginal costs, then welfare may increase when these prices rise to the level of marginal costs

Third, with increasing returns and no losses in the regulated firm, a necessary condition to maximize welfare is that the deviation of prices from marginal cost in each market should be inversely related to the price elasticity of demand in each market.[9] That is, in markets with welfare maximization as the goal, price discrimination is appropriate. It also means that prices will be higher than average costs for some consumers, and lower for others. This means there are cross subsidies among consumers, which redistribute income away from low-elasticity groups toward consumers in high-elasticity groups.[10] Thus, if consumers have different elasticities, then optimal prices are not subsidy free, according to the average cost criterion. This result does not say whether optimal prices hold for the stand-alone and the incremental cost criteria for pricing schemes to be subsidy free.

---

[9] A formal proof of this can be found in Boiteux (1971). If nonlinear prices are allowed, then price discrimination is not a necessary condition for maximizing welfare (Willig 1978).

[10] Optimal prices will improve income distribution if low-elasticity groups are the wealthier consumers. Although this is an empirical matter, it seems plausible that wealthier consumers could have a lower price elasticity.

This third point relies on increasing-return technologies and the no-losses restriction for the regulated firm. Nevertheless, it is relevant as a guide for pricing policy of public services because increasing-return technologies are the main reason for regulating the prices of infrastructure services. The case for public sector intervention in infrastructure services is the presence of market failures caused by increasing returns (decreasing average cost structures). In fact, if infrastructure services lack these features, regulators should not control prices, but only promote competition.

Can Cross Subsidies Destroy Markets?

The above results suggest that one cannot make a case against all price schemes with cross subsidies on a welfare basis. Furthermore, cross-subsidy schemes, according to the average cost criterion, are a necessary condition for maximizing welfare when increasing returns are present and losses are forbidden. Therefore, reasons other than welfare should determine whether price schedules with cross subsidies are rejected.

One reason for rejecting cross subsidies is that they may lead overpriced consumers to abandon the regulated firm or force the exclusion of under-priced consumers. Overpriced consumers may realize that their payments to the regulated firm are larger than they would otherwise be. Also, overpriced consumers may observe that excluding underpriced consumer groups would reduce their payments to the regulated firm. Thus, overpriced consumers may force the splitting of the service, causing the entire community to lose the benefits of technologies with economies of scale.

Voluntary Sustainability

The notion of voluntary sustainability characterizes price schemes under which all consumer groups in a community are better off when the public service is jointly provided. Therefore, no consumer is willing to change to another provider. A price discrimination scheme for a community is volun-tarily sustainable if the following two conditions hold:

- *Stand-alone criterion.* Each consumer group pays less for provision of the service than it would otherwise. Thus, separation of a group will not improve the welfare of its members. This condition sets an upper bound for revenues from a consumer.

- *Incremental cost criterion.* Revenue from each consumer group covers the incremental cost that occurs when the service is provided to that group, as opposed to not being provided at all. This condition sets a lower bound for revenue from a consumer group.

When the first condition holds, no group is willing to separate because doing so would increase its payments. However, if the second condition holds, no group is willing to exclude other groups, since exclusion of one group would hurt the remaining consumers.

Observations

A number of observations on the above conditions should be made. First, a pricing scheme is sustainable only if it is free of cross subsidy, according to both the stand-alone and incremental criteria. Second, the incremental cost condition requires that prices should be above marginal costs; therefore, price over marginal cost should hold for both welfare and sustainability reasons. Third, price schedules meeting the conditions for voluntary sustainability may have implicit cross subsidies, according to the average cost criterion; therefore, prices with cross subsidies according to the average cost criterion may be compatible with both welfare and sustainability requirements. Fourth, sustainability of a price scheme closely depends on the alternatives for service provision of each consumer or consumer group. That is, checking sustainability requires information about the alternative technologies available to every group of consumers. Fifth, the notion of voluntary sustainability is strong because all groups should be checked; however, in the real world, it is often difficult for consumers to join in to achieve other alternatives of service provision, even if they can technically achieve them.

This chapter's example can be used to illustrate these notions. The manager's proposal is voluntarily sustainable because neighborhood c pays its incremental cost. Also, because neighborhoods a and b share the common costs, hotel payments are less than the costs of self-provision using wells. Thus, the stand-alone criterion holds. However, the manager's proposal has cross subsidies according to average costs because the price of water for neighborhood c is less than total average costs. By contrast, the consultant's proposal is better than the manager's in terms of welfare. However, hotels have cheaper alternatives than receiving water from the regulated firm at prices that cover the total cost of tanks and pumps. Therefore, the consultant's proposal is not voluntarily sustainable, and most hotels split off.

This chapter's example can be modified to illustrate that voluntary sustainability may be too strong. For example, one can assume that the cost of water provision for each group of hotels is greater than payments to the regulated firm; however, a coalition of one hotel and a thousand consumers may obtain water at a cost lower than its actual payments. One can also assume that the new water supply alternative for this coalition requires large initial investment and that consumers do not have the financial capacity to pay their share of the initial investment. This coalition of one hotel and a thousand consumers, while technically feasible, would be unlikely to make the required investment. Modifying the example shows that the consultant's pricing schedule is still not voluntarily sustainable, according to our definition, because it meets the stand-alone criterion; however, the separation does not occur.

Regulatory Approaches

The economics of regulation deals mainly with three topics. The first is market failure to reach efficiency and the corrective actions that regulators should take. The second involves equity issues and measures for improving income distribution. The third (and most innovative) involves compatibility between regulatory frameworks and the behavior of economic agents for achieving welfare and equity goals. For the issues addressed in this chapter, research on optimal prices with a no-losses condition falls within the first topic, while the sustainability of a pricing scheme falls within the third. Modern theory drives regulators who jointly deal with welfare and incentive issues. In the context of this chapter, this means that regulators should seek prices that are both optimal and sustainable, but may take different approaches to reach this goal.

In one approach, the regulator sets a price schedule that maximizes welfare, subject to a nonnegative profit restriction (see, for example, Baumol and Bradford 1970; Boiteux 1971; Ramsey 1927). However, the optimal price schemes may not be voluntarily sustainable.[11] If not, then the public service may split, which, with scale economies, leads to larger social costs. To defend this approach while avoiding service splitting, regulators should restrict entry. By doing so, the optimal price schedule may be sustainable, but not voluntarily so. However, it may be difficult to control entry effectively since regulators

---

[11] The Weak Invisible Theorem states the conditions under which optimal prices are voluntarily sustainable. See Baumol, Baily, and Willig (1977).

may easily prevent entry into new markets, but may not prevent consumers from providing their own service. Nevertheless, whatever the reason for splitting, the scale economy advantages are lost. The case in which optimal prices are not voluntarily sustainable should be common. The reasons are, as discussed previously, that optimal prices depend on demand elasticities and the cost schedule of joint community provision, whereas voluntarily sustainable prices depend on the cost alternatives of each consumer group.

In the example, hotels have a lower price elasticity of demand; therefore, the optimal price schedules, from a welfare perspective, should set hotel prices higher than those for other consumers. Nevertheless, these price schemes are unsustainable because hotels have wells, an alternative source of water supply. This means that hotels can block optimal price policy. The annex to this chapter provides a numerical example with no sustainable optimal prices.[12]

In a second approach, regulators choose the price scheme that maximizes welfare within the set of voluntarily sustainable prices. Entry may be free because price conditions prevent competitive entry. If revenues from all groups cover total costs, then entry would not improve the current position of any consumer group. Regulators consider consumer incentives, and communities benefit from the advantages of economies of scale through incentives. In the first approach, the economy of scale benefits the community through regulator prohibitions. It requires that regulators have information on coalitions and the technologies available to them. Such information is difficult to gather. As managers often have more of such information than do regulators, discriminatory price schedules that are proposed by managers and supervised by regulators may be appropriate for implementing this approach. The regulators check the optimal properties of the manager's proposal that likely will be sustainable since managers usually wish to avoid separation.

Comparing these two approaches leads to the following conclusions. First, the first approach favors efficiency over voluntary sustainability. Second, the first approach relies on regulator intervention to avoid service splitting, while the second approach relies on consumer incentives. Third, in choosing an approach, regulators should balance efficiency gains against the losses of splitting the service that the first approach entails. Fourth, it is easier to split the service when consumer coalitions are feasible in a communi-

---

[12] Although complete information is unavailable, figures suggest that optimal prices are unsustainable in the Bahamas because hotels can obtain water from wells at a total cost close to their payments when the price is set to the average total cost of jointly servicing the whole island. The price schedule, which charges the hotels above average cost, encourages hotels to split off, which most do.

ty because coalitions make it easier to share common costs. For example, hotel and large industrial consumers easily split off because they do not need to join with other consumers to share the costs of a provider different from the regulated monopoly.

Conclusions and a Final Observation

This chapter reaches several main conclusions:

- Price discrimination and cross-subsidy schemes may be suitable from an efficiency standpoint. Furthermore, price schemes where certain prices are below average cost and others are above—that is, cross subsidies, according to one of its many definitions—are a necessary condition to maximize welfare in public services with increasing returns and no loss constraints.
- Price discrimination and cross-subsidy schemes may not be voluntarily sustainable because a group of consumers may be better off separating from the public service. The overpriced consumers may force the community service to split off, causing the overall community to lose the benefits from the increasing-return technologies.
- If optimal prices are incompatible with voluntary sustainability, then a choice must be made between sustainable and efficient prices. The appropriate choice depends on the likelihood that entry will be prevented, efficiency losses from service splitting, and alternatives for providing service.

These conclusions lead to a final observation: centralized pricing policy through regulators is a complex matter because regulators often lack the information required to set appropriate prices. Therefore, even with increasing returns and the no-losses restriction, the pricing policy should rely, to some extent, on information that markets provide. Market agents, consumers, and producers are better than regulators at gathering the information required to set price discrimination schedules to maximize profit without losing customers.[13] Regulators may set limits to these prices, but not

---

[13] A necessary condition for gathering appropriate information is consumption measurement; however, a large meter program may be difficult to implement, not for technical or economic reasons, but because large consumers may be reluctant to accept meter consumption.

forbid them. Finally, if entry is free, then markets will signal unsustainable pricing policies to regulators. However, restrictions are sometimes required from private operators. In particular, concessions of traditional monopolies with large investment requirements demand exclusivity of market entry to make a trade-off. As Friedman (1962) laments, there is, unfortunately, no good solution for technical monopoly.

Annex. Optimal but Unsustainable Pricing Scheme

In the following case, optimal prices are not voluntarily sustainable. Thus, the Ramsey rule that prices should be lower for high-elasticity consumers contradicts the sustainability rule that, in this example, would require lower prices for low-elasticity consumers.

Consider two neighborhoods (1 and 2) for which the cost schedules for providing water are as follows:

Neighborhood 1: $C(X_1) = X_1 + 5$

Neighborhood 2: $C(X_2) = X_2 + 4$

Neighborhoods 1 and 2: $C(X_1 + X_2) = X_1 + X_2 + 6$

where X_1 and X_2 stand for the quantity of water used in each neighborhood.

The demand schedules and consumer surplus for neighborhoods 1 and 2 are as follows:

Indirect demand: $P_1 = 2 - \frac{1}{5} X_1$ and $P_2 = 10 - X_2$

Consumer surplus: $S(X_1) = 2X_1 - \frac{1}{10} X_1^2$ and $S(X_2) = 10X_2 - \frac{1}{2} X_2^2$.

where P_1 and P_2 stand for prices in each neighborhood.

Optimal prices are obtained by solving the following optimization problem:

Maximize: $\iota_1 S(X_1) + \iota_2 S(X_2) - X_1 - X_2 - 6$

subject to: $P_1 X_1 + P_2 X_2 - X_1 - X_2 - 6 = 0$

where ι_1 and ι_2 are consumer surplus weights.

First, consider a solution for ι_1, and ι_2 equal to 1. That is, the welfare of both neighborhoods is equally weighted. A pair (X_1, X_2) solves the above problem if, and only if, $9X_1 = 5X_2$. This equation implies the following relationships between prices:

$P_1 = 2 - \frac{1}{9} X_2$ and $P_2 = 10 - X_2$, which, in turn, implies that $P_1 = \frac{1}{9} P_2 + \frac{8}{9}$.

Annex table 7-1 summarizes the figures corresponding to the solution of this problem. Consumers in neighborhood 1 pay 4.9715 units, while those in neighborhood 2 pay 13.9716 units. Neighborhood 1 payments cover marginal and variable costs (4.6225 units) and a small portion of common costs. neighborhood 2 payments also cover marginal and variable costs (8.3206 units) and a large portion of common costs.

It is noteworthy that this solution is in accordance with the elasticity rule of Ramsey pricing because the price for neighborhood 1 is lower than that for neighborhood 2, and the price elasticity of neighborhood 1 is larger than that for neighborhood 2. This solution, which is optimal from a welfare

ANNEX TABLE 7-1. COST SCHEDULE FOR PROVIDING WATER, USING THE ELASTICITY RULE OF RAMSEY PRICING

Neighborhood	Optimal prices	Quantities under optimal prices	Elasticity	Payments under optimal prices	Current costs	Alternative costs
1	1.0755	4.6225	1.1633	4.9715	-	9.6227
2	1.6791	8.3206	0.2018	13.9716	-	12.3209
Total	-	12.9431	-	18.9431	18.9431	21.9436

standpoint, is unsustainable because neighborhood 2 would be better off splitting off and providing service with its own company. The cost of water consumption for neighborhood 2 would be 12.30 units (the new company cost schedule is $C(X_2) = X_2 + 4$). Thus, if the new producer reduces neighborhood 2's price to 1.5, revenue will be sufficient to cover total cost and produce a profit.

References

Baumol, W. J., and D. E. Bradford. 1970. "Optimal Departure from Marginal Cost Pricing." *American Economic Review* 60: 265–83.

Baumol, W. J., E. E. Bailey, and R. D. Willig. 1977. "Weak Invisible Hand Theorems on the Sustainability of Prices in a Multiproduct Monopoly." *American Economic Review* 67: 350–65.

Boiteux, M. 1971. "On the Management of Public Monopolies Subject to Budgetary Constraints." *Journal of Economic Theory* 3: 219–40.

Braeutigam, R. R. 1989. "Optimal Policies for Natural Monopolies." In *Handbook of Industrial Organization*, Vol. 2, eds. R. Schmalensee and R. Willig, 1289–343. New York: Elsevier Science Publishers.

Friedman, M. 1962. *Capitalism and Freedom*. Chicago: University of Chicago Press.

Panzar, J. C. 1989. "Technological Determinants of the Firm and Industry Structure." In *Handbook of Industrial Organization*, Vol. 1, eds. R. Schmalensee and R. Willig, 4–56. New York: Elsevier Science Publishers.

Ramsey, F. P. 1927. "A Contribution to the Theory of Taxation." *The Economic Journal* 37: 47–61.

Willig, R. D. 1978. "Pareto Superior Nonlinear Outlay Schedules." *The Bell Journal of Economics* 9: 56–69.

Chapter 8

Power Sector Reforms in Central America: Challenges of Regional Convergence

Richard Tomiak and Jaime Millan

The 1990s is often referred to as the decade of privatization and deregulation—a strategy largely pioneered in mature Western economies; however, the notion that liberalization could improve economic efficiency and, at the same time, generate income streams to alleviate fiscal imbalances has rapidly extended to developing countries. Private sector investors would pay to acquire publicly-owned assets and assume certain government obligations. A regulatory framework that enabled market forces to deliver efficient decisions in competitive market sectors and simulated market forces in monopolistic ones would ensure that these obligations continued to be met responsibly. As the decade progressed, governments, business people, consultants, and lending agencies around the world embraced the concept of energy market liberalization as a cornerstone of economic policy. Such enthusiasm for liberalization, however, sometimes overlooked asking whether liberalization was, in fact, an appropriate policy for all countries, regardless of their circumstances.

Call for Change

In Central America, the initial impetus for change had its origins in the deteriorating situation faced by the state-owned, vertically integrated utilities during the early 1990s. In most countries, finances were in disarray, inefficiency was rife, and resources were scarce. Consultants and advisors were brought in to help resolve these problems, but, without fully understanding the special circumstances of the region's countries, they often recommended the indiscriminate transfer of solutions that appeared to be working successfully in other economies. In hindsight, it is clear that many reforms originally planned for Central America were overly optimistic, both in terms of what could be achieved and how soon.

In four Central American countries—El Salvador, Guatemala, Nicaragua, and Panama—fundamental electricity sector reforms have been implemented (table 8-1). These have resulted in a significant level of privatization and the unbundling of companies. Guatemala and Panama have introduced competition at the level of the wholesale market; El Salvador has opened up the entire sector, at least in terms of legal infrastructure; and Nicaragua has accomplished privatization of distribution. Though reforms in Honduras are incipient, progress is being made. Only Costa Rica remains reluctant to proceed beyond contracting a limited number of Power Purchase Agreements (PPAs) within the private sector.

For more than 20 years, economic integration has been an elusive goal in Central America. In recent years, a desire for unity across the region has emerged, which is replacing past conflicts and rivalries, brightening prospects for integration. Increasingly, countries realize that future economic prosperity depends not only on their relationships with one another, but also on their relationships with larger neighbors to the north: Mexico, the United States, and Canada (members of NAFTA); as well as the emerging economies of South America. Many social agents recognize that only through joint initiatives will the region be able to exploit its geographic advantages and participate actively in the global energy economy.

Significant progress has already been made, with the establishment of a free-trade agreement between Guatemala, Honduras, El Salvador, and Mexico and, in a separate initiative, with the agreement to create a customs union to include Guatemala, Honduras, Nicaragua, and Belize. Furthermore, the Plan Puebla Panama has become the focus of infrastructure integration in Central America. These developments fit well with plans for a free-trade pact with Central America, which President Bush outlined at the summit meeting held in Quebec in March 2001. As encouraging as these steps toward integration may appear, the region still has much work ahead to reach levels such as those already achieved by Mercosur, for example.

This chapter assesses Central American power sector reforms and suggests an integrated framework for promoting sustainability of electricity sec-

TABLE 8-1. ELECTRICITY SECTOR REFORMS IN CENTRAL AMERICA

Competition type	Costa Rica	El Salvador	Guatemala	Honduras	Nicaragua	Panama
Single buyer with PPA	1990 Law 7200 & 7508 Qualifying Facilities	1994 PPA CEL-Nejapa Power	1991 PPA EEGSA-Enron	1993 PPA ENEE-ELCOSA	1996 PPA ENEL-Amfels	1997 PPA IRHE-Petroeléctrica
Wholesale	None	1996 Law	1996 Law	None	1998 Law	1997 Law
Retail	None	1996 Law	None	None	None	None

Source: IDB.

tor reform in the six countries of the Central American isthmus.[1] While experiences from other parts of the world are taken into account, the region's unique characteristics are explicitly considered. Competition in these six countries—constrained both technically and institutionally—can be stimulated by establishing appropriate regulatory regimes and pursuing a policy of regional market convergence that ultimately results in full regional integration.

Prospects for Regional Integration

Full regional integration of Central American electricity markets, initiated by the signing of the Central American Market Framework Treaty in Guatemala in December 1996, must be viewed as a longer-term goal.[2] While the treaty provided the foundation for integration, implementation has been delayed by the absence of a formal timeline defining specific milestones. Advancing the process requires a continuous commitment to achieving at least two key long-term goals that condition a sustainable sector reform. Furthermore, as illustrated by the European example, bringing the integration dream to fruition may require significant work in many areas.

Conditions for Sustainable Sector Reform

First, social acceptance and clear public commitment to the longer-term goal of developing a free and competitive energy market are needed from the out-

---

[1] Belize has not participated in the integration effort.

[2] The history of integration dates back some 20 years, when the first studies were performed.

set. Inevitably, compromises will be made along the way; however, if there are doubts that liberalization is the goal, the reform process will be seriously jeopardized. One important challenge in this respect is to re-energize the overall drive toward liberalization, which, in the eyes of some involved parties, has become a worn-out, and even discredited, initiative.

Second, a mature institutional framework—encompassing political, legal, regulatory, and commercial issues—is essential to facilitate the smooth operation of a free market and to minimize the national and political risk that potential investors perceive. Forcing through liberalizing reforms in a country where such a framework does not exist can cause serious problems that threaten long-term success. Creating institutions that are sufficiently flexible and robust to support a free, competitive market is an enormous, but vital, task (von der Fehr and Millan 2001).

Evolution of Market Integration: Lessons from the European Experience

In drawing parallels between Europe and Central America in how the market integration process evolves, it is helpful to recall that the idea of a common European market began nearly 50 years ago as a purely sectoral initiative. Although driven by a broader political vision, the Schuman Plan for establishing a common market in coal and steel was embodied in a treaty and ratified by member countries in 1952. The European Coal and Steel Community, which the treaty initiated, allowed its members to cooperate in these two industrial sectors without having to enter into broader, more demanding commitments. However, the benefits of economic cooperation were demonstrated, and, in 1957, the Treaty of Rome was signed, resulting in the formation of the European Economic Community (EEC). Since then, the EEC has been enlarged and strengthened, as initially recalcitrant countries gradually came to realize that their economic and political interests would be best served by joining the European Union.

> The first lesson from the European experience is that cooperation, at a sectoral level, can precede full economic integration and, indeed, can provide a valuable learning platform for participating states.

A main feature of the market restructuring process adopted by the European Union is the binding character of the Electricity and Gas Directives. Adopted in 1996 and 1998, respectively, these directives provide an overall binding, legal framework for the European Union, setting out the basic rules and minimum requirements for market openings in gas and electricity. They require member states to open a specified minimum level of demand to Europe-wide competition, give third parties access to the transportation network, and partially unbundle networks from other parts of the electricity and gas industries. This overall framework is significant since, with interconnected systems, decisions and actions in one country can affect markets and consumers in other countries. Of course, the European experience has not been without its problems. France, for example, has occasionally been reluctant to conform to measures contained in the energy directives. But over time, the explicit and implicit pressures that fellow member states can exert, combined with a degree of compromise, are gradually moving toward the objective of a creating a single European energy market. Whether setting binding rules for all countries is an acceptable course within the context of Central American politics is an issue for debate.

The second lesson from the European experience is that effectiveness of the directive's binding approach should not be underestimated.

While the energy directives issued by the European Commission in Brussels have driven European deregulation, this process has been reinforced by the creation of new industry organizations, the following of which are particularly significant:

- Council of European Energy Regulators (CEER), which has both gas and electricity sections that meet quarterly to coordinate and advance implementation of the principles of the energy directives
- Independent System Operators, whose role is to ensure that national transmission grids are operated in a commercially and technically efficient manner to facilitate Europe-wide movement of energy
- European Federation of Energy Traders Regulators (EFET), established by energy traders in 1998 to develop processes and mechanisms to enable trading on a pan-European basis.

To encourage joint action at the European Community level, the European Commission, in 1998, initiated the European Regulatory Forum for electricity, known as the Florence Forum. The Florence Forum brings together representatives of the Commission, national administrations, European Parliament, Council of European Regulators, and Association of European Transmission System Operators (ETSO), as well as producers, consumers, traders, and other players. The Forum's goal is to discuss and clarify possible solutions with all key players, particularly on cross-border tariffs and congestion management.

While the Forum is a proven, highly effective tool for developing consensus on complex, controversial, and rapidly evolving issues, recent experience has also revealed a number of weaknesses. For example, it holds only two meetings annually and is poorly equipped to make firm decisions on many issues. Unanimity in decisionmaking is required, but no procedures are in place to enforce implementation. As a result, the Commission decided to adopt a directive to finalize decisions on cross-border transmission tariffs and congestion management on interconnectors.

The third lesson from the European experience is the important role that diversity of institutions plays in the deregulation process.

In the early 1990s, the Norwegian and Swedish Transmission System Operators (TSOs) were formally separated from their integrated utilities. As impartial, apolitical players, these TSOs were able to identify common interests and develop strong mutual links so that, by 1996, the Swedish grid operator logically took a 50-percent stake in NordPool, the Nordic power exchange. Ongoing differences between Norway and Sweden—not only on electricity issues and government policy, but also as the result of their long history of mistrust and conflict—has many parallels in the relationships between Central American countries. However, the Scandinavian experience shows that the neutral operation of a cross-border electricity market can coexist with national political differences and continue to deliver integration and competition in the best interests of both parties.

The fourth lesson from the European experience is the extent to which fully independent TSOs may facilitate closer regional cooperation. This lesson is particularly relevant to the Central American context since the institutional organization of the transmission system is still a point under discussion.

These four lessons from Europe's experience should be considered when planning the integration of electricity markets. Nevertheless, the extent to which the lessons apply to the conditions of the Central American Electricity Market requires a thorough understanding of the constraints and peculiarities unique to these countries.

TABLE 8-2. CHARACTERISTICS OF THE CENTRAL AMERICAN ELECTRICITY MARKET, 2000

Market characteristic	Costa Rica	El Salvador	Guatemala	Honduras	Nicaragua	Panama	Total
Peak demand (MW)	1,121	758	1,017	702	397	777	4,772
Installed capacity (MW)	1,699	1,114	1,668	918	633	1,071	7,104
Energy sold (GWh)	5,750	3,638	4,620	3,289	1,505	3,797	22,599
Annual per capita consumption (kWh)	1,429	580	406	499	297	1,329	624
Electricity coverage (%)	95	76	72	58	46	68	69

Note: MW = megawatt, GWh = gigawatt hour, kWh = kilowatt hour.

Market Constraints and Regional Convergence

With the exception of Costa Rica, levels of electrification coverage in Central America remain relatively low (table 8-2). This highlights the importance of ensuring that government priorities are agreed on and understood. For example, consensus must be reached that liberalization will not jeopardize the goal of rapidly obtaining full electricity coverage.

Market Size

Within the context of electricity markets, "small" is best defined as a size that provides an insufficiently large demand base to support a competitive generation sector (for example, five or six companies, each accounting for some 500 MW of capacity). As table 8-2 shows, peak demand in the region ranges from less than 400 MW in Nicaragua to more than 1,000 MW in Costa Rica. Such "small" markets risk being dominated by one or two larger players or having to limit the size of participants to levels at which they cannot realize economies of scale. Enlarging the market by encouraging interconnection of national markets, thereby developing a regional market, will produce a more robust, diverse market. Total demand of the six Central American countries, which currently totals about 4,500 MW, would be capable of supporting a competitive industry, as defined above. Moreover, demand in these countries

**TABLE 8-3. SUMMARY OF LEGAL ARRANGEMENTS
IN CENTRAL AMERICAN COUNTRIES**

Status of legal arrangements	Costa Rica	El Salvador	Guatemala	Honduras	Nicaragua	Panama
Legal framework for liberalization and deregulation	No	Yes	Yes	Analyzing future reform	Yes	Yes
Antitrust laws	Yes	No	No	No	No	Yes
Deregulation program, with detailed timetable	No	No	No	Analyzing future reform	No	5-year transition period
Degree of legal market opening	No	Total	Wholesale competitive	Wholesale competitive	Wholesale competitive	Wholesale competitive

is currently growing at rates close to 6 percent a year. Thus, the potential for future market growth should not be underestimated.

Market Convergence

Generally, all Central American countries may be moving toward a deregulated future; however, it would be useful to know whether their market structures—wholesale market arrangements, trading rules, and company structures—are together moving toward a standard regional model. If convergence does not occur, it will be more difficult and costly to bring about the degree of homogeneity and consolidation required to expedite the creation of a single Central American energy market. While this appraisal is inevitably subjective, key parameters can be used to assess the state of liberalization in each country.

Legal Arrangements

First, suitable legal arrangements should be in place. These must include an appropriate legal framework through which the necessary structural changes can be implemented, enforced, and underpinned by related supporting systems, such as contract law and antitrust laws. Whether detailed plans exist for market opening, the level already implemented (both theoretically and in practice), and other relevant factors also need to be considered (table 8-3). The spectrum of reform ranges from Costa Rica, whose government is reluctant to pursue reform because of a lack of consensus and opposition of inter-

TABLE 8-4. SUMMARY OF OWNERSHIP STRUCTURE

Legal framework indicator	Costa Rica	El Salvador	Guatemala	Honduras	Nicaragua	Panama
Market share of the three largest companies (%)						
Generation	100	90	70	90	90	100
Transmission	100	100	100	100	100	100
Distribution	80	100	100	100	100	100
Extent of vertical integration	No separation	Separation, but no limits	Separation, but no limits	No separation	Legal separation	Legal separation
Legal freedom of entry	No	Yes	Yes	Yes	Yes	Yes

est groups, to Panama, which has an appropriate legal framework, a well-developed transition plan, and a strong regulatory regime.[3]

Ownership Structure

Given the legal arrangements in place, it is interesting to observe the degree to which the ownership structure of the electricity industry has changed, particularly in terms of private sector participation, market concentration, and ownership mix. Other indicators of whether the legal framework is delivering the desired outcomes include the extent that vertical and horizontal integration of companies is permitted and whether new entrants enjoy legal freedom of entry (table 8-4).

In all countries of the region, transmission continues to be a state-owned monopoly; increasingly, however, distribution companies are falling into private hands. Vertical re-integration in small systems is likely to result in establishing dominant positions, especially for companies that already have a strong existing position in the distribution sector. Allowing incumbents to move from distribution to production enhances their market power and discourages new players from market entry.

---

[3] It should be noted that El Salvador, which has a fully deregulated electricity sector, has no antitrust laws with which to manage the situations that an open market can induce.

TABLE 8-5. WHOLESALE ARRANGEMENTS IN CENTRAL AMERICAN COUNTRIES

Wholesale arrangement	Costa Rica	El Salvador	Guatemala	Honduras	Nicaragua	Panama
Type of contract	Physical	Physical	Financial		Financial	Financial
Spot market price	Not market, but SOE buys at SRMC from qualified generators	Marginal bid to serve the residual market (after contracts have been dispatched)	SRMC by dispatching available capacity at declared cost; transmission constraints		SRMC by dispatching available capacity at declared cost	SRMC by dispatching available capacity at declared cost
Capacity charge	No	No	Regulated	Contracted	Regulated	Market based

Note: SOE= state-owned enterprise, SRMC= short-run marginal cost.

Wholesale Arrangements

A deregulated market needs to provide mechanisms that facilitate development of the liberalizing forces that the reform program envisaged. In the electricity industry, efficient wholesale arrangements that link energy producers with retailers and enable the effective management of price risk are crucial factors in the competitive market. Thus, it is important to determine whether such arrangements exist; the rules for dealing in such markets; and whether there are any impediments to the use of wholesale markets, such as existing long-term contracts (table 8-5).

With the exceptions of Costa Rica and Honduras, Central American countries have introduced some form of wholesale market (ECLA 2000). El Salvador's pooling arrangements, which allow free bids, have already proven difficult to implement. It appears that cost-based pools are more appropriate for Central American countries. They represent a natural progression from traditional, merit-order dispatching methods; because they require transparency, they should ensure that dispatching remains economically efficient. Hedging instruments can develop around a cost-based pool, and no constraints (other than size) should prevent such arrangements from eventually evolving into bid-based spot markets.

TABLE 8-6. REGULATION STATUS IN CENTRAL AMERICAN COUNTRIES

Characteristic	Costa Rica	El Salvador	Guatemala	Honduras	Nicaragua	Panama
Regulatory authority structure[a]	MS	MS	S	S	S	MS
Pass through of generation cost to regulated customers	Not applicable; traditional utility	Quarterly average of spot prices	Average of contracts and spot-market purchases; yearly forecast adjusted quarterly	Long-term marginal cost	Yearly purchases	Weighted average of contracts and spot market
Rebalanced tariffs	No	No; subsidies maintained	No; subsidies maintained	No; subsidies maintained	Yes	Yes; subsidies withdrawn

[a] MS = multisector; S = sector.

Regulation

Even in successfully deregulated electricity markets, monopolistic segments must be regulated to ensure open access and appropriate prices. As table 8-6 shows, Panama appears to have a sufficiently robust regulatory structure in place. While this observation may call for the pooling of regional expertise, the Panamanian regulator may not wish to risk its position by becoming involved with other regulators in the region. Moreover, Central American states have been experimenting with various price-setting mechanisms for regulated customers. Unless reversion to a common standard occurs over an extended period, any rebalancing of tariffs could produce severe socioeconomic disturbances in countries of the region.

Generation

In most countries, generation is the first sector of the electricity industry affected by liberalization, since it is relatively easy for international players to enter this area of activity. Relevant expertise is internationally transferable, and standard contractual arrangements can, to a great extent, isolate overseas investors from the risks associated with working in an uncertain economic and political environment. Table 8-7 shows the Central American countries

TABLE 8-7. FREEDOM OF ENTRY IN THE ELECTRICITY GENERATION SECTOR

Factor	Costa Rica	El Salvador	Guatemala	Honduras	Nicaragua	Panama
Freedom of entry	No	Yes; market power of incumbents is restrictive	Yes; market power of incumbents is restrictive	Yes	Yes	Yes; single buyer
Number of major companies	1	2 + imports	4	4 + imports	4 + imports	4 + imports

where freedom of entry is possible and the extent to which new entrants have taken advantage of it.

As the experiences of El Salvador and Honduras show, the problems of small markets are most evident in generation. To achieve economies of scale, individual generation projects are often large enough to meet the entire demand of a single country, thereby restricting new entry. Other difficulties associated with market entry include limited upside potential, high start-up costs, and inability to find reliable local partners. However, once new entrants have overcome these hurdles to secure market access, they then become the automatic choice for future projects, thereby discouraging other companies from market entry. Moreover, providing the stability that private sector investors seek creates a regulatory burden for authorities, who, in difficult circumstances, must find the financial and human resources to support a skilled, stable regulatory regime. Establishing a regional grid, along with the facility to trade electricity between countries, alleviates many of these problems.

Transportation

An interconnected regional grid has been proposed as the medium-term solution to problems resulting from the small size of Central American countries' electricity markets. Although new entrants can only participate in a deregulating market if they can access the transportation network on the same terms as incumbents, a physical transmission grid is a necessary, but insufficient, condition for integrating markets, as European Union experience shows.

Access to electricity transportation systems in Central America, at least in theory, is open to all market participants (table 8-8). System operators are

TABLE 8-8. ACCESS TO ELECTRICITY TRANSPORTATION SYSTEMS

Transportation factor	Costa Rica	El Salvador	Guatemala	Honduras	Nicaragua	Panama
Grid access	Open	Open	Open	Open	Open	Open
Interconnector capacity	[a]	[a]	[a]	[a]	[a]	[a]
System and market operators	Vertically integrated	1, independent	Independent company	1, vertically integrated	1, independent	1, grid owned
Grid ownership	State	State	State	State	State	State
Number of distribution companies	8	5[b]	2	1	1	4

[a] Limited; two isolated segments to be united next year; SIEPAC line will enhance capacity in 2006.

[b] AES, with 80-percent market share, controls three companies.

accountable to the government, but their responsibilities have not yet been extended to include resolving issues that arise as a result of cross-border movement of electricity (for example, tariff structures, congestion management, and allocation of existing capacity). Just as regional regulatory bodies need encouragement, coordination between national transmission system operators also needs strengthening.

Overall Assessment

Of the six Central American countries, Panama has developed the strongest and most independent electricity sector, while Costa Rica, at the other extreme, has delayed introduction of market reform, largely because of political considerations. Across the region, the power of regulators remains weak. In Guatemala, for example, the regulator reports directly to the ministry of energy. All countries except El Salvador, whose pooling arrangement follows the Nordic model, have adopted cost-based pooling. El Salvador's government was forced to intervene to control high consumer prices driven by an artificial supply shortfall that resulted from exploitation of market power in a duopolistic wholesale market. Panama is the only country to have introduced phased competition, during whose initial five-year period, the grid operator acts as a single buyer on behalf of the market.

As evidenced above, there is no trend toward regional convergence of electricity markets. This is not surprising, given that no decision confirms that, in light of the SIEPAC project, convergence is a desired strategic objective. Any movement away from the planned program of reform will inevitably be difficult—even painful—to drive through. Expectations have been created and commercial decisions made. However, creation of a competitive, regionally integrated electricity market will be all the more difficult to achieve unless measures are taken now to direct national programs toward the goal of regional convergence in the medium term.

Private companies have expertise and resources that are often superior to those found in the countries in which they plan to invest; however, these potential investors frequently appear recalcitrant and reluctant to divulge key information. Hence, it is vital that regulators and governments in Central America work to achieve a balance of negotiating strength with potential investors. This might involve drawing on the European model and pooling regional resources; harmonizing regional regulatory and competition strategies; and making use of informed, objective advice.

Toward an Integrated Electricity Market

Within the context of the conditions outlined above, numerous factors must be considered to facilitate a smooth transition toward an integrated regional electricity market. These include realistic expectations of the role and strategies of foreign investors, scope for competition and regulation in small markets, the fundamental role that transmission plays as a market enabler, the institutions required for the market to function, and the need for regional planning. These five factors are discussed below.

Strategies of Foreign Investors

Observers have noted that relatively few overseas companies appear interested in investing in the Central American region; even when they do, it is only under certain conditions that are not always compatible with building a competitive market. The needs of potential investors, as well as what is and is not acceptable to host governments and regulators, must be understood.

The largest energy companies—their small number will further diminish as global consolidation and restructuring progress—are now operating at a global level. They are cash rich and need to invest their funds to produce reliable future income streams for their shareholders. In searching for investment opportunities, these companies aim to diversify their portfolios, not only by moving along the energy chain and into other utility-related areas (such as telecommunications, water, and even financial services), but also into geographic areas that extend beyond their traditional North American and European markets (Millan, Micco, and Lora 2001). Nonetheless, companies investing in overseas markets balance potential gains against the risks they run; where risks are perceived as high, projected returns must compensate. Within this context, it is significant that many international companies are constantly looking to identify opportunities for "regulatory arbitrage;" that is, moving operations overseas to escape harsh regulatory regimes in their home markets.

However, a pragmatic approach must be taken with respect to the question of actual price levels versus levels expected under perfect competition. Occasionally, the impression is that any imbalance between theoretical and actual prices is simply the result of private sector "rip-offs," whereas a more realistic view is that a certain premium is economically justifiable, according to the level of risk being taken. Of course, if regulators are insufficiently empowered or informed, private firms may be tempted to exploit their weaknesses and try to justify excessive margins in their prices. Central American countries' experiences with poorly negotiated PPAs prior to reforms are painful reminders of what may be expected when large asymmetries in negotiation power exist.

Market Structure and Competition

Having acknowledged that Central American markets are relatively small and immature, it is difficult to envisage how a competitive energy market could develop in each country in the near future. On the other hand, regulatory systems in those countries are weak. Combined, these factors make the threat of regional market dominance by a few large players particularly relevant. Although regulators in Central American countries need to be concerned about the potential mismatch between their size and that of companies entering their markets, this does not necessarily mean they should insist on developing a sector with only small units unable to profit from optimal power plant sizes. If investment is to be encouraged, then sensible compromises must be made. Regulators across Central America should ensure that they share a vision of how and when to achieve a competitive market. Furthermore, they need to present a unified, consistent regional structure to potential entrants; though challenging, this would not necessarily destroy their incentive to invest.

Properly regulated, vertical integration may be preferable to competition in a small market because of its few players and limited scope for competition. However, this argues for a process that results in large economic groups controlling all power sector segments. Unbundling had already been undertaken on the basis that limiting vertical integration could enhance competition. However, relinquishing this control without making corresponding changes in regulation could result in the worst of both worlds. The regulatory frameworks already being implemented or discussed in the region, with the exception of Costa Rica, are based on unbundling transmission, distribution, and generation.

It is vital to understand the crucial importance of convergence in regulatory frameworks. Individual decisions, such as mandating distribution companies to open bids for long-term contracts, having a cost-based pool, and imposing price caps on the pool or the forward markets are important; even more important, however, is the need for all Central American countries to make similar decisions—regional convergence. A consolidated regional market can occur only if there is a marked degree of convergence. Moreover, commonality of decisionmaking reduces the potential for regulatory arbitrage. Hence, for example, cost-based pooling arrangements, open bids for long-term contracts, single buyer arrangements, and accounting unbundling of integrated firms will provide regulators the mechanisms to monitor private sector investors. Relying on quasi-competitive forces where they do not really exist or forcing physical unbundling to a level consistent with the small size of Central American markets is impractical.

Crucial Role of the Regional Grid

The European Union and U.S. markets are painful reminders of the importance of having an independent, properly regulated transmission segment. To comply with the Directive, incumbent European electricity utilities are obligated to unbundle the TSO activity in accounting and management terms and demonstrate that it operates at arm's length from other competitive parts of their business, such as generation and supply. Unbundling is essential not only for eliminating cross subsidies, but also to ensure nondiscriminatory access. System operators must protect the interests of potential entrants by allowing freedom of access to the transmission network. Progress toward unbundling has already been made in most Central American countries; this should continue in order to achieve full managerial, accounting, and legal separation of the TSOs from their parent companies.

Nearly all European Union member states have implemented the Directive, and transmission capacity, in most cases, is physically available; however, for many eligible customers, it remains organizationally and economically difficult to choose a supplier located in another European Union country. Because of differences in tariff structures among member states, the amount payable for cross-border access to the system can vary considerably, depending on the TSOs involved, without there necessarily being a link to actual costs. In addition, in cases where several countries have to be transited, accumulation or "pancaking" of tariffs can occur.

Furthermore, given the limitations of existing interconnector capacity, the principles of allocation of capacity to market operators will be important in determining which players profit from trading in the internal market. Without transparency rules, discrimination between market players may occur. Incumbents might deter new entrants, particularly if substantial volumes of capacity are tied up in long-term contracts. This would hinder the development of trade and produce fewer benefits from the establishment of the internal market.

Hence, electricity liberalization with open network access and transparent pricing facilitates the development of free trade. This, in turn, will promote better use of Central America's transmission infrastructure and stimulate reinforcement of networks. To achieve these goals, a proper framework for cross-border charging, interconnector access, and congestion management should be established at the regional level. Where possible, commercial solutions should be used to deal with constraints. For example, network operators should have commercial incentives to develop their networks and optimize the management of congestion. In this area, it may be useful to bear in mind the principles adopted by European legislators and regulators.

Transmission and distribution charges must be published and subject to independent regulation. Indeed, published transmission charges and nondiscriminatory access to ancillary services are essential for the development of competition. It is important to clarify what is covered by the published charges. Long and short-term transmission charges must be separated out, and losses should not be included in them. In some European markets, access to distribution markets has proven problematic, and relevant provisions have had to be reinforced, particularly since nondiscriminatory access to distribution is likely to become increasingly important with the development of embedded generation. Cross-border transmission charges should reflect costs, but they should also be simple and facilitate trade. In Central America, as in Europe, a pragmatic regional solution is needed to ensure progress toward a single market.

Congestion of transmission networks should not be viewed primarily as a physical problem. When the institutional framework can support them, market-based approaches should be used for congestion management. These could include not only auctions, but also market splitting and counter trade, which work well in the Nordic market.[4] Eventually, for a liquid market to develop, traders will need access to clear and timely information on likely transmission capacity and periods of availability. Such forecasts will be needed on a day-ahead basis and should be complemented by accurate ex post information on actual flows to enable traders to predict load flows over time.

Institutions for the Integrated Market

If raising the level of competition in the region is the desired result, then regulatory regimes in Central America must be customized to reflect the special circumstances prevailing in individual countries. Since markets are too small and immature to support competition, regulators must accept that a significant degree of integration is inevitable and strive to contain it by setting appropriate limits and simulating market forces. The initial effort, therefore, must center on creating or strengthening national regulatory institutions and developing a vigorous regulatory culture. This involves securing high-quality resources for the regulator's office and ensuring that the regulator has access to all relevant information and enjoys symmetry of negotiating power. Subsequently, plans and timetables should be outlined, and details of regulatory structures and processes proposed, negotiated, and agreed on. A transition plan and timetable for introducing competition, balancing the negotiating strength of all parties involved, and creating a regulatory model that simulates competitive pressures should also be developed.

Furthermore, if global regulatory gradients are not to lead to exploiting less well-developed or regulated energy markets, a regional organization should be established to serve as a discussion and knowledge-sharing forum for Central American regulators. Such an organization would provide the perfect platform from which to develop a consistent regional strategy; equally important, it would serve as an influential power base for individual regulators who are otherwise exposed to myriad pressures in their home markets.

---

[4] However, lack of liquidity in small markets may delay implementation of these methods.

Need for Regional Planning

A key element missing from the existing plans for regional integration in Central America is an agreed on timetable against which to measure progress. Lacking a plan with target dates allows the process to drift aimlessly and risks the possibility of divergence in each country's structural evolution. The U.K. liberalization program, for example, followed an eight-year plan that, at its outset, laid out a timetable for a phased opening of the electricity market.

Any decisions that are made must promote convergence of the six national markets and ensure that transition to increased competition, in terms of delivering institutional change and making the required compromises and trade-offs, is properly managed and executed according to a detailed schedule. An initial outline of the plan might be structured in the following five phases.

Phase I: Agreement on Strategy

At the outset, it is essential to ensure that a genuine appreciation of and desire for the benefits of liberalization exist. Commitment to the liberalization process results from education and informed debate, not political ideology. This debate must be accompanied by a parallel debate on the desirability of regional integration and the timeframe in which it can be achieved. As all relevant issues are already familiar to the parties involved, it should be possible to reach consensus in a relatively short period of time. Then, if liberalization of the electricity sector through regional integration is accepted as the desired goal, the process can move forward. However, if it is rejected, then separate national plans that address the problems associated with poor efficiency in small markets must be put in place.

Phase II: Preparation

Within each Central American country, deficiencies in the existing institutional endowment must be recognized, remedies identified, and a program of change that delivers regional convergence established. Such an analysis of institutional endowment must encompass the judiciary, financial and banking sectors, contractual arrangements, and regulation.

Phase III: A Common Agenda

After regional integration is agreed on and country preparations have been made, implementation of a convergent market framework becomes the highest priority. Pushing through the changes in individual countries that will lead to regional convergence is a complex task that may involve terminating existing arrangements. However, it should be made easier if all countries agree on a common agenda that includes the following:

- Changing market rules so they conform to a regional standard (for example, plant bidding rules or treatment of renewable resources)
- Unbundling vertically integrated companies into legally separate generation, transmission, distribution, and retail businesses
- Phasing out or restructuring existing contracts, which addresses the difficult question of how to deal with stranded costs
- Rebalancing tariffs to more cost-reflective levels
- Divesting assets or imposing harsher regulatory intervention if certain ownership thresholds are reached.

Phase IV: Implementation

Transition from six national electricity markets to a single regional entity must be planned, both in terms of timing and sequence of events. The transitional framework must be sufficiently robust to withstand shocks to the system, whether the causes are physical (such as damage to generation and transmission systems), commercial (such as high prices or dominance by large global players), or political (such as undermining the commitment to reform or not making decisions according to appropriate business principles).

Phase V: Consolidation

Once these basic changes have been implemented, it will be necessary to fine-tune the system in response to any minor deficiencies and inconsistencies. In this regard, it is interesting to note that Panama has set up market monitoring groups, composed of independent outside experts, whose objective is to institutionalize change.

Final Remarks

Integrating Central American electricity markets has long been on the agenda of energy planners. Despite progress to date, including the Central American Treaty and the SIEPAC project, achieving this ambitious goal remains elusive, largely because of the magnitude and complexity of the tasks required to overcome institutional, political, and technical constraints. Parallel to this process, most countries in the region have adopted power sector reforms, seeking private sector participation and competition. However, they are now facing problems in implementation because of lack of local institutional capacity and technical constraints.

This chapter suggests that building a regional electricity market in Central America may help to overcome certain barriers that small countries face in implementing sector reforms. To this end, experience of the European electricity market is instructive. However, it would be naïve to think that integration could resolve all the difficulties inherent in reforming small markets. The same or similar institutional, political, and technical constraints that limit development of competitive private markets in small countries may conspire against development of a regional integrated market. Moreover, it may be impossible to achieve an integrated market before reforming individual markets first. The challenge is how to move simultaneously on both fronts: acknowledging local constraints without jeopardizing future prospects for integration and competition.

References

ECLAC. 2001. "Evolución reciente y desafíos de los mercados mayoristas de electricidad en El Salvador, Guatemala, y Panamá." United Nations, April 17. Mimeographed.

Millan, J., E. Lora, and A. O. Micco. 2001. "Sustainability of the Electricity Sector Reforms in Latin America." Inter-American Development Bank, March. Mimeographed.

Nils-Henrik M. von der fehr, University of Oslo, and J. Millan. 2001. "Sustainability of Power Sector Reform: An Analytical Framework." Inter-American Development Bank, January. Mimeographed.

Chapter 9

Competition Policy in Latin American Infrastructure: Lessons from Six Countries

Carmen Fuente

Over the last two decades, most Latin American countries have introduced important reforms in infrastructure services, encompassing changes in ownership patterns and operations. An environment in which unregulated monopolies and public ownership prevailed has evolved into a context of private participation, in which competition and regulation play complementary roles. Although competition is a key feature in designing public service reform processes, vertical and horizontal concentration still pervade the industrial structure of many countries in the region. Absence of vertical unbundling and industry restructuring during the early stages of liberalization has hindered the efficiency of competition policy, making strong regulatory efforts necessary. In fact, inappropriate industry structures may explain, in part, the shortcomings of reforms in Latin America.

Restructuring Monopolist Sectors

Introducing competition into formerly monopolist infrastructure sectors requires a process of sector restructuring, whereby old regulations are eliminated and new ones are established and applied. It requires altering sector structures characterized by high levels of horizontal concentration and vertical integration. Promoting competition in one or more sector segments involves a degree of vertical unbundling of natural monopoly segments into potentially competitive industry segments. Such separation is key to leveling the network access playing field and preventing abuse of dominant position. At the same time, a sufficient number of participants in competitive segments is needed to ensure market competitiveness.

Undertaking restructuring encompasses the divestiture of generation assets; obviously, this vertical decoupling is an extremely difficult process. Most difficulties can be explained by the substantial political and economic transaction costs involved (Dixit 1996). However, country experience has shown that, when politically feasible, structural measures should be applied in advance of liberalization to ensure successful reform (Fernández-Ordóñez 2000). Furthermore, undertaking such measures at the appropriate time helps clarify the rules for private investors, thus reducing the likelihood of subsequent litigation.

A well-designed competition law is a basic tool to ensure that competition occurs and continues to work effectively as the reform process proceeds and unexpected events unfold. Therefore, competition regulations should cover infrastructure services. Moreover, proper control of mergers and acquisitions should avoid reverting to industrial structures with large horizontal concentration or vertical integration. In Latin America, infrastructure sectors are covered under the competition regulations of Argentina, Brazil, Chile, and Peru. In Mexico, competition regulations do not fully apply to infrastructure sectors because that country's competition law states that control exercised exclusively by the state in the strategic sectors described in the constitution does not constitute a monopoly; therefore, it is not covered by competition law.

In Latin American countries, a major privatization concern has been attracting private finance in the face of investor fear of the risks involved. While structural reforms have been implemented in certain countries, in most, private investors continue to enjoy monopoly power. On the other hand, reforms in some countries have left publicly-owned enterprises either totally or partially untouched, giving them dominant power in their respective sectors. Among the countries studied, public monopolies in infrastructure industries persist in Brazil, Mexico, and Venezuela. Furthermore, mergers and acquisitions occurring in an increasingly global economy without appropriate legislation aimed at promoting competition and restraining market control have often led to reduced levels of competition.

Structural Provisions and Merger Control

Structural provisions foster a market structure hostile to concentration to prevent abuse of dominant position in terms of number of players. The aim of controlling market concentration is not to avoid large firms, but to avert concentrated market power, whereby a firm can raise prices over a large time span without being rivaled by other firms (Fernández-Ordóñez 2000). The primary structural provisions of competition law relate to mergers, acquisitions, and joint ventures. Since such agreements can irreversibly alter the structure of an industry, some regulations require prior notification and approval of such business arrangements. Among the countries studied in this chapter, Chile, Peru, and Venezuela do not require prior notification, while Argentina, Brazil, and Mexico do. To avoid an unnecessary regulatory burden, only the largest transactions or proposals must be screened. A commonly adopted approach in administering and enforcing merger and acquisition provisions in competition laws is to specify size thresholds in terms of market share, assets, sales, and employment of the parties involved. Differences in the approach to merger control correspond to different thresholds for requiring merger notification. In Argentina, thresholds are based on absolute size of sales, while in Mexico, they are determined by the ratio of sales to the minimum wage. In Europe, thresholds for merger notification have traditionally been considerably higher than those in the United States.

Assessing a merger usually involves a trade-off between an increase in companies' internal efficiency and a decrease in competition, which may reduce the likelihood of passing on efficiency gains to consumers. This means that merger transactions significantly reduce the number of independent firms and increase market concentration, thereby reducing or preventing competition. On the other hand, these transactions are generally motivated by the pursuit of efficiency. A rule-of-reason approach, generally advocated for evaluating mergers, permits mergers to proceed on a restructured basis if economic efficiency gains are likely to be greater than losses from reduced competition. This policy facilitates structural adjustment and more efficient use of resources because it allows for the closure of suboptimal plants through mergers and acquisitions.

This approach is not without its risks. A major one is abusing recourse to concentration legislation, with the aim of protecting domestic players against foreign, hostile takeovers. Conversely, globalization seems to push national competition authorities toward complacency regarding domestic infrastructure mergers, thereby strengthening incumbent providers of national infrastructure services. Other risks include high legal costs and the complex process of proving efficiency gains and contestable markets. These risks require limiting authorities' discretion to authorize mergers by setting limits. Authorization may be given, even if limits are surpassed, conditioned on the sale of some assets. The appropriate value of such limits may vary across countries and sectors, depending on technological conditions and entry barriers. In this regard, limits are not established in competition laws, but in those of each sector. For example, Chile's new power sector regulations state that an economic group cannot hold more than 40 percent of market share.

Other structural provisions include horizontal restraints and structural powers. Horizontal restraint instruments aim to measure limits in market share and evaluate the adequacy of horizontal structure in terms of effective competition and market contestability outcomes. Structural powers entitle competition authorities to impose divestiture measures on existing monopolies to reduce their market power. In Argentina, for example, the competition tribunal may ask the courts to order the dissolution, liquidation, or breakup of companies who violate the law. These provisions are complemented by restraints established in infrastructure sector laws. For example, in the electricity sector, an economic group cannot control companies that own more than 40 percent of distribution assets within a municipality or metropolitan area. In Mexico, the law empowers the competition agency to order a partial or total divestiture of what has been improperly concentrated, regardless of the applicable fine.

Behavioral Provisions

The behavioral provisions in competition laws and policies aim to avert monopolistic behavior, which could result in misallocating resources and reducing economic welfare. The main monopolistic behaviors that such provisions seek to avoid are horizontal and vertical agreements and abuse of dominant position, which are discussed below.

Horizontal Agreements

Horizontal agreements are those entered into between two or more firms that would otherwise compete at the same level of production. Horizontal agreements tend to distribute markets geographically or by customer segments and negatively affect consumers and competition.

While economic theory does not provide efficiency or consumer welfare reasons for horizontal agreements between firms, it does support the view that firms engaging in such behavior interfere with the competitive process and the societal benefits of competition. Among economists and lawyers, there is a virtual consensus that horizontal agreements should be strictly prohibited; that is, considered illegal and subject to serious penalties and fines.

However, not all horizontal agreements are anticompetitive. For example, firms can agree to share research or promote cost reduction and competition. Currently, a lively debate is under way to decide whether export agreements should be permitted as an effective means of penetrating foreign markets or prohibited on the basis that they could lead to collusion in domestic markets.

Although difficult to prove, price fixing, market sharing, and bid rigging are considered serious violations in most regulations. Some competition laws include provisions that give participants and injured parties incentive to provide authorities evidence of these activities. Other regulations impose tough penalties as a deterrent. In this regard, the competition laws of Argentina, Chile, Mexico, and Peru specifically prohibit horizontal agreements that harm competition.

Vertical Agreements

Vertical agreements—those between firms at different levels of the production process—are less likely to harm competition. Increasingly, practitioners advocate a rule-of-reason approach, on the grounds that vertical restraints are more likely to affect competition adversely if the firms involved have a dominant market position and there are barriers to entry.

Because of network requirements, vertical agreements pose particularly acute competition problems in infrastructure services. For example, in the electricity, gas, telephony, and rail transport sectors, owner of the sole distribution network might give, through vertical agreements, monopoly power to a particular retailer or generator, even in cases where regulations establish full separation between owners of networks and companies that provide services in the competitive segment of the sector.

Abuse of Dominant Position

Abuse of dominant position implies anticompetitive business practices in which a dominant firm engages to maintain or increase its market position or profit. Exploitative abuses allow firms to benefit from their market power by charging excessively high prices, discriminating against customers, or paying suppliers low prices. Exclusionary abuses suppress competition by refusing to deal with a competitor, raising market entry costs for competitors, or charging predatory prices. Although the definition of abusive business practices varies by country, the most widely contested practices are as follows:

- Charging unreasonable or excessive prices
- Price discrimination
- Predatory pricing
- Price squeezing by integrated firms
- Refusal to sell
- Tied selling or product bundling
- Preemption of facilities.

Abuse of dominance in the infrastructure services sector is one of the most challenging areas of competition law because such abuse may occur in practices that are common in utilities provision, such as network access restrictions or setting prices with implicit cross subsidies. Moreover, the application of regulations in certain infrastructure sectors may involve practices that nonregulated sectors consider abuse of dominant position. For example, power consumer tariffs in Mexico imply cross subsides from industrial to residential consumers; therefore, the company applying such a tariff would have dominance, according to widely accepted definitions of this concept. Nevertheless, the Mexican competition agency may not prosecute the publicly-owned monopoly because it is excluded from the scope of the Mexican competition law.

Although most competition laws contain provisions aimed at preventing abuse of dominant position, there is no clear determinant of what constitutes dominance. In this regard, a firm's size is not a determining factor. On the one hand, there are small firms operating in closed markets that hold sizeable market power. On the other hand, there are large firms operating in large, open markets with no market power. Therefore, analysis should focus on a firm's behavior and its ability to strategically deter others from entering the market. The demarcation between business practices that may or may not be abusive or anticompetitive is not always clear; thus, the rule-of-reason approach is often advocated.

Decisions regarding abuse of dominance typically involve three steps. First, the market in which the potential abuse occurs must be defined. Second, existence of dominant position must be evaluated in terms of the market share of the firm in question and the extent of entry barriers. As Ordover and Saloner (1989) note, in some cases, the behavior under investigation can be the most significant barrier to entry. Third, alleged abuses of dominant position—whether exploitative or exclusionary—must be identified and investigated.

Among the countries studied in this chapter, Argentina and Brazil explicitly deal with abuses of dominant position. The competition laws of both countries penalize abuse of dominance, not simply the existence of dominant power. The laws of Chile and Mexico do not refer explicitly to abuse of dominance, while Peru's Decree on Competition describes dominant practices as the unfair or discriminatory treatment of customers.

Structural and Behavioral Provisions: Complements or Substitutes

Market Structure and Business Conduct

While the structure and behavioral provisions of competition policy tend to be applied separately, the relationship between market structure and business conduct is interactive. For example, in markets where the corresponding technologies do not show scale or scope economies, many firms behave competitively. As such, a firm that sets prices above competitors will undoubtedly lose customers. Similarly, technologies with increasing returns push market participants to gain market share in order to increase profits, which, in turn, increases market concentration. Furthermore, the interaction between market structure and business conduct requires complementary structural and behavioral approaches; however, significant disagreements can arise over how competition policy treats structural provisions.

Opponents of structural provisions argue that competition policy should promote economic efficiency and that optimal firm size should be favored, regardless of a firm's size and market share. Therefore, contestable markets would promote efficiency and consumer welfare since the efficiency gains derived from concentration are transferred to consumers.

However, given the lack of pressure from international trade and the poor threat of new entrants, this argument does not apply to infrastructure services because firms have no incentive to transfer efficiency gains to consumers. Advocates of structural provisions argue that, because a firm's behavior depends on market structure, preventing concentration is the best way to avoid abuse of dominance. Additionally, they argue that efficiency gains from larger market concentration will never reach consumers. However, in those sectors where technologies have large, increasing returns, this view is risky. That is, when efficiency gains from concentration are excessive, consumer welfare may be larger in concentrated markets than in nonconcentrated ones with competitive firms, even when the behavior of concentrated firms is not entirely competitive.

Structural Provisions in Emerging Countries

Economies with large domestic markets have little difficulty implementing structural measures since their large market size allows many large firms to operate, thus making vigorous competition and increasing returns compatible. In emergent countries with small markets, the dilemma is whether to promote firms with optimal size or enough firms to ensure competition. Thus, the potential risks of misapplying competition law tend to be greater. Applying structural measures to ensure competition may prevent domestic firms from achieving the minimum size needed to compete in international markets. When trade is possible, governments can best alleviate worries about high concentration by removing barriers to foreign trade and investment and by lifting regulatory barriers to entry, such as licensing. However, when the pressure of trade is low, as is the case with infrastructure services, solutions are not easy.

Allowing large, local firms to operate may increase internal efficiency and reduce costs. However, lack of domestic competition may prevent a transfer of efficiency gains to consumers. It might be argued that a sound competition law that adequately provides for preventing abuse of dominant position might preclude such behavior, but proving abuse of dominance in developing countries is a difficult, lengthy process. One case in point is the evolution of competition regulation in Argentina. The country's 1980 competition law did not include structural provisions. In 1998, the Energy Regulatory Commission (Comisión Reguladora de Energía) addressed the issue of lack of competition in the wholesale gas market; yet, abuse of dominant position could not be proven, given the then-prevailing competition legislation. In 1999, this situation was remedied when a new law that included structural provisions was approved.

Competition Authorities

The Independence Issue

The general consensus is that sound policy outcomes are possible if institutions are designed to give independent agencies a degree of policymaking power free of political influence and appropriate incentives. This idea was first put into practice or implemented when monetary policy was delegated to independent central banks. Later, antitrust agencies emerged because of the need to promote and preserve competition in liberalized markets. While delegating monetary policy to independent central banks has been widely accepted, delegating powers in competition policy has been more partial in nature. For example, Argentina's former National Competition Commission could only issue nonbinding reports, while its Secretary for Competition Defense, a government department, issued the final resolution. More recent legislation revoked delegating competition policy to other government agencies (see annex).

Competition laws customarily establish the independence of competition agencies, although the meaning of independence varies by country. Board appointments and removals, as well as budgetary autonomy, have been considered indicators of both functional and financial independence. Political independence, viewed as the absence of government interference in the agencies' decisionmaking, is difficult to assess. Of the six countries studied in this chapter, independence is established through the process of selecting and removing commissioners; only in Argentina is the concept of financial independence clearly stated (see annex).

Argentina's National Tribunal for the Defense of Competition (Tribunal Nacional para la Defensa de la Competencia) is organized as a self-financing agency. Proceeds from fees paid by those bringing matters before the Tribunal cover its ordinary, reasonable expenses. The national executive appoints board members on the basis of a public call for candidates. Selection takes place by means of a competitive examination by a jury. The commissioners serve one six-year term; misconduct, negligence, disability, felony, and violations of incompatibility are causes for removal.

In Brazil, only one of three agencies is supposed to be independent. Nevertheless, the short, two-year terms of council members; the rather trivial causes for their removal; and lack of permanent staff work against independence. In Chile's 1973 decree, no reference to agencies' independence is made. In Mexico, commissioners are appointed for 10-year periods and can only be removed for serious reasons. In Peru, the competition agency enjoys limited managerial freedom in terms of setting salaries and financial resources. As for its functional autonomy, the president, board members, and judges of the tribunal are appointed by the national executive for fixed, five-year terms and can only be removed on grounds of incompetence, negligence, or dishonesty. In Venezuela, the 1992 law established the Agency for the Promotion and Protection of Free Competition (Procompetencia), an operationally autonomous body attached to the Ministry of Commerce. The Agency is headed by a chairman (appointed by the president for a four-year term), a vice-chairman, and five directors; yet, causes established for their removal do not appear substantive or supportive of independence.

Functions and Procedures

Competition laws usually focus on preventing restrictive business practices undertaken by private agents. However, public policies and institutional arrangements may also work in favor of or against competition. Therefore, in addition to enforcing competition laws, competition agencies' mandate must also encompass competition advocacy.

Enforcement

The effective enforcement of competition laws is a complex, demanding task, even in countries where competition is well established on both legal and regulatory grounds. The additional obstacles that Latin American countries face stem from lack of an antitrust culture and weak institutional capacity. Thus, it is understandable why competition laws in these countries are usually written in general terms. Enforcement officials face the challenge of determining whether a particular conduct is harmful, friendly, or neutral to competition, which requires a good command of competition and economic principles. A series of analytical guidelines have been developed to remedy insufficient capacity among competition authorities. For example, Brazil established simple guidelines for investigating anticompetitive behavior, and Peru's government set limits to market share in the power sector.

Competition agencies are usually in charge of investigating and adjudicating cases, with each phase being conducted separately by bodies within the agency. Functional separation of case preparation and preliminary investigation from ruling decisions within the competition commission are key to preserving stakeholders' guarantees. This functional separation exists in all six of the countries studied. In Argentina, Mexico, and Peru, investigations are conducted by technical units within the competition agency, who follow well-established procedural rules. Their results are submitted to the agency head or board of directors for ruling. In Brazil, investigation and decision-making are undertaken by different agencies; however, the country's current plans are to unify them. In Chile, the administrative unit (Comisión Preventiva) conducts investigations, which are then sent to a specialized court for ruling (Comisión Resolutiva).

Competition authorities enjoy more discretion than most government enforcement agencies. The courts, therefore, are supposed to exert control over their exercise of discretion. The judiciary, whether specialized or general, is usually involved in the final phase of the process. In fact, in most countries, competition cases are subject to judicial review. Therefore, the outcomes of courts' reviews of cases are instrumental in shaping the agency's enforcement decisions and competition policy itself. In Argentina, the new law establishes that tribunal resolutions involving the application of penalties, conduct modification, or abstention, and opposing or changing the conditions of concentration transactions can be appealed. In Chile, the law establishes the judiciary's involvement at every stage of the proceedings. Peru's law establishes that the commission's decision may be appealed before the Court of Competition Defense (Corte de Defensa a la Competencia).

Advocacy

The broad aims of competition advocacy are promotion and creation of competitive environments. The first pillar of the competition agency's advocacy role is to participate in the legislative and regulatory processes to ensure that norms are consistent with competition principles. Second, it should contribute to the shaping of government policies by posting efficiency and consumer-friendly policy alternatives. Third, it should make accurate information on the benefits of competition available to private and corporate citizens.

Mexico's competition agency plays an important role in the design and implementation of sector-specific regulatory mechanisms. The competition law empowers the commission to weigh in on the contents of other laws and regulation that involve competition. In addition, several sector-specific laws and regulations assign an explicit role to the competition agency in matters related to determining the presence of effective competition or market power. Furthermore, the commission is empowered to authorize the participation of economic agents in privatization or concession operations, having exercised such power in railway privatization and auctions for radio or seaport concessions.

Recent legislation enacted in Argentina explicitly empowers the competition tribunal to issue nonbinding opinions on antitrust and free competition features of laws, regulations, and administrative proceedings, and to issue general or sector-specific recommendations on competition modalities in the markets. These provisions, together with public hearings and media exposure, set the stage for strengthening antitrust advocacy.

In Peru and Chile, the advocacy functions of competition authorities are not explicitly defined in competition laws. Nevertheless, in Peru, competition advocacy is considered a key ingredient in consolidating the gains derived from market reforms (Jatar 1999).

Balancing Advocacy and Enforcement

According to Rodríguez and Hoffman (1998), competition agencies in emergent countries should divert resources from traditional antitrust enforcement to competition advocacy. The institutional characteristics of most Latin American countries have been shaped by decades of pervasive state participation in economic life, which have traditionally favored monopoly, rent seeking, and other anticompetitive practices likely to erode market reform efforts. These historical trends may shift focus after market reforms, but they will not disappear. Against such a backdrop, the competition agency must pursue a balanced strategy of advocacy and antitrust enforcement. Unless the pervasiveness of anticompetitive mechanisms and incentives is clearly understood, the benefits of liberalization may be elusive. For example, if competition agencies act exclusively on the basis of traditional antitrust enforcement, this could provide an incentive for rent-seeking behavior. In addition, the strategy of diverting resources to competition advocacy results from a lack of enforcement-related statutes in competition laws.

In countries that lack a social antitrust tradition, the competition agency's advocacy role is instrumental in creating and consolidating a competition culture by showing society its benefits. Target groups of this advocacy are consumers, academia, court systems, and productive sectors.

Competition advocacy fosters increasing transparency, leading to reasonably competitive market structures and corporate behavior. This could be achieved by lessening direct intervention of competition authorities under antitrust law enforcement. Such direct intervention poses a threat to foreign investment and fosters regulatory uncertainty.

Competition Agencies and Sector Regulators

Competition and sector regulatory agencies are usually involved in enforcing competition in infrastructure industries. Although these institutions differ in coverage and performance timing, consistency among their activities is key to enabling competition in infrastructure industries.

Competition agencies are virtually economywide in coverage and administer laws primarily intended to protect consumers by preventing firms from reducing competition through collusion, mergers with rivals, or eliminating competitors by means other than offering superior products to consumers. Regulatory agencies cover a small number of infrastructure services—those that, in the government's view, would inadequately serve the public interest if private markets supervised by a competition agency were relied on. In this case, the government empowers an institution to safeguard competition in a particular sector or sector group.

In terms of timing, competition agencies operate ex post (with the exception of merger review), while regulation operates ex ante and throughout. However, measures aimed at shaping adequate market structures should be implemented before initiating the deregulation process. Typically, regulation is applied under the assumptions that market forces cannot be relied on to produce a satisfactory outcome and that attempting to change a firm's incentives is insufficient. In such situations, firms may be better served by ex ante instructions, rather than being surprised by unexpected requirements once sunken costs have been incurred.

Functional Roles

Regarding the ex post functional division between regulatory and competition agencies, a simple approach would suggest that competition agencies address issues related to competitive segments, while regulators consider issues in noncompetitive segments. However, this approach ignores the fact that pricing and access practices in the noncompetitive segment may be the best tool for destroying competition. Therefore, competition authorities, in conjunction with sector regulators, should ensure that such practices favor competition. Another approach recommends that competition agencies be entitled to prosecute practices that are contrary to competition, while sector regulators are responsible for investigating this conduct.

In Latin American countries, infrastructure sector reforms have been implemented within a context where vertically integrated firms have enjoyed government mandated monopoly positions and have been obligated to supply services at below cost to certain customer groups because of universal service obligations. The initial measures needed to change this situation are not particularly suited to a competition authority or regulator; instead, the government should take these steps, with the agencies playing an advisory role. Initial measures should include privatizing previously restructured state-owned utilities; removing legal barriers to entry; leveling the playing field among publicly-owned incumbents and new entrants; providing access to government or incumbent-controlled networks; and restructuring or eliminating universal service obligations.

Once these initial steps have been taken, introducing competition into infrastructure services requires a broad range of skills and experience to deal with competition protection as well as access, economic, and technical regulation. According to the OECD (1999), competition agencies or sector regulators should take five essential steps to enhance competition: ensure nondiscriminatory access to essential facility networks; control other anticompetitive behavior and review mergers; conduct technical regulation to ensure that compatibility, privacy, and environmental concerns are addressed; conduct economic regulation to control monopoly pricing and ensure consumer protection; and periodically reassess the scope and degree of remaining market power in markets where competition is being introduced to determine whether any sector-specific laws or regulations should remain in place.

Guidelines for Assigning Tasks

- Where the need for access and economic regulation is expected to be temporary and the main task is to introduce competition, entrusting both access and competition regulation to the general competition agency may be best. Where the need for access and economic regulation is expected to be permanent, as is the case with natural monopoly transmission and distribution networks, the sector regulator should be responsible for these tasks.
- Responsibility for protecting competition should remain with the general competition agency since it has a comparative advantage in this area, especially in prosecuting anticompetitive behavior and reviewing mergers. Competition agencies should prosecute practices contrary to competition in infrastructure sectors, while sector regulators should be in charge of investigating such conduct.

- Attention must be given to the fact that economywide agencies are supposedly less vulnerable to regulatory capture than are sector-specific regulators.
- In terms of expertise and institutional culture, competition agencies are better suited to safeguarding against anticompetitive behavior and mergers. For these same reasons, sector-specific regulators are better able to deal with technical regulation. However, the division of labor in economic and access regulation is less clear, leaving ample room for institutional collaboration.
- If the task of safeguarding competition is separated from access and economic regulation, cooperation and coordination are required to avoid inconsistent application of the two sets of policies, which would discourage investment. Various approaches—from informal to legally required consultation, to general oversight of the competition office—can be used to ensure cooperation and coordination. Whenever access and economic regulation are located outside the competition agency, that agency should be fully involved in any periodic reviews of the regulation. Cooperative links are also needed to ensure that technical regulators appropriately consider the ways in which adoption and enforcement of technical standards may distort or restrict competition.

The Mexico Case

Mexico typifies how the division of labor between the competition agency and infrastructure sector regulators and ministries may be organized (OECD 1999). In that country, the functioning of market forces in former monopolist sectors is now simultaneously regulated (under the 1993 Law of Economic Competition, which is enforced by the Competition Commission, and under sector-specific laws enforced by independent regulatory entities). The telecommunications, electricity, and natural gas sectors have independent regulators. Although the Commission ensures compliance with the law and sector regulators deal with sector-specific technical and economic regulations, some functional overlap exists because the Commission is empowered to investigate and sanction anticompetitive activity in these sectors.

In addition to its enforcement role, the Commission plays a key advocacy role in designing and implementing sector standards. These roles are grounded both in the competition law and in the natural gas and telecommunications sector laws. Under these provisions, specific responsibilities of the Commission determine the competitiveness of a market and authorize participation in privatization or concession processes in the infrastructure sectors. Moreover, the Commission plays a critical role in fostering private participation of natural gas transport, storage, and distribution.

Final Remarks and Lessons Learned

In Latin America, as in many other world regions, a tradition of anticompetitive behavior, resulting from pervasive state intervention, has contributed to creating an intricate web of widely accepted, collusive practices. This trend has been especially pervasive in infrastructure sectors, where, until 1980, state-owned monopolies were considered the norm. In addition, privatization processes, driven by public deficits, have transformed publicly-owned monopolies into private ones.

Confusion has surrounded the issue of applying competition laws to infrastructure services. Given that the aim of most infrastructure reforms has been the introduction of competition, provisions that apply to other competitive sectors should also apply to the competitive segments of infrastructure sectors. Moreover, while sector regulations may detail some provisions related to market structure and regulate the monopolistic segment of the industry, competition authorities should consistently be able to prosecute noncompetitive practices in infrastructure services and evaluate the appropriateness of mergers that may give dominance to firms that provide infrastructure services.

In countries that lack a competition culture, a sound, pro-competition constituency needs to be fostered. The broad aims of competition advocacy are promotion and creation of competitive environments. Moreover, an extensive public education program should be launched to lay the foundation for understanding the objectives of competition policy in infrastructure sectors. Competition agencies should oversee public policies that affect competition, particularly market entry conditions, sector regulations of natural monopolies, and privatization processes.

In competition matters, competition agencies should prevail over sector regulators, although the competition functions of sector agencies should not be excluded. Given that regulatory agencies are well suited to identifying issues related to third-party access and other technical matters, they should be charged with investigating the anticompetitive behavior of infrastructure service providers.

Competition laws usually establish independent enforcement agencies in charge of preserving competition. However, such a goal is difficult to achieve because of the enormous economic power and political clout of those who head dominant utilities, whether appointed privately or by the government. Furthermore, industry or economy ministries retain significant enforcement functions, thereby preserving preferential links with industry interests. Efforts should be made to increase enforcement agencies' capacity and strength.

The interaction between market structure and business conduct requires competition laws that encompass both structural and behavioral provisions. In promoting competition in infrastructure services, this approach is particularly relevant. Devoid of pressure from international trade or the threat of new market entrants, infrastructure service providers (who hold a large market share) lack incentive to reduce costs and prices. Moreover, is it often difficult to prove that their practices are monopolistic.

Striking an appropriate balance between competition advocacy and enforcement of antitrust laws by competition authorities is crucial in emergent economies (World Bank and OECD 1998). In such countries, a few dominant firms typically engage in anticompetitive business practices or lobby government authorities for preferential treatment. Greater transparency would foster the conditions leading to reasonably competitive market structures and corporate behavior. Although advocacy alone may not suffice and intervention of competition authorities is likely required, it should be emphasized that excessive direct intervention would threaten foreign investment and create regulatory uncertainty.

In closing, the scope of competition laws for infrastructure services provision, although potentially significant, tends to be scant in practice. Even with well-designed laws, events may prove difficult to tackle because of the sizeable economic and political transaction costs involved in policy implementation. Increased globalization renders elusive the task of providing well-substantiated, enduring recipes for developing countries. Finally, applying competition regulations requires large economic and legal expertise, which are not always easily available. A transnational policy approach would be instrumental in setting guidelines for regulators and limiting the power of interest groups.

Annex. Summary of Competition Laws in Six Latin American Countries

Argentina

Historical Framework

In 1923, Law 11.210, one of the first antitrust bills in Latin America, was passed. Subsequently, this law was modified several times and then replaced by Law 12.906. Both laws focused on monopoly issues and were seldom enforced (only two cases were presented under each). In 1980, in an attempt to remedy the ineffectiveness of Law 12.906, Law 22.262 came into force. Its aims were to ban acts and behaviors that limit, restrict, or distort competition or constitute abuse of dominant position in ways that may affect general economic interests. The enforcement body for Law 22.262 was the National Commission for the Defense of Competition. As time passed, both the Commission and Law 22.262 proved inadequate in dealing with the increasing complexity of competition issues.

Since the early 1990s, economic institutions in Argentina have undergone profound transformations as a result of market deregulation and the opening to international competition, privatization of public service firms, and elimination of intervention mechanisms. Since the post-war period, reforms have resulted in a radical change in the economic regime, which remained unchanged until the 1990s. The main consequence of reshaping economic rules was the private sector's enhanced role in allocating and administering resources, combined with a redefinition of public sector responsibilities aimed at safeguarding the outcomes of liberalization. Within this context, privatization of public firms gave rise to competition policy measures aimed at controlling privatized firms' abuse of dominant position, as well as the establishment of regulatory bodies responsible for surveying monopoly segments of privatized public service firms.

By the mid 1990s, the dynamics of globalization and, more specifically, the wave of mergers driven by an increased flow of direct foreign investment to privatized utilities, created an apparent need to readjust current standards. A new law dealing specifically with these circumstances was passed; it provided for the creation of a more independent enforcement authority with powers and responsibilities suitable to address the current situation. In 1998, the National Congress started debate on a new antitrust bill, which came into force September 29, 1999 as Law 25.156. Compared with the previous law, certain general elements in Law 25.156 remained unchanged, as is typical of behavioral policy instruments. However, the new law made important inroads by featuring merger and acquisitions control.

Scope and Infrastructure Services

Article 3 of the competition law states that the law applies to all economic agents. Furthermore, one of the new law's main purposes was to address concentration processes under way in infrastructure services, namely gas and electricity. Therefore, all provisions of the law apply to infrastructure services. Under the law, competition jurisdictional powers conferred to other agencies were revoked and transferred to the new competition agency. However, if the economic concentration involves firms or persons whose economic activity is regulated by a sector or regulatory agency, the National Tribunal for the Defense of Competition, prior to issuing its resolution, requires the sector regulatory agency to submit a report and substantiated opinion on the economic concentration's effects on competition in the respective market or its compliance with the relevant regulatory framework.

Behavioral Provisions

The new law deals with these practices in terms similar to the previous law. As such, unlawful practices and horizontal and vertical agreements are described as acts and behaviors related to the production of goods and services that limit, restrict, or distort competition or abuse dominant position in a market. If these acts result in damage to the general economic interest, they are prohibited and are penalized. It is noteworthy that the mere threat, albeit solidly grounded, of damage to the general economic interest is considered unlawful. The general economic interest is deemed equivalent to economic efficiency. It should also be noted that the law considers no conduct per se as illegal. Therefore, it is necessary to evaluate the conduct's economic effects in order to determine its competition-restricting character. Obtaining significant competitive advantages through violation of other regulations is also deemed anticompetitive behavior.

Dominant position is dealt with under the same terms as the previous law; that is, abuse of dominance, not its mere existence, is penalized. However, entry into force of a compulsory notification regime for economic concentrations renders highly unlikely the chance of obtaining authorization for a transaction that involves or strengthens dominance. Under the new law, it is understood that one or more agents may enjoy a dominant position when, for a certain type of product or service, that agent is the only supplier or buyer in the national market. This also holds when the agent is not the only supplier or buyer in the national market, in which case the agent is able to determine the economic viability of a market competitor to his or her detriment.

Unlike the previous law, the new law explicitly describes the circumstances to be considered when determining a dominant market position. These include the following: the extent to which relevant goods or services may be replaced by other national or foreign goods or services and the conditions and time required for such replacement; the extent to which regulatory restrictions limit access of products, suppliers, or buyers to the relevant market; and the extent to which the presumed liable subject can unilaterally affect price formation or restrict market supply or demand and the extent to which its competitors can offset said power.

Economic Concentration and Merger Control

The new law significantly strengthens control of economic concentration operations, which, because of their size, may negatively affect market performance. The former law did not provide an explicit scheme for controlling mergers and acquisitions; it simply provided behavioral measures that the new law complements by means of a double set of prescriptions.[1] On the one hand, Article 7 generically prohibits economic concentrations whose aim or effect is to reduce, distort, or restrict competition in a way that is biased against the general economic interest. On the other hand, to effect that prohibition, the law dictates that the Tribunal for the Defense of Competition must be notified of operations that exceed certain established parameters. Thus, the court has the power to object to or limit particular transactions when their social costs are deemed to outweigh their benefits.

However, the law does not provide rules to determine whether a specific concentration transaction should be authorized, prohibited, or contingent on certain conditions. Nevertheless, contrary to previous legislation, which was based on strengthening dominant position as the rationale for decision-

---

[1] Article 3 of Law 25.156 states that economic concentration is the takeover of one or several firms by the merger of firms, transfer of good will, acquisition of the property or any right over the shares when such acquisitions grant the purchaser control of or substantial influence over the capital stock, and any other agreement or act that transfers (in fact or legally) a firm's assets or decisionmaking powers to a person or economic group.

making, the new law (following European legislation) has adopted the rationale prevalent in the United States, which is the possibility to exercise market power (De Quevedo 2000). The general guidelines for controlling economic concentration, which are embodied in Resolution 726 of 1999, are designed to reflect the methodological sequence to be applied when evaluating concentrations.[2]

Three steps are required. First, a description of the effects of the concentration transaction on general economic interest is required. If the resulting concentration level does not endanger general economic interest, the transaction is cleared. Otherwise, analysis will proceed. Once a high degree of concentration has been determined, its consequences, in terms of exercising power in the relevant market, must be evaluated. Factors to be considered are the countervailing potential of market participants; likelihood of eliminating a vigorous, effective competitor; and flow of information within the relevant market. The last step is to determine the gains in productive efficiency resulting from concentration. Lower prices, improved quality, better service, and new product development may follow. If such gains materialize, their significance should be compared with the potential harm inherent in the concentration transaction.

Filing is mandatory for all parties involved in the transaction. The transaction's implementation must be suspended prior to its clearance. Thresholds entailing compulsory notification of the transaction to the Competition Tribunal are established at US$200 million in revenues within the country for the companies involved or US$2.5 billion worldwide. Neither the transaction volume nor the merging companies' market share is used as a criterion for notification. Notification must occur either prior to or during the week following execution of the agreement. In all cases subject to notification, the Tribunal, on substantiated resolution, decides within 45 days after submitting the relevant application and documentation, whether to approve the operation, subordinate the act to comply with conditions to be established by the Tribunal, or refuse authorization. If no resolution is issued after 45 days, the transaction is deemed implicitly approved. Implicit approval has the same legal effect as explicit approval. The following operations are exempt from mandatory notice and excluded from the scope of merger control: acquisition of companies in which the acquirer owns more than 50 per-

---

[2] See Lineamientos para el Control de las Concentraciones Económicas (National Commission for the Defense of Competition, 1999).

cent of shares; acquisition of a company by a foreign investor that does not own shares or assets in Argentina; acquisition of bonds, debentures, shares with no voting rights, or certificates of indebtedness of firms; and acquisitions of liquidated companies that have no registered activity in the country over the last year.

Competition Authorities

The new law establishes the transfer of decisionmaking capacity from the public administration to the Competition Tribunal through creating a new antitrust body as an autonomous agency empowered to impose sanctions that can be appealed in the corresponding federal court. Formerly, the National Competition Commission was entitled only to issue nonbinding reports, while the Secretary for Competition Defense pronounced the final resolution. The new law evidences a great institutional leap forward, whereby the official channel ends with Tribunal sentences, with no need for a political authority's decision. Furthermore, the law abolishes every attribution of authority on competition issues granted to other government agencies or entities.[3]

Independence

The National Tribunal for the Defense of Competition is organized as a self-financing agency. Proceeds from the fees paid by interested parties for the proceedings brought before the Tribunal are used to cover the Tribunal's ordinary and reasonable expenses. Although its headquarters are located in Buenos Aires, the Tribunal, acting through delegates appointed by its president, can act or meet anywhere in the country. Its delegates can be national, provincial, or municipal officers. The Tribunal comprises seven (formerly five) members with satisfactory personal records and qualifications to perform their duties; at least two must be lawyers and two must be economists, each with more than five years of experience. Tribunal members are not permitted to perform any other activity during their commission, except for teaching. The national executive appoints the members, and selection takes place by means of a competitive examination by a jury. With the aim of guar-

---

[3] Section 59 of the Competition Law revokes the conferring of any jurisdictional powers concerning the subject matter and purpose of this law on other government agencies.

anteeing transparency, the jury is composed of the following representatives of executive, legislative, and judicial powers and academia: National Treasurer, Secretary of Industry, Chairmen of the Trade Commissions (of both legislative chambers), President of the National Court of Appeals for Commercial Matters, and Presidents of the National Academies of Law and Economic Sciences. The commissioners serve six-year terms, can be partially renewed every three years, and may be re-elected in accordance with the law's provisions. Causes for removal include misconduct, negligence, disability, penal sentence, and violation of incompatibility.

Procedures

The Tribunal's ability to hold public hearings enhances transparency of the antitrust process overall. It can decide to hold a public hearing whenever it is deemed convenient for the course of the investigation. Its decision to hold hearings involves identifying the investigation under consideration; nature and purpose of the hearing; date, time, and place of the hearing; and requirements for attendance and participation. Hearings must be convened with at least 20 days prior notice, and the parties involved must be given not less than 15 days prior notice of the date appointed for the hearing. Notice of public hearings must be published in the official gazette and two newspapers of national circulation no less than 10 days prior to the said date. The Tribunal may allow participation of third parties in the proceedings brought before it; these include individuals involved in the events investigated, consumer and business associations having a legal standing, and any other person having a legitimate interest in the investigated events. Finally, the Tribunal may request expert opinions on the investigated events.

Punitive Powers

The Competition Law strengthens commission powers in terms of the amount of fines and imposition of conditions aimed at re-establishing competition. The available sanctions for closing a transaction before clearance are potentially draconian. Monetary penalties range from US$10,000 to $50 million, depending on the damage caused, the benefits obtained, and the value of the assets involved. If recidivism occurs, the fines are doubled. In addition, the Tribunal may impose certain conditions to neutralize the detrimental effect on competition of the transaction, or ask the courts to order the dissolution, liquidation, de-concentration, or breakup of the companies in violation of the law. When an individual commits violations, the monetary sanctions will be imposed on board members, auditors, or attorneys of the companies, both jointly and severally. In such a case, a supplementary penalty, consisting of disqualification to engage in commerce for one to ten years, may be imposed. It should be noted that the new law eliminates prison penalties, which, though never implemented, had been formerly established by Law 22.262.

Advocacy Role

Section 24 of the law establishes enhancement of the advocacy function, empowering the Tribunal to issue nonbinding opinions on antitrust and free competition features of laws, regulations, and administrative proceedings, and to issue general or sector recommendations on competition modalities in the markets.

Brazil

Historical Framework

Brazil's first competition law (Law 4,137), passed in 1962, merely survived in an environment characterized by government intervention in the economy and protectionism. Price controls were prominent, and most of the country's largest industrial, transportation, and financial firms were either public or private monopolies. Little room was left for competition policy until the late 1980s when a liberalization process was launched with the enactment of the 1998 constitution.[4] At that time, trade barriers were removed, and privatization made some inroads. In 1991, a second competition law (Law 8,158) was passed, paving the way toward stronger competition enforcement. In 1994, another new law (Law 8,884) reinforced control of merger and anticompetitive conduct and antitrust agency independence. The pace of privatization increased; price-controlling agencies were abolished; and independent regulatory agencies for telecommunications, electricity, oil, and natural gas were created.

---

[4] The Brazilian Federal Constitution of 1988 states that "the law shall repress the abuse of economic power that is directed toward market control, elimination of competition, and the arbitrary increase of profits."

Scope and Infrastructure Services

Brazil's competition law does not specifically exempt any infrastructure sectors. However, even if Law 8,884 fully applies to infrastructure services provision, the interface between sector regulations and the general competition law is not yet well defined. Therefore, implied exemptions to the competition law may arise when regulations conflict with general competition provisions; in this regard, competition enforcement may have to yield to sector regulations. To date, however, few competition cases have dealt with infrastructure industries. Recently established, ad hoc working groups are currently dealing with the issue.

The Brazilian System for Competition Defense (SBDC) works in cooperation with federal regulatory agencies dealing with telecommunications, power, oil, and gas sectors. For example, Article 7 of the General Telecommunications Act of 1997 explicitly provides for applying Law 8,884 to the telecommunications sector. Article 19 states that the telecommunications regulator, ANATEL, "shall have the legal authority to control, prevent, and curb any breach of the economic order in the telecommunications industry, without prejudice to the powers vested in the Competition Agency." The electricity law requires the sector regulator, ANEEL, to promote competition in the industry, wherever feasible.

Behavioral Provisions

Law 8,884 of 1994 was mainly designed to curb "abuse of economic power" by targeting competition-restricting practices as possible manifestations of such power. Articles 20 and 21 (under the heading of "violations of economic order") are ambiguous about all types of anticompetitive conduct, other than mergers.

Article 20 prohibits any act either intended to produce or capable of producing effects that limit competition, control the relevant market, increase profits on a discretionary basis, or abuse market control. Paragraph 1 specifically excludes from violation the achievement of market control as a result of competitive efficiency. Paragraph 3 further provides that a dominant position is presumed when a company or group of companies controls 20 percent of the relevant market; this is subject to change by the Council of Economic Defense (CADE) for specific sectors of the economy. Article 21 lists 24 restrictive practices considered violations of "economic order," as set forth in Article 20, if they produce any of the outcomes enumerated in Article 20. These 24 practices can be grouped into four main categories of competition restrictive practices: cartels, noncartel agreements, vertical restraint, and abuse of dominance.

In many of its decisions, CADE has emphasized that Law 8,884 specifically promotes the adoption of a rule-of-reason approach when dealing with violations of economic order. CADE endorses the view that Article 20 does not allow competition authorities to deem any agreement as presumably illegal. A thorough investigation of the market effect of every restrictive practice is mandatory. In 1999, CADE issued Resolution 20, thereby establishing a framework for analysis of rule-of-reason cases, consistent with mainstream principles on this matter. Principles underlying the resolution are: the necessity of taking into account the specific context in which the practice occurs, the costs incurred, and the benefits expected; applying strict standards to the conduct of cartels,[5] while dealing with noncartel agreements on a rule-of-reason basis; and defining steps for evaluating behavior.

Economic Concentration and Merger Control

Article 54 states that "any acts that may limit or otherwise restrain open competition, or that result in the control of relevant markets for certain products or services, shall be submitted to CADE for review." In practice, most notifications submitted involve mergers. Thus far, the threat of compulsory notification of all restrictive agreements persists.[6]

Article 54 sets forth the requirements to be met by concentration transactions authorized by CADE and the thresholds for notification of such transactions. Transactions should be approved if they meet the following criteria: they intend to increase productivity, improve the quality of a product or service, or result in increased efficiency; the resulting benefits are allocated among all stakeholders; and they do not drive competition out of a substantial portion of the relevant market for a product or service. However, paragraph 2 states that any action under the article may be considered lawful if, whenever taken in the public interest or otherwise required, it benefits the Brazilian economy, provided no damages are caused to final consumers or end users. This paragraph clearly opens the door to transactions that restrict competition and protect Brazilian industries.

---

[5] Since joining the OECD Council, Recommendation Concerning Effective Action Against Hard-core Cartels, Brazil's anticartel efforts have increased.

[6] According to Clark (1997), since the enactment of Law 8,884, the three competition agencies have devoted large, increasing proportions of their resources to merger control.

CADE must be notified of mergers that satisfy one of two tests: the resultant company accounts for 20 percent of the relevant market or any participant has posted an annual gross revenue of at least 400 million Reais in its latest balance sheet. However, these thresholds give rise to various ambiguities in interpretation. The minimum of 400 million Reais applies to worldwide revenues, thus imposing the obligation to notify CADE of transactions involving minimal effects on Brazilian markets. On the other hand, the threshold of 20-percent market share might introduce ambiguity since definition of the term *relevant market* has not been agreed on, posing doubts as to whether notification of a transaction is required.

Article 54 (paragraph 4) requires that merger notifications occur not later than 15 days after the transaction. It should be noted that litigation concerning the appropriate trigger date has been increasing.

Another source of merger review inefficiency lies in its being conducted by three agencies—two within the government and one independent entity. In practice, a minimum of six months elapses before a merger review is completed. Because each agency conducts its own fact finding and investigation, CADE has been unable to profit from its sister agencies' expertise, thereby furthering inefficiency.

In infrastructure industries, sector regulators are legally involved in merger reviews. However, since the process of energy sector liberalization is still at an early stage, most cooperation deals with privatization issues. In the telecommunications industry, mergers are subject to specific pre-merger control by the sector regulatory agency, as established by the Telecommunications Act. Since the competition law also applies to mergers exceeding established notification thresholds, in such cases, the sector regulator is responsible for conducting the investigation.

Competition Authorities Organization

CADE, the Secretariat for Economic Law (SDE) of the Ministry of Justice, and the Secretariat for Economic Monitoring (SEAE) of the Ministry of Finance constitute the SBDC. CADE is an administrative tribunal, while SDE and SEAE have analytical and investigative functions.[7]

---

[7] On August 11, 2000, a presidential decree created a cross-ministries working group to review the SBDC; according to the decree, the working group's main task was to prepare a law that would integrate the SEAE, SDE, and CADE.

Law 8,884 reshaped CADE into an independent federal agency, linked to the Ministry of Justice and consisting of a president and six board members. Brazil's president appoints CADE's chairperson and commissioners, after the Senate approves their two-year terms, which may be extended once. CADE's powers are those typically associated with a competition enforcement agency. Article 7 enumerates, among others, the following functions: to hear and decide cases involving breaches of the substantive provisions of the Law; to issue orders requiring the cessation of unlawful activity and the implementation of the corresponding performance commitments; to require the submission of information from both public and private entities in the course of its proceedings; and to impose fines on corporations. However, since most investigation and analysis functions are performed by CADE's two sister agencies, it has no permanent staff.

Law 8,884 also provides for creation of the Office of the Attorney General within CADE, which is responsible for rendering legal assistance, providing for defense in court, arranging for judicial execution of CADE decisions and sentences, arranging court settlements, and rendering opinion on cases. Some 20 attorneys work in this office.

Under Article 13, the SDE is entitled to investigate functions and certain preliminary enforcement proceedings. SDE can, ex-officio or on request of an interested party, initiate preliminary investigation and therefore request data from individuals, agencies, or authorities and determine the action required for exercising its duties. Preliminary investigation should not exceed 60 days, after which the SDE may either close the investigation, following CADE approval, or begin administrative proceedings. At this stage, SDE has full information-gathering powers, including the power of obtaining testimony from witnesses. At the end of the information phase, SDE will either send CADE a substantiated report ascertaining violation of economic order and suggesting recommendations, or sign a cease-and-desist commitment when it concludes that there are no grounds for indictment. The order can be appealed to CADE.

The SEAE also has important responsibilities in competition enforcement. Article 38 establishes that CADE will inform SEAE of the initiation of any administrative proceedings and that the secretariat may decide to render an opinion on the matters within its sphere of authority, before the investigation phase concludes. Law 9,021 provides SEAE with powers to investigate possible violations of competition law; therefore, SEAE may conduct preliminary investigations, either independently or in cooperation with SDE. However, under the competition law, SEAE has no adjudication or enforcement functions. The institution is headed by a secretariat and has 200 employees.

Independence

Of the three competition agencies, only CADE is officially independent. Nevertheless, at first glance, the institutional setting under conventional independence criteria sends a mixed message. First, commissioners are appointed by Brazil's president and are approved by the senate for two-year terms. This relatively short appointment period (even if renewed for one two-year term), combined with lack of permanent CADE staff, does not favor institutional independence.

However, according to Article 5 (paragraph 1), Council members may only be removed under extreme and unlikely circumstances, indicating a type of independence. Yet, it should be noted that the second part of Article 5 provides for rather trivial causes terminating office terms, including absence from 3 consecutive or 20 intermittent ordinary meetings, which seems to work against independence. As for the competition agency's financial independence, this is not clearly stated in any of the sources consulted.

Procedures

Cases begin in SDE, which, with the assistance and advice of SEAE, conducts preliminary investigations and administrative proceedings before submitting the file and its recommendations to CADE for final ruling.

Articles 42–51 deal with CADE judgment on administrative proceedings. Once proceedings have been found admissible, the reporting official has 20 days within which to render an opinion. The attorney general also provides an opinion on the legal aspects of the matter within 20 days. A 60-day supplementary period is provided, at CADE's request. However, a supplemental investigation is seldom undertaken since CADE sends the matter back to SDE when it needs further information. After the 60-day period ends, the case is submitted to CADE "to be judged as soon as possible." Furthermore, its decision must be announced at a public meeting, where a quorum of five members is required. In case of a tie, the president is given an extra vote. Article 50 provides that CADE decisions do not qualify for executive branch review; accordingly, any such decisions must be promptly executed, the attorney general's office being then advised so that it can take all legal actions within its sphere of authority. Special procedures apply to merger review.

Punitive Powers

CADE has considerable powers to fashion remedies where it holds that the law has been violated. Fines on corporations that violate substantive provisions of the law prohibiting anticompetitive conduct amount to 1–30 percent of the gross pretax revenue for the previous year. Fines on individual managers responsible for such unlawful conduct are penalized 10–50 percent of the corporate fine. Fines on recurring violations are doubled. Article 24 sets forth a series of penalties to be imposed whenever the severity of the violation or the public interest so requires. In addition to fines, companies that violate antitrust law may have their tax incentives and public subsidies cancelled. Sale of assets and other divestiture measures are also considered.

Imposition of fines for late notification of mergers reflects the severity exhibited by CADE in interpreting the corresponding section of the competition law. In 1998, late notification represented 70 percent of total fines.

Advocacy Role

Brazil's three competition agencies aim to promote free competition and disseminate competition culture. To meet its capacity-building target, CADE, in coordination with education authorities, recommended the introduction of antitrust studies in the undergraduate and graduate programs of law, economics, business, engineering, and related majors. In addition, since the 1998 passage of Resolution 18, which was intended to ease consultations, CADE's contribution to the national competition debate has been reinvigorated. Finally, by decentralizing such activities as public hearings, advocacy has been greatly enhanced (Oliveira 2000).

With regard to infrastructure industries, the agencies have made special efforts, despite serious resource constraints. Foremost among these initiatives has been establishment of working groups with sector regulators to collaborate on efforts to deregulate electricity, gas, oil, and telecommunications.

Chile

Historical Framework

In Chile, antitrust regulation was first enacted in 1959, although it remained ineffective until 1973, when a comprehensive process of economic liberalization, encompassing privatization of most public firms and across-the-board deregulation of economic activity, was launched. Since 1973, liberalization policies have pursued similar paths in Chile, despite significant political changes. The main objective of the first privatization wave, which occurred in 1974–78, was to maximize revenue; it did not include privatization of public services, but rather their restructuring and deregulation.

During the second wave of privatization (1984–1990), some 30 infrastructure companies were sold, including Endesa (electricity sector) and Entel and CTC (telecommunications sector). To gain political support, this second wave of divestiture focused on improving ownership distribution. This concern was particularly acute with regard to utilities, which had been considered fairly efficient since their restructuring and deregulation. Therefore, utilities were transformed into public companies subject to standard commercial and audit procedures, with shares quoted in the stock market.

The third wave of privatization, which started in 1994, is still under way. Its goals—to improve regulation and competition—have proven difficult to achieve, mainly because of institutional reasons and lack of an updated antitrust law.

Scope and Infrastructure Services

Although Competition Decree Law 211 (Article 1) states that it applies to all economic agents, according to Article 5, infrastructure services may be regulated by sector-specific regulations. However, anticompetitive behavior is subject to the competition law, and competition authorities are entitled to and are responsible for reporting or providing their opinion on new regulations of infrastructure services.

Behavioral Provisions

Articles 1–4 deal boldly, yet inadequately, with practices that restrict competition, establishing jail penalties for acts aimed at hampering free competition. Articles 5–30 deal, in great detail, with competition enforcement institutions.

The law's general provisions establish that anyone executing any action tending to impede free competition within the country's economic activities will be punished by imprisonment. When offenses affect essential articles or services, such as those related to food, housing, clothing, or health, the punishment will be increased by one degree. Acts considered anticompetitive include quotas on production, transport, or distribution; price-setting agreements; and limiting access to any activity or work. In the case of legal entities' involvement in anticompetitive activities, dissolution of these entities may be ordered.

Economic Concentration and Merger Control

Although Chile's competition law does not refer specifically to economic concentration, legal grounds for its control can be found in Articles 8, 16, and 24, which state the respective functions of the Preventive Commission, Resolution Commission, and National Economic Prosecutor. Despite their broad powers conferred by the law, the authorities' behavior has been one of moderation and restraint. In this regard, there is insufficient evidence of commission rulings dealing with cases of economic concentration (Serra 1995). One case involves acquisitions intended to hamper competition in the gas distribution sector, where incumbent wholesalers acquired newcomer rivals in their attempt to eliminate market contestability. The office of the National Economic Prosecutor conducted a thorough investigation of the case and proposed adequate corrective measures. However, the Resolution Commission's 1993 report (no. 876) did not impose any penalty. In another case, the Preventive Commission, on grounds of lack of market contestability and empirical evidence of price increases, objected to Chile's flagship international airline acquiring the dominant domestic airline.

Competition Authorities Organization

The Regional Preventive Commissions, Central Preventive Commission, Resolution Commission, and office of the National Economic Prosecutor comprise the institutions responsible for safeguarding and promoting competition.

The role of the Regional Preventive Commission is to ensure competitive behavior, handle complaints regarding anticompetitive behavior, and implement preliminary investigations to determine whether behavior is anticompetitive. The Central Preventive Commission intervenes if the case is national in scope or involves more than one region. It also acts as the preventive commission for the metropolitan area of Santiago. Opinions expressed by these commissions can be appealed before the Resolution Commission, which supervises application of the competition law and the work of the preventive commissions.

The Resolution Commission handles cases of anticompetitive behavior ex officio or at the request of the National Economic Prosecutor. If the Commission determines that a violation of the law has occurred, it may apply a fine or recommend that the office of the National Economic Prosecutor pursue a penal case. It is also within this Commission's jurisdiction to determine whether a market requires regulation because of lack of competition.

Despite their regulatory empowerment, Chile's antitrust institutions have implemented their functions with restraint. When facing complex cases, these agencies are reluctant to apply sanctions or take preventive actions. Several considerations may help to explain their attitude (Serra 1995). First, it might be that hypothetical prejudices arising from monopolies are considered less significant than damages incurred by an active antitrust policy. A second reason for the agencies' inefficiency might be lack of resources. Judges are not paid for their work, which may guarantee independence, but may also mean that they devote little time to their tasks, thereby lengthening the process. However, the main drawback lies in the commissioners' lack of an appropriate background in economic regulation, which seriously hampers sound decision making. Other institutional weaknesses include neighborhood association representatives' participation in the Precautionary Commission and appointing those who lack specific qualifications or training to high-ranking positions on the Resolution Commission.

Mexico

Historical Framework

Although Mexico's Constitution (Article 28) has, since 1917, prohibited monopolies, this prohibition has never been reflected in government policies or put into practice. In fact, until the 1980s, price and entry controls and public monopolies have prevailed in the Mexican economy. The crisis of the mid 1980s called the country's economic policies into question by replacing control with market competition. A reform process was also fueled by Mexico's joining the General Agreement on Tariffs and Trade (GATT) and the North American Free Trade Agreement (NAFTA).

Mexico's competition policy is part of a larger reform effort initiated in the mid 1980s that aimed to move the country from protection and state intervention toward a market economy. Major elements of the reform were ending price controls, liberalizing trade and investment, privatizing public enterprises, changing regulation, and adopting a sound competition policy. At the heart of the policy is the stated objective of consolidating the entire liberalization process, while simultaneously increasing efficiency (Wise 1999).

In 1993, the Federal Law of Economic Competition was passed, and the Federal Competition Commission was subsequently established to enforce it. Article 2 states: "The purpose of this law is to protect the process of competition and free market participation, through the prevention of monopolies, monopolistic practices and other restrictions that deter the efficient operation of the market for goods and services."[8] The law's design benefits from the most advanced ideas and practices, as its drafters in the Ministry of Trade and Industry consulted with leading academic and legal experts. However, the level of support among the business community and general public remains difficult to determine. Until recently, the Commission's contribution to increasing that support has been called into question (Rodríguez and Williams 1995; Wise 1999).

Scope and Infrastructure Services

According to Article 3, the competition law applies to all economic agents, including those subject to sector-specific regulations. However, Article 4 points out that faculties exercised exclusively by the state in the strategic sectors described in Article 28 do not constitute monopolies.

In recent years, Mexico's government has introduced competition and private participation into several activities, some of which have traditionally been considered natural monopolies. Some segments have been opened to competition; however, the extent to which the gas and electricity sectors are covered by the law's provisions remains unclear.

Behavioral Provisions

The competition law implements constitutional provisions by preventing and penalizing anticompetitive conduct. It does not provide for monopoly correction, but addresses particular practices to strengthen monopolies.

Horizontal agreements. Absolute monopolistic practices that are subject to prohibition encompass four types of horizontal agreements among competing agents: price fixing, output restriction, market division, and bid rigging. Article 9 specifies particular types of conduct in these categories. The price fixing clause prohibits fixing, raising, or manipulating the purchase price or sale of

---

[8] Federal Law of Economic Competition, official gazette of the Federation (APEC, December 24, 1992).

goods or services supplied or demanded in the markets, as well as the exchange of information with the same purpose or effect. The output restriction clause prohibits the establishment of an obligation to produce, process, distribute, or market a restricted or limited amount of goods that restricts the number, volume, or frequency of service. The market division clause protects both potential and actual markets by prohibiting the division, distribution, assignation, or imposition of portions or segments of a present or potential market of goods and services, by means of a determinable group of customers, suppliers, time, or locations. The bid rigging clause covers agreements on participation and bid levels, such as bid establishment or coordination or bid abstention in tenders or public auctions. The listing of relative monopolistic practices includes only one specific type of horizontal agreement—collusive boycotts. It also includes a general provision whereby other types of horizontal agreements are subjected to economic treatment on a case-by-case basis.

Provisions that prohibit horizontal agreements set the stage for eliminating publicly sanctioned, but privately arranged, price controls established by business chambers. The laws providing for these organizations were revised in order to limit their powers of membership exclusion and price fixing. These horizontal monopolistic practices are prohibited per se and are legally void. Parties to these practices cannot claim they are efficient since their inherent inefficiency is taken for granted. Violators are subject to administrative sanctions, and the Competition Agency may report associated criminal conduct to the public prosecutor.

Vertical agreements. Vertical agreements are considered relative monopolistic practices and are subject to case-by-case analysis. Article 10 identifies market division, resale price maintenance, tied sales, and exclusive dealing. Relative monopolistic practices are considered illegal only when they positively harm competition by displacing other agents from the market, limit their access, or provide certain agents advantages. The responsible party must have substantial power in the relevant market and may base its defense on efficiency grounds. In the presence of sufficient horizontal competition, vertical agreements are permitted.

Abuse of dominant position. Although both the competition law and the Constitution prohibit monopolies, no separate section of the law deals with monopolies or abuse of dominant position. If a firm abuses its market power by charging its clients prices above competitive levels, such an attitude is considered self-correcting insofar as other competitors are attracted by that market. Only if the dominant firm tries to exclude competitors will the Competition Commission step in.

Economic Concentration and Merger Control

The competition law prohibits mergers whose objective or effect is to reduce, distort, or hinder competition. Article 16 establishes that the Commission shall contest and penalize those concentrations whose purpose or effect is to diminish, impair, or impede competition and free market participation regarding equal, similar, or substantially related goods and services. Concentration is understood as a merger, acquisition of control, or any other act whereby companies, partnerships, shares, equity, trusts, or general assets are concentrated among competitors, suppliers, customers, or any other economic agent. Article 17 states that the Commission, when investigating concentrations, will interpret as evidence the following acts or attempts: price fixing, restricting supply, displacing or preventing other agents from entering the relevant market, or permitting participants to engage in monopolistic practices. Article 19 empowers the Commission to impose appropriate legal measures or penalties, to subject such acts to compliance with the conditions established by the Commission, to order partial or total divestiture of what has been improperly concentrated, and to terminate the control or the act, as required. Article 20 quantifies the value of transactions of which the Commission deserves in terms of the minimum wage in the Federal District.

The Commission must be notified of the following concentrations in advance of their implementation: if the value of a single transaction or series of transactions amounts to more than 12 million times the minimum general wage prevailing in the Federal District; if a single transaction or series of transactions implies accumulation of 35 percent or more of the assets or shares of an economic agent, whose assets or sales amount to more than 12 million times the minimum general wage prevailing in the Federal District; or if two or more economic agents take part in the transaction, and their assets or annual volume of sales, jointly or separately, total more than 48 million times the minimum general wage prevailing in the Federal District, and such transaction implies an additional accumulation of assets or capital stock in excess of 4.8 million times the minimum general wage prevailing in the Federal District.

Article 21 establishes a 45-day period during which the Commission issues a decision. If no decision has been given the interested parties by the end of the period, it is understood that the Commission has no objection. It has been questioned whether a merger transaction can be undertaken during the waiting period prior to clearance (Moguel 2000). This issue has not been fully settled by Mexican law.

Article 39 states that an appeal for reversal may be filed before the Commission, against its own decisions; it must be filed within 15 working days following the date of notification of such decisions. Filing of the appeal suspends enforcement of the contested decision. In case of suspension of penalties, and where third parties may sustain damage or loss, the appeal can be admitted only if the petitioner provides sufficient guarantee to restore the damage and to compensate losses. The Commission issues and notifies the interested parties of its decision within 60 days following the date of filing the appeal.

In recent years, merger activity in Mexico, as in many other countries, has increased considerably. In its first year of operation, the Commission undertook 34 merger reviews, 89 cases in its second year, 218 in 1997. Few of these mergers have been challenged. In 1997, the Commission objected to two cases and imposed conditions on three others (Wise 1999).

Competition Authorities Organization

According to Article 23, the Federal Competition Agency is a technically and operationally autonomous administrative entity of the Ministry of Trade and Industry Promotion. It is responsible for the prevention, investigation, and contesting of monopolies, monopolistic practices, and concentrations.

Independence

The Agency's decisionmaking authority is the Plenum, which consists of five commissioners, including a commissioner president; their appointments by Mexico's president are staggered over 10-year periods. The Commission conducts its debates as a collegiate body, and its decisions are reached by a majority vote; in the event of a tie, the chairman casts the deciding ballot. The commissioners must be Mexican citizens, professionally qualified in matters related to competition law, 35–75 years old, and distinguished professionally in public or academic services. Independence of decisionmaking is protected by the commissioners' insulation from the practice of complete personnel turnover following presidential elections.

Unlike certain sector agencies, the Commission's independence is based on the law, not lower-level regulations. In addition, commissioners are appointed by the president rather than by ministers.

Procedures

Article 24 empowers the Commission to investigate the existence of monopolies, practices, or concentrations prohibited by the competition law, to which end it may require from individuals and other economic agents the relevant information or documents; establish mechanisms of coordination to contest and prevent monopolies, concentrations, and illicit practices; solve cases of competition practice and impose administrative penalties; and report to the Public Prosecutor criminal practices regarding competition and free market participation.

Article 31 establishes that the Commission may begin legal or other enforcement in response to the request of an interested party or on its own initiative. Increasingly, the Commission is treats complaint-based issues ex officio. Any individual can file complaints about absolute monopolistic practices, while the affected party must file complaints about relative monopolistic practices and mergers. The Commission is obligated to deal with all complaints that meet the conditions established by the law. When exercising its powers, the Commission may request the necessary information or documents in order to carry out investigations, as well as to summon those involved in the relevant cases.

Appeals of decisions issued by the Commission may be filed before the Commission within 15 working days following the date of their notification. Filing of an appeal suspends enforcement of the contested decision. The Commission then issues and notifies the interested parties of its decision within 60 days following the date of filing the appeal. Absence of a ruling from the Commission during this time implies that the contested decision has been sustained. Some observers have criticized the Commission for slowness in its decision-making; however, the cause for their delay has often been constitutional appeals or strict observation of procedures intended to reduce the risk of losing appeals.

Punitive Powers

The Commission is empowered to impose administrative penalties for infringements of the competition law. Major penalties include fines of up to 7,500 times the minimum wage, which can be imposed for making false statements or submitting false information to the Commission, regardless of the responsible party's criminal liability. Other penalties include suspension, rectification, or elimination of the practice in question or total divestiture of the concentration.

When imposing fines, the Commission must consider the seriousness of the violation, damage caused, degree of intentionality, violator's market share, size of the market affected, length of the practice or concentration, and violator's background, as well as its financial capacity. In cases of particularly serious infringements, the Commission may impose fines of up to 10 times annual sales or assets, whichever is higher.

Advocacy Role

The Competition Agency plays an important role in the design and implementation of sector-specific regulatory mechanisms. The competition law empowers the Commission to give its opinion on the contents of other laws and regulations concerning competition. For the most part, the relevant authorities have taken these opinions into account, despite some problems in the telecommunications sector, where the regulator has rejected the Commission's views.

Several sector-specific laws and regulations assign the Commission an explicit role in matters related to determining the presence of effective competition or market power. In addition, the Commission is empowered to authorize the participation of economic agents in privatization or concession operations, having exercised such powers in railway privatization and auctions for radio or seaport concessions.

Relationship of Competition Agency with Other Regulatory Bodies

The Competition Commission exclusively enforces matters related to competition law, while sector regulators have exclusive responsibility for sector-specific regulations (OECD 1999). Strategic areas are not considered monopolies under the Constitution and are therefore exempt from competition law. Despite this clear division of labor, significant overlaps persist in infrastructure sectors, examples of which are telecommunications and natural gas.

In the telecommunications sector, both the competition and sector laws have provisions about monopolistic practices, such as cross subsidies and discriminatory treatment. However, the sector-specific law squarely prohibits these practices, while the competition law provides a rule-of-reason approach.

In the natural gas sector, the Energy Regulatory Commission enforces regulations. However, parties interested in obtaining a permit for natural gas transport, storage, or distribution need authorization from the Competition Commission. Gas sector regulations also give the Competition Commission a role in determining competitive market prices and tariff regulations. As a result, whenever the Competition Commission determines that effective competition exists, gas terms of sale can be freely negotiated. Furthermore, if the Competition Commission determines that such free negotiations lead to discriminatory treatment, the Energy Regulatory Commission can re-establish regulation of prices and sales conditions.

Peru

Historical Framework

During significant periods of its recent history, Peru's economic policies have been based on strong state intervention. In 1963, a program of import substitution industrialization and fiscal expansion was launched in an effort to mitigate external shocks and improve income distribution. These interventionist policies persisted until the late 1980s, coexisting with adjustment periods aimed at counteracting the crisis derived from exhaustion of the import substitution model. Anticompetitive, government-sponsored policies became the rule; they adversely affected the structure and performance of all economic sectors, paving the way for the 1980s crisis and economic collapse of 1989 (Rodríguez and Hoffman 1998).

In Peru, as in most transitional economies, competition policy is part of a broader liberalization process and regulatory reforms launched during the early 1990s. Trade creation and investment promotion were at the core of the economic reform program launched in 1991 by the Fujimori administration. Aggressive trade liberalization and privatization efforts were supported by across-the-board sector deregulation, leading to sizeable increases in trade and investment. Both foreign investment and competition laws were enacted in 1991, setting the stage for market access promotion. The foreign investment law establishes basic guarantees to free initiative, competition, and access to sectors traditionally controlled by state-owned firms, with some exceptions in the natural resources and energy sectors. The law also liberalizes all prices, with the exception of public utility rates.

Scope and Infrastructure Services

The competition law (Legislative Decree 701 of 1991), according to Article 2, applies to all economic agents without exception. Cases of investigation or punishment in infrastructure services have not been found.

Behavioral Provisions

The competition law is a development of a constitutional prohibition against monopolistic practices (Jatar and Tineo 1998). It focuses on anticompetitive conduct, with efficiency and consumer welfare its main objectives. It primarily addresses behavioral matters—those business practices aimed at restricting or hampering competition.

The two main anticompetitive practices are those that restrict free competition and abuse dominant position. Those that restrict free competition are price fixing and discrimination, output restraints, and market allocation. Vertical agreements, dealt with through a rule-of-reason approach, may be authorized if it is determined to improve efficiency and help consumers. Abuse of dominant position is dealt with more flexibly. The competition agency determines dominant position by measuring market share, market concentration, entry barriers, and potential competition. Once dominance is determined, the agency must decide whether abuse of dominance has occurred through anticompetitive practices, such as refusal to deal, price discrimination, and tying arrangements.

Economic Concentration and Merger Control

Mergers and other economic concentrations are not subject to competition law. Firms may freely merge, integrate assets, and engage in joint ventures without being subject to official scrutiny based on market structure reasons. However, merging firms may be examined under conduct standards. Energy and telecommunications sectors are subject to merger review. However, while limits to market share are well defined for the energy sector, no specific limits have been set for the telecommunications sector.

In November 1997, a merger control mechanism was established in the electricity sector (Law 6876 of 1997). Both vertical and horizontal mergers that occur in electricity generation, transmission, and distribution activities are subject to a prior permission procedure to avoid acts of concentration that tend to diminish, damage, or prevent market competition. Authorization of the Competition Commission is required before undertaking concentration activities in the generation, transmission, and distribution segments of the power industry. In cases of horizontal concentration, previous or resulting market share must be equal to or greater than 15 percent; in cases of vertical concentration, a 5-percent market share threshold must be established. The Competition Commission is empowered to order total or partial devolution of what has been concentrated illegally, terminate control, or remove the acts, as appropriate. The Commission can also impose fines of up to 10 percent of sales or gross income of the electricity companies involved in the transaction under investigation. Breach of the resolution that establishes devolution authorizes the National Institute for the Protection of Free Competition and Intellectual Property (Indecopi) to take actions that leave the concentration intact, such as sale of assets or stock shares.

Competition Authorities Organization

Indecopi is a multifunctional agency in charge of promoting and enforcing a variety of market regulations. It has jurisdiction over competition laws, antidumping, consumer protection, unfair competition and advertising, technical barriers, and intellectual property rights. Governed by a board of directors, Indecopi covers economic policy and jurisdictional matters. Its economic policy functions deal mainly with advocacy, while its jurisdictional role centers on enforcement.

The jurisdictional area is divided into two chambers: market competition and intellectual property. The market competition chamber consists of eight commissions, and the intellectual property chamber has three offices. The Free Competition Commission, which has a technical secretariat, is in charge of enforcing and administering the law in cases of business conduct intended to restrict or limit competition.

The jurisdictional area has an authority above the commissions and offices, known as the Tribunal. An administrative-judicial body of second instance, the Tribunal hears appeals decided by commissions and offices and has authority to uphold or overrule them; its decisions can be appealed directly to the Supreme Court.

Independence

The agency enjoys limited managerial freedom in terms of salary setting and financial resources. Regarding its political autonomy, the president, board members, and tribunal judges are appointed by the National Executive for fixed, five-year terms; they can only be removed on serious grounds of incompetence, negligence, or dishonesty.

Enforcement Functions

The Free Competition Commission is empowered with investigative, decisionmaking, and punitive powers. Nevertheless, a certain degree of separation between investigative and decisionmaking activities exists. The Technical Secretariat is responsible for administrative proceedings ex officio or at the request of interested parties, while the Free Competition Commission resolves in the first instance, adopts corrective measures, and imposes the corresponding sanctions. Monetary sanctions are limited to up to 105 percent of total company revenues.[9]

The Technical Secretariat can initiate the investigation on its own initiative, by previous consent of the Free Competition Commission, or acting on a third-party petition. If it believes there are reasonable signs of violation of Legislative Decree 701, the Technical Secretariat must notify the party presumed responsible for the investigated actions and inform it of the facts attributed to it. Replies to the charges must be submitted within 15 working days, and any evidence deemed necessary may be offered; other parties with a legitimate interest may become party to the proceedings during this period. The Technical Secretariat issues an opinion on the factual requirements of the claim, suggesting pertinent sanctions, and submits the case to the Free Competition Commission, which must issue a decision within five days.

The Commission's decisions can be appealed to the Tribunal for the Defense of Competition and Intellectual Property, which must decide the appeal within 30 days. The Tribunal's rulings, in turn, can be challenged judicially before the Civil Division of the Supreme Court of Justice. The decisions of the Division may also be appealed to the Constitutional and Social Law Division of the Supreme Court.

Venezuela

Historical Framework

Venezuela's economic liberalization process was launched in 1989. It attempted to counter the fiscal and external crisis stemming from an ill-

---

[9] Rodríguez and Hoffman (1998) point out that Indecopi's enforcement activity appears limited and is decreasing. For example, in 1994, 31 cases were processed and 22 were solved; in 1998, only 8 cases were processed and 6 solved. Resource shortages and political interference might partially explain such scant activity.

managed reduction in oil revenues, which had resulted from a sharp decrease in oil prices, coupled with increased production costs. A newly elected government designed an economic strategy aimed at shaping a market economy through replacing traditional interventionist, economic policy with liberalizing market reforms and opening of external trade.

In December 1991, as part of the reform program, the Law to Promote and Protect Competition (also known as the Pro-Competition Law) was passed. The intention of legislators was to establish maximum consumer welfare and economic efficiency as the goals of antitrust enforcement. This focus on efficiency requires intensive economic analysis, using a rule-of-reason approach; involves significant judiciary requirements; and places a heavy burden on qualified human resources (Olivo Valverde 1993). Under this Law, the agency responsible for its enforcement, known as the Agency for the Promotion and Protection of Free Competition (or Pro-Competition Agency), was created. It became operational in May 1991.

In December 1998, a new administration took office, and a new constitution containing significant antitrust provisions was drafted in 1999. Article 113 of the new constitution establishes that "monopolies will not be permitted." It also bans abuse of dominant position and activities aimed at establishing monopolies. Article 114 stipulates that cartels will be heavily punished. Provisory measure 18 provides that all civil servants and judges must abide by Article 113 of the Constitution, enforce it on a priority basis, and avoid laws or regulations contrary to that article. The same measure rules that, in compliance with Article 113, the National Congress will pass a law creating a controlling and supervisory agency responsible for enacting the principles embodied in that article. In subsequent sections, reference is made to both the Law to Promote and Protect Free Competition of 1991 and the Draft Bill to Reform the Law to Promote and Protect Competition (September 14, 2000).

Scope and Infrastructure Services

Venezuela's Competition Law applies to all private or public entities and individuals engaged in profitable and nonprofit economic activities. Although infrastructure services are not excluded, the law has never been applied to them. However, the Draft Competition Bill devotes an entire section (Chapter II) to infrastructure services competition and regulation. Article 7 establishes that the Competition Agency, in collaboration with sector regulators, is responsible for the promotion and protection of competition in economic activities deemed public services. For purposes of the Draft Bill, public services or general interest economic activities are gas, transport, telecommunications, electricity, water, and waste management. Article 8 of the Draft Bill states that public service firms that own distribution or inter-connection networks are obligated to provide all interested agents access, taking technical limitations into account. Such access, set forth in Article 9, is offered on the basis of nondiscrimination, transparency, neutrality, and good faith. Article 10 deals with concentration transactions in infrastructure services, establishing the need to obtain pre-merger authorization from the competition agency, and prohibiting concentrations leading to creation of dominant position or generating effects that restrict competition.

Behavioral Provisions

Under the current law, cartel agreements are prohibited if they fix prices, limit production, divide markets, or impose unequal or unfair conditions. Abuse of dominance is prohibited, particularly when it involves price discrimination, production limitation, and refusal to meet demand. A dominant position exists when a single person or group of associated persons conducts a specif-ic economic activity and when more than one agent conducts a specific type of activity where no effective competition exists between them. Associated persons means individuals who own 50 percent or higher share of the capital of the other or exercise any form of control. Control refers to one person's decisive influence on the activities of another, be it through exercise of prop-erty rights, use of all or a portion of the assets of that person, or exercise of rights that decisively influence the decisions of ruling bodies.

These practices are considered unlawful when they harm competition. Therefore, the practices at stake must be evaluated according to Competition Agency guidelines as the basis for applying a rule-of-reason procedure, as stipulated in the law.

The Draft Bill includes behavioral provisions similar to those of the current bill. However, a new provision is included that, if applied, would require changing the structure of the gas, oil, and power sectors. According to Article 51 of the draft bill, competition-restricting acts of the public pow-ers are considered invalid.

Economic Concentration and Merger Control

The former law dealt generally with concentration control, by means of a single article. Article 11 of the Law to Promote and Protect the Exercise of

Free Competition states that economic concentrations are prohibited, especially if they arise from the exercise of a single activity, when, as a result of the transaction, free competition is restricted or dominance results. Notification of mergers is not required. Therefore, competition authorities can only take ex post actions if they consider that a merger breaches Article 11.

The Draft Bill devotes three chapters in Article 20 to control of concentration. Such increased attention to this issue may be an answer to recent events.[10] Those articles most relevant to mergers and acquisitions are 34–38 and 40. Article 34 indicates which aspects of an action under investigation may constitute presumptions of competition restrictions. These include price fixing; hampering other agents' free access to and exit from favorable, competition restricting practices; and promoting increased market concentration. Article 35 describes which factors should be considered when determining whether a concentration transaction warrants investigation. These are the relevant market and entry and exit conditions of agents who operate within it. Article 36 stipulates pre-merger notification according to thresholds determined by the Commission Resolution. However, the minimum total turnover of firms engaged in the transaction is set at 50,000 times the current minimum monthly wage. Articles 37 and 38 state that parties to the transaction must notify the competition agency. In order to safeguard third-party rights, the competition agency might order that a summary of proposed concentration transactions be published in daily newspapers and the official gazette. Article 40 states that, if an economic concentration transaction occurs without prior notification or without Commission or Tribunal declaration of agreement, the Tribunal can initiate an investigation. Declaring a transaction absolutely invalid follows if the concentration results in competition-restricting effects.

Independence

The Agency for the Promotion and Protection of Free Competition (Procompetencia) is an independent body attached to the Ministry of Commerce. The Agency is led by a chairman, appointed by Venezuela's president for a four-year term; a vice-chairman; and five directors. Competition proceedings are handled by the Proceedings Chamber, which is presided over by the vice-chairman.

---

[10] Takeover of Electricidad de Caracas by the U.S. firm AES.

Article 52 of the 2001 Draft Bill stipulates that the competition agency shall enjoy functional, technical, operating, administrative, financial, and budgetary autonomy while exercising its powers. In fact, a reasonable degree of independence seems to emerge from relevant articles of the bill. Venezuela's president appoints commissioners for renewable six-year terms, and these commissioners can only be removed under extreme conditions. In addition, Article 63 describes the sources of finance for the agency: yearly budget contributions, extraordinary contributions occasionally granted by the executive, grants from public or private sources, income from revenue stamps and any other income or contributions received. Article 64 states that the Comptroller General of the Republic will supervise the agency's administrative activities.

Procedures

The Proceedings Chamber has broad powers to investigate anticompetitive conduct, including the right to summon any person to give evidence in an investigation, as well as to require the production of any information or documents. Once it has sufficient evidence of anticompetitive practice, the Proceedings Chamber notifies the parties involved, who have a maximum of 30 working days to present their arguments and counter evidence. At the end of this period, the agency must rule on the case within 30 days. However, in cases of voluntary prior notification of transactions, the period can be extended up to four months. During the investigative stage, the Agency for the Promotion and Protection of Free Competition can issue preliminary injunction to order suspension of the conduct under investigation.

The Draft Bill provides for the new agency to act as a prosecutor before a special tribunal of single instance; it is empowered to pass orders and measures; impose and collect compulsory fines; and, if necessary, seize the goods of a firm in violation. To avoid power being concentrated in a single individual, the Tribunal is composed of three justices appointed by the Supreme Court of Justice.

Punitive Powers

The Agency can impose fines of up to 20 percent of the offending party's sales. In cases of repeat offense, the fine can be increased 40 percent. Any decision issued by the Agency can be appealed before the First Administrative Court within 45 days. Court procedures can last a minimum of two years, during which period, the Agency's measure is pending. In practice, this means that measures taken by competition authorities cannot be implemented, thereby allowing breaching agents to continue their unlawful conduct. By the same token, fines can only be collected after completion of a special judicial procedure, since neither the Agency nor the administrative court is empowered to collect fines.

References

Clark, J. 1997. Background Note on Judicial Enforcement of Competition Law Competition Policy Roundtables, OECD/GD.

Comisión Nacional de Defensa de la Competencia. 1999. *Lineamientos para el control de las concentraciones económicas.* Buenos Aires: Argentina Competition Agency.

De Quevedo, L. 2000. "Reformas a la legislación de defensa de la competencia en Argentina." *Boletín Latinoamericano de Competencia* 9, Febrero.

Dixit, A. 1996. The Making of Economic Policy: *A Transaction Cost Politics Perspective.* Cambridge, MA: MIT Press.

Fernández-Ordoñez, M. A. 2000. *Competencia.* Madrid: Alianza Editorial.

Jatar, A. J. 1999. "Competition Policy in Venezuela: The Promotion of Social Change." In *Competition Policy, Deregulation and Modernization in Latin America,* eds. Moises Naim and Joseph S. Tulchin. London: Lynne Rienner Publishers.

Jatar, A. J., and L. Tineo. 1998. "Five Years of Competition Policy in Peru: Challenges in the Transition to a Market Economy." In *Peru's Experience in Market Regulatory Reform. Lessons from the First Five Years of Indecopi: 1993–1998,* ed. B. Boza. Lima: Sello Editorial, Indecopi.

Moguel, M. 2000. "Análisis del capítulo de concentraciones en la Ley Federal de Competencia Económica Mexicana." *Boletín Latinoamericano de Competencia* 10: 61–70.

OECD. 1999. "Relationship between Regulators and Competition Authorities." Directorate for Financial, Fiscal, and Enterprise Affairs/Committee on Competition Law and Policy (DAFFE/CLP) 99(10): 8.

Oliveira, G. 2000. "Recent Trends and Prospects for Brazilian Antitrust." *Boletin Latinoamericano de Competencia,* Issue No. 9.

Olivo Valverde, C. 1993. *The Venezuelan Experience on Antitrust.* Caracas: Procompetencia Publications.

Ordover, J., and G. Saloner. 1989. "Predation, Monopolization and Antirust." In *The Handbook of Industrial Organization,* eds. Richard Schmalensee and Robert Willig. Amsterdam: North-Holland.

Rodríguez, A., and K. Hoffman. 1998. "Why Is Indecopi Focused on Competition Advocacy?: A Framework for Interpretation." In *Peru's Experience in Market Regulatory Reform. Lessons from the First Five Years of Indecopi: 1993–1998,* ed. B. Boza. Lima: Sello Editorial, Indecopi.

Rodríguez, A., and M. Williams. 1995. "Economic Liberalization and Antitrust in Mexico." *Revista de Análisis Económico* 10(2): 165–18.

Serra, P. 1995. "La política de competencia en Chile." *Revista de Análisis Económico* 10(2): 63–88.

Wise, M. 1999. *Review of Competition Law and Policy in Mexico.* Paris: Organisation for Economic Co-operation and Development.

World Bank and OECD. 1998. *A Framework for the Design and Implementation of Competition Law and Policy.* Washington, D.C.: World Bank.

Chapter 10

The Role of Competition Law in Infrastructure Industries: The European Energy Market

Salomé Cisnal de Ugarte

For most of the latter half of the 20th century, the prevailing market structure for Europe's infrastructure services has been monopoly. This is notably the case for network industries, including air transport, electricity, and natural gas; postal services; telecommunications; and railways. Traditionally, these industries have been sheltered from competition and operated within national or regional boundaries. As a result, European consumers have had little or no choice of network service supplier, and prices have remained relatively high.

Only in recent years has competition been introduced into Europe's network industries. During the late 1980s and 1990s, liberalization of traditionally monopoly industries was an essential step toward establishing an internal market structure. However, not all formerly monopoly industries have been liberalized to the same degree; in fact, levels of deregulation have differed markedly by sector.

Overview of Sector Liberalization

Liberalization of Europe's energy sector has been slow compared with other sectors, such as telecommunications. Nonetheless, recent adoption of the Electricity and Gas Directives has changed the legal framework for achieving liberalization of the energy sector, initiating a process toward creating an internal energy market and effective competition.

The electricity and gas industries, which traditionally have been publicly owned, vertically integrated monopolies with exclusive rights, are not easy to liberalize. Indeed, liberalized energy markets require rules for both market participants and the regulators who enforce these rules to avoid circumventing competitive liberalization measures to replace existing monopolies with other types of monopolies.

The oil sector has not been targeted to the same extent as the gas and electricity sectors for an internal energy policy initiative. Liberalization measures in that sector were not considered necessary since effective commodity markets in both crude oil and petroleum products already existed. The oil market is characterized by price transparency, global integration of markets, multiple operators, ample supply of petroleum products, and numerous ways of transporting products. Perhaps its most salient feature is the absence of a network structure, which enables the consumer to have a choice of supplier.

Although formally applicable, enforcement of competition rules in the energy sector has been limited by the need to accommodate public interest factors. However, this has changed as liberalization has progressed. In the past, for example, security-of-supply arguments could justify exclusive or long-term supply contracts; in the post-liberalization era, however, other methods less restrictive of competition (such as contracts with several suppliers or risk cover instruments) might be used to meet the same objectives.

This chapter assesses the role of competition law in infrastructure services. It illustrates, using the example of the European energy market, that competition rules are an essential complement to regulatory measures since they monitor the behavior of market participants and avoid potential abuses by dominant incumbents. It also reveals that the broad range of legal instruments that competition policy provides may not suffice to handle all post-liberalization situations, such as a market failure. Thus, additional regulatory measures might be necessary to complement competition rules.

Milestones in Market Liberalization

Europe's energy sector is, on the one hand, comprised of primary energy sources: coal, oil, natural gas, hydroelectric power, nuclear power, and renewables. Electricity is an important source of energy that can be produced from various primary fuels. Because of this characteristic, electricity links and allows a degree of competition between the primary fuel markets.

Oil remains Europe's predominant, primary energy source. The price of oil is the standard used for other primary sources, particularly natural gas. Because of its environmental advantages over other hydrocarbon sources as a primary fuel, natural gas is being consumed far faster than any other fuel in the European Community. It depends heavily on the availability of transmission grids; furthermore, its network-bound character creates special regulatory issues that, with regard to liberalization, require striking a balance between general competition rules and sector specific regulation.

Electricity constitutes 20 percent of the European Community's final energy consumption. Although the European Commission has noted that the network-bound character of the electricity sector inevitably leads to dominant positions for grid companies, the Commission has applied Articles 81 and 82 in only a few cases.

Key liberalization measures for the electricity and gas sectors are:

- Directive 96/92/EC of the European Parliament and the Council of 19 December 1996 concerning common rules for the internal market in electricity.[1] This Directive had to be implemented prior to February 19, 1999 (with the exceptions of Belgium and Ireland, which had an additional year, and Greece, which had two additional years).
- Directive 98/30/EC of the European Parliament and the Council of 22 June 1998 concerning common rules for the internal market in natural gas.[2] This Directive had to be implemented prior to August 10, 2000.

Electricity Directive

The Electricity Directive, which forms part of the framework for the internal energy market, establishes common rules for electricity generation, transmission, and distribution. It concerns three key aspects of liberalization: competition in generation, third-party access (TPA) to transportation networks, and the unbundling of accounts of vertically integrated firms.

Emphasis on these areas corresponds to the goal of opening up specific sector segments that are amenable to competition. This means that the Directive preserves the natural monopoly status of the transmission and distribution segments, but introduces a degree of consumer choice in genera-

---

[1] Official Journal L27 of 30 January 1997.

[2] Official Journal L204 of 21 July 1997.

tion and supply—two areas that are logically connected because competition in generation would have a limited effect if consumers were not given a choice of electricity supplier.[3]

Article 4 of the Directive considers two alternative procedures for constructing new generation capacity: authorization and tendering. Regardless of which procedure the implementing member state chooses, the criteria that national authorities apply must be objective, transparent, and nondiscriminatory. Under the authorization procedure, which most member states have adopted, the generation sector of the implementing member state's electricity industry is opened completely to competition, subject only to standard licensing requirements that the national authorities must make public.

Articles 16 and 17 seek to ensure network access for producers and consumers by requiring member states to adopt either a TPA or single-buyer system. If a member state opts for a TPA system, it must choose between the *negotiated* and the *regulated* TPA. Negotiated access means that a producer will be able to sell its electricity directly to eligible consumers after negotiating with a state-designated Transmission System Operator (TSO) for the right to use the network. To date, only Germany has opted for this type of TPA. Regulated access, on the other hand, means that third parties who meet the relevant technical standards are automatically eligible to access the network on payment of regulated tariffs. Regardless of which TPA system a member state chooses, procedures must be carried out according to objective, transparent, and nondiscriminatory criteria.

Articles 13-15 require unbundling accounts to make cross subsidization across product markets more transparent. Transparency aims to prevent cross subsidies and discriminatory practices of vertically integrated utilities. The accounts of vertically integrated companies must be accessible to the national authorities,[4] and must be published annually in accordance with national rules.[5] More specifically, the unbundling provisions require the company to maintain separate accounts for generation, transmission, and distribution by recording their costs and revenues on a differentiated basis for each stage of production.

---

[3] In naturally monopolistic markets, it would be inefficient or undesirable for two or more firms to compete.

[4] See Article 13.

[5] See Article 14(2).

Article 19 provides for the gradual opening of the market in three successive steps to occur in 1999, 2000, and 2003. The minimum market opening corresponding to the first step is calculated as a share of the total consumption of final consumers, with annual consumption exceeding 40 gigawatt hours (GWh). This corresponds to 26 percent of consumption in 2000 and 35 percent in 2003.

Gas Directive

The Gas Directive establishes common rules for the transmission, distribution, supply, and storage of natural gas. It lays out rules related to the organization and functioning of the natural gas sector, including market access; system operation; and criteria and procedures granting authorization for transmission, supply, and storage.

Adopted nearly two years after the Electricity Directive, the Gas Directive resembles the Electricity Directive in many ways. Certain provisions are nearly identical; for example, Article 3 of both Directives allows member states, in the general economic interest, to impose public service obligations (PSOs) on natural gas undertakings. These PSOs may relate to security, regularity, quality, and price of supply, as well as environmental protection. Such obligations must be clearly defined, transparent, nondiscriminatory, and verifiable; in addition, they must be published, of which the Commission must be notified. The unbundling provisions of the Gas Directive are also similar to those of the Electricity Directive. Provisions in both directives allow for derogations (Articles 24-26 of the Gas Directive; Article 23 of the Electricity Directive).

Articles 14-16 of the Gas Directive give member states three possibilities for organizing access to the system: negotiated access based on publication of at least the main commercial conditions that apply, regulated access based on published tariffs, or a combination thereof.

With regard to the level of market opening, Article 18 states that all gas-fired power generators, irrespective of their annual consumption, as well as other final customers consuming more than 25 million cubic meters (cu m) per year, are eligible for access to the system, from initial market opening.[6] The Gas Directive requires an absolute minimum market opening of 20 percent, which will gradually increase, but which will still allow member states to impose limits on market opening.

---

[6] This consumer threshold will be lowered to 15 and 5 million cu m by 2003 and 2008, respectively.

Implementation Update

Electricity

The Commission's communication of 15 May 2000 assesses progress made toward achieving the goal of an internal electricity market.[7] All member states have adopted national legislation implementing the Electricity Directive. Two member states (France and Belgium) have yet to adopt the secondary legislation (implementing decrees) needed in order to apply the laws.

With regard to raising the required market opening from 26 percent of consumption in 2000 to 35 percent in 2003, many member states are exceeding these requirements. For example, Finland, Germany, Sweden, and the United Kingdom are opening 100 percent of the market. As a result, implementation of the Directive has already opened up 65 percent of the consumer market for electricity in the European Union.

In anticipation of implementing the Directive, electricity prices have fallen about 6 percent on average and, in some cases, as much as 20 percent between 1996 and 1999. Cross-border trading is also increasing, with a total volume equivalent to about 8 percent of the total European Community electricity produced.

The Commission's communication highlights two issues that must be re-examined before a fully integrated market can be achieved. First, it states that unbundling of the network from production and distribution is necessary, with member states ensuring that the commercial interests of the parent company are fully separated from grid operation activities. Second, it states that the TPA must be regulated in a transparent way to exclude discrimination of any kind. It stresses that the ultimate aim is a truly integrated market, not a patchwork of 15 more or less liberalized markets.

Progress has been made to establish a cross-border pricing mechanism and congestion management. In March 2000, the Fifth Meeting of the European Electricity Regulatory Forum (Florence Forum) agreed on a provisional pricing mechanism for cross-border trade in electricity. (The Forum included representatives of the Commission, national administrations, Council of European Regulators, Association of European TSOs, producers, consumers, operators, and the European Parliament). This mechanism pro-

---

[7] European Commission (2000a).

vides for compensation between system operators for the transmission of electricity through their systems by setting up a compensation fund.[8] The Eighth Meeting of the European Electricity Regulatory Forum held in Florence 21-22 February 2002 made substantial progress on the subject. It was agreed that a provisional cross-border pricing system would enter into force on 1 March 2002 and be operative until 1 January 2003. In addition, agreement was reached on the basic principles and operational guidelines for a more cost-oriented pricing mechanism to enter into force 1 January 2003. The Forum emphasized that this progress represents important steps toward providing nondiscriminatory, cost-reflective trading mechanisms, ensuring security of supply and contributing to completion of the internal electricity market.

Furthermore, the Association of European Transmission System Operators has developed various congestion management mechanisms that involve publishing data on available interconnector capacity, information exchange to ensure system security, and allocation of available transfer capacity for specific congested lines (notably those of France-Spain and Germany-Denmark).

Gas

Article 29 of the Gas Directive required that member states bring into force the laws, regulations, and administrative provisions needed to comply with the Directive no later than 10 August 2000. The aim was not merely to have legislation passed by this date, but also to have administrative and other procedures in place to allow market opening to take effect.

By the end of May 2000, most member states had passed legislation that, to a large extent, implemented the Gas Directive. Only Greece and Portugal lagged in the implementation process. Member states are obliged to implement at least parts of the Directive over time, while other parts may be derogated from if such derogation is applied for and the Commission is notified.

As regards the choice for organizing system access, the Directorate General for Energy and Transport stated that eight member states (Austria, Spain, Finland, Italy, Ireland, Luxembourg, Sweden, and the United Kingdom may be expected to choose regulated TPA based on published tariffs, while three member states (Denmark, France, and the Netherlands) would

---

[8] This fund came into force 1 October 2000 for an initial one-year period.

choose hybrid systems. Only two member states (Belgium and Germany) were expected to choose negotiated access. None of the negotiated access systems would be purely negotiated as the applicable tariffs were subject to prior regulatory approval or agreements between associations.[9]

The Directive required an absolute minimum market opening of 20 percent, which would gradually increase, but still allowed member states to impose limits on market opening. In general, member states are exceeding the Directive's requirements. For example, the United Kingdom market has been fully liberalized since 1998; Germany intends a 100-percent opening by the deadline; and as many as seven member states will fully open to competition by 2008. It was expected that, by 10 August 2000, approximately 78 percent of the total gas demand of the European Union would be eligible.

With regard to unbundling, nearly half of all member states intend to exceed the Directive's requirements. Germany and Sweden do not foresee specific PSOs, while other member states have laid out PSOs related to connection, supply of connected customers, gas quality, and safety. Article 23 of the Directive requires that member states ensure access to upstream pipeline networks. Member states are allowed a degree of discretion in how to implement this Article and have chosen slightly different approaches. With regard to storage access, for example, the approaches selected range from regulated storage access in Italy to auctions in the United Kingdom; member states also vary regarding the conditions under which such access is given.

Applicability of Treaty Rules

European Community Treaty rules are generally applicable to electricity supply, although relatively few European Court of Justice (ECJ) cases or Commission decisions deal expressly with this sector. Nonetheless, general points can be made on the Treaty's applicability, as follows:[10]

- Electricity has been determined to be a good subject for the rules on free movement of goods, as set out in Articles 28-31 of the European Community Treaty.[11]

---

[9] European Commission (2000b).

[10] While this analysis focuses mainly on the electricity sector, it should also apply to the gas sector, as the two sectors should be treated similarly under Treaty rules.

[11] Case C-6/64, Judgment of the Court of 15 July 1964: *Flaminio Costa versus Enel.*

- Provisions on state aid contained in both the European Community and European Coal and Steel Community (ECSC) Treaties are applicable to the energy sector. State aid may involve schemes applicable not only to the energy sector, but also through it; for example, member states may support their domestic coal industry by promoting or requiring arrangements designed to ensure use of domestic coal at prices well above the marginal import price. Such forms of downstream aid are covered under Article 87(1) of the European Community Treaty.
- Firms operating in the electricity sector are subject to the competition rules contained in Articles 81 and 82 of the European Community Treaty.[12]
- General rules on free movement and competition are subject to the exceptions provided for in the Treaty, which, in certain cases, may mean that the electricity sector would not be subject to such rules.

Decisions Establishing Applicability of Competition Rules

Various Commission decisions have determined that its competition rules are applicable to agreements involving all aspects of the electricity supply sector. Several decisions—*Jahrhundervertrag*,[13] *Scottish Nuclear*,[14] and *IJsselcentrale*[15]—illustrate how these rules apply.[16]

In the *Jahrhundervertrag* decision, the agreement under review had been concluded between the Association of the German Public Electricity Supply Industry and the General Association of the German Coalmining Industry. This agreement established a quota system, whereby the electricity companies agreed to buy a fixed quantity of German coal. In its decision, the

---

[12] Case C-363/92, Judgment of the Court of 27 April 1994: *Municipality of Almedo and others versus NV Energierbedritjflisselmij.*

[13] 93/126/EEC: Commission Decision of 22 December 1992 relating to a proceeding under Article 85 of the Treaty and Article 65 of the ECSC Treaty (IV/33.151, Jahrundertvertrag).

[14] 91/329/EEC: Commission Decision of 30 April 1991 relating to a proceeding under Article 85 of the EEC Treaty (IV/33.473, Scottish Nuclear, Nuclear Energy Agreement).

[15] 91/50/EEC: Commission Decision of 16 January 1991 relating to a proceeding under Article 85 of the EEC Treaty (IV/32.732, IJsselcentrale and others).

[16] Not discussed here are two other decisions: Pego in Portugal (which, like the Scottish Nuclear case, relates to long-term PPAs) and Grangeville (which relates to minor price-fixing agreements between French [EdF] and Italian [ENEL] utilities).

Commission concluded that the agreement was restrictive in that it prevented the electricity companies from seeking cheaper inputs from businesses in other member states; in addition, it induced the companies to produce their own, rather than import, electricity. Although the *Vertrag* violated Article 81(1) of the European Community Treaty, the fact that the quotas served to prop up a mining sector in serious decline added another dimension to the case. The Commission granted a series of short-term exemptions to the agreement under Article 81(3), on the grounds that it safeguarded electricity supplies.[17] However, to ensure that the restrictive terms of the agreement did not prevent competition indispensable to improving generation and distribution, the Commission noted that, by the end of 1995, preferentially supplied coal was to account for no more than 20 percent of the overall primary fuel needed for Germany's gross electricity consumption. That percentage was to have dropped to 15 percent by the year 2000.[18]

In the *Scottish Nuclear* decision, the Commission was similarly influenced by the overall context surrounding the challenged agreement. The United Kingdom had restructured the Scottish electricity industry, creating two vertically integrated competing utilities; namely, Scottish Power and Scottish Hydro-Electric (which later became part of Scottish and Southern Energy). Pursuant to the notified agreement, these two companies were to purchase, on a take-or-pay basis, all of the power generated by two of Scottish Nuclear's production facilities. Scottish Power was obligated to buy about 75 percent of Scottish Nuclear's output, while Scottish Hydro-Electric had to buy the other 25 percent. At the same time, Scottish Nuclear was not permitted to supply other firms without the consent of the parties. Furthermore, the parties were committed to each other for a 30-year period. The Commission decided that these arrangements were contrary to Article 81(1). On the one hand, the agreement limited Scottish Nuclear's ability to sell its output on better terms to third parties; on the other hand, it prevented Scottish Power and Scottish Hydro-Electric from choosing their supply sources. The fixed supply ratio also prevented the two firms from competing for Scottish Nuclear's output. The question, therefore, was whether the agreement was eligible for exemption under Article 81(3).

---

[17] While the Commission was willing to grant exemptions under Article 81(3), it rejected the argument that Article 81(1) was rendered inapplicable by Article 86(2). See Section 28 of the decision.

[18] Article 8(4) of the Electricity Directive states: "A Member State may, for reasons of security of supply, direct that priority be given to the dispatch of generating installations using indigenous primary fuel sources, to an extent not exceeding in any calendar year 15 percent of the overall primary energy necessary to produce the electricity consumed in the Member State concerned."

The Commission pointed out that the agreement enhanced electricity production and distribution because it facilitated the long-term planning necessary to ensure security of supply. In the Commission's view, the agreement was a guarantee that Scottish Nuclear would continue to steadily generate power, which would help to open up an independent supply market. Based on that theory, the agreement was pro-competitive because, after a reasonable start-up period, the sector would become more competitive than it had been before. Moreover, the agreement made it possible for Scottish Nuclear's power stations to perform at full capacity, which would offset investment costs and promote economies of scale. However, the Commission also required the parties to shorten the duration of their agreement by half (from 30 to 15 years).

The *IJsselcentrale* decision demonstrates the applicability of Article 81(1) within the context of a private agreement that created an import-export monopoly that was nonexempt on public service grounds. The agreement at issue, *Overeenkomst van Samenwerking* (OVS), was concluded in 1986 between four Dutch production companies and a joint venture wholesaler, Samenwerkende Elektriciteits Produktiebedrijven (SEP), which operated the transmission system in the Netherlands. The Commission was not notified of the agreement. Under Article 21 of the OVS, the producers agreed not to import or export electricity, giving those activities exclusively to SEP. Furthermore, the producers agreed that, when entering into supply contracts with distributors, they would require the distributors to refrain from importing and exporting. SEP thereby gained a monopoly over those activities; distributors and large industrial customers were unable to import electricity, even though certain large customers located near the Dutch border did not need access to the transmission network. These facts gave rise to the *Almelo* dispute, whereby local distributors, having been forced to purchase all of their required electricity from the regional distributor, challenged the validity of the OVS agreement.

The Commission concluded that the agreement was in violation of Article 81(1) because the OVS prevented all but SEP from importing and exporting electricity. The agreement was enforced horizontally among the Dutch producers, and vertically by requiring producers to impose the same ban on distributors. This web of exclusive purchasing obligations was clearly anticompetitive. Since the parties had forfeited the possibility of obtaining an exemption under Article 81(3) by failing to notify the Commission, the parties sought to invoke Article 86(2).

SEP argued that it was obligated to guarantee supply, and that it was therefore necessary to have control over imports and exports. The Commission accepted that the obligation to supply qualified as a public service within the meaning of Article 86(2). However, the public service exception did not apply because the application of Article 81(1) did not prevent SEP from performing such obligations. The Commission distinguished between SEP's obligation to supply the general public and the separate matter of supplying large industrial customers.[19] This latter category, nonpublic supply, could not legitimately be regarded as part of SEP's public service mission.

Article 86(2) Exception

Article 86(2) states that companies entrusted with operating services in the general economic interest may be exempt from the Treaty rules if such application obstructs the performance, in law or in fact, of the particular task assigned to them. On various occasions, electricity supply has been held to fall under this exemption.

In the 1994 *Almelo judgment*, which involved Dutch distribution utilities, the ECJ made it clear that Articles 81 and 82 of the European Community Treaty apply to the electricity sector, as they do to any other sector, provided that Article 86(2) is taken into account.

The *Almelo* judgment focuses on the extent to which electricity supply firms, entrusted with public supply duties, are exempt from Treaty rules on free movement and competition. The Almelo dispute arose from a Royal Order of the Dutch Government that granted a nonexclusive concession to IJsselcentrale (IJM) to function as a regional distributor of electricity in the Netherlands. As such, IJM was required by a separate contractual arrangement with the Dutch electricity producers to purchase electricity intended for public supply (that is, small, captive customers) exclusively from those producers. In turn, IJM contracted various local distributors who agreed to purchase their electricity intended for public supply exclusively from IJM. This put IJM in the middle of an exclusive purchasing chain.

When IJM began to impose an equalization surcharge on the local distributors, those companies initiated arbitration proceedings to challenge the legality of the agreements. The Dutch Court, referring to Article 234 of the European Community Treaty, questioned how far the Treaty rules apply to a ban on imports for the public supply of electricity imposed on local distributors by the regional distributor.

---

[19] See paragraphs 39 et seq. and 49 et seq.

The Court held that both Articles 81 and 82 were clearly relevant, as the practices had restrictive effects, and the exclusive purchasing agreement was evidence of abuse, granted that the parties were jointly dominant. The Court then addressed the question of whether IJM could rely on Article 86(2) to exempt it from the application of Articles 81 and 82. The Court accepted that IJM had an important public service function to perform. Accordingly, the question of whether the Article 86(2) exception applied depended on whether the ban on imports was necessary for IJM to fulfil its obligation to provide universal service. This question would have to be determined by the Dutch Court, taking into account the economic and regulatory conditions under which IJM operated, including the costs arising from compliance with environmental protection rules. The Court would thereby be positioned to evaluate what degree of restriction on imports was necessary to enable IJM to carry out its public service mission.

In the electricity sector, the Commission took action against four member states, with the aim of establishing the illegality of their exclusive import and export regimes for electricity and natural gas.[20] According to the Commission, the exclusive rights granted to certain undertakings by France, the Netherlands, Italy, and Spain were contrary to Articles 28, 29, and 31 of the European Community Treaty.

In France, the government had given Electricité de France (EDF) a monopoly over electricity imports and exports. Similarly, the French government had granted exclusive rights over natural gas imports and exports to Gaz de France and two other firms. In the Netherlands, electricity intended for public supply could only be imported by SEP. In Italy, the sole importer-exporter was Ente nazionale per l'energia elettrica (ENEL). In Spain, the theory that the government had created a *de facto* monopoly for Redesa, the state electricity company, was summarily dismissed due to the Commission's failure to show the existence of such a monopoly.

The stakes were high because a victory for the Commission would have enabled it to apply substantial pressure in negotiations concerning the terms and conditions of the Electricity Directive. The ECJ upheld the rights of member states to maintain such exclusive concessions, on the grounds that the public service exception of Article 86(2) rendered the free-trade rules inoperable.

---

[20] See cases C-157/94, Commission versus Netherlands, [1997] ECR I-5699; C-158/94, Commission versus Italy, [1997] ECR I-5789; C-159/94, Commission versus France, [1997] ECR I-5815; and C-160/94, Commission versus Spain, [1997] ECR I-5851. All four decisions were rendered by the full court 23 October 1997.

Competition Law's Role in a Liberalized Energy Market

The liberalization required by Europe's Electricity and Gas Directives does not demand a fully liberalized market. This factor, together with the fact that member states have much room in which to maneuver when implementing the Directives, has meant that problems of competition remain in the market. While some problems may be solved by existing or future regulations, others require applying competition laws.

When considering the relationship between regulation and competition, one has to bear in mind that the Electricity and Gas Directives do not change the basic framework of the Treaty rules and therefore may not be applied in a way that is inconsistent with European Union competition rules. Liberalization means that the market will restructure, with increased application of competition rules to the new realities. While the European Union internal market and energy policy are geared toward removing legal obstacles to competition (such as eliminating special or exclusive rights of production, transmission, and distribution), European Community and national competition laws mainly remove behavioral obstacles to competition. Enforcing competition laws in the energy sector therefore aims to complement sector rules by preventing private arrangements or practices that limit emerging competition or that favor national markets.

Principles of Competition Law

Most competition frameworks promote a competitive environment in which companies operate on a level playing field and consumers can choose from a variety of suppliers and pay low prices for their services and products. Besides these purely economic goals, European Union competition rules strive for political integration, a goal that is unique to this political structure. Competition authorities, at both national and continentwide levels, have several competition policy instruments at their disposal. The instruments most likely used to ensure a healthy level of competition in the energy market are antitrust rules (Articles 81 and 82 of the European Community Treaty) and merger control and state aid rules (Articles 87-89 of the European Community Treaty).

Applying Competition Rules to Energy Markets

Prohibition of Anticompetitive Agreements and Practices

At the continentwide level, Article 81 of the European Community Treaty deals with anticompetitive cooperation between companies. It prohibits companies from entering into agreements or concerted practices whose object or effect is to prevent, restrict, or limit competition and that affect interstate trade. Hard-core restrictions are cartels; that is, agreements or practices aimed at price-fixing, market sharing, or quota allocations. In the energy sector, this provision can be applied to various situations, as outlined below.

Structural agreements. Structural agreements are arrangements aimed at organizing a specific market either by means of bilateral agreements or through a pool arrangement. In some cases, a market can have both features. The Commission is usually notified of these agreements for its scrutiny and exemption. Typical examples that the Commission handles are reorganization of the electricity industry in England and Wales, reorganization of the electricity industry in Scotland, privatization of the electricity industry in Northern Ireland, and coding of the United Kingdom gas transmission network.

The main competition concerns of structural agreement contracts are ensuring that operational rules and conditions of membership are objective, transparent, and nondiscriminatory, and that no anticompetitive information exchange occurs between market members.

Connection agreements. Connection agreements deal with use of networks. They may raise competition concerns if they contain restrictive clauses related to calculating transmission fees or the capacity use of the network (capacity allocation agreements).

Access to interconnector capacity may become a key element in a liberalized market since, in some member states with a monopolistic supply structure, interconnectors may be the only source of competition. The Commission's past relatively liberal attitude, whereby agreements of indefinite duration that provided for exclusive use of an interconnector were accepted (for example, the reorganization of Scotland's electricity industry), has started to change. It appears that long-term contracts enabling the TSO to make interconnector construction commercially feasible will still be acceptable to the Commission.

Duration of the exclusivity that the Commission will be willing to accept will ultimately depend on the time required to ensure a proper return on the investment of the parties. New guidelines on applying competition law to capacity reservation agreements (concerning electricity) have been outlined.[21] Article 81 may also apply to transportation and related agreements negotiated by electricity suppliers and TSOs. The German *Verbande-vereinbarung* is an example of a tariff system agreed on by competitors that has attracted much criticism from competition authorities.

Long-term exclusive agreements. Long-term exclusive supply agreements, exclusive purchase agreements, and similar arrangements may also raise competition concerns because such agreements may foreclose the market. For example, in the case of Electricidade de Portugal/Pego Project,[22] ISAB Energy,[23] and REN/Turbogas,[24] the Commission accepted exclusivity in such agreements for periods of up to 15 years. Justification for the long periods was often based on concerns about supply security and sunk investment costs.

However, it is likely that the period for which the Commission will accept exclusivity in this type of agreement will be reduced in the future because these objectives could be met by other, less competition-restrictive means.

Exclusive distribution agreements. Exclusive distribution agreements guarantee the distributor a local retail monopoly over a specific geographic area. In this type of agreement, potential competitors agree not to enter each other's area.

The German competition law (GWB) previously exempted such agreements. The ECJ was to rule on the validity of these agreements in the *Ruhrgas AG/Thyssengas GmbH*, but, because of the 29 April 1998 changes in the GWB, in which exemption for distribution agreements was abolished, the case was removed from the ECJ register.[25]

---

[21] European Commission (1999b).

[22] Notice pursuant to Article 19 (3) of Council Regulation No 17/62 (Case No IV/34.598, Pego) (OJ No C265).

[23] Notice pursuant to Article 19 (3) of Council Regulation No 17/62 (Case No IV/E-3/35.698, ISAB Energy) (OJ No C138).

[24] Notice pursuant to Article 19 (3) of Council Regulation No 17/62 (Case No IV/34.598, Pego) (OJ No C265).

[25] Case C-365/96: Reference for a preliminary ruling by the Kammergericht, Berlin, by order of that court of 30 October 1996 in the case of *Ruhrgas AG and Thyssengas GmbH versus Bundeskartellamt* (OJ No C009).

Upstream cooperation. Upstream cooperation agreements, such as joint exploration and development in the oil and gas sectors, may be justified by the need to spread risk during the exploration phase.

Other related situations in which gas production companies cooperate may include sale of pipeline capacity or decisions to stop production or reinject. Such situations are more complicated and should be considered on a case-by-case basis.

Joint purchasing and sales agreements. Joint purchasing and sales agreements have also been dealt with under Article 81. In 1996, the Commission cleared a set of joint sales arrangements between owners of the Britannia field on the basis of lack of effect on trade. However, it indicated that joint sales arrangements are likely to fall within Article 81(1), whereby they have an appreciable effect on competition and trade between member states.

Prohibition of Abusive Dominance

Another essential antitrust rule for ensuring a liberalized energy market is Article 82 (formerly Article 86) of the European Community Treaty. It prohibits abuse by any company having a dominant market position. Given that transmission activity has long been considered a natural monopoly in many countries, this type of rule is important, and may become more so. In the European context, Article 82 is the instrument that controls the abusive exercise of monopoly power. It is possible to envisage the following situations in which application of Article 82 (and similar provisions in the national legal systems) could be used in the liberalized energy sectors.

Refusal of access. Refusal of access by a dominant company acting as the system operator of the national grid or downstream pipelines without justified reasons is a key situation in which Article 82 can be used.

The Commission has not yet intervened in a case of refusal of access; however, it intends to control network access closely in the electricity and gas markets. Application of the doctrine of essential facilities, as redefined by the ECJ in the *Oscar Bronner* judgment, will be crucial for applying Article 82.[26]

---

[26] Case C-7/97, Judgment of the Court (Sixth Chamber) of 26 November 1998: *Oscar Bronner GmbH & Co. KG versus Mediaprint Zeitungs und Zeitschriftenverlag GmbH & Co. KG*, Mediaprint Zeitungsvertriebsgesellschaft mbH & Co. KG and Mediaprint Anzeigengesellschaft mbH & Co. KG., ECR 1998 p. I-07791.

According to this doctrine, a company that owns infrastructure, whose access by other companies is vital to their ability to compete in the upstream or downstream markets in which the infrastructure owner operates, must allow nondiscriminatory access. The infrastructure owned and controlled exclusively by one entity is, in such a case, the only practical means of providing a particular service.

In cases where there is no reasonable alternative for supplying the service (or where it is not economical to replicate the infrastructure), the company that controls the infrastructure has a dominant position. Abuse of dominant position would occur if the owner refused access to third parties, thereby preventing them from competing, or if it allowed them access under terms less advantageous than its own, thereby conferring on itself a competitive advantage in the services market.

However, there could be legitimate justification for refusing access: lack of sufficient capacity, lack of technical qualifications, need to meet public service obligations, and need to honor existing contractual commitments. Most of these principles are reflected in the provisions of the Electricity and Gas Directives. Interestingly, the Directives allow TPA without having to qualify that the facility is essential.

To date, national competition authorities have been more active than the Commission in dealing with cases of refusing access. Examples include *Enron versus Elektromark and Bewag* in Germany, *SEP versus Norsk Hydro* in the Netherlands, and *SNAM versus Edison* in Italy.

Unfair transmission tariffs. Unfair—either excessive or predatory—transmission tariffs are likely to become another key application of Article 82.

A transmission price may be considered excessive within the meaning of Article 82 if the price exceeds the value of the service provided. With regard to predatory prices (prices below variable costs), it is important for vertically integrated suppliers to ensure that their price includes a transmission fee, which is the same as for any third party.

However, assessing transmission tariffs might be complex. The experience of Swedish regulators, for example, has shown that the process is difficult and demanding in terms of time and resources to determine what constitutes a reasonable price for transmission. National cases regarding excessive transmission fees include *Helsingin Energia* in Finland and *Enher/HEC/Eléctrica de Llémanà* in Spain.

Tying arrangements. Article 82 is potentially applicable to tying situations in the energy market. In Sweden, for example, Tekniska Verken i Linköping was found to have abused its dominant position in the market for electricity supply in the Municipality of Linköping on this ground. It applied a loyalty rebate scheme by which the customer received a rebate on district heating if it bought all its electricity requirements from Tekniska Verken as well. The Swedish Competition Authority ordered Tekniska Verken, under threat of a penalty of SEK1 million, to stop the abusive conduct.

Penalty clauses. Penalty clauses, through which a dominant firm keeps consumers from switching to another supplier, are also likely to violate Article 82. A priority of the Commission will be to ensure that consumers are not unduly restricted in their choice of supplier.

Limiting market development. Other cases where Article 82 may apply are those that limit market development. In the Commission's recent investigation of Gas Natural, for example, the Commission investigated a long-term gas supply agreement, whereby the leading Spanish electricity generator, ENDESA, would cover virtually all of its gas requirements for the foreseeable future through Gas Natural. The Commission found that the contract would bar entry into the newly liberalized Spanish gas market. After the parties agreed to amend the contract, the Commission decided not to pursue its action against Gas Natural.[27]

Merger Control

As witnessed previously in the telecommunications industry, gradual liberalization of the energy sector has triggered a series of strategic alliances, mergers, acquisitions, and joint ventures between suppliers and distributors or between competitors. Companies may merge for various reasons: economies of scale, national-level consolidation, market extension, or market entrance. Whatever the reason, merger control rules at either the European Union or national level will be available to competition authorities to ensure that mergers do not obstruct competition in a liberalized energy sector. Specifically, merger control rules prevent individuals or concentrated groups of individuals from exercising a dominant market position that would lead to structural changes in the market.

---

[27] Commission's press release of 27 March 2000 (IP/00/297).

Since 1994, the Commission has dealt with some 30 mergers, acquisitions, and joint ventures in the electricity sector, under the European Community Merger Regulation (ECMR).[28] The number of notifications doubled in 1998 and 1999, following liberalization of the electricity markets. Examples of acquisitions, mergers, and joint ventures handled under the ECMR during late 1999 and early 2000 include *EdF/South Western Electricity*,[29] *EdF/Louis Dreyfus*,[30] *Preussen Elektra/EZH*,[31] *Sydkraft/Hew/Hansa Energy Trading*,[32] *Fortum/Elektrizitätswerk Wesertal*,[33] *TXU Europe/EdF-London Investments*,[34] *Eletrabel/EPON*,[35] and *Vattenfall/Hew*.[36] The *VEBA/VIAG*[37] merger was the first case in the electricity sector in which the Commission opened an in-depth investigation. Following the second phase of its investigation, the Commission approved the merger, subject to stringent conditions.

In the oil and gas sector, there have been fewer mergers, acquisitions, and joint ventures (about 15, if the upstream market is included). Examples of oil mergers include *Bayernwerk/Isawerke*,[38] *BP/Sonatrach*,[39] *BP/Amoco*,[40] *Texaco/Chevron*,[41] *Bayernwerk/Gaz de France*,[42] *Kelt/American Express*,[43]

---

[28] Council Regulation (EEC) 4064/89 on the control of concentrations between undertakings [1989] OJ L395/1 (amended [1990] OJ L257/13).

[29] Case No IV/M.1606, EDF/Southwestern Electricty of 19 July 1999, Official Journal C248, 01/09/1999.

[30] Case N IV/M.1557, EDF/Louis Dreyfuss of 28 September 1999, Official Journal C323 of 11/11/1999.

[31] Case No IV/M.1659, Preussen Elektra/EZH of 30 September 1999, Official Journal C074, 15/03/2000.

[32] Case No IV/M.0028, Sydkraft/HEW/Hansa Energy Trading of 30 November 1999, Official Journal C078, 10/03/2001.

[33] Case No IV/M.1720, Fortum/Elektrizitaetswerk Wesertal of 5 January 2000, Official Journal C056, 29/02/2000.

[34] Case No IV/M.JV36, TXU Europe/EDF-London Investments of 3 February 2000, Official Journal C049, 22/02/2000.

[35] Case No IV/M.1803, Electrabel/Epon of 7 February 2000, Official Journal C101, 08/04/2000.

[36] Case No IV/M.1842, Vattenfall/HEW of 20 March 2000, Official Journal C145, 25/05/2000.

[37] Case COMP/M.1673, Veba/Viag of 13 June 2000, Official Journal L188, 10/07/2001.

[38] Case No IV/M.808, Article 9 of the ECMR referral.

[39] Case No IV/M.672, BP/Sonatrach of 12 February 1996, Official Journal C072, 12/03/1996.

[40] Case No IV/M.1293, BP/Amoco of 11/12/1998, Official Journal C 112, 23/04/1999.

[41] Case No IV/M.1301, Texaco/Chevron of 30 October 1998, Official Journal C 130, 11/05/1999.

[42] Case No IV/M.745, Bayernwerk/Gaz de France of 1 July 1996, Official Journal C266, 13/09/1996.

[43] Case No IV/M.116, Kelt/American Express of 20 August 1991, Official Journal C223, 28/08/1991.

Elf/Enterprise,[44] *Elf/Occidental,*[45] *Amoco/Repsol/Iberdrola/Ente Vasco de la Energía,*[46] *and Norsk Hydro/Saga.*[47]

A recent gas merger was the case *Gaz de France/BEWAG/GASAG.*[48] In the upstream market, *Exxon/Mobil,*[49] *BP Amoco/Atlantic Richfield,*[50] and *Totalfina/Elf Aquitaine*[51] are examples of mergers that were cleared only after an in-depth investigation, mainly because the Commission was concerned that consolidation in the oil market would risk creating an oligopolistic structure, which would eventually lead to collective dominance by a few major oil companies.

Cooperative agreements and mergers between suppliers of the same fuel may be pro-competitive to the extent that they allow these companies to enter into new product or geographic markets. Examples include *Sydkraft/Hew* (trading and exchanges), *TXU/EdF London Investments* (network services), and *Preussenelektra/EZH, Vattenfall/HEW, EdF/ESTAG/EDG/London Electricity, EdF/EDISON/ISE,* and *Electrabel/EPON* (new geographic markets). However, when suppliers who are former monopolists merge or cooperate, concerns are inevitable because these suppliers risk consolidating the parties into a strong market position in their formerly exclusive supply area.

Mergers between suppliers of different fuels may be pro-competitive if they allow for new market entry. However, mergers between gas and electricity suppliers must be assessed on a case-by-case basis because, to a certain degree, these fuels are exchangeable. In addition, mergers between dominant companies in the gas and electricity sector may raise concerns because they might allow the electricity supplier to gain control of the upstream market for supplying gas to electricity generation. Examples of such cases include *Tractebel/Distrigas*[52] and *Neste/IVO.*[53]

---

[44] Case No IV/M.0088, Elf/Enterprise of 24 July 1991, Official Journal C203, 02/08/1991.

[45] Case No IV/M.0085, Elf/Occidental of 13 June 1991, Official Journal C160, 20/06/1991.

[46] Case No IV/M.1190, Amoco/Repsol/Iberdrola/Ente Vasco de la Energía of 11 August 1998, Official Journal C288, 16/09/1998.

[47] Case No IV/M.1573, Norsk Hydro/Saga of 5 July 1999, Official Journal C221, 03/08/1999.

[48] Case No IV/M.1402, Gaz de France/Bewag/Gasagentscheidung of 20 January 1999, Official Journal C032, 06/02/1999.

[49] Case No IV/M.1383, Exxon/Mobil of 29 September 1999.

[50] Case No IV/M.1532, BP Amoco/Arco of 29 September 1999, Official Journal L018, 19/01/2001.

[51] Case COMP/M. 1628, TotalFina/Elf of 9 February 2000, Official Journal L143, 29/05/2001.

[52] Case No IV/M.493, Tractebel/Distrigaz (II) of 1 September 1994, Official Journal C249 of 07/09/1994.

[53] Case No IV/M.931, Neste/Ivo of 2 June 1998, Official Journal C218, 14/07/1998.

State Aid Control

Articles 87-89 of the European Community Treaty prohibit any aid granted by state or public authorities to companies that may distort competition. As former Competition Commissioner Karel Van Miert anticipated in 1997, state aid rules will become increasingly important in a liberalized energy market, as the stranded-cost issue exemplifies.

Stranded costs may arise in a liberalized market when the compulsory investments former state utilities made earlier on, which often were linked to public service obligations, become uneconomical. Examples of stranded costs include investments of the state, outside standard commercial activities, in its role as regulator or shareholder of production, transport or distribution, and fuel and power purchase agreements effective beyond 1999.

The Electricity Directive recognized that utilities may have commitments or guarantees of operation made before the Directive entered into force that the Directive's provisions may not honor. In these cases, member states could be granted a derogation from certain provisions in the Directive; for example, those concerning TPA during a period of transition.

However, among the member states that notified the Commission of transitional regimes, only the German and Luxembourg schemes were dealt with under the Directive. The remaining countries proposed levy-based systems in order to compensate their national power companies. In July 2001, when the Commission conditionally approved the systems of Germany and Luxembourg, it also decided that levy-based compensation schemes should be dealt with under state aid rules, rather than under the Electricity Directive. No formal investigation procedure in accordance with Article 88(2) has been opened related to any of the schemes, but the Commission has been negotiating informally with countries that have notified it of schemes, in accordance with state aid procedures.

All schemes of which the Commission is notified will be assessed according to guidelines that the Commission is developing on applying state aid rules to stranded costs.[54] It appears that aid aimed at compensating stranded costs can be authorized, provided that the costs under consideration result from well-identified and qualified historical commitments linked to the introduction of liberalization. However, aid must be digressive and limited to the strict minimum allowed.

---

[54] Commission's communication relating to the methodology for analyzing state aid linked to stranded costs, adopted by the Commission 26 July 2001.

Regarding renewable energy resources, state aid is likely to be carefully assessed in light of future competition law. To date, such aid has fallen under Commission guidelines on state aid for environmental purposes.[55] Although the scope for granting such aid has gradually become tighter, the Commission has been generous regarding aid to renewable energy production. However, the XXVIIth Report on competition policy (European Commission 1997) stressed the following: "Projects giving priority to renewable sources of energy, district heating systems, and indigenous energy sources will be scrutinized to ensure that they are compatible with the Treaty's competition rules." A stricter approach was indicated with the opening of an investigation into the effect of the German electricity tax (introduced 1 April 1999) on the amount to be paid, pursuant to the Grid Feed-in Law regarding renewable energy sources. The Commission's concerns related to the increased feed-in price resulting from the electricity tax.

Public Service Obligations and Competition Laws

One factor that has hindered progress toward a single energy market has been the disagreement between member states and the Commission over the meaning, scope, and importance of the public service obligation entrusted to most European Union electricity and gas companies. This term generally refers to the obligation to provide customers basic services on demand and on a continuing basis at a reasonable price that is uniform across consumer categories.

Article 86(2) of the European Community Treaty recognizes that a company assigned with a public service obligation imposed by a member state in its general economic interest may, under certain strict conditions, disregard the application of competition rules if applying these provisions would obstruct performance of such obligation. For example, a company may refuse a third party access to the system where such access would prevent it from carrying out a public service obligation.

Interestingly, the Electricity and Gas Directives recognize that member states may impose public service obligations; however, the obligations must be clearly defined and verifiable, and member states must notify the Commission of them. However, as a piece of secondary legislation, the Directives cannot overrule or detract from Treaty provisions; thus, the public service obligations provided for in the Directives could be viewed only as an example of services of general economic interest within the meaning of Article 86(2).

---

[55] Community guidelines on state aid for environmental protection, OJ C37 of 3 February 2001.

Final Thoughts

Competition policy will play an important role in European energy markets in ensuring that restrictive measures will not be put in place to offset the benefits of the liberalization process. Competition policy will complement legislative measures for market opening, principally on a case-by-case basis, but also through guidelines or other legal instruments, as witnessed in liberalization of the telecommunications sector. Enforcement efforts will likely focus on transmission, long-term supply and purchase agreements, and TPA to ensure suppliers can deliver goods.

It is thought that complaints will play an increased role in the new system the Commission envisages in the White Paper on modernization of rules for implementing Treaty Articles 81 and 82.[56] As a result, enforcement of competition law in the energy sector may become more decentralized. In principle, the Commission may decide to take action only in cases of particular political, economic, or legal significance for the European Community or in which national regulators or competition authorities have erred.

An interesting question regarding TPA is whether the Commission will be prepared to pursue complaints about refusing noneligible customers access to a grid or pipeline. The Electricity and Gas Directives specifically give eligible customers access to the grid or pipeline, while general competition rules give access to both eligible and noneligible customers. Clearly, European Community competition rules are applicable, irrespective of measures taken by the Commission to complete the internal energy market.

However, intervention must be motivated by European Community interest. Its interest in the electricity sector is defined in Article 3(3) of the Directive as including, inter alia, competition with regard to eligible customers (the Gas Directive includes a similar provision). Strictly interpreted, this article may suggest that it is not in the European Community's interest, at this stage of liberalization, to protect noneligible customers from being refused access to a grid or pipeline. However, since member states are free to liberalize energy markets beyond what is provided for in the Electricity and Gas Directives, it is likely that national regulators and competition authorities will intervene to ensure that full competition is guaranteed in these newly liberalized markets.

---

[56] European Commission (1999a).

References

European Commission. 1997. *XXVIIth Report on Competition Policy*. Brussels.

_____. 1999a. "White Paper on Modernisation of the Rules Implementing Articles 85 and 86 [now 81 and 82] of the EC Treaty." Commission Programme No. 99/027. Brussels.

_____. 1999b. *Second Report to the Council and the European Parliament on Harmonization Requirements*. SEC 1999/470, 16 April. Brussels.

_____. 2000a. "Communication from the Commission to the Council and the European Parliament: Recent Progress with Building the Internal Electricity Market." COM(2000) 297 final, 16 May. Brussels.

_____. 2000b. "State of Implementation of the EU Gas Directive." 98/30/EC, May. Directorate Generale for Energy and Transport. Brussels.

Epilogue

A Regulator's Views

Miguel A. Fernández-Ordóñez

Introducing competition and liberalization into network industries is an emerging paradigm. Although experience in this area is still limited, the lessons learned to date lend perspective to the dimensions of the challenge. Accordingly, this epilogue considers issues that are relevant to network industries: the breakup of monopolies and competitive businesses; the importance of having in place infrastructure conducive to competition; structural measures to promote competitive business activities; antitrust instruments that regulate monopolistic practices; the achievement of social objectives without jeopardizing competition mechanisms to ensure adequate, ongoing service; and the comparative advantages and disadvantages of general antitrust enforcement bodies and sector-specific regulatory agencies.

A New Paradigm

Many countries around the world still lack competition in network industries. Even in countries reasonably successful in introducing competition into such sectors as telecommunications and air transport, results in other sectors, such as gas and electricity, remain questionable. In the United States, for example, consumers in most states are not free to choose their electric utility company, despite this country's long-standing free market tradition. Despite this limited experience, useful lessons have been gleaned along the way.

Since the 1970s, when economists like Stigler first questioned why competition could not be introduced into these sectors, progress has been made. In fact, U.S. President Jimmy Carter was the first government leader to introduce competition into regulated sectors, which, for the most part, were network based. Deregulation of the airline industry and the events leading up to the decision of Harold Green, U.S. Federal District Court Judge, to break up AT&T were spearheaded by Carter democrats; Carter's successor, President Ronald Reagan, picked up the banner (albeit more in word than in deed). British Prime Minister Margaret Thatcher was the first European leader to introduce competition into these sectors. Thanks to her tenacious efforts, the United Kingdom became the first European nation to deregulate many of these sectors. Certain countries have made progress in specific areas. Norway, for example, has made pioneering efforts in the electricity sector. Similarly, Latin American countries, together with New Zealand and Australia, have been an experimental laboratory in this regard. In Asia, however, efforts to introduce competition into network industries have lagged significantly. Similarly, countries of the former Soviet block, with the exception of Poland, have emphasized privatization at the expense of competition, for which most of these countries are now paying the price.

Differences between Liberalization and Deregulation

Introducing competition into network-based industries (what we call deregulation) differs vastly from introducing competition into conventional or nonnetwork industries, where competition is promoted simply by market liberalization and privatization, followed by enforcement of antitrust law. Structural measures, such as placing constraints on mergers or rulings on abuse of dominant position, may also be taken in conventional sectors to promote competition; but these measures must be a posteriori.

In network-based industries, conversely, pro-competition measures are implemented in reverse order; that is, restructuring mechanisms must be adopted in advance to enable these sectors to begin operating under a competitive model. Antitrust enforcement is only effective when anticompetitive behavior is not the natural result of the existing business structure. For example, if vertical integration is kept in place, network owners will take advantage of this edge, making it impossible for any competition to emerge. Another distinguishing characteristic of network industries is that it is impossible to have total loosening of regulatory constraints: a certain degree of market regulation must remain in effect because not every productive segment is able to work properly under a system of competition. Lastly, the need to transition gradually to a competitive market is usually greater in network-based industries than in conventional sectors. Given the unique characteristics of network sectors, the competition policies applied to them should not mirror those designed for conventional (nonnetwork) sectors; any attempt to do so will inevitably fail. In short, deregulation implies much more than liberalization.

Heterogeneity of Network Industries

Network industries not only differ from nonnetwork industries; they also differ significantly from one another. Although bound by the common thread of networks, the peculiarities of each sector demand unique competition policy solutions. For example, in the electricity networks, no competition exists because it is economically not feasible; in the telecommunications sector, on the other hand, some degree of competition between networks is apparent in certain segments. Thus, regulations to keep networks separate from competitive businesses in the telecommunications industry do not need to be as stringent as those in the electricity sector.

Similarly, the competitive components of the electricity and airline sectors differ markedly. Electric power generation and air passenger and cargo transport require major capital investment, which would lead one to assume that the sectors are similar. In electric power generation, establishing a business in a particular location is paramount and requires a heavy investment in sunk costs. However, capital investment in the airline industry is highly mobile; new airlines can be quickly established simply by moving airplanes to locations where they are needed. For this reason, it makes no sense to place restrictions on market share in the airline business since it is a more flexible market in which companies' major concern is attaining choice slots at airports.

Need for Vertical Separation

Separation of competitive and monopolistic businesses must be even more far-reaching than what was believed necessary five to 10 years ago. In fact, liberalization of these sectors has its roots in asserting the right to compete in essential facility sectors; that is, third-party access to networks. Today, there is proof that allowing companies to operate simultaneously as both monopoly and competitor obstructs, or at least delays, the start-up of competition. Third-party access to monopoly-owned networks is only viable in sectors where the potential for competition between networks exists. Lacking such potential, the presence of any other competitor firms in the market would be merely symbolic. One case in point is Spain's electricity sector, a segment of which was opened to competition. An even clearer example is the United Kingdom's gas sector, which had no true competition until the Gas Act of 1996 forced British Gas to break up its monopolistic businesses into independently owned companies, thereby separating them from the competitive businesses.[1]

Other Restructuring Needs

Restructuring should not only focus on vertical measures, but should also seek to provide businesses a competition-friendly structure. In order for competition to thrive, former monopolies must first undergo a process of horizontal breakup. Such measures as the rule enacted in Argentina that prohibits any one company from holding more than 10 percent of generation assets are appropriate and have met with favorable results compared with countries that have not adopted such measures. However, the feasibility of their implementation will require a case-by-case study in each particular sector. The need for such measures is perhaps greatest in the electricity sector because of its deregulated business activities, which are not particularly conducive to competition. Therefore, if the objective is to ensure a degree of competition between companies, these segments must adopt restructuring measures.

Because the electricity sector is characterized by inflexible demand and electric power production does not always match capacity, it is critical for the market to function effectively during peak periods of demand. Furthermore, potential entrants into this sector face multiple challenges: the large scale of the initial investment, locating the site and gaining approval for constructing a power generation plant, limited potential for international trade, inability to store the product, ability to predict demand, and rival competitors' mutual awareness of each other's business profiles. All of these factors, combined with the usual problems inherent in any network-based sector, hamper competition in the power generation market. For these reasons, structural measures targeted also at competitive markets must be adopted, regardless of whether far-reaching separation of business activities is implemented in response to network-related problems.

---

[1] A particularly interesting discussion of this topic is contained in the OECD document "*Structural Separation in Regulated Industries*" (Paris, 2001).

Infrastructure Investment: Prerequisite for Success

The link between commerce and transportation infrastructure has long been established. Commerce can occur only to the extent that exchange is physically possible. This point is best illustrated by the electricity sector, where the legacy of the regulated monopoly has always been a blanket of isolated monopolies. Spain is a clear example in this regard. Another striking example is California, whose recent predicament illustrates what can happen when infrastructure—in this case, electric power transmission lines—is approached from the perspective of regional monopolies rather than a business standpoint. Design of electric power lines connecting regional monopolies of the grid was limited to concerns about safety; hence, it was incapable of transferring energy from areas with excess production to those experiencing shortages and vice versa. This case shows that the scope of the public sector's infrastructure development role should not be limited to safety concerns, but should be expanded to facilitate competition.

New Regulatory Approaches

The inefficiency that often characterizes regulation of monopolistic activities is the underlying rationale for introducing competition. Nonetheless, specific segments of business activities must continue being regulated, either because competition is inappropriate for a particular type of activity or because ways to compete have not yet been designed.

Today, there is more skepticism about new regulatory mechanisms, such as price caps. It has been proven that price caps add little to the traditional approach of return on investment or cost of service. The new methods, still hampered by the disadvantages of the old ones, may serve only to delay the review process.

This was proven to be the case in the United Kingdom, the first country to implement these practices, and more recently in California, where electric utility companies proposed price caps and regulators approved them. If a price cap is much higher than the level that would have resulted through competition, then the consumer loses while the electric power company reaps hefty profits. Of course, the price cap will not be set at a lower rate since that would run counter to the principle of regulatory stability and curb incentives to improve efficiency. If, however, the level of the price cap is proven inadequate, as was the case in California, then regulated firms will immediately ask the regulator for a rate increase because private companies cannot be expected to operate at a loss.

If only one lesson has been learned over the past decade, it is this: There is a regulatory procedure, which, if implementation is feasible, is slightly better than cost of service or price caps—that is, the transfer of a monopoly on a competitive basis, also known as *franchise bidding*. This method has worked well in transferring concessions of long-distance passenger bus transport lines (in Spain, for example) and in awarding licenses for using the telecommunications spectrum (key examples are the United States and the United Kingdom). It is therefore possible, even in a monopoly situation, to use competition to award that monopoly. Another lesson learned, exemplified by Italy's failure at awarding spectrum licenses, is that auction design is essential to success.

Social Policy and Competition

In recent years, much has been learned about how to ensure fulfillment of social objectives in network industries. During Spain's dictatorship, for example, few social objectives were attached to monopolistic arrangements; however, in many countries, regulation of monopolies has helped protect elderly, disadvantaged, and rural populations through policy mechanisms that guarantee delivery of various public services at affordable prices. The current global focus on the digital divide between those who have and do not have access to computers and the Internet is bringing this debate to the forefront again.

The idea is to design policy mechanisms aimed at achieving these objectives while taking care not to hinder competition. Traditionally, these objectives were met through a system of swapping favors, whereby monopolies agreed to meet social objectives in exchange for the government guaranteeing their monopoly. This explains why monopolies were eager to defend social objectives, claiming they would no longer be adequately fulfilled if their monopolies were terminated.

Today there exists a wide array of alternatives from which to choose, ranging from self-regulation, under which the incumbent firm is responsible for ensuring that social objectives are met in exchange for a significant market share, to establishment of funds financed by mandatory user fees, which are then used to meet the needs of those not served by the market. There are also pay-or-play systems, under which firms either provide or pay for these services, as well as public tender systems, which are designed to accurately reflect the costs of these social policies. Finally, experience in the field of environmental objectives has shown that secondary markets can be created to swap social obligations. As mentioned above, such debt instruments can be financed through user-financed funds or various other ways, including connection fees, government budgeting, an operator income-based or fixed-amount arrangement, and direct billing or charges based on traffic volume.

Guarantee of Supply

Guarantee of supply, similar to a social objective, merits special consideration.[2] While various lessons have been learned in this regard, two are most salient. The first, and perhaps most important, lesson is the need to develop network infrastructure conducive to doing business. The second lesson, pertaining to electric power generation, is that the two approaches implemented thus far to guarantee supply have proven useless. These approaches relied on market forces to provide the necessary levels of investment to guarantee electric power supply, and charged a premium to guarantee power generation capacity (the model used in Spain and the United Kingdom). A consensus is now emerging that governments need to stimulate and promote the creation of markets to cover such risks. Undoubtedly, this coverage will increase the cost of supply through a premium, as was the case in Spain and the United Kingdom, but instead of receiving nothing for one's money, it will provide for a true guarantee of future supply.

The worst part of California's problem was not the blackouts themselves, but the reaction they caused. Apart from the need for adequate network infrastructure, it is clear that any system operating on January 1, 1998 would have failed to prevent the blackouts in that state. In fact, even if the world's best regulatory system had been in place, the blackouts still would have occurred. This is because it takes four years to build a power plant: two years of construction, plus two years to secure the necessary permits. Consequently, even if all of the required permits had been secured and environmental concerns adequately addressed, California would not have escaped the rash of rolling blackouts.

---

[2] Guarantee of adequate supply is particularly critical in the electricity sector; recently, California's rolling blackouts have raised concerns about introducing competition in this sector.

The troublesome part of the California debacle is that the state came to the rescue of consumers and electric power companies alike—a response that runs counter to market logic. Nevertheless, in the absence of a consumer education program and inadequacies in oversight and regulation of electric power companies, California's fate was most probably sealed.

There is a striking parallel between this situation and the U.S. banking crisis of the late 20th century, where guaranteeing all bank deposits, coupled with lax banking supervision, conspired to make the frequency and scope of bank failures inevitable. Raising consumer awareness about the risks that the service entails, ensuring that electric power companies adequately provide for such risks, and stimulating and promoting markets that make it possible to cover them are integral to guaranteeing supply.

Sector-specific Regulatory Agencies and Antitrust Institutions

What role should sector-specific and antitrust institutions play with respect to introducing competition into network industries? In general, antitrust institutions have several disadvantages related to regulating competition in sectors undergoing deregulation. The most obvious disadvantage is lack of sector-specific knowledge. In addition, these institutions are relatively slow in taking action. Moreover, competitive firms are entitled to more procedural guarantees than monopolies because of their unique relationship with the government. General regulatory agencies provide firms the utmost guarantee that any state intervention will be fully justified and that these agencies will therefore move deliberately in all of their proceedings. While this deliberate pace may be justified in conventional sectors, it is an obvious liability in safeguarding competition in network industries.

Another shortcoming of general antitrust institutions is that any measure they adopt is usually meant to impose punishment or order a company to refrain from engaging in a certain type of behavior; this is because these institutions usually lack the legal authority to issue affirmative orders of conduct. This is relevant to network industries because problems often arise in these sectors that require compelling the monopolist or company with a dominant position to do something that is not being done rather than forcing it to stop doing something or to punish it for something it has already done.

Finally, general antitrust institutions are ill suited to sector regulation because they largely lack the legal authority or ability to perform such duties as changing regulations or setting rates. In fact, these types of tools can be useful complements to antitrust measures and, occasionally, may even substitute for them. For example, setting a maximum rate can be used to alleviate network congestion after both competition and administratively setting an interconnection rate have failed. Attempting to resolve such problems by conducting proceedings on charges of abuse of dominant position would be futile.

Notwithstanding these disadvantages, general antitrust institutions enjoy an advantage over their sector-specific counterparts: They are less likely to become captive to network-based sector firms. With few exceptions, sector-specific agencies tend to rule in favor of the firms they regulate, thereby shortchanging the best interests of both consumers and the overall economy. This situation has led some countries, including Australia, to eliminate sector-specific regulatory institutions altogether.

One compromise solution might be to have sector-specific agencies run the regulatory process initially, with the understanding that all responsibility for competition-related matters, with the exception of monopolies, would eventually be transferred to general antitrust institutions, in accordance with a pre-established timetable.

About the Authors

Cécile Aubert is a lecturer in the Faculty of Economics and Politics at the University of Cambridge, United Kingdom. A graduate of the Université des Science Sociales of Toulouse, France, she worked at the University of California at Berkeley as a research associate in the Department of Agricultural and Resource Economics (2000–2001) and as a visiting lecturer in the Department of Economics (2001). She held internships at the OECD (1996) and the Contrôle d'Etat de France Télécom (1998) and was a World Bank consultant in 1997 and 2000. Her research interests include the economics of regulation and competition policy, with a particular focus on institutions and developing economies; the economics of cultural goods; and micro-credit in poor countries.

Paulina Beato is a principal economist in the Infrastructure and Financial Markets Division of the Inter-American Development Bank's Sustainable Development Department. She received her doctorate in economics from the University of Minnesota. Previously, she worked at the International Monetary Fund and held several senior executive and management positions in industrial and financial companies in Spain. Her research on regulation, competition, and pricing policies in infrastructure and financial services has appeared in a variety of journals, including the *Journal of Economic Theory, Quarterly Journal of Economics,* and *Journal of Project Finance.*

Diego Bondorevsky is a senior economist at the Center for Regulation Economic Studies of the Universidad Argentina de la Empresa. He holds a master's degree in economics from the London School of Economics. Previously, he worked as a consultant on competition policy for several institutions.

Salomé Cisnal de Ugarte is a lawyer in the Brussels office of Freshfields Bruckhaus Deringer. She holds a law degree from Harvard University and a doctorate in law from the European University Institute in Italy. Previously, she taught at the University Carlos III of Madrid. She also served as an advisor to and representative of international companies, trade associations, and governments. Her research focuses largely on European Community law.

Miguel A. Fernández-Ordóñez is a consultant on regulation and competition policy. He is a graduate of the Universidad Complutense of Madrid, where he majored in law and economic science and taught economic policy. At the Ministry of Economy and Finance in Spain, he served as state secretary for economy and state secretary for commerce. Other key positions held include executive director of the International Monetary Fund, president of the Office for the Defense of Competition, and president of the National Electric System Commission of Spain.

Carmen Fuente is an economist and consultant in the Infrastructure and Financial Markets Division of the Inter-American Development Bank. Previously, she taught applied economics at the Universidad Complutense of Madrid, where she graduated, and did graduate work in economics and statistics at Stanford University. Other key positions held include chief of staff at the Electricity Regulatory Commission in Madrid, chairperson of Tabapress, economic counselor of the Spanish delegation to the OECD, and chief of staff for the Secretary of State for Economy. In addition, she served in the Ministry of Commerce's Research Division.

Alfredo García is an assistant professor of systems and information engineering at the University of Virginia. He received both doctoral and master's degrees in operations research from the University of Michigan, a DEA Automatique from the University of Toulouse III (France), and an undergraduate degree in electrical engineering from Universidad de los Andes in Colombia. From 1996 to 1999, he worked for Colombia's Energy and Gas Regulatory Commission and Fundesarrollo, a think tank, on public policy issues, including deregulation of the electricity and natural gas industries.

Jean-Jacques Laffont, professor of economics at the University of Toulouse, received his doctorate from Harvard University. He held visiting positions at the California Institute of Technology, University of Pennsylvania, Harvard University, and Australian National University. He served as president of the Econometric Society and the European Economic Association. In addition, he created and continues to direct the Institut d'Économie Industrielle. His published works include 12 books and more than 200 scientific articles.

Jaime Millan is an energy economist at the Inter-American Development Bank, in charge of coordinating implementation of the Bank's energy strategy and conducting research and advising on the sustainability of power sector reform in Latin America and the Caribbean. Since joining the Bank, he has supervised the economic inputs of energy projects, drafted public utilities policy and energy strategy, and initiated a program on sustainable energy. Previously, he served as president of a consulting firm and professor at the Universidad de los Andes in Bogotá, Colombia. He holds a doctorate in water resources planning from Colorado State University.

Diego Petrecolla is executive director of Centro de Estudios Económicos de la Regulación (CEER) of the Universidad Argentina de la Empresa. He holds a doctorate in economics from the University of Illinois at Urbana-Champaign. Prior to joining CEER, he served as president and chief economist of the National Antitrust Commission, research director at the Argentine Foundation for Equity Development, and professor at the Universidad Torcuato di Tella.

Pablo Serra is chair of the Department of Industrial Engineering at the University of Chile and regularly consults for regulators, public utilities, and such international organizations as the World Bank and the International Monetary Fund. He holds a doctorate in economics from Yale University and a master's degree in industrial engineering from the University of Chile. He is a member of the Chilean Antitrust Commission; specializes in economic regulation and public economics; and has authored articles for the *International Economic Review, Quarterly Journal of Economics, Journal of International Economics, World Development,* and *Energy Economics.*

Richard Tomiak, a consultant who specializes in South American and East European energy markets, has more than 20 years of energy sector experience in Europe and the Americas and has lectured widely on energy and deregulation issues. Formerly a vice president of TXU Europe, he served as TXU representative to various European organizations, including the European Federation of Energy Traders, EURELECTRIC, and GEODE (Groupement Européen des Enterprises et Organismes de Distribution d'Énergie). For eight years, he was electricity purchasing manager at Midlands Electricity.

David Wood is a partner in the law firm of Howrey Simon, in the firm's Brussels office. He is a former official of the Directorate General for Competition at the European Commission in Brussels, having served as head of the Financial Services Unit, deputy head of the Media and Music Publishing Unit, and administrator in the Transport and Transport Infrastructure Unit. He holds a law degree from the University of Buckingham in the United Kingdom, and received his undergraduate training in politics from the University of Sussex's School of English and American Studies. He is admitted as a solicitor to the Supreme Court of England and Wales, the High Court of the Supreme Court of England and Wales, and the High Court of Ireland.